The Future of Banking

The Future of Banking

Edited by BENTON E. GUP

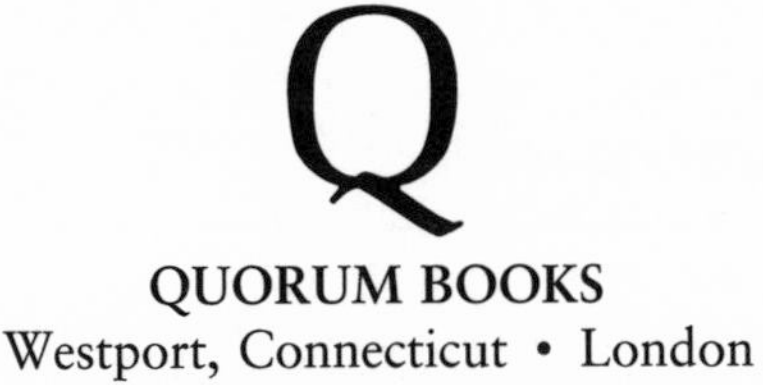

QUORUM BOOKS
Westport, Connecticut • London

Library of Congress Cataloging-in-Publication Data

The future of banking / edited by Benton E. Gup.
p. cm.
Includes bibliographical references.
ISBN 1–56720–467–8 (alk. paper)
1. Banks and banking. I. Gup, Benton E.
HG1601.F88 2003
332.1—dc21 2002023035

British Library Cataloguing in Publication Data is available.

Library of Congress Catalog Card Number: 2002023035
ISBN: 1–56720–467–8

First published in 2003

Quorum Books, 88 Post Road West, Westport, CT 06881
An imprint of Greenwood Publishing Group, Inc.
www.quorumbooks.com

Printed in the United States of America

The paper used in this book complies with the Permanent Paper Standard issued by the National Information Standards Organization (Z39.48–1984).

10 9 8 7 6 5 4 3 2 1

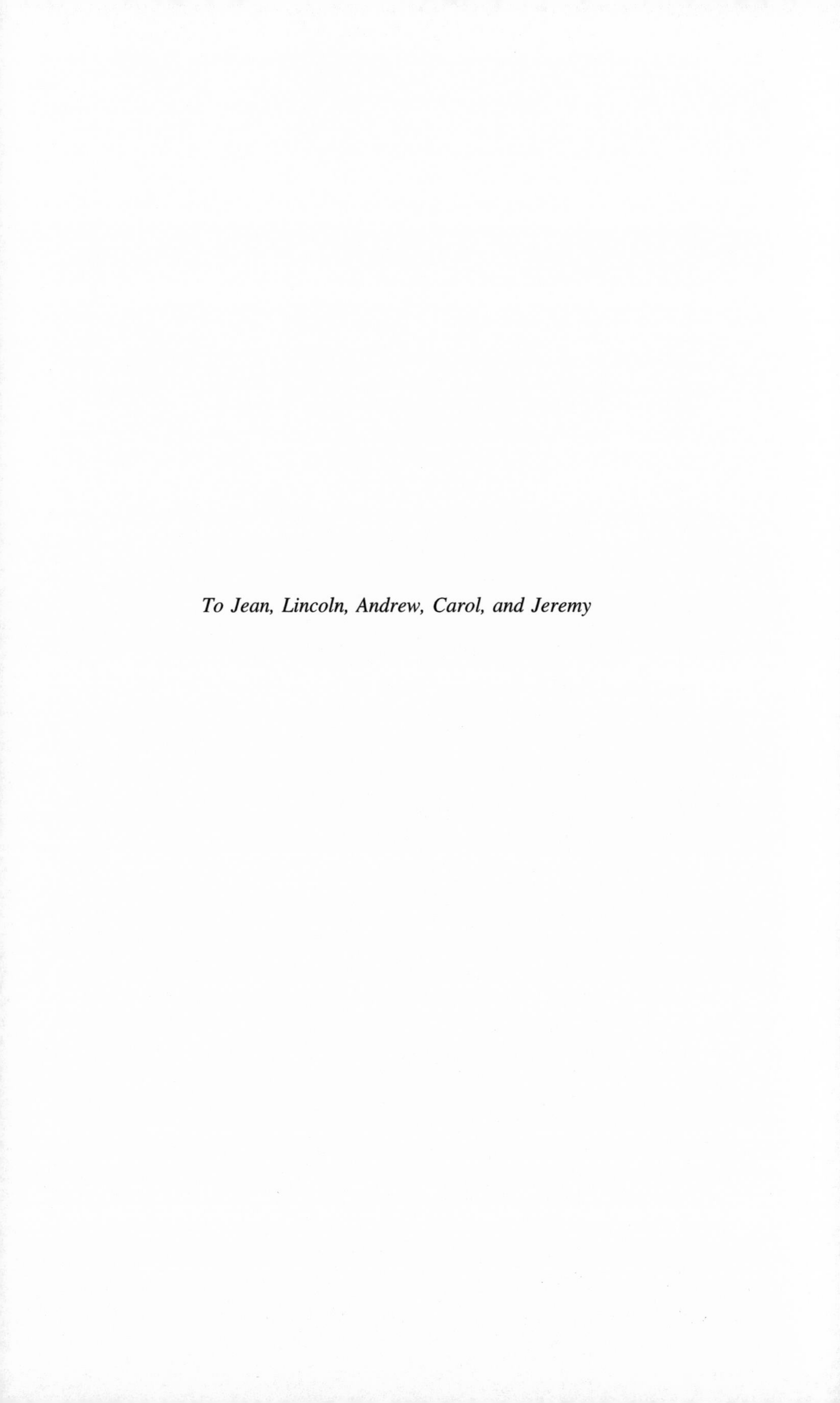

To Jean, Lincoln, Andrew, Carol, and Jeremy

Contents

Preface

This is the fifth in a series of books published by Quorum Books which began with one about bank failures (*Bank Failures in the Major Trading Countries of the World*, 1998) and continued with *International Banking Crises* (1999), *The New Financial Architecture* (2000), and *Megamergers in a Global Economy* (2002). The first book was a result of research done while I was at the Office of the Comptroller of the Currency in connection with the Gramm-Leach-Bliley Act. As that book was being written, a financial crisis began in Thailand, and then it spread around the world, providing interesting fodder for research. While working on books about failures and banking crises around the world, it became clear to me that bank regulation was not effective in preventing either failures or crises and that changes must be made in a new financial architecture. One of the more visible changes was increased consolidation and megamergers. The next topic dealt the outcomes of these and other events. Thus, this book is about the future of banking in the broad sense of that word.

It is obvious that banks are evolving in response to changes in competition, globalization, laws, technology, and other factors. Nevertheless, the long-run effect of these factors on banks and financial systems is not clear. Will banks and other financial service firms continue to consolidate on a global basis? Will electronic banking become the dominant form of retail banking? Will nonbank competitors replace banks? These are a few of the questions that are addressed here.

This book consists of a collection of writings by academics, practitioners, and regulators from around the world who were asked to give their perspective of the future. The chapters cover such diverse topics as banking laws, electronic banking, microcredits in poor countries, relationship lending, stock exchanges in Europe, and more. Collectively, they provide unique insights into changes we can expect to see in the future.

Earlier versions of some of these chapters were presented at the annual meeting of the Financial Management Association held in Toronto, Canada, in October 2001, and at other venues.

Chapter 1

Creative Destruction

Benton E. Gup

CHANGES IN FINANCIAL SERVICES

Joseph A. Schumpeter, the Austrian-born economist who died in 1950, left us with two concepts that are alive and well today. He is best known for the concept of creative destruction, which refers to the process whereby new products and processes render the older ones obsolete in "wave-like" periods of innovation that contribute to booms and busts in the economy.[1] Schumpeter also recognized that technological change can revolutionize economic structures.[2] Today we are participating in the ongoing process of creative destruction and change that is being spurred by deregulation, globalization, and technological change. Although these changes are affecting all segments of the economy, our particular interest is in global financial services. In that regard, Robert C. Merton and Zvi Bodie (1995) observed that the basic functions of the financial system are stable across time and place, but the institutional ways in which they are performed are not constant. Those functions—payments, intermediation, managing risk, and price information—can be performed by banks as well as a wide variety of nonbank organizations such as Merrill Lynch, Fidelity Funds, and General Electric Credit. Simply stated, form follows function—and the forms of the financial service industry are changing.

As an illustration of the changes that took place in the financial system from the time of Adam Smith in the eighteenth century until the early twentieth century, we can point to the *real bills* or *commercial loan theory* which was the way banks operated in the past. That theory held that banks should make short-term self-liquidating loans to finance current production, transportation, or storage of physical goods (Meyer, 1986). Banks matched the maturities of their assets and liabilities. Banks no longer practice the real bills theory. They make

Table 1.1
Banking Structure in the United States

Year	Number of Banks	Total Assets ($ billion)	Number of Banks with Assets Greater than $10 Billion	Percentage of Assets Held by Large Banks
2000	8,315	$6.2	82	70%
1980	14,769	$1.9	18	34%

Source: FDIC.

loans for any legal purpose with maturities of 30 years for some real estate loans, and their liabilities still tend to be short term. The two-century-old *real bills* approach to bank management is so out of date that most modern texts on banking do not even mention it, even in an historical context.[3]

Consolidation

Consolidation in the banking industry in the United States from 1980 to 2000 is one of the most noticeable changes. As shown in Table 1.1, the number of banks declined by more than 6,000, while the percentage of total assets held by the largest institutions doubled. The result is that 82 large banks—less than 1 percent of the total number of banks—hold more than two-thirds of all bank assets. Consolidation in the banking industry is not unique to the United States. A study by the central banks of the Group of Ten Nations (G-10) found a high level of concentration in the 13 countries they examined.[4] The consolidation is the result of deregulation of geographic markets, changes in financial technology (e.g., securitization and derivatives), communications technology, changes in information technology, the desire to achieve economies of scale, high stock prices used as currency in mergers, and other factors.[5] The consolidation usually involves large banks within one nation, cross-border bank consolidations, and consolidations between banks and other types of financial institutions.[6]

Although the number of banking organizations declined during the 1988–2000 period, the number of branches increased from 59,449 to 71,647.[7] This suggests that bank customers want to use branches, which has some implications for electronic banking. Electronic banking may complement physical banks, but it is not a substitute for them.

Consolidation is global, as reflected in the cross-border mergers and deals between financial service firms in recent years: Deutsche Bank (Germany) and Bankers Trust (U.S.); Credit Suisse (Switzerland) and DLJ (U.S.); Abbey National (UK) and Scottish Provident (Scotland); HypoVereinsbank (Germany) and

Bank Austria (Austria). Spanish banks have been particularly active in cross-border deals. Banco Bilbao Vizcaya Argentaria (BBVA) acquired a small stake in the privatization of France's Crédit Lyonnais and Italy's Banco Nazionale del Lavoro. Banco Santander Central Hispano (BSCH) has a stake in the Royal Bank of Scotland, which in turn owns part of Italy's Sanpaolo IMI and Germany's Commerzank. BSCH and Sanpaolo IMI signed an agreement to jointly offer products to small and medium-sized businesses in Italy and Latin America. BSCH is one of Sanpaolo's largest stockholders ("Sanpaolo," 2000). In 2001 Royal Bank of Canada (RBC) bought the United States' Centura Banks, Dain Rauscher—a Minneapolis-based brokerage firm. Its other U.S. operations include Bull and Bear Securities, an online broker, and Liberty Life Insurance ("Royal Bank of Canada," 2001). Finally, Lone Star Fund (a private equity fund) of Dallas, Texas, bought the failed Japanese Tokyo Sowa Bank Ltd. (Singer, 2001).

The pace of consolidation might be faster in Europe, but the European Central Bank has blocked some cross-border acquisitions. For example, BBVA wanted to acquire Unicredito in Italy, but it was blocked by the central bank of Italy (Crawford, 2001).

Bank consolidation has some unintended side effects. Cetorelli and Gambera (2001) examined the relationship between bank consolidation and long-run economic growth in 41 countries. They found that increased concentration depresses the industrial growth of the economy as a whole. However, it promotes growth in younger industries that are in need of credit.

Unbundling

Although global consolidation has taken place in the banking industry, there are several related trends that deserve mention. First, the traditional services offered by commercial banks are being unbundled and offered by brokers, insurance companies, and other types of firms. By virtue of their size, banks are still the dominant financial institutions, and they will probably remain so in the near term as they expand their offerings of financial services through acquisitions and strategic alliances. However, size per se is not a sustainable competitive advantage. In the past, banks had information about customers that others did not have. As we go to real-time systems with both transactions and knowledge, the advantage that banks had is disappearing. According to Alan Greenspan (2000), "The continued success of banking organizations . . . is dependent on their ability to reinvent themselves by providing new and different services and creating new and different ways to lend and to manage assets." One new way to manage assets and information is through the use of strategic alliances. To some extent, strategic alliances can be used in lieu of mergers and to deal with cross-border relationships.

Demutualization

Second, demutualization was widespread in the U.S. thrift industry in the 1980s, and now it is occurring in the insurance industry.[8] Major policyholder-owned insurance companies are changing their mutual form of ownership through *demutualization* to become stockholder owned. This gives them greater access to the capital markets and the flexibility to use stock to make acquisitions. Prudential Insurance Company of America, MetLife Inc., MONY Life Insurance Company Inc., John Hancock Mutual of New York, and the Principal Financial Group[9] are a few examples of insurance firms that demutualized ("Prudential to Go Public," 2000; "Diving into Demutualization," 2000). Not all insurance companies are willing to do so. In 1999, New York Life announced that the company had considered its options, and it had elected to remain a mutual.

The number of mutual insurance companies in the United States declined from 135 in 1980 to about 90 at the turn of the century (Crenshaw, 2000). Likewise, the major insurance companies in Canada demutualized following amendments to the Insurance Companies Act in 1999. The driving force behind the recent conversions is access to the capital markets and ownership of stock to make acquisitions. Demutualization of mutual life insurance companies has occurred in the United Kingdom as well. There the rationale was a troubled life insurance industry.[10]

Privatization

Third, some government-chartered/owned financial institutions have been privatized. Fannie Mae (Federal National Mortgage Association), Freddie Mac (Federal Home Loan Mortgage Corporation), Sallie Mae (Student Loan Marketing Association) in the United States, Credit Lyonnais in France, and Banespa in Brazil are examples of government-owned financial institutions that have been privatized. The privatized banks, in turn, can acquire or be acquired by other banks or financial service firms.[11] A study by Bortolotti, Sinscalco, and Fantini (2000) revealed that privatization is widespread. From 1977 to 1997 there were 1,865 deals in more than 100 countries. They also found that few governments completely gave up their ownership.

Nationalization

Finally, the trend toward globalization may not be sustainable. Most of the globalization referred to here occurred when the economies of the United States and the European Union (EU) were booming. In 2001 the economies of the United States, the EU, and Japan were growing at a slower pace. Jurgen E. Schrempp, chairman and chief executive officer of DaimlerChrysler, claimed that there would be a tremendous backlash against globalization in the twenty-first century (Garten, 2001). Similarly, Rolf-E. Breuer, CEO of Deutsche Bank, stated that nationalization, not globalization, was the fastest growing trend. In Japan, the economy has shown no signs of recovery, and there is a growing sense of nationalism in connection with trade with China.[12] For example, Credit Suisse First Boston (CSFB) and other investment banks scaled back their contact with Taiwan after CSFB was penalized for doing business there. China dropped CSFB as an underwriter of its second largest telecom company, Unicom Group.[13]

The Law

Laws and court decisions are two of the most important factors affecting financial services. For example, the National Bank Act of 1864 created the Office of the Comptroller of the Currency (OCC) and national banks, which are banks with a national charter issued by the OCC.[14] This law stated that national banks had the power to carry out "the business of banking" and had "incidental powers" necessary to carry out that business. At that time, banking was defined as discounting and negotiating promissory notes, drafts, bills of exchange, and so on, but the incidental powers were not clearly defined. It was not until 1995, in *NationsBank v. Variable Annuity Life Insurance Co.*, that the court ruled that the business of banking is not limited to those powers expressed in the National Bank Act.[15] Instead, the business of banking is an expansive concept, and the powers listed in the Act are merely illustrative. The effect of the ruling is to broaden banking powers. Accordingly, the task of the federal bank regulators is "to allow innovation in a safe and sound manner, without smothering new activities with unnecessarily burdensome restrictions that undermine the benefits—to banks and their customers—of allowing banks to develop and offer new products and services" (Williams and Jacobson, 1995).

In November 1999, the Gramm-Leach-Bliley Act (GLB) was signed into law. It marked the end of the 1933 Glass-Steagall prohibitions concerning the separation of banks from investment banking and rescinded the 1956 Bank Holding Company Act's prohibitions against insurance underwriting. It allows banks, securities firms, and insurers to be affiliated, thus opening the door to further consolidation and increased competition in financial services in the United States and abroad. Regions Financial Corporation acquired Rebsamen Insurance Inc., a full-line general insurance broker, and Morgan Keegan, a large investment firm.[16] Some insurers, such as Allstate Insurance, Metropolitan Life, Principal Financial Group, and State Farm Insurance, have started their own Federal Savings Bank (State Farm Bank) to retain their existing customers and to get new ones (Gogoi, 2001). E*TRADE, an online brokerage firm, owns E*TRADE Bank which offers a full array of banking services.[17] In Canada, the Bank of Montreal owns InvestorLine, an online discount brokerage firm. And a private equity fund—Lone Star Fund of Dallas, Texas—bought a failed Japanese bank, Tokyo Sowa Bank Ltd. In addition, Ripplewood Holdings LLC of New York purchased the Long Term Credit Bank of Japan (Singer, 2001).[18] And Allianze

AG, the large German insurance company, increased its control over Dresdner Bank AG.[19]

The combination of banks with other types of financial service firms does not necessarily add to profitability. Many relatively small banks have found that running their own mutual funds hurts earnings and growth (McReynolds, 2000). Owning mutual funds works better for large banks that can take advantage of economies of scale. The reason for this is the high fixed costs such as legal fees, directors fees, and marketing costs. The breakeven point is about $50 million in assets.

The combination of banking and securities firms may also lead to competition within the same banking organization. Consider AmSouth Bank which has both a Trust Division and AmSouth Investment Services.[20] The Trust Division and AmSouth Investment Services (a registered investment advisor—RIA—service) compete to provide investment services and annuities for some of the same customers. In addition to brokerage services, the RIA sells mutual funds as well as annuities offered by insurance companies.

Merrill Lynch, Amex, General Electric, Pitney Bowes, and BMW own industrial loan corporations (ILCs) chartered in Utah.[21] ILCs are nonbank banks that are FDIC insured, but they are not regulated by the OCC or the Federal Reserve. The ILCs provide a link between commerce and banking, and they avoid most federal oversight.

Despite the liberalization of powers provided by the GLB, there are still limitations on banks' nonfinancial commercial activities. To some extent, the distinction between financial and nonfinancial commercial activities is becoming blurred as financial institutions form strategic alliances with telecommunications companies and others to deliver financial services online and by wireless means.

The globalization of financial services requires international cooperation among regulators in various countries. The Basel Committee on Banking Supervision's proposal for a New Capital Accord in 2001 is one example of international cooperation among regulators.[22] The New Capital Accord is expected to be implemented in 2004, replacing the first one in 1988. This illustrates that international cooperation is possible, but it is very slow and incomplete.

THREE CASE STUDIES

The following short chronologies/case studies illustrate the dynamic process of change in three global financial institutions: Citigroup, Deutsche Bank, and Credit Lyonnais. Both Citigroup and Deutsche Bank chose different paths for growth, while Credit Lyonnais was contracting. Because these are large, complex international organizations, these chronologies/case studies do not cover all aspects of their business.

Citigroup Inc.

1998

In 1998, two major financial organizations—Citicorp[23] and Travelers Group—announced that they would merge and create Citgroup Inc. Citicorp had assets of about $700 billion. It was a global bank with branches in 40 countries and the world's largest issuer of credit cards, with more than 60 million credit cards. Travelers Group, known mainly for its life and property casualty insurance activities, also owned Salomon, Smith Barney (investments), Salomon, Smith Barney Asset Management, Primerica Financial Services (consumer finance), and Commercial Credit (business finance). At the time of the merger, the two organizations announced that they would focus on traditional banking, consumer finance, credit cards, investment banking, securities brokerage and asset management, and property casualty and life insurance. In April 1998, before the merger, Citibank had acquired AT&T Universal Card Services. By 2001, the new company was serving more than 120 million customers in about 100 countries. It also has 10 million online accounts.

Following the merger, there was a reorganization and the introduction of SSBC Asset Management Group. SSBC combined what was Salomon Brothers Asset Management, Smith Barney Asset Management, and Citibank Global Asset Management. The new group had about $290 billion in managed assets and catered to institutional and high net worth retail clients around the world.

Later that year, Citigroup acquired the credit card business and branches of Banco Mayo Cooperative, Ltda., in Argentina.

1999

In 1999, Citigroup made four acquisitions to strengthen its consumer lending. It acquired Mellon Bank's credit card business, bringing Citibank's credit cards up to 70 million in the United States. Its total number of credit and charge cards was about 96 million. It also acquired Financiero Atlas in Santiago, Chile.

Commercial Credit acquired the loans and branches of Associates First Capital Corporation. Associates First Capital specialized in subprime lending and provided consumer financing and home equity loans in more than 1,000 offices located in 45 states.[24] In 2001, Citigroup settled a lawsuit claiming that Associates engaged in predatory lending.[25]

Finally, Citigroup bought the principal operating assets of Source One Mortgage Service Corporation. Source One focused on low- to moderate-income borrowers.

2000

Salomon, Smith Barney acquired Schroders PLC, a leading British investment banking and asset management firm. The European operations will be known as Schroders Salomon, Smith Barney. Citigroup acquired AST StockPlan, Inc., a provider of stock benefit plan services that will complement Salomon, Smith Barney's Stock Plan Services Group.

Citigroup and America Online announced an alliance to provide personal financial services and products for online customers. This includes banking, mortgage, credit cards, investment, and insurance products and services. The services include some payment options. Citigroup and America Online also launched Myciti, providing online access to accounts registered with the service.[26]

Continuing to expand its online activities, Citibank e-Business launched the World Chemical Exchange, a global Internet market for chemicals, plastics, and gasses. Citibank introduced Cititrade, a discount, stand-alone online investment service.[27] Citibank formed alliances with Oracle to facilitate B2B financial payments and introduced a web dealing with ADRs (American Depository Receipts).[28]

2001

Citibank acquired European American Bank (EAB) from ABN Amro. EAB is a retail bank with deposits of $11.5 billion. The acquisition makes Citibank the largest bank in terms of deposits in Long Island, New York. It also strengthens Citibank's retail operations in the New York City area. Citibank also entered into negotiations with Mycal, a Japanese supermarket operator, to buy its credit card operations.[29]

Citigroup expanded its online activities by signing an agreement with Microsoft allowing Microsoft Network (MSN) customers to use the Internet to transfer money.[30] About 230 million people use MSN each day.

Citigroup moved into Mexico by acquiring Grupo Financiero Banamex-Accival, which is better known as Banacci. Banacci is Mexico's second largest bank. The new group will operate under the "Banamex" name.

Deutsche Bank AG

In February 2001, Deutsche Bank was the second largest bank in the world in terms of assets. It was founded in 1870 to transact banking business of all kinds and to promote trade between Germany, Europe, and overseas markets. It's still doing that and more. But the recent history of Deutsche Bank AG reveals a shift away from universal banking in general, and retail banking in particular, toward corporate banking, investment banking, and asset management. One reason for the shift is due to the competition from the state-owned Sparkassen savings banks and regional Landesbanks ("Deutsche's Big Gamble," 2000; "Europe's Banking Blues," 2000). According to the European Competition Commission, the German government's backing of these institutions causes the "distortion of competition rising from state guarantees which are unlimited both in duration and amount and are provided free."[31] Deutsche Bank's share of the 6 million retail customers in Germany is less than 5 percent. Collectively, the four biggest private sector banks hold only 5 percent of total deposits.[32] The small market share and low returns from retail banking have forced the banks to look elsewhere for growth.

Following acquisitions in Belgium, Italy, and Spain, Deutsche Bank established a strategic relationship with EFG Eurbank Group in Athens, Greece, in 1998. It also spun off its direct industrial holdings into subsidiaries in the legal form of private limited partnerships with a joint stock company as general partner. The joint stock company is called DB Investor.

In 1999, Deutsche Bank acquired Bankers Trust Corporation. Bankers Trust had a strong position in asset management and securities custody. It also had acquired two investment firms, Wolfensohn & Co., and Alex Brown & Sons, Inc., and had combined them into a major merger advisory and equity underwriting business. A decade earlier it acquired the UK's Morgen Grenfell. The acquisition of these firms is part of Deutsche Bank's aim to become a leading global investment bank.

In March 2000, Deutsche Bank and its Frankfurt rival, Dresdner Bank, Germany's third largest bank, planned to merge and form the biggest bank in Europe. However, the following month the proposed merger with Dresdner Bank collapsed, in part, because the Deutsche investment bankers wanted to keep the branch and online brokerage outlet distribution channels that would have been turned over to Allianze as part of the deal. Allianze AG, a German Insurer, is a major stockholder in both banks, and Deutsche Bank owns stock in Allianze as well.[33] Those distribution channels gave Deutsche Bank access to about 60 million Europeans who could switch from low-yielding deposit accounts into securities and investment funds (Major, September 16, 2001). Another major problem was the proposed sale of Dresdner Kleinwort Benson, Dresdner's investment banking union. That unit did not want to be sold, and the merger was called off.

As previously noted, Deutsche Bank wanted to change from a conventional universal bank into a global investment bank that could challenge U.S. investment banks such as Goldman Sachs. Goldman Sachs is a major competitor in Europe and globally.

In February 2001, Deutsche Bank reorganized its business into a "two-pillar" structure to improve profitability. The two groups are the Corporate and Institutional Clients Group and the Asset Management & Private Clients Group. The Corporate group includes investment banking, institutional businesses, and real estate. According to Deutsche Bank's CEO, Rolf Breuer,[34] the main growth potential for the bank is in asset (wealth) management and private banking because the growth of investment banking cannot be sustained at past rates (Cameron, February 1, 2001). The Asset Management group includes DB Alex Brown, Private Client Services for high net worth individuals, Deutsche Bank 24, and other retail distributions. Bank 24 is a retail banking business targeted at customers in Germany who want advice at branches or who would like to do business online. It also has a retail network in Italy, France, Poland, and Spain.

In addition, it has formed strategic alliances with Yahoo!, Nokia, SAP, AOL, and others to deliver their Global E-strategy for electronic commerce. Rolf Breuer (2000) said that E-business is the key to future success and forms an integral part of the bank's strategy; the bank is using its highly advanced technical infrastructure to reach customers even more effectively. In 2001, *Global Finance* magazine ranked Deutsche Bank as the best Internet bank.[35] As part of the retail strategy, an online brokerage service, Maxblue, opened in 2001.[36] This service is an attempt to combine traditional retail banking with funds management. Unfortunately for Deutsche Bank, profits from asset management fell sharply in the first half of 2001.[37] The bank's response was to cut costs, which means getting rid of people—especially high-cost people. Deutsche Bank claims that the multimillion salaries paid to investment bankers were too high, and so the chairman of their Alex Brown unit was replaced. In the second half of 2001, Deutsche Bank wrote down 408 million Euros in assets after the September 11 terrorist attack in the United States.[38] It also increased its provision for loan losses due to a slowing economy. It was not a good year for the bank.

Deutsche Bank expanded its pan-European market by acquiring the asset management and corporate banking activities of the French Bank of Worms Group in 2001. To make further inroads in France, Deutsche Bank was holding talks with Axa, the French Insurance Group, over a possible distribution agreement.[39] It also acquired National Discount Brokers, an online broker, giving it access to U.S. retail brokerage markets.

Deutche Bank's UK subsidiary, Morgan Grenfell Private Equity, acquired 3,000 British bars (pubs) for $2.3 billion.[40] The venture capital firm is interested in cash flow. Income from the pubs can be securitized by issuing bonds backed by the pub's real estate. The company that sold the pubs, however, claims that Britons are spending less of their income on beer. This type of investment reveals the range of investments made by the parent company. While the company expanded in some markets, it sold holdings in banks in Poland and Australia. Nevertheless, it still operates in more than 60 countries.

A slowdown in global economic activity adversely affected Deutsche Bank's profits, and in August 2001, Chief Executive Rolf Breuer announced job cuts, the sale of some assets, and the acquisition of others. Part of the strategy included purchasing the part of the National Discount Brokers (NDB) Group Inc. that it did not own for about $1 billion. NDB is a U.S. online retail broker. However, the decline in the U.S. stock market hurt retail brokers and NDB. In July 2001, Deutsche Bank sold NDB's online retail business to Ameritrade Holding Corporation for $154 million in stock, but it still retained NDB Capital Markets Corp.[41] Deutsche Bank also planned to sell its life insurance unit (Deutsche Herold Life) to help pay for the acquisition of Zurich Financial Services' U.S. asset management affiliate—Zurich Scudder Investments.[42] As part of the deal, Deutsche Bank also wanted to acquire Zurich Invest, ZFS's fund manager.[43]

Despite the slowdown in profits, Deutsche Bank's desire for global expansion did not decrease. For example, it attempted to acquire a failed bank in Korea, but the deal fell through when the Korean government refused to take back bad loans.[44]

Credit Lyonnais

Credit Lyonnais was incorporated as a private bank in France in 1863, and it was nationalized in 1946.[45] It was France's largest bank. Under the chairmanship of Jean Yves Haberer from 1988 to 1993, the bank expanded aggressively and recklessly.[46] One goal was to build a global bank that would rival Germany's Deutsche Bank. To help achieve that goal, Credit Lyonnais acquired banks in Belgium, Italy, Germany, and the Nertherlands. It also financed loans that went bad in a Canadian real estate group, Olympia and York, and the Metro-Goldwyn-Mayer movie studios in California.

Credit Lyonnais's subsidiary, Altus Finance, SA, indirectly acquired the junk bond portfolio from Executive Life Insurance Company that failed in 1991 after its $9 billion junk bond portfolio collapsed in value and the company was taken over by the California Insurance Department.[47] An independent insurer, Aurora National Life Insurance Company, offered to buy the junk bonds for $3.25 billion. Aurora was controlled by Altus and the MAAF group.[48] However, Altus did not properly disclose its relationships with Aurora, and it was under investigation by the Federal Reserve in 2001 for violation of U.S. regulations.[49] At that time, banks and their subsidiaries were prohibited from buying life insurance companies. Finally, most banks were prohibited from owning junk bonds, but that does not apply to insurance companies.[50]

Furthermore, Credit Lyonnais is being sued by a private group of U.S. investors who claim the bank fraudulently took control of Executive Life (Mackintosh and Larson, 2001). It is also being sued by the California Insurance Commissioner who claims that French investors profited unduly from Executive Life's junk bond portfolio when the takeover of the insurance group was illegal. A criminal investigation of potential fraud in this deal has been initiated.

Credit Lyonnais financed these failed activities with high-cost debt. Even though Haberer left in 1993, the problems did not go away. In 1997, employee fraud in Credit Lyonnais Belgium resulted in a loss of $100 million, five times the bank's profit. In 1998, Deutsche Bank bought Credit Lyonnais Belgium.

"Meglomania and mismanagement are the main reasons for the bank's losses, fraud is also to blame" ("Banking's Biggest Disaster," 2001). The huge losses required several government rescue plans, downsizing, and privatization in 1999. Part of the bailout agreement stipulated that the bank would put its losing assets in a holding company, and the government would grant a below-market rate loan to fund those assets ("Credit Lyonnais Warns," 2001). As part of the downsizing, the bank sold assets worth $88 billion. The cost of the rescue plans to French taxpayers is estimated to be about $20 billion.

In the privatization, the public held 50 percent of the stock, core shareholders held 33 percent, the French state kept 10 percent, and the rest was shared by employees and the company. The core shareholders (*groupe d'actionaires partenaires*) included Crédit Agricole (10%), Allianz-AGF (6%), Axa (5.5%), Commerzbank (4%), Banco Bilboa Viscaya Argenartia (BBVA) (3.75%), and Crédit Commercial de France (1%).

The bank sold some or all of its retail operations in Argentina, Brazil, Chile, the Netherlands, Peru, the Philippines, and Sweden, and their Dublin-based financial services firm. Nevertheless, the bank is still present in more than 60 countries.

In 2000, the bank was reorganized into three major lines of business: Corporate and International Banking, full-service French Commercial Banking, and Asset Management. It also opened a fully remote online bank (e.creditlyonnais.fr). Credit Lyonnais was once again on the growth path. It acquired ABF Capital Management, a small fund manager, and Systeia Capital Management, a hedge fund (Mackintosh, December 6, 2000, and January 31, 2001). It also formed a pan-European investment banking joint venture with the Italian Banca Intesa and Spanish BBVA (Iskander, June 27, 2001).

Due to its increased performance, the bank was concerned that it might be a target for a hostile takeover from other banks or insurance companies (Iskander, September 12, 2001). The French mutual bank, Credit Agricole SA, and the German insurer, Allianz AG, are considered the front-runners as takeover candidates (Wrighton and Carreyrou, 2001). However, Lyonnais's chairman, Jean Peyrelevade, told reporters that he did not believe that a takeover would happen before July 2003 (Barkin, 2001).

VIEWS FROM THE TOP

Against this background of change, Dr. David Morgan, chief executive officer of Wespac (Australia), made the following comment about the future of banking:

> It will be the interplay between the financial, social and environmental factors driving our industry, that will ultimately determine the future of our industry. We truly do live in extraordinary times with frontiers of change rolling through the business environment and society at large with relentless and unstoppable force. The current transformation promises to be as profound as the industrial revolution that reshaped the world.[51]

The net result of these and other changes, according to Richard M. Kovacevich, president and chief executive officer of Wells Fargo & Company, is that "There is no longer a banking industry, a securities industry and an insurance industry. There is a $2.4 trillion financial services industry" (Kovacevich, 2000). While that may be so, banks are by no means passé. In an interview with *U.S. Banker*, Hugh McColl, Jr., then CEO of Bank of America Corporation, stated that institutions retain their bank charters for two reasons (Bennett, 2000). First, they can attract funds because of their FDIC insurance. Second, they can borrow funds from the Federal Reserve when they need to do so in order to create liquidity. McColl went on to say that while these two things are not as important today as they were in the past, banks are getting out of the banking business.

Dennis O'Leary, executive vice president of Chase Manhattan Bank, provides further insights about change. He argues that business architecture is driven by technology and that changes are taking place (O'Leary, 2000). The business architecture of large U.S. banks consists of three major areas: distribution of services through many different channels; competence in manufacturing digital factories that produce economies of scale and efficiencies; and competence in information mastery. He argues that the distribution of services and economies of scale businesses are becoming commodities. The value to be added in the future is combining those two to take advantage of information about consumers. O'Leary goes on to say that the model is not proprietary. It often involves joint ventures and alliances. Lehman Brothers demonstrates how to use different channels and alliances. Lehman owns Lehman Brothers Bank (Delaware), but it does not plan to offer banking services directly ("Lehman to Offer Baking to Clients," 2000). Instead, it made an agreement with Corillian Corporation to use its Voyager eFinance Suite to bring Internet banking services to institutional clients who, in turn, will offer them to their retail customers.

CONCLUSIONS

Change is the operative word in the global financial markets. Changes in financial markets are a result of changes in technology, deregulation, and globalization. But what are the implications of these changes? Andrew Crockett (2000), general manager of the Bank of International Settlements, argues that there will be an erosion of geographic barriers between markets, a blurring of distinction between different types of financial institutions, further consolidation, and completeness of markets—referring to the increased use of derivatives to disaggregate, price, and trade risk. While that may be so, it may not be a smooth transition. Krugman (2000) stated that one implication of these changes is that they predispose the world economy to more crises because they pressure governments to relax financial restrictions that have made 1990s-style crises less likely. He also maintains that dollarization or euroization may help solve the problem and that in the long run, integration of the markets may solve the problems it created. However, dollarization may have helped Argentina, for example, with its hyperinflation problems, but it hampered it in recovering from an economic crisis in 2001 (Wessel, 2001).

NOTES

1. Schumpeter (1934).
2. Schumpeter (1942).

3. Real bills is, however, mentioned in connection with monetary policy. See Mishkin (1995).

4. *Consolidation in the Financial Sector* (2001). Also see Robertson (2001).

5. For additional discussion of megamergers in financial institutions, see Gup (2001). For a discussion of other changes in the banking industry, see Berger, Kashyap, and Scalise (1995).

6. For additional discussion of the types of consolidations, see Berger (2000).

7. Data are from the FDIC, *Statistics on Banking, 2000.*

8. See Colantuoni (1998) for a discussion on demutualization in the thrift industry.

9. The Principal Financial Group went public in 2001. See www.principal.com/about/demut.htm (visited 2/18/01).

10. See "The Blame Game" (2001) and "Low Life" (2001) for an overview of the problems with the life insurance industry in the UK; "Friends to Float on LSE," CNNfn, May 2, 2001 (visited 5/2/01).

11. Although not discussed here, legislation was introduced (HR 3703, in 2000) to reduce the lines of credit to Fannie Mae and Freddie Mac, government-sponsored enterprises (GSE) that are very active in the home mortgage markets. Baer and Miles (2000) edited a special edition of the *Quarterly Review of Economics and Finance* that focused on bank privatization and restructuring in Brazil.

12. "Japan Starts Picking on China," *Economist*, February 10, 2001, 43–44.

13. "China Ban Spooks Banks," September 3, 2001.

14. National Bank Act, 12 USC, 24 (7).

15. *NationsBank v. Variable Life Insurance Co.*, 1995, U.S. Lexis 691, 115 S. Ct. 810 (January 18, 1995).

16. www.regionsbank.com; "Fourth Quarter 2000 Update."

17. See www.etrade.com.

18. The name of the bank has been changed to Shinsei Bank Ltd.

19. Walker, Handelsblatt, Landgraf, and Busse, April 3, 2001.

20. See www.amsouth.com.

21. "From Mormon to Mannon" (2001).

22. The new Basle Capital Accord can be found on www.bis.org.

23. Information about Citigroup is from their press releases or other sources that are cited. See www.citigroup.com for more information.

24. The acquisition was completed in November 2000.

25. Beckett, September 7, 2001.

26. See www.myciti.com.

27. See www.citibankonline.com.

28. See www.citibank.com/adr.

29. Hijino, January 18, 2001; "Citigroup to Buy Banacci," May 17, 2001.

30. Beckett, May 1, 2001.

31. Part of a statement by European Competition Commissioner, Mario Monte (Walker and Mitchner, January 29, 2001).

32. "Co-operative Spirit," 2001.

33. In June 2000, Deutsche Bank reduced its holdings of Allianze to 4.1 percent. Allianze owned about 22 percent of Dresdner and 5 percent of Deutsche Bank.

34. Breuer is the "Speaker for the Board" of Deutsche Bank, which is the equivalent of the chief executive officer.

35. "World's Best Internet Banks," *Global Finance*, October 2001, 72. Also see www.deutschebank.com, www.db-business-direct-de, and www.dbmarkets.com.
36. Walker, May 4, 2001.
37. Major, September 16, 2001.
38. "Duetsche Bank Profits Fall," October 31, 2001.
39. Cameron, March 5, 2001.
40. Cowell, March 21, 2001.
41. "Ameritrade Buys NDB.com."
42. Wollrab, September 7, 2001.
43. Major, October 30, 2001.
44. Kirk, October 11, 2001.
45. For a detailed history, see www.creditlyonnais.com.
46. Gup (1998).
47. See "The Curse Continues" (2001) for information about Executive Life; see "Credit Lyonnais Probe Widens" (2001) for information about Altus.
48. MAAF is an acronym for a French auto insurance company. MAAF Vie (a subsidiary of MAAF) and a Swiss company form the MAAF group. For additional information, see "Conservation & Liquidation: Executive Life Insurance Company," California Department of Insurance, www.insurance.ca.gov/CLO/Clohome.htm (visited 9/10/01). Another member of MAAF was Fimalack, a firm owned by Marc Ladreit de Lacharriere, a French businessman who was a director of Credit Lyonnais ("Credit Lyonnais: The Curse Continues").
49. Rossant, July 30, 2001.
50. Winninghoff (1994).
51. Morgan, December 2000.

REFERENCES

"Ameritrade Buys NDB.com." CNNfn, cnnfn.com, July 31, 2001 (visited 7/31/01).

Baer, Werner, and William Miles, eds. *Quarterly Review of Economics and Finance* (special edition: Focus: Privatization and Restructuring: The Case of Brazil), Vol. 40, 2000.

"Banking's Biggest Disaster." Economist.com, www.economist.com, July 5, 1997 (visited 1/18/01).

Barkin, Noah. "Lyonnais Grows, No Alliance Imminent." CNNfn, cnnfn.com, September 7, 2001 (visited 9/7/01).

Beckett, Paul. "Citigroup, Microsoft Sign Pact Allowing MSN Users to Make Web Money Transfers." *Wall Street Journal*, May 1, 2001, B6.

Beckett, Paul. "Citigroup Sets Accord to Settle Associates Probe." *Wall Street Journal*, September 7, 2001, A3, A6.

Bennett, Robert A. "McColl Sees the Future." *U.S. Banker*, September 2000, 34–91.

Berger, Allen N. "The 'Big' Picture of Bank Diversification." *The Changing Financial Industry Structure and Regulation: Bridging States, Countries, and Industries*. Federal Reserve Bank of Chicago, Proceedings of the 36th Bank Structure Conference, May 2000, 162–174.

Berger, Allen N., Anil K. Kashyap, and Joseph M. Scalise. "The Transformation of the U.S. Banking Industry: What a Long, Strange Trip It's Been." *Brookings Papers on Economic Activity*, 2, 1995, 55–218.

"The Blame Game." *Economist*, January 20, 2001, 70–71.

Bortolotti, Bernardo, Domenico Sinscalco, and Marcella Fantini. "Privatisation and Institutions: A Cross Country Analysis." CESifo Working Paper No. 375 (Germany), November 2000.

Breuer, Rolf-E. Speech at the Annual Shareholders Meeting of Deutsche Bank AG, Frankfurt am Main, June 9, 2000.

Cameron, Doug. "Deutsche Bank Talks to Axa." FT.com, *Financial Times*, www.ft.com, March 5, 2001 (visited 3/5/01).

Cameron, Doug. "Deutsche to Cut 2,000 Jobs." FT.com, *Financial Times*, www.ft.com, February 1, 2001 (visited 2/2/01).

Cetorelli, Nicola, and Michele Gambera. "Banking Market Structure, Financial Dependence, and Growth: International Evidence from Industry Data." *Journal of Finance*, Vol. 56, No. 2, April 2001, 617–648.

"China Ban Spooks Banks." CNNfn, cnnfn.com, September 3, 2001 (visited 9/3/01).

"Citigroup to Buy Banacci." CNNfn, cnnfn.com, May 17, 2001 (visited 5/17/01).

Colantuoni, Joseph A. "Mutual-to-Stock Conversions: Problems with the Pricing of Initial Public Offerings." Federal Deposit Insurance Corporation, *FDIC Banking Review*, Vol. 11, No. 4, 1998, 1–9.

"Conservation & Liquidation: Executive Life Insurance Company." California Department of Insurance, www.insurance.ca.gov/CLO/Clohome.htm (visited 9/10/01).

Consolidation in the Financial Sector. Group of Ten, Basel, Switzerland, Bank for International Settlements, January 2001.

"Co-operative Spirit." *Economist*, February 17, 2001, 75.

Cowell, Alan. "Deutsche Bank Unit to Pay $2.3 Billion for 3,000 Pubs." *The New York Times on the Web*, March 21, 2001, www.nytimes.com (visited 3/21/01).

"Crawford, Leslie. "BBVA Attacks Central Banks." FT.com, *Financial Times*, www.ft.com, March 12, 2001 (visited 3/12/01).

"Credit Lyonnais: The Curse Continues." *Economist*, January 13, 2001, 67–70.

"Credit Lyonnais Probe Widens." news.bbc.co.uk, September 6, 2001 (visited 9/6/2001).

"Credit Lyonnais Warns." CNNfn, cnnfn.com, May 2, 2001 (visited 5/2/01).

Crenshaw, Albert B. "Own a Share of the Rock." *Washington Post*, December 22, 2000, E01.

Crockett, Andrew. "Commentary: How Should Financial Market Regulators Respond to the New Challenges of Global Economic Integration?" *Global Economic Integration: Opportunities and Challenges*, Federal Reserve Bank of Kansas City, 2000, 121–129.

"The Curse Continues." *Economist*, January 13, 2001, 67–70.

"Deutsche Bank Profits Fall." CNN.com, www.money.cnn.com, October 31, 2001 (visited 10/31/01).

"Deutsche's Big Gamble." *Economist*, March 11, 2000, 74–75.

"Diving into Demutualization." *Financial Executive*, November/December 2000, 19–21.

"Europe's Banking Blues." *Economist*, March 11, 2000, 22–23.

"Friends to Float on LSE." CNNfn, cnnfn.com, May 2, 2001 (visited 5/2/01).

"From Morman to Mammon." *Economist*, June 9, 2001, 74–76.

Garten, Jeffrey E. "The Mind of the C.E.O." *BusinessWeek*, February 5, 2001, 106–110. (Contains excerpts from Jeffrey E. Gartan, *The Mind of the C.E.O.* [New York: Basic Books/Perseus Publishing, 2001].)

Gogoi, Pallavi. "I'll Take a CD with That Life Policy, Please." *BusinessWeek*, January 22, 2001, 92.

Graham, Robert, and Victor Mallet. "France Seeks US Intervention over Credit Lyonnais Problems." FT.com, *Financial Times*, www.ft.com, June 18, 2001 (visited 6/28/01).

Greenspan, Alan. "Remarks by Chairman Alan Greenspan before the American Bankers Association, Washington, D.C." September 18, 2000.

Gup, Benton E., ed. *Bank Failures in the Major Trading Countries of the World: Causes and Consequences*. Westport, Conn.: Quorum Books, 1998.

Gup, Benton E., ed. *Megamergers in a Global Economy*. Westport, Conn.: Quorum Books, 2001.

Hijino, Ken. "Citigroup in Talks to Buy Japan's Mycal Credit Card." FT.com, *Financial Times*, www.ft.com, January 18, 2001 (visited 1/18/01).

Iskander, Samer. "CL Presses for Joint Venture." FT.com, *Financial Times*, www.ft.com, June 27, 2001 (visited 5/2/01).

Iskander, Samer. "Lyonnais Becomes Scared of Success." FT.com, *Financial Times*, www.ft.com, September 12, 2001 (visited 5/2/01).

Kirk, Don. "Deutsche Bank's Negotiations for a Korean Bank Collapse." *New York Times*, www.nytimes.com, October 11, 2001 (visited 10/11/01).

Kovacevich, Richard M. "Privacy and the Promise of Financial Modernization." Federal Reserve Bank of Minneapolis, *The Region*, March 2000, 27–29.

Krugman, Paul. "Crises: The Price of Globalization." *Global Economic Integration: Opportunities and Challenges*. Federal Reserve Bank of Kansas City, 2000, 75–106.

"Lehman to Offer Banking to Clients." *FutureBanker*, June 2000, 18s.

"Low Life." *Economist*, January 20, 2001, 72.

Mackintosh, James. "Credit Lyonnais Buys Hedge Fund." FT.com, *Financial Times*, www.ft.com, January 31, 2001 (visited 1/31/01).

Mackintosh, James. "Credit Lyonnais Purchases ABN News Digest." FT.com, *Financial Times*, www.ft.com, December 6, 2000 (visited 1/31/01).

Mackintosh, James, and Peter Thal Larsen. "Credit Lyonnais Faces Suit over Executive Life." FT.com, *Financial Times*, www.ft.com, January 31, 2001 (visited 5/2/01).

Major, Tony. "Deutsche Bank in Talks with Zurich Financial Services." FT.com, *Financial Times*, www.ft.com, October 30, 2001 (visited 10/30/01).

Major, Tony. "Deutsche Bank Launches Cost-cutting Program," FT.com, *Financial Times*, www.ft.com, September 16, 2001 (visited 9/17/01).

Major, Tony. "With the Shake-Up Announced This Week, A Symbol of German Finance Has Donned the Garb of Wall Street." FT.com, *Financial Times*, www.ft.com, December 8, 2000 (visited 1/22/01).

McReynolds, Rebecca. "A Drag on Earnings." *U.S. Banker*, www.us-banker.com, January 2000 (visited 1/31/01).

Merton, Robert C., and Zvi Bodie. "Financial Infrastructure and Public Policy." In *The Global Financial System: A Functional Perspective*, edited by D. B. Crate, et al. Boston: Harvard Business School Press, 1995, 263–282.

Meyer, Paul A. *Money, Financial Institutions, and the Economy*. Homewood, Ill: Irwin, 1986.

Mishkin, Frederic S. *Financial Markets, Institutions, and Money*. New York, HarperCollins College Publishers, 1995.

Morgan, David. "Banks and the Bigger Picture." *Journal of Banking and Financial Ser-*

vices, Australasian Institute of Banking and Finance, Vol. 114, No. 6, December 2000, 6.

O'Leary, Dennis. "All the Answers Are Different." Federal Reserve Bank of New York, *Economic Policy Review*, Vol. 6, No. 4, October 2000, 61–65.

"Prudential to Go Public." CNNfn, cnnfn.com, December 18, 2000 (visited 12/18/00).

Robertson, Douglas D. "A Markov View of Bank Consolidation: 1960–2000." *Economic and Policy Analysis Working Paper 2001–4*. Washington, D.C.: Comptroller of the Currency, September 2001.

Rossant, John. "The Sword over Lyonnais." *BusinessWeek Online*, www.businessweek.com, July 30, 2001 (visited 8/3/01).

"Royal Bank of Canada to Buy Centura Banks for $2.3bn." FT.com, *Financial Times*, www.ft.com, January 26, 2001 (visited 1/26/01).

"Sanpaolo, BSCH to Link in Two Markets." *Wall Street Journal*, July 13, 2000.

Schumpeter, Joseph A. *Capitalism, Socialism and Democracy*. New York: Harper & Bros., 1942.

Schumpeter, Joseph A. *The Theory of Economic Development*. German edition 1911; English translation, Cambridge, Mass.: Harvard University Press, 1934.

Singer, Jason. "Japan Allows Texas Fund to Buy Bank." *Wall Street Journal*, January 26, 2001, C10.

Statistics on Banking, 2000. Washington, D.C.: FDIC, 2001.

Walker, Marcus. "Deutsche Bank Posts Profit of $920 Million." *Wall Street Journal*, May 4, 2001, A13.

Walker, Marcus, Handelsblatt, Robert Landgraf, and Busse Caspar. "Deal for Dresdner Won't Satisfy an Acquisitive Allianz." *Wall Street Journal*, April 3, 2001, A16, A19 (Editor's Note: No first name was given for Hanelsblatt).

Walker, Marcus, and Brandon Mitchner. "EU Competition Panel Says German Banks Violate Law." *Wall Street Journal*, January 29, 2001, A18.

Wessel, David. "A Default in Slow Motion." *Wall Street Journal*, November 9, 2001, A1.

Williams, Julie L., and Mark P. Jacobsen. "The Business of Banking: Looking to the Future." Office of the Comptroller of the Currency, Memo, March 6, 1995.

Winninghoff, Ellie. "Smart Buyer, Dumb Seller." *Forbes*, March 14, 1994, 71.

Wollrab, Mirko. "Deutsche Offers Swap for Scudder." CNNfn, cnnfn.com, September 7, 2001 (visited 9/7/01).

"World's Best Internet Banks." *Global Finance*, October 2001, 72.

Wrighton, Jo, and John Carreyrou. "Positioning for Control of Credit Lyonnais Begins." *Wall Street Journal*, May 22, 2001, A23.

Chapter 2

The Future of Banking in Developed and Less Developed Countries

Steven A. Seelig

INTRODUCTION

The development of financial markets, and banking in particular, has been evolutionary. Developed economies have seen the number of banking organizations shrink, the size of the largest institutions grow, a move toward internationalization of financial services, and the blurring of institutional boundaries by product. This trend has led some to believe that the future of banking will be very different from that of the past century. However, an examination of trends in much of the world, particularly in the less developed countries, shows financial markets at a very early stage of development and a future for banking that is very different from what has been observed for developed countries.

This chapter examines some of the data on financial depth and the relationship between macroeconomic conditions and the development of banking markets. It also discusses the precursors necessary for change to come in the less developed countries. The chapter also points out that while a number of structural changes are critical for the development of robust banking sectors, one cannot ignore the overall macroeconomic environment in analyzing the prospects for a country's financial sector. Although the chapter does not provide any definitive conclusions that would allow a reader to predict the state of a nation's banking sector, it does suggest the types of economic influences that are important for financial sector development. There is a clear need for more research in this area. The literature on the future of banking should not continue to ignore what is happening in much of the world.

This chapter reviews the literature on the trends that have been observed in the more developed economies; presents data on the degree of financial depth for a variety of countries and highlights the disparities across countries; discusses some of the things that need to happen to encourage a more robust banking system in those countries that lack financial depth; and provides some concluding thoughts and observations on policy issues.

THE DEVELOPED WORLD

During the early to mid-1990s, the banking literature began to focus on the changes occurring in the financial sector and raised the issue of whether banking was on the decline. In May 1994, the Federal Reserve Bank of Chicago focused its annual Conference on Bank Structure and Competition on "The Declining Role of Banking." Franklin Edwards (1996) devoted a chapter in his book to the decline of traditional banking and the rise of nonbank financial intermediaries. He noted that the role of commercial banks as a source of funds to nonfinancial firms had been declining in the United States. He went on to explain this trend as well as other measures of the diminishing role of banks.[1] Edwards also noted that "traditional banking is on the decline in other countries as well" (p. 42). However, the data he presents to support his views concentrates exclusively on developed countries. Other authors who focused on developed countries have also pointed to a need for changes in regulation and powers for banks in order to stem their demise.[2]

Although the demise of traditional banking had become a popular theme among some researchers and commentators on the banking scene, others found the reports of banking's death to be greatly exaggerated. Boyd and Gertler (1994, p. 85) found no evidence of "a significant decline in banking" after empirically adjusting for the growth of off-balance-sheet items. Similarly, the Organization for Economic Cooperation and Development (OECD) (1995) found that although securitization had replaced some lending, banks still played a key role in marshalling savings and in the payment system.

While the debate on the future of banking is interesting, both the trade and research literature has looked only at the developed countries and ignored what is happening in much of the world. In many less developed nations, the role played by banks and the state of development of the banking sector is very different from that in the developed world.

FINANCIAL DEPTHS—EMPIRICAL EVIDENCE

One approach to examining the depth of a country's financial system is to look at the ratio of broad money to gross domestic product (GDP) (see Table 2.1). The data presented in Table 2.1 is for the year 2000. The ratio of broad money to GDP provides a measure of financial activity relative to a country's income. This measure of monetization is only about 10 percent for those countries with extremely low levels of financial activity, compared to between 40 and 80 percent for the formerly centrally planned economies of Central Europe

Table 2.1
Broad Money as Percentage of GDP, 2000[1]

Country	Ratio	Country	Ratio	Country	Ratio
Albania	0.1	Sao Tome & Principe	28.1	Djibouti	53.5
Equatorial Guinea	4.6	Solomon Islands	28.4	Dominica	54.7
Tajikistan	5.9	Guinea-Bissau	28.4	Indonesia	55.0
Congo, Dem. Rep. Of	7.0	Togo	28.6	Tunisia	56.6
Lao People's Dem. Rep.	7.4	Mexico	29.5	South Africa	57.3
Niger	7.5	Haiti	29.6	St. Lucia	57.7
Georgia	10.4	Benin	29.7	Syrian Arab Republic	57.8
Belarus	10.0	Bulgaria	29.7	India	58.6
Sudan	10.8	Gambia, The	30.0	Maldives	59.5
Guinea	11.1	Latvia	30.2	Barbados	60.3
Gabon	11.2	Paraguay	30.4	Bahamas, The	60.7
Azerbaijan	11.6	Dominican Republic	30.6	Kuwait	63.0
Kyrgyz Republic	11.7	Oman	31.6	Guyana	63.5
Congo, Republic Of	11.7	Bangladesh	31.7	Germany	64.1
Armenia	11.8	Colombia	32.4	Uruguay	64.3
Chad	12.3	Argentina	33.6	Netherlands Antilles	64.7
Uzbekistan	12.4	Estonia	33.9	France	64.8
Kazakhstan	12.5	Yemen, Republic of	34.1	Slovak Republic	65.2
Malawi	13.5	Costa Rica	36.0	Cape Verde	65.2
Turkmenistan	14.1	Denmark	37.6	St. Vincent & Grens. St.	67.1
Uganda	14.4	Sri Lanka	38.1	Kiribati	67.9
Mauritania	14.5	Zimbawe	38.2	Australia	68.2
Tanzania	14.7	Tonga	39.4	Antigua and Barbuda	68.3
Angola	15.2	Qatar	40.1	Portugal	71.6
Cambodia	15.7	Kenya	40.2	Bahrain	72.1
Zambia	15.9	Algeria	40.7	Luxembourg	73.5
Cameroon	15.9	Croatia	41.6	St. Kitts and Nevis St.	76.9
Rwanda	16.2	Jamaica	42.5	Egypt	77.4
Central African Rep.	16.4	Turkey	42.9	Netherlands	77.6
Russia	16.5	Philippines	43.0	Morocco	78.2
Nicaragua	16.9	Samoa	43.1	Czech Republic	79.8
Sierra Leone	18.0	Pakistan	43.2	Korea	79.9
Ukraine	18.1	Iran, I.R. of	43.8	Austria	80.0
Venezuela, Rep. Bol.	18.4	Ethiopia	44.0	Israel	80.3
Burundi	18.6	Italy	44.5	Mauritius	81.1
Romania	18.7	Iceland	44.5	Ireland	81.9
Moldova	19.7	Poland	44.9	Belgium	87.5
Mali	20.4	Sweden	45.2	New Zealand	89.2
Liberia	20.5	United Arab Emirates	46.2	Panama	89.3
Peru	20.8	Suriname	46.4	United Kingdom	93.9
Lithuania	21.8	Trinidad and Tobago	47.0	Spain	95.7
Botwana	21.8	Hungary	47.0	Seychelles	99.2
Madagascar	21.9	Honduras	47.2	Singapore	107.4
Swaziland	22.9	Nepal	47.7	Brunei Darussalam	107.5
Ghana	23.1	Bolivia	47.9	Thailand	108.3
Comoros	23.4	Canada	48.2	Chile	109.1
Nigeria	23.5	Bhutan	48.4	Jordan	110.8
Mongolia	23.8	El Salvador	48.9	Cyprus	114.1
Macedonia, FYR	23.8	Namibia	48.9	Switzerland	122.8
Senegal	24.2	United States	49.3	Japan	125.0
Myanmar	24.3	Saudi Arabia	49.4	Vanuatu	131.9
Cote D'Ivoire	25.1	Slovenia	51.2	Malaysia	132.5
Burkina Faso	26.2	Grenada	51.3	China, P.R. Mainland	150.6
Mozambique	26.8	Belize	51.5	Eritrea	162.6
Papua New Guinea	26.9	Norway	52.2	Malta	168.8
Guatemala	27.2	Vietnam	52.3	Taiwan Prov. Of China	191.0
Lesotho	27.7	Libya	52.4	Lebanon	196.7
Brazil	27.7	Finland	52.6	China, P.R. Hong Kong	286.9
Ecuador	27.9	Fiji	52.8		

[1]1998 data for Austria, Belgium, Finland, France, Germany, Ireland, Italy, Netherlands, Portugal, and Spain; 1999 data for Luxembourg.

Sources: WEO and IFS.

and a broad range of other countries in various stages of economic development, including the United States. Some of the countries traditionally thought of as international financial centers, or offshore centers, have ratios over 100 percent. It should be noted that the United States has averaged approximately 50 percent over the last decade, and this is consistent with the results observed in the literature cited above.

If one wishes to focus on the relative importance of the banking sector, an alternative measure is to examine the ratio of bank deposits, or bank assets, to GDP. This measure captures the impact of the public's preference for either using or avoiding banks. An examination of the data for 2000 indicates that the countries with the shallowest banking sectors are several African countries and Georgia.[3] The five lowest ratios are all 5 percent or less. Other countries range widely from the United States with 28.1 percent (consistent with the rise of nonbank financial institutions) to Hungary at 39.1 percent. The depth of the banking sector is considerably greater in the developed Asian economies of Korea and Japan. Hong Kong, with its role as a financial center for Asia, had deposits equaling two to three times GDP.

In some of those countries that are considered to lack financial depth, a partial cause is the public's desire to hold cash rather than deposits.[4] To some extent, this preference for cash over deposits can be observed by comparing the data in Table 2.1 with that in Table 2.2. However, it can be seen more vividly in Table 2.3 which presents the ratio of currency (outside the central bank) to deposits. As one can see, most countries have relatively low ratios, indicating that either wealth is held in deposits or, more likely, that deposits are tied to the medium of exchange used in a country, whether it be checks, debit cards, credit cards, or some other means of making retail and wholesale payments. However, the data also show that some of the countries with the shallowest banking systems also have the highest ratios of currency to deposits.

INCREASING FINANCIAL DEPTH

Importance of Financial Depth

Empirical evidence showing the linkage between economic growth and finance was first emphasized in the work of McKinnon (1973) and Shaw (1973). They showed that high-growth economies tended to have well-developed financial markets. Recent research has demonstrated that the size and depth of an economy's financial system is positively correlated with its future real income per capita (King and Levine, 1993a and 1993b). Despite recent research by Gerard Caprio (2001), which show a positive correlation between growth and financial depth, the debate over the causality between economic growth and financial sector development remains unresolved. Cross-country correlations should be viewed with some skepticism since correlation does not prove causality. Nevertheless, the empirical work suggests that improving the performance

Table 2.2
Deposits as Percentage of GDP, 2000[1]

Country	Ratio	Country	Ratio	Country	Ratio
Cambodia	0.4	Senegal	19.7	Qatar	45.2
Central Africa Rep.	3.3	Swaziland	20.1	Tonga	45.4
Equatorial Guinea	3.4	Latvia	20.5	India	45.5
Chad	4.0	Zambia	20.5	Trinidad and Tobago	46.0
Georgia	5.2	Zimbabwe	21.7	Slovenia	46.2
Comoros	5.2	Colombia	21.7	Uruguay	46.2
Kyrgyz Republic	5.3	Turkey	22.7	Chile	46.5
Niger	5.3	Bulgaria	23.0	United Arab Emirates	46.9
Guinea	5.4	Lesotho	24.2	Norway	47.8
Sudan	6.4	Botswana	24.9	Belize	48.7
Armenia	8.9	Mozambique	25.5	Indonesia	51.4
Vietnam	9.0	Paraguay	25.7	South Africa	54.4
Sierra Leone	9.1	Peru	26.1	Philippines	55.0
Congo, Republic Of	9.9	Brazil	26.2	Cape Verde	55.2
Romania	10.4	Gambia, The	26.7	Guyana	55.4
Azerbaijan	10.6	Algeria	26.9	Nicaragua	55.5
Ukraine	10.6	Argentina	27.3	Greece	57.0
Kazakhstan	11.0	Papua New Guinea	27.4	Canada	60.0
Burundi	11.1	Oman	27.9	Slovak Republic	60.2
Gabon	11.4	Dominican Republic	28.1	St. Lucia	63.2
Moldova	11.8	United States	28.1	Australia	64.0
Mauritania	11.8	Bangladesh	28.5	Barbados	64.5
Uganda	12.2	Haiti	29.0	Czech Republic	64.9
Rwanda	12.6	Costa Rica	30.3	Egypt	65.4
Malawi	12.6	Estonia	31.3	Morocco	65.9
Cameroon	12.6	Iran, I.R. Of	31.6	Dominica	66.2
Guinea-Bissau	13.1	Pakistan	31.8	Kuwait	66.8
Ghana	13.2	Ethiopia	32.6	Bahamas, The	67.3
Tanzania	13.9	Sri Lanka	33.5	St. Vincent & Greens. St.	69.5
Madagascar	14.0	Samoa	33.8	Bahrain	70.2
Angola	14.6	Suriname	33.8	Korea	76.4
Venezuela, Rep. Bol.	14.7	Fiji	34.6	Antigua and Barbuda	77.3
Mali	15.0	Liberia	34.7	Mauritius	80.4
Belarus	15.0	Maldives	35.5	Panam	82.2
Mongolia	15.1	Libya	35.9	Seychelles	84.3
Burkina Faso	15.2	Kenya	36.7	New Zealand	87.7
Cote D'Ivoire	15.2	Namibia	37.7	Grenada	88.5
Russia	15.9	Poland	37.9	Israel	88.9
Lao People's Dem. Rep.	16.2	Honduras	38.7	St. Kitts and Nevis	91.3
Benin	16.2	Hungary	39.1	Jordan	91.8
Macedonia, FYR	16.2	Bolivia	39.2	Malaysia	91.9
Togo	16.7	Bhutan	40.3	Thailand	94.3
Lithuania	17.3	Jamaica	41.7	Singapore	100.4
Mexico	17.5	Syrian Arab Republic	41.7	Cyprus	106.6
Saudi Arabia	17.7	Croatia	41.9	Vanuatu	108.5
Nigeria	17.8	El Salvador	42.9	Japan	110.8
Myanmar	17.9	China, P.R. Mainland	43.0	Switzerland	120.7
Yemen, Republic Of	17.9	Iceland	43.5	Malta	137.4
Netherlands Antilles	18.1	Djibouti	44.2	Lebanon	191.4
Guatemala	18.8	Tunisia	45.1	China, P.R. Hong Kong	229.6

[1]According to IFS classification, deposits are the sum of demand deposits and time savings and foreign currency deposits.

Sources: WEO and IFS.

Table 2.3
Currency as Percentage of Deposits, 2000[1]

Country	Ratio	Country	Ratio	Country	Ratio
Ecuador	0.87	Indonesia	10.92	Gabon	28.31
New Zealand	2.16	Japan	10.92	Romania	31.22
Lebanon	2.99	Iran, I.R. Of	10.93	Uganda	31.59
Israel	3.09	Samoa	11.06	Malawi	32.47
Lao People's Dem. Rep.	3.11	Turkey	11.26	Lithuania	34.14
China, P.R. Hong Kong	3.15	Belize	12.01	Cameroon	35.97
Korea	4.46	Fiji	12.22	Nigeria	36.86
Bahamas, The	4.61	Slovak Republic	12.56	Kazakhstan	37.18
South Africa	5.00	Oman	13.01	Russia	37.31
St. Kitts and Nevis	5.24	Poland	13.10	Gambia, The	37.46
Kuwait	5.38	Greece	13.21	Pakistan	38.78
Cyprus	5.71	Jamaica	13.49	Tanzania	39.03
Canada	5.73	Czech Republic	13.50	Bulgaria	40.55
Vanuatu	5.78	Honduras	13.90	Libya	41.58
Trinidad and Tobago	5.88	Zambia	14.08	Algeria	44.98
Bahrain	6.01	Zimbabwe	14.38	Niger	45.63
Antigua and Barbuda	6.09	Bhutan	14.65	Equatorial Guinea	46.45
Qatar	6.18	Sri Lanka	14.89	Burundi	47.54
Norway	6.25	Kenya	15.03	Bk. Cen. Afr. Sts. (BEAC)	48.03
Botswana	6.36	Mozambique	15.84	Latvia	48.21
Slovenia	6.37	Argentina	16.14	Ghana	48.63
Australia	6.41	Venezuela, Rep. Bol.	16.55	Madagascar	48.81
Chile	6.42	Bangladesh	16.56	Liberia	54.12
Uruguay	6.50	Dominican Republic	16.65	Azerbaijan	54.18
St. Lucia	7.01	Egypt	17.21	Suriname	55.39
Singapore	7.07	Hungary	17.28	Burkina Faso	56.11
Malaysia	7.11	Belarus	17.50	Mali	56.57
Grenada	7.25	Tunisia	18.34	Syrian Arab Republic	58.83
Dominica	7.35	Malta	18.58	Cote D'Ivoire	61.09
Mauritius	7.54	Cape Verde	18.85	Congo, Republic Of	63.05
Aruba	7.57	Mexico	19.13	Mongolia	63.90
Switzerland	7.68	Paraguay	19.67	Armenia	64.66
Swaziland	7.95	United States	19.79	Togo	64.76
El Salvador	8.01	Guyana	19.91	Ukraine	69.54
St. Vincent & Grens.	8.11	Colombia	20.82	Moldova	69.90
United Arab Emirates	8.57	Djibouti	21.21	Sierra Leone	73.36
Thailand	8.81	India	21.23	Sudan	74.44
Tonga	8.89	Jordan	22.85	Yemen, Republic Of	80.44
Lesotho	9.06	Estonia	23.18	Benin	81.07
Seychelles	9.09	Angola	23.23	Myanmar	83.02
Costa Rica	9.21	Mauritania	24.11	Guinea	99.70
Peru	9.31	Haiti	24.87	Georgia	102.43
Barbados	9.32	Morocco	24.98	Kyrgyz Republic	124.48
Brazil	10.04	Guatemala	26.27	Vietnam	134.62
Croatia	10.06	Maldives	26.57	Chad	205.47
Nicaragua	10.24	Macedonia, FYR	27.06	Guinea-Bissau	210.47
Philippines	10.59	Ethiopia	27.29	Central African Rep.	397.61
Bolivia	10.64	Rwanda	27.91		
Papua New Guinea	10.88	Senegal	27.98		

[1]Currency includes Monetary Authorities' currency outside Deposit Money Banks.

Source: IFS.

of the financial sector is desirable, even if high-growth economies require a strengthening of their financial systems prior to a growth spurt.

The debate on the mechanism by which financial institutions affect the real economy has focused on the relative importance of two influences. One is that improved financial intermediation increases the level of investment by lowering transaction costs and allowing for a more efficient mobilization of savings into investment. In addition, financial markets provide an effective hedge for savers against the risk associated with parting with liquidity by enabling them to indirectly invest in more productive (but illiquid) assets and technologies.

The second mechanism by which improved financial intermediation affects the real economy is to improve the quality or composition of the investment projects that are financed. Banks have been viewed as providing value, in part, by their ability to screen and monitor borrowers. Borrowers who do not have access to capital markets (as is the case in many less developed countries) are dependent on the banking sector for capital.

Causes of Cross-Country Variation

Cross-country variations in the depth of banking markets are caused by a combination of macroeconomic and institutional factors. Economic theory suggests that there should be a positive correlation between wealth and the depth of a banking system. Basic supply–demand relationships for the asset and liability sides of bank balance sheets determine the equilibrium level of banking that will be found in a country.

A population's ability to hold deposits is clearly influenced by its income. In those countries where per capita income is so low that most citizens can barely survive, savings is almost nonexistent, and for much of the population there are no funds available to be put in a bank. The converse would be expected in countries with higher income and a positive savings rate.

Countries that are heavily engaged in international trade, as is the case with the more developed Asian countries, are more reliant on banks to conduct international transactions. Hence, one would expect to find a positive correlation between the relative importance of trade and the depth of the banking system. The role of inflation is more difficult to include. Clearly, inflation erodes the value of savings. Nevertheless, where expectations include a steady state of inflation, economic behavior will adjust and people will continue to use banks, though they are less willing to hold long-term fixed-rate instruments. However, where a country has experienced hyperinflation of an extreme magnitude, savings will have been wiped out and the public may lose confidence in public institutions.

To measure the impact of these macroeconomic effects on financial depth, regression equations were estimated for a cross section of over 100 countries using macroeconomic variables to try to explain the variations in the depth of the banking sector across countries. The functional relationship tested was:

Figure 2.1
Regression Statistics

Dependent Variable:	*BM*		*DEP*	
	coef.	*t-stat.*	*coef.*	*t-stat.*
b_0	–43.39	3.29*	–56.78	5.50*
b_1	24.65	6.01*	25.67	8.03*
b_2	0.73	1.05	0.02	0.03
b_3	0.21	4.16*	0.17	4.33*
b_4	–16.87	2.44**	–12.14	2.21**
Summary Statistics:				
Number of observations	120		123	
Adjusted R-squared	0.406		0.495	
S.E. of regression	26.772		21.320	
Mean dependent variable	46.299		37.203	
S.D. dependent variable	34.731		30.013	

*Significant at the 99 percent level.
**Significant at the 95 percent level.

$$FD = f(GDPPC, ERVAR, TRADE/GDP, HYPER)$$

where:

FD is the measure of financial depth used, either broad money to GDP or deposits to GDP,

GDPPC is GDP per capita,

ERVAR is the variation in the exchange rate over time,

TRADE/GDP is the ratio of trade to GDP,

HYPER is a dummy variable reflecting whether a country experienced inflation 100 percent in its Consumer Price Index during the past decade.

The regressions equations estimated took the following form:

$$FD = b_0 + b_1 * \log GDPPC + b_2 * \log ERVAR + b_3 * TRADE/GDP + b_4 * HYPER$$

and were estimated using both the ratio of broad money to GDP (*BM*) and deposits to GDP (*DEP*) as dependent variables. As can be seen in Figure 2.1, all of the variables, except the variation in the exchange rate, were significant in explaining either measure of financial depth.

These results indicate that macroeconomic factors clearly are important in explaining relative differences in financial depth. Other macroeconomic factors that influence the supply and demand for bank assets and liabilities also are important determinants of the depth of a banking sector. However, consistent data are not always available to allow broad-based cross-sectional empirical research on a large number of countries.

Lack of confidence in the banking system can also contribute to a low level of financial depth. If the public believes that their funds are at risk when deposited in banks, they will show a decided preference for holding cash or other types of assets. This is evident in countries that have experienced large numbers of bank failures where the depositors have suffered losses or seen their funds frozen for a lengthy period of time.

The practice found in some countries of accumulating arrears in public sector domestic payments can also help to inhibit financial sector growth. These arrears form an involuntary type of private financing of the government and thereby reduce the available supply of funds that otherwise might be deposited in banks. These arrears also reduce the public's confidence in economic policy and, hence, economic stability. This loss of confidence likely will spill over to economic organizations operating under the supervision of the government, such as banks.

Institutional Factors

Although macroeconomic factors play a key role in explaining differences in the depth of banking systems across countries, they are not the sole determinants. As the results presented above show, one can only explain about 50 percent of the variation using macroeconomic variables. Microeconomic factors that affect the supply and demand for bank assets and liabilities are also important. Unfortunately, data that are consistent across countries are not readily available for many of these influences. Nevertheless, they are important when one examines a specific country's situation. The discussion below is not meant to be all-inclusive but rather suggestive of the types of institutional factors that vary from country to country.

The efficiency of payment system is one of the critical determinants of the effectiveness of financial intermediation. A number of factors influence the efficiency of the payment system, including the types of settlement systems, the central bank's liquidity management policies, and the development of money markets. In some countries with very shallow financial systems, the only settlement system, other than cash, is an interbank market. If there are no checks, or other medium of exchange, both banks and their customers tend to hold greater amounts of cash (or other liquid assets). This in turn reduces the supply of funds available for lending. Although the conventional wisdom in developed countries is that a move toward electronic payments systems and avoidance of the use of checks reduces costs and improves payment efficiency, such a move may be very difficult to accomplish in some countries, especially those without a steady source of electricity.

Bankers in many countries rely on *secured lending as the means of assuring repayment on loans*, especially when businesses do not have an extended credit history or when financial reporting is unreliable. For a bank to engage in secured lending, the legal structure has to allow liens to be recorded and lenders to enforce them. Where this does not occur, lenders are limited to possessory pledges as the sole source of collateral. In this situation, the bank takes physical possession of the collateral and holds it until the loan is repaid. Clearly, only certain types of collateral lend themselves to such a practice. Small objects, such as jewelry or gold, which are not used in business, can be pledged in this fashion, but plant and equipment, not to mention real estate, cannot. Hence, the absence of collateralized lending hinders the supply of credit in countries that lack the appropriate legal infrastructure for such types of credit.

When one looks at the future of banking in developed countries, research such as that presented by Berger and Udell (Chapter 10 in this volume) focuses on *the development of banking relationships*. The term *relationship lending* has a whole different meaning in countries with less developed financial markets. In these countries the term refers to connected lending, where banks lend to companies and affiliates of the owners of the bank. In some countries, this makes up a significant portion of the commercial loans at many banks. Hence, the immediate policy issue is a very different one. In these countries, the issue is one of prudential standards and risk diversification rather than the competitive issues surrounding developing banking relationships that will allow banks to extend their product lines. Nevertheless, the practice of exclusive connected lending is also detrimental to the growth of a banking sector and the economy as a whole because it prevents unaffiliated potential borrowers from obtaining credit. These frequently will be small entrepreneurs who thus can get credit only if micro-finance ventures are created.

CONCLUSIONS

Although it has become fashionable to write about the globalization of banking and the demise of traditional banking with the growth of multiproduct financial conglomerates, this debate is relevant only to the developed world. As the data presented above show, the banking sector is not well developed in many countries. Research on financial globalization and discussions of financial engineering and "asset-backed securities" are totally irrelevant in these economies.

For a large part of the world, the future of banking is bright. In many countries, banking is at an early stage of development and is going through the growing pains once experienced in developed countries. As economic conditions improve and structural improvements are made in the legal and regulatory environments, banking will flourish in these countries. In fact, banking may be the only meaningful financial intermediary that can spur economic growth. However, banks will have to be encouraged to meet the needs of all creditworthy customers.

Of equal importance to developing financial depth in underdeveloped countries is the development of the payment system. As long as economies are fundamentally cash oriented, financial markets will not acquire sufficient depth to help fuel economic growth. Hence, more needs to be done in designing alternative media of exchange that are appropriate for poorer countries and encourage the populace to hold deposits.

In terms of research agenda, there is a need for more research on banking in less developed countries. Although data may be more readily available in developed countries, researchers would be amazed at what is available on the web from central banks all over the world. An example of one of the issues facing policymakers is whether it is better to broaden the financial sector by introducing a plethora of financial institutions, such as credit unions, micro-finance firms, leasing companies, and securities firms, or to encourage the development of the banking sector by providing the stimulus to encourage banks to meet the needs of those segments of the population that are served by specialized financial firms. There is no one answer that will fit every country. Rather, the authorities in each country will have to develop a strategic view if they are to deepen the financial sector in their country.

NOTES

The author is a Financial Sector Advisor at the International Monetary Fund. The views expressed are those of the author and not those of the IMF, nor does the discussion in this chapter reflect IMF policy.

This chapter was presented as a paper at the 2001 FMA meeting in Toronto, Canada.

1. See Edwards (1996), pp. 10–42.
2. See, for example, Pierce (1991) and Litan and Rauch (1998).
3. While data is reported for Albania, the relative magnitude is so low as to be suspect.
4. This measure was tracked by Friedman and Schwartz (1963) in their study of the history of the U.S. monetary system.

REFERENCES

Boyd, John, and Mark Gertler. 1994. "Are Banks Dead? Or Are the Reports Greatly Exaggerated?" *Proceedings of the 30th Conference on Bank Structure and Competition*. Chicago: Federal Reserve Bank of Chicago, pp. 85–117.

Caprio, Gerard. 2001. *Finance for Growth: Policy Choices in a Volatile World*. Washington, D.C.: The World Bank and Oxford University Press.

Edwards, Franklin R. 1996. *The New Finance*. Washington, D.C.: AEI Press.

Federal Reserve Bank of Chicago. 1994. "The Declining Role of Banking." *Proceedings of the 30th Annual Conference on Bank Structure and Competition*. Chicago: Federal Reserve Bank of Chicago.

Friedman, Milton, and Anna Schwartz. 1963. *A Monetary History of the United States 1867–1960*. Princeton, N.J.: Princeton University Press.

King, Robert, and Ross Levine. 1993a. "Finance, Entrepreneurship and Growth." *Journal of Monetary Economics* 32: 513–542.

King, Robert, and Ross Levine. 1993b. "Finance and Growth: Schumpeter Might Be Right." *Quarterly Journal of Economics* 108: 717–738.

Litan, Robert, and Jonathan Rauch. 1998. *American Finance for the 21st Century*. Washington, D.C.: Brookings Institution Press.

McKinnon, Roland. 1973. *Money and Capital in Economic Development*. Washington, D.C.: Brookings Institution.

OECD. 1995. *The New Financial Landscape*. Paris: OECD.

Pierce, James. 1991. *The Future of Banking*. New Haven, Conn.: Yale University Press.

Shaw, Edward. 1973. *Financial Deepening in Economic Development*. New York: Oxford University Press.

Chapter 3

The Future of Banking: A Global Perspective

Ian R. Harper and Tom C. H. Chan

INTRODUCTION

The combined forces of demography, technology, regulation, and globalization are driving far-reaching change in the financial services sector. The banking industry in particular has been severely affected. To understand the future of banking, we must first appreciate how these forces for change bear upon banks and the markets in which they participate. We can then understand the reasons behind the major trends in the industry. Following these trends to their logical conclusions helps us to discern the future of banking.

In Part 1 of this chapter, we examine the foundations of banking by considering what it is that banks do. Understanding the theory of financial intermediation shows just how fundamental current challenges to the business of banking really are. Banks are at risk of losing the very basis of their role as intermediaries.

Part 2 identifies key forces for change bearing on the banking industry. These include changing consumer tastes and preferences, especially in light of population aging, rapid advances in technology, developments in the regulation of financial systems, and the overarching influence of globalization.

In Part 3, we examine the current state of play in banking in light of the forces for change. Four clear trends are identified, which have their roots in the forces for change outlined in Part 2: competition, consolidation, convergence, and connectedness. Together these trends define the trajectory of the banking industry as it drives toward the future.

Part 4 is an attempt to discern the future of banking. Taking the trends outlined in Part 3, Part 4 attempts to deduce what banks might look like and what they might do if current trends continue into the future.

PART 1—WHAT BANKS DO

Banks perform six broad functions: (1) conducting exchange (clearing and settling claims); (2) funding large-scale enterprises (pooling and dividing resources); (3) transferring purchasing power across time and distance; (4) providing risk management (hedging, diversification, and insurance); (5) monitoring borrower performance (mitigating adverse incentives); and (6) providing information about the relative supply and demand for credit (Jordan, 1997).

These functions are the practical outworking of banks' role as financial intermediaries. At base, banks bring borrowers and lenders together. In a world free of information inefficiencies, banks would have a greatly reduced role, if any at all. Borrowers and lenders would interact of their own accord in open financial markets, exchanging financial claims at agreed prices. Banks come into their own when information inefficiencies abound—in particular, when information is asymmetrically held by the two parties to a financial transaction.

Theory of Financial Intermediation

Information asymmetry induces a fundamental lack of trust. When two parties to a contract cannot independently observe the same set of outcomes at identical cost, there is the potential for one party to dissemble and, in so doing, to induce the other party to make a decision contrary to his or her self-interest (Harper and Eichberger, 1997, 244). Financial intermediaries aim to raise the level of trust between parties by designing contracts to mitigate the most basic incentive problems. In this sense, "intermediation is a response of market-mediated mechanisms to efficiently resolve information problems" (Bhattacharya and Thakor, 1993, 14).

The first step is for intermediaries to interpose themselves between ultimate borrowers and lenders, so that each party deals with the intermediary and only indirectly with its counterpart on the other side of the intermediary's balance sheet. In this way, the intermediary can attempt to match the demands of the two sides by accommodating their needs on its own account. Thus, we speak of intermediaries *matching* the differing demands for maturity, liquidity, and risk-bearing held by ultimate borrowers and lenders.

Furthermore, the intermediary can attempt to reconcile the lack of trust between the two ultimate parties by inviting each to trust the intermediary in place of the ultimate counterparty. To generate trust between itself and ultimate borrowers and lenders, the intermediary must employ some distinctive contractual arrangements.

The Debt Contract

The debt contract is a device for aligning the divergent interests of borrowers and lenders arising from the inability of lenders to observe all states of nature costlessly and the incentive for borrowers not to reveal their true circumstances.

The debt device sorts risky borrowers from less risky borrowers. Borrowers who cannot meet the terms of the contract—including the collateral required and the schedule of repayments—are denied funds. This screens out borrowers who may have been happy to promise repayment of capital plus interest upon maturity but who in fact have a high probability of default.

By insisting that all borrowers sign a debt contract, the bank raises the average credit quality of its loan book and assures lenders (its depositors) that their funds are secure. Moreover, the fact that the bank writes a debt contract between itself and the lenders (the deposit contract) provides additional assurance to lenders that the bank faces the same discipline as a borrower that it places upon its loan customers. The deposit contract offers depositors a first charge over the assets of the bank in the event of default.

The "Banker-Customer" Relationship

Banks strengthen the risk-mitigating effect of the debt contract by building a "banker-customer" relationship with their clients. The core of this relationship is confidentiality. By credibly committing to confidentiality, a bank induces reluctant borrowers to reveal private information that would damage them commercially if it were to be released publicly. Superior information assists in the appropriate risk classification (and pricing) of loans and hence in building the confidence of ultimate lenders that the bank knows its loan book. Similar confidentiality on the deposit side helps banks to encourage ultimate lenders to reveal their financial circumstances and allow the bank to better meet their needs.

Significance of the Payments Function

In screening borrowers, banks act as "delegated monitors" on behalf of lenders (Diamond, 1996). In this function, banks benefit from scale economies and risk pooling that are not available to individual lenders. Not only do banks sort borrowers according to their default risk *ab initio*, but they also maintain continual vigilance over the performance of borrowers during the term of a loan.

This is facilitated by banks' provision of loan monies in the form of checkable deposits with themselves. When a borrower is obliged to operate a checking account with the bank, the bank obtains up-to-the-minute information on the cash flows of the borrower and is in a prime position to investigate a borrower whose cash flows signal imminent default.

Banks' participation in the payments process grants them unique access to information and the possibility of intervention, both of which are directly relevant to their monitoring and risk mitigation roles. This adds to the assurance of trustworthiness conveyed by banks to their borrowers.

Disintermediation

If intermediation is founded on information asymmetry, then based on that logic, the creation of greater symmetry in information between borrowers and lenders ought to undermine the utility of intermediation. This is precisely the impact of the digital information revolution and is the genesis of so-called disintermediation.

With greater symmetry of information, borrowers and lenders are better placed to interact directly through the exchange of financial claims on organized markets. The rationale of intermediated finance, such as that provided through bank balance sheets, is undermined. Market exchange substitutes for bank intermediation as financial activity is "disintermediated."

Disintermediation is driven by the changing dynamics of markets in the wake of the information revolution.

> The threat of disintermediation is real enough. . . . Go back 20 years, and banks could extract high margins on corporate loans based on exclusive knowledge of their clients' credit standing. As that information became broadly available, big companies could go direct to lenders through the bond markets, and the banks' margins evaporated. (Anon., 1998)

Digital technology has greatly reduced the costs of compiling, processing, and distributing information. Information and communications technology (ICT) invigorates markets by enhancing the flow of information, not in creating certainty, but making information more symmetric. The rise of the Internet, for example, has increased transparency, improving the ability of all market participants to determine the available range of prices for financial instruments and financial services (Clemons and Hitt, 2000, 4). Indeed, information-driven disintermediation is not limited to the financial sector: "The the flow of information turns client relationships into markets. This phenomenon is cropping up in fields as diverse as travel agencies, real estate and the auctioning of flowers in Amsterdam" (Anon., 1998).

The new markets that hand information to consumers also tend to push down prices. This is a dangerous prospect for branded goods like banking products and services, which behave increasingly like commodities. Moreover, technology has continually lowered the transaction costs of direct financing, facilitating the emergence of new electronic markets, payments and settlement networks, and new market-based risk and wealth management systems.

Disintermediation is accompanied by *securitization*. Large firms increasingly raise finance directly from the financial markets. Companies with secure cash flows create securities from (or "securitize") these "assets," the value of which is determined by the volume and reliability of the cash flows (Holland et al., 1998, 222). The securities are then sold publicly or privately to institutional investors.

Securitization of assets disintermediates banks from their traditional role of lenders to the corporate sector. Financial deregulation and information technology have both contributed to the growing dominance of capital markets by facilitating access for new issuers and investors.

Retail banking is also subject to disintermediation, although the impact has been slower to materialize. A bank's primary role in retail markets has been to act as intermediary between the customer and wholesale financial markets, typically using its own products. New electronic delivery channels bring customers closer to wholesale providers, creating the prospect of the bank itself being bypassed.

Disintermediation is a threat to the very foundations of what banks do. Its genesis lies in the information revolution and the resulting erosion of information asymmetry. But technology is not the only force bearing down on banks. Other factors, some themselves linked to the ICT revolution, are also at work.

PART 2—FORCES FOR CHANGE

Powerful forces for change are forging the future shape of the banking industry. These include demographic, technological, and regulatory factors. Undergirding these developments is the continuing closer integration of national economies and financial systems through the process known as globalization.

Changing Customer Needs and Preferences

Populations are aging rapidly, at least in the developed Western democracies. The prospect of rising aged-dependency ratios is focusing governments and individuals on alternative means of funding retirement incomes. "Pay-as-you-go" pension schemes, under which the younger (working) generation funds the retirement incomes of the older (retired) generation, are not viable when the aged-dependency ratio rises beyond certain limits.

Governments are responding by inducing individuals to make greater provision for their own incomes in retirement, restricting the availability of publicly funded pensions to the genuinely indigent. A mixture of incentive and compulsion characterizes the efforts of most Western governments to date.

The banking industry is affected as individuals seek higher rates of return on their savings. By their nature, banks offer a low-risk, low-return savings vehicle. Increasingly, those forced to fund their own retirement must earn higher rates of return on their savings. This in turn requires them to accept higher levels of commercial risk than have traditionally been offered through the banking system.

Riskier investment products have been sought in the nonbank sector, including various forms of collective investment vehicles, such as mutual funds and equity trusts. Banks have found their traditional deposit products increasingly less attractive to savers and have been obliged to offer investment-linked savings products. As a result, banks have moved into the burgeoning field of wealth management, in which they offer higher-risk, higher-return savings products through their funds management subsidiaries. This has reoriented the focus of banks' retail operations away from the passive receipt of idle balances to the active pursuit of funds under management.

As customers' needs have changed, so have their preferences become more sophisticated. The typical bank customer is now more attuned to the basics of financial analysis. They are more aware of the options available and are much better tutored in the means of discerning value for money. Although customers need a more sophisticated mix of products to meet their financial needs in retirement, they are generally also better informed. This makes the task of attracting savings far more challenging for banks. This trend can be expected to continue.

Technology

Advances in ICT have profoundly altered the banking business. This is not surprising given that banking is an information-intensive industry. Technology has enabled banks to innovate in a range of areas, including products, distribution channels, organizational structures, internal processes, and customer relations management.

These changes create both new threats and new opportunities. In particular, technology has increased the competitiveness of banking as an industry, not least because it facilitates comparison-shopping and the entry of new providers.

Some areas in which technology is changing the face of banking include:

- Automation/computerization of standard transactions; for example,
  —automating payment services, thus reducing the need for paper checks, paper records, and bricks-and-mortar branches;
  —standardizing credit analyses for loan applications.
- Decentralization of back-office support
  —modern communications networks allow back-office support and operations (including call centers) to be located at a distance from retail points of delivery (sometimes even offshore).
- Creating value for customers
  —integrating different types of financial accounts—across multiple vendors, checking and mortgage accounts, car loans, mutual funds, and so on;
  —customizing products to specific needs and circumstances;
  —improving service times and sales capabilities (e.g., cross-selling).
- Making payments
  —facilitating customer-initiated electronic payments;
  —creating digital cash.
- Customer information and data-mining systems
  —improving services to existing customers or bundling information for sale to other players.

Regulatory Developments

The banking industry has been subject to significant government regulation since at least the 1930s. The shape of the banking industry is as much determined by regulation as the shape of regulation is influenced by the evolution of the banking industry. During the 1970s and 1980s, banking systems around the world were substantially deregulated, reflecting a prevailing view that regulation had become a distorting influence on the industry, no longer serving its original public policy goals.

Since that time, there has been a change in the form and purpose of bank regulation. Regulation was originally aimed at harnessing the banking industry to the ends of monetary policy. Banks were subject to controls on the interest rates they could offer on deposits and charge on loans, and were also often subject to quantitative and qualitative controls on their lending. The intention was to allow central banks to manage the volume and direction of bank lending so as to control aggregate credit conditions.

Bank regulations of this type were removed when it became clear that they were increasingly ineffective and inefficient instruments of public policy. Central banks switched to market-oriented mechanisms for the implementation of monetary policy, mechanisms that relied on interest rates being free to move and banks being free to lend as they saw fit. Such a change in the *modus operandi* of central banks required the abolition of direct controls on banks.

Nowadays bank regulation focuses primarily on safety and soundness (so-called prudential regulation) rather than on monetary policy. Since 1988, most countries have adopted a version of the risk-weighted capital adequacy regulations promulgated by the Bank for International Settlements in Basel, Switzerland. A revised regime for capital adequacy regulation is currently under review by the Basel Committee on Banking Supervision. This will refine and extend the original framework first developed in 1988. It is proposed that the new system be in force by 2005.

The evolving regulatory framework within which banks operate influences the scope and shape of their activities. Strengthening controls on balance-sheet activities has tended to encourage banks to move their business off-balance sheet. This has in turn stimulated banks' involvement with market-oriented activities, including investment banking and securities trading, where the regulatory burden is comparatively light.

The most recent regulatory developments include the emergence of so-called integrated regulation and the growing emphasis on disclosure. Given the increasing convergence of financial activity across traditional boundaries (about which more is said below), governments in many developed countries have moved to integrate or combine the regulation of banking, insurance and, to some extent, funds management. The emphasis is on *functional* rather than *institu-*

tional regulation. Financial functions (e.g., deposit-taking) are subject to regulation as opposed to specific institutional forms (e.g., banks and insurance companies).

In most countries, separate regulatory agencies were involved in the regulation of different parts of the financial system. Recognizing the increasing difficulty of separating these activities in practice, let alone conceptually, governments have moved to rationalize their regulatory regimes by combining regulatory responsibility in a single integrated agency. Integrated regulators now exist in Britain, Germany, Japan, the Scandinavian countries, Canada, Singapore, Australia, and, since the Gramm-Leach-Bliley Act, the United States.

There is also a growing emphasis on disclosure as an alternative to standards-based regulation. This development reflects the increasing complexity of financial institutions as well as the trend toward market-oriented (and away from balance-sheet-based) financial products and services. The more financial institutions base their operations on the exchange of financial claims, the less they rely on balance-sheet intermediation. In sympathy with this evolution, it becomes more appropriate for regulators to rely on market conduct and disclosure regulation in preference to prudential standards. The former is better attuned to market exchange while the latter is designed to govern balance-sheet intermediation.

Globalization

The freer flow of goods, services, capital, and labor across borders is heightening competition in national markets. This is especially true of information-based services, including financial services. The ICT revolution has created a global communications network across which it is increasingly easy to exchange information and trade financial claims.

Globalization offers enormous opportunities to efficient and innovative participants. It also threatens the inefficient and those who resist change. Competition intensifies as its scope becomes increasingly global.

The demands of increasingly global customers are pushing banks to create new organizational structures, offering bank products, knowledge, and expertise, and managing relationships on a global scale. Networked information systems and electronic delivery channels facilitate global coordination and management of banking business (Holland et al., 1998, 220).

PART 3—STATE OF PLAY

The forces for change, including the underlying drift from intermediaries to markets, have produced four clear trends in the banking industry: increasing competition, consolidation, convergence, and connectedness.

Competition

The various forces for change have combined to create a vastly more competitive environment for banks. Until recent moves to deregulate financial systems, banking was, in most countries, explicitly protected from "excessive" competition. Banks were required to be stable and profitable so as to provide a reliable fulcrum for monetary policy. Too much competition would undermine both the profitability and the stability of banks to the detriment of monetary control.

This was the prevailing orthodoxy until the mechanism for implementing monetary policy shifted from bank balance-sheet controls to "open market operations," using capital markets and interest rates. Once this transition was complete, there was no particular reason to protect banks from competition. Indeed, more competitive banks would transmit interest rate changes more rapidly throughout the financial system. Hence the push for bank deregulation and the end of the quiet life for banks.

Deregulation has not only intensified competition from within the banking industry, but it has also allowed nonbank financial institutions to invade territory formerly reserved to banks. Furthermore, nonfinancial institutions have found it easier to offer financial services as a result of technological developments. Banks' customers have added to competitive pressure by opting to "go it alone" through securitization and other forms of disintermediation. Top off the list with the impact of globalization on cross-border competitive entry and it is clear that the competitive environment for banks is many times greater than at any time in living memory.

Apart from deregulation itself, technology is by far the most potent force serving to increase the intensity of competition in banking. Technology has a *democratizing* effect in opening up the banking sector—anybody who can afford the technology can implement it, and new players may even have an advantage in this respect as they are not encumbered with dated, even obsolete, "legacy systems" (Engler and Essinger, 2000, 6).

Electronic networks allow an international bank or nonbank organization to offer services to domestic customers online, and "cherry pick" the most profitable customers by employing sophisticated information gathering and processing technologies. Enhanced systems for analyzing and identifying revenues and costs are forcing prices to reflect cost. Meanwhile, the ability of full-service providers to cross-subsidize loss-making products, such as transaction services, has diminished.

Consolidation

Since the late 1980s and 1990s, there has been a remarkable spate of merger and acquisition activity involving banks. Banks are growing both in size and in complexity. The world's top 20 banks now account for about half of global financial sector capitalization. In the United States alone, the top 10 banks account for approximately 70 percent of financial sector capitalization. Most of these banks have been created via multiple mergers (UBS Warburg, 2001, 3).

The trend toward consolidation reflects banks' need to respond to a business environment demanding greater competitiveness and efficiency—to compete better in a market transformed by precisely the forces discussed in Part 2. It is also clear that the shift from intermediation to markets leaves banks with excess capital (discussed further in Part 4). This obliges institutions to improve the rate of return to the capital they retain or to face pressure from the capital markets to repay shareholders. Increasing size and scope have also been seen as necessary to improve service quality to an increasingly global clientele, to enable risk diversification, to facilitate the purchase of expensive and lumpy computer technology, and to attract and retain the best human resources (Engler and Essinger, 2000, 16).

Larger banks can supply the breadth of resources needed to solve increasingly sophisticated and global client problems. This requires broad skills such as portfolio consulting, education, marketing, and financial structuring. In addition, a global presence is required to fulfill the increasing demand for offshore investments and the need to accompany clients into markets wherever they go (Engler and Essinger, 2000, 19).

Falling regulatory barriers and monetary integration have facilitated cross-border consolidation.

> Transnational consolidation is the natural tendency of banking in an integrated monetary area. We are already seeing this in the US, where the elimination of the restrictions on inter-state bank mergers has given way to an unstoppable process of mergers and acquisitions. (Engler and Essinger, 2000, 17)

Harmonization of laws and regulations will likewise stimulate consolidation within the EURO-11 countries.

The trend toward consolidation looks set to continue. Empirical studies of scale economies in banking generally support claims that the future of banking points to larger, diversified companies operating across national boundaries (Hogan, 1999, 417). On the other hand, the challenge for consolidating banks is, "getting the fit right, and making all the pieces yield the synergies they are supposed to yield, especially in terms of personnel issues" (Engler and Essinger, 2000, 18). Cross-border consolidation may yet be arrested by the difficulties of managing huge cultural differences, and different return-on-equity thresholds.

Convergence

Blurring of Boundaries

Traditional distinctions between different types of financial institutions are eroding. Institutions that have traditionally operated in separate markets are increasingly offering an undifferentiated set of products and services. As Alan Greenspan has observed: the "evolution of financial technology alone has changed forever our ability to place commercial banking, investment banking, insurance underwriting, and insurance sales into neat separate boxes" (Sicilia and Cruikshank, 2000, 217). For example, life companies are offering products that have many of the characteristics of deposits, while pensions and market-linked products are being offered by banks though their subsidiary operations. Banks have felt the pressure to diversify product offerings as customers demand the convenience of dealing with one entity for a wide range of financial needs.

Changes in government regulations, introduced primarily to encourage competition, have been partly responsible for this blurring of boundaries. Indeed, notable megamergers between insurance and other financial institutions have occurred in the United States with the passage of the Gramm-Leach-Bliley Act of 1999 (Koco, 2001). Citigroup was the first U.S.-based company permitted to operate in all sectors of financial services—investment banking, commercial banking, and insurance.

Thus far, the transformation to "one-stop" financial institutions has not been fast and furious, but rather has been quietly gaining momentum (Anon., 2001b). This is understandable, given the complexity of the integration process.

Arising from the wave of cross-industry activity, the advent of hybrid financial products—which combine elements of banking, investing, and insurance in one package—is another sign of blurring lines between industries. Such products can be modified to allow typical bank customers to customize their portfolios. For example: "Insurance producers can now offer clients a Certificate of Deposit with a rate of return linked to a major stock market index, similar to some equity indexed annuities, yet backed by the Federal Deposit Insurance Corporation up to the coverage limits" (Blowers, 2001).

Convergence products allow banks to strengthen their relationships with existing clients and to compete more aggressively with other financial services providers for new customers. They are a defense against single-line niche players from within or outside the financial services sector.

Market Widening and Nontraditional Players

Nontraditional players are entering markets that have traditionally been the preserve of banks and other financial institutions. The boundaries already extend to include:

- nonfinancial companies, such as utilities (postal, telecommunications, and electricity groups) that can utilize a considerable physical and communications infrastructure for the delivery of transaction services;
- retail organizations or consumer product companies (airlines, motor vehicle manufacturers) that can use a strong brand name, large customer networks, and a well-developed marketing and segmentation capability to offer a wide range of financial services and products to consumers; and

- software companies that can develop sophisticated software able to act as a customer "gateway" or "digital agent" for search and delivery of financial services and products (Financial System Inquiring, 1997, 156–157).

A prime example is Ford Financial Services, which generates over a billion dollars in profit for the automaker and disintermediates the banks from their traditional role of providing finance for automotive purchases (Kapoor, 1995). The U.S. telecoms giant, AT&T, became the world's second largest issuer of credit cards within five years of entering the market (Gosling, 1996, 60). Niche operations such as Virgin Direct, an operation of the Virgin Airline group, now offers savings accounts, investment products, personal pensions, insurance, and mortgages (through a partnership with Royal Bank of Scotland).

Technology is a major force driving convergence. The growth of online banking will further enhance the capability of nontraditional players to offer stiff competition for traditional banks. Indeed, the broadening of the traditional banking industry in the context of the networked economy may provide the greatest challenge of all—how to hold on to a customer and instill loyalty when your competitor is just a mouse-click away.

Connectedness

Heightened competition, consolidation, and convergence in financial markets are forcing greater integration at all levels—financial systems are increasingly *connected.* The increasing connectedness of different segments of national financial systems has forced a rethinking of regulatory strategy and has given rise to the phenomenon of integrated regulation.[1] A number of countries, including the United Kingdom, Germany, Japan, the Scandinavian countries, Canada, Australia, and, since 1999, the United States, now operate integrated regulatory regimes under which the regulation of banking, insurance, and funds management is overseen by a single agency.

The aim behind this development is to harmonize regulatory requirements across traditionally distinct industry segments. Acknowledging that the industry itself is experiencing convergence, regulators are also attempting to bridge gaps and eliminate overlaps in regulatory coverage so as to minimize regulation-induced distortion.

The same development is occurring at the supranational level. The increasing connectedness of the global financial system mandates a greater degree of cooperation and coordination among national regulators. Supranational regulatory agencies—including the Basel Committee on Banking Supervision, the International Association of Insurance Supervisors, and the International Organization of Securities Commissions—are attempting to coordinate regulatory efforts within their own domains and also across domains.[2] The aim is to promote as far as possible a seamless regulatory framework within which the ongoing globalization of financial services can occur with minimum regulatory distortion.

Globalization has spurred a massive growth in cross-border asset holding and trading, credit flows, and the creation of global financial markets. However, the greater connectedness of the global financial system has also magnified potential shocks and increased exposure to financial "contagion." "Regrettably, the very efficiency that contributes so much to our global system also facilitates the transmission of financial disturbances far more effectively than ever before" (Dr. Alan Greenspan, quoted in Sicilia and Cruikshank, 2000, 206).

The consequences of ill-conceived policies are exacerbated when they are transmitted internationally.

> These global financial markets, engendered by the rapid proliferation of cross-border financial flows and products, have developed a capability of transmitting mistakes at a far faster pace throughout the financial system in ways that were unknown a generation ago. (Dr. Alan Greenspan, quoted in Sicilia and Cruikshank, 2000, 206)

> The "contagion" of financial panics used to be constrained by poor communications and more or less impenetrable national borders. Today there are far fewer constraints. (Sicilia and Cruikshank, 2000, 216)

The increasing connectedness of the global financial system will require ever greater cooperation among national regulatory and monetary authorities to contain disturbances, staunch contagion, and promote stability. However, the extent of global financial contagion following recent events in Asia, South America, and Russia bears testimony to the nascent state of developments in this arena.

PART 4—THE FUTURE

"If you want to know what the next 125 years will be like for banking, look at the last 125—and add in the computer and the Internet" (Johnson, 1999, 11). This is the view of Hjalma Johnson, former president of the American Bankers' Association. Johnson seems to imply that the Internet will not fundamentally alter the business of banking. In fact, the ICT revolution strikes at the very heart of what banks do. By undermining information asymmetry, the Internet has the potential to eliminate banking as surely as the advent of steamships eliminated sailing ships from commercial shipping lanes.

While *banking* may well go the way of tall ships and stagecoaches, *banks* as corporations need not. The Wells Fargo Company once operated stagecoaches. It exited the transport business and is now in banking. Whether Wells Fargo chooses to change industries again remains to be seen, but the company could stay in the financial services business and just give up banking. People's need for transport services survived the transition from stagecoaches to railroads to automobiles. People's need for intertemporal exchange, payments services, and a trusted third party will similarly survive the demise of banking.

Why Banking Will (Almost) Disappear

Banking adds value when information is asymmetric. For the reasons discussed in Part 1, the business of banking developed as a substitute for missing financial markets. The markets went missing because information was insufficiently symmetric between potential borrowers and lenders, leading to an absence of trust. Without trust, the two parties were not prepared to deal.

Banks resolved this dilemma by interposing a balance sheet between ultimate borrowers and lenders. By writing separate agreements between themselves and lenders, and themselves and borrowers, banks eliminated the need for the two parties to trust each other. But why would the parties trust the banks instead? Through judicious use of debt contracts on either side of a balance sheet, maintaining confidentiality through the "banker-customer" relationship and participating directly in the payments system, "banking" was born. Balance-sheet banking allowed banks to plug the gap and replace missing markets for financial claims.

But the basis of banking is asymmetric information. As information becomes more symmetric, thanks to the Internet and ICT, the reason financial markets went missing in the first place no longer applies. While balance-sheet banking is an effective substitute for markets, it is expensive. Balance sheets require equity capital—indeed, a minimum amount must be subscribed by law in most jurisdictions. Financial markets operate without the need for capital to be held in reserve. If they exist, financial markets will therefore operate more cheaply and at least as effectively as their substitute—balance-sheet banking.

The spate of merger activity within the banking industry and between banks and other financial institutions, discussed in Part 3, can be traced to the same evolution away from balance-sheet intermediation. As banking declines and financial market exchange arises in its place, banks (and to some extent also insurers) find themselves with excess capital. Capital that once supported balance-sheet intermediation is now surplus to requirements as banks move their business toward investment banking, securities trading, and other forms of off-balance-sheet, market-linked activities.

Banks have three options to deploy the surplus capital: repay their own shareholders (which many banks have done in recent years); acquire the business of a competitor, in the process repaying its shareholders; or merge two or more institutions in the hope of reaping cost and revenue economies of scale. The third strategy does not reduce the capital base of the merged institution but aims to improve the rate of return on invested funds. The intention is to extend the life of balance-sheet activity for as long as possible in the face of increasing competition from market-based financial activity.[3]

But there will probably always be some residual information asymmetry. Wherever information asymmetry persists, balance-sheet intermediation will always have a role. Retail finance suggests itself as the obvious final stronghold of information asymmetry. Unlike wholesale finance, retail borrowers and lenders may always be sufficiently lacking in sophistication as to warrant the use of traditional banking products. Nevertheless, one should not push the point too far—after all, retail mortgages and consumer credit loans were among the first to be disintermediated.

What Will Banks Do?

The future of *banking* is one of steady retreat into the remaining pockets of information asymmetry. The more ubiquitous ICT becomes, the more redundant traditional balance-sheet intermediation will become. An analogous pattern will be observed in the insurance industry, with the gradual demise of balance-sheet insurance products and their replacement by market-based instruments. Accompanying this transition will be a substantial reduction in the capital requirements of banks and insurance companies. Both industries will shed capital as they evolve away from capital-intensive balance-sheet intermediation.

The future of *banks* will not be in banking but rather in the market exchange of financial instruments. Banks will retain their expertise in financial matters and exploit this advantage by becoming expert in the use of financial markets to achieve the objectives of ultimate borrowers and lenders. Although this seems an obvious transition for banks to make, and it is already well under way, we should not underestimate the cultural challenge involved. Traditional bankers are managers of balance-sheet claims; they are not traders. The culture of the trader is quite foreign to the dyed-in-the-wool banker. Indeed, there is something bordering on mutual contempt between the two traditional rivals.

For banks to embrace the future, they must accept the need for a complete attitude makeover. The future for banks will revolve around financial markets, and their success will be governed by their expertise as traders and advisers to those who trade. Banks that understand this point have already sought to acquire or merge with funds managers and brokers. The aim is to infuse the culture of the finance house throughout the bank. Unless bankers start to think and act like traders, the transition will never be made and banks will go the way of banking—or leave the financial services industry, a possibility canvassed below.

While the future belongs to the markets and not the balance sheet, there is one dimension in which the balance sheet will remain important, at least for a time. Banks engaged in the creation and marketing of securities for clients ("investment banking" as it is known) can add value not just through the ingenuity of the design of the securities and the skill with which they are traded. Indeed, much of the value to be added in investment banking resides in the originality of the structure of the deal. But it is equally important when securities are new to the market for an investment banker to be able to reassure a client that the funds will be forthcoming, even if the market turns down. One way in which this can be done is to use the balance sheet.

At least until markets are so complete that the creation of genuinely new securities is a rarity, if not an impossibility, there will be a continuing role for the balance sheet to complement trading activity. Banks with strong balance sheets will have an edge on those without, precisely because they can "warehouse" claims that prove difficult or costly to sell. The balance sheet will still offer a means of providing liquidity insurance or a capital guarantee, at least until financial markets become so ubiquitous and complete that the same can be achieved through market exchange.

As long as banking exists, it will be done by banks. The same cannot be said of the other functions currently performed by banks. We saw in Part 3 that nonbanks and even nonfinancial firms are entering markets traditionally served by banks. This is feasible where the advance of the market has superseded the balance sheet or where the function did not rely on balance-sheet skills in the first place. An example in this latter category is payments services.

The provision of payment services is an area in which banks have rapidly lost their competitive advantage. This is due in part to the advance of technology and in part to financial deregulation, which has opened the way for nonbanks to clear and settle payments through the central bank. But at base the provision of payments services was always just an "add on" for banks.

Any institution with a large customer base and regular cash flow can create a payments service, as many telcos and utilities have demonstrated. The underlying claims can be settled using accounts with a bank or with the central bank or, depending on the regulatory regime, with a private clearinghouse established for the express purpose. Accounts do not even need to be kept in standard units of account. Loyalty points schemes operated by retailers, airlines, and credit card companies can easily become a substitute payments system as points are exchanged for an ever-widening array of goods and services.

At present, banks are still at the core of the payments system. This is unlikely to continue far into the future. The Internet provides the ultimate opportunity for nonbanks to develop cashless payments systems without the involvement of banks (or even central banks). PayPal is a rapidly growing, Internet-based cashless payment service that operates increasingly independently of the banking system. Obligations are settled through PayPal and are effectively claims to the assets of PayPal. Similar schemes offering claims to gold and portfolios of securities have also been developed. The point is that this is an area in which the uniqueness of banks is fast disappearing. The future of banks will not be as dominant players in the provision of payments services.

Whereas some banks will successfully evolve from balance-sheet managers into expert financial traders, others may withdraw from financial markets altogether. If the quintessential banker's skill is the creation of trust and this can no longer be done cost-efficiently through the use of balance sheets, some banks may choose to find other means of continuing in the trust business outside the financial services industry. This would make sense if e-commerce grows as fast as expected, since the need for a trusted third party is essential in online market exchange.

Banks could leverage their existing brands to establish verification and certification businesses based on the collection and reliable storage of important financial and other data. The "banker-customer" relationship could evolve into a relationship in which individuals and companies pay banks to act as trusted third parties, verifying reputations and other data when requested as part of commercial exchange. Given that banks have traditionally managed relationships based on resolving information asymmetry, a translation of their role in this way keeps faith with their historical roots and plays to their time-honored competitive strengths.

Even if this were to be the haven into which old "square-rigged" banks sail, they will not have the harbor to themselves. Many firms, including credit ratings agencies and security firms—even some online operators like eVerify—have spied out the same opportunity. Wherever banks turn, the story will be the same—a crowded marketplace.

For with the death of banking, banks have forever lost their uniqueness. Balance-sheet banking was a technique for its time—a remarkably successful technique, responsible in large part for the economic development of the West. The ICT revolution has brought the era of banking to a close. There is no reason to believe that individual banks will not proceed to greater glory in a range of activities, some of which may well involve a departure from the financial services industry. But they will not be banking—and they will no longer be unique.

NOTES

1. There are many different models of integrated regulation. These include models that put market integrity and prudential regulation under one regulator, placing some but not all prudential regulation under one regulator, and putting parts of market integrity and competition regulation in with prudential regulation. In Australia, one regulator is assigned functionally to each source of market failure.

2. The pressure for more integrated working among regulators internationally is beginning to be met by existing initiatives, such as those established under the auspices of the Financial Stability Forum and the Joint Forum (of banking, insurance and securities regulators) (Financial Services Authority Press Release, "Securities Regulators Have a Key Role to Play in Global Financial Stability," June 27, 2001).

3. For further discussion of the motivations behind recent bank merger activity, see Harper (2000).

REFERENCES

Anon. (1998). "Plugged into the IT Revolution." *The Financial Times*, October 13. Available from http://pages.britishlibrary.net/blwww3/misc/disintermediation.htm.

Anon. (2001a). "Citigroup Chairman: Scale Boosts Chance for Success." *Best's Review*, 101(12) (April), 14.

Anon. (2001b). "Clarifying Convergence." *Bank Systems & Technology*, 38(5) (May), A2.

Bhattacharya, S., & Thakor, A. V. (1993). "Contemporary Banking Theory." *Journal of Financial Intermediation*, 3(1), 2–50.

Blowers, S. (2001). "Crossing Industry Lines: Convergence Products Target Convenience." *National Underwriter*, 105(33) (August 13), 14.

Clemons, E. K., & Hitt, L. M. (2000). "The Internet and the Future of Financial Services: Transparency, Differential Pricing and Disintermediation." Working Paper Discussion Draft, Wharton Financial Institution Center, September.

Diamond, D. W. (1996). "Financial Intermediation as Delegated Monitoring: A Simple Example." *Economic Quarterly*, 82(3) (Summer), 51–66.

Engler, H., & Essinger, J. (2000). *The Future of Banking*. London: Reuters.

Financial Services Authority. (2001). "Securities Regulators Have a Key Role to Play in Global Financial Stability." Press Release FSA/PN/081/2001, June 27. Available from http://www.fsa.gov.uk/pubs/press/2001/081.htmlhttp://www.fsa.gov.uk/pubs/press/2001/081.html.

Financial System Inquiry (Australia). (1997). *Financial System Inquiry Final Report*. Canberra: Australian Government Publications Service.

Gosling P. (1996). *Financial Services in the Digital Age*. London: Bowerdean.

Harper, I. R. (2000). "Mergers in Financial Services: Why the Rush?" *Australian Economic Review*, 33(1) (March), 67–72.

Harper, I. R., & Eichberger, J. (1997). *Financial Economics*. New York: Oxford University Press.

Hogan, W. P. (1999). "The Future of Banking: A Survey." *Economic Record*, 75(231) (December 1999), 417–427.

Holland, C. P., Lockett, A. G., & Blackman, I. D. (1998). "Global Strategies to Overcome the Spiral of Decline in Universal Bank Markets." *Journal of Strategic Information Systems*, 7, 217–232.

Johnson, H. (1999). "Embrace Technology, Preserve Trust." *ABA Banking Journal*, 91(11) (November), 11.

Jordan, J. L. (1997). "The Functions and Future of Retail Banking." *Economic Commentary—Federal Reserve Bank of Cleveland*, September 15. Available from http://www.clev.frb.org/research/com96/091596.htm.

Kapoor, M. (1995). "Making Cars—and Money." *Asset Finance and Leasing Digest*, London, Issue 212 (March), 14–15.

Koco, L. (2001). "Convergence Products Are Coming." *National Underwriter*, 105(21) (May 21), 20.

Sicilia, D. B., & Cruikshank, J. L. (2000). *The Greenspan Effect: Words That Move the World's Markets*. New York: McGraw-Hill.

UBS Warburg LLC. (2001). "The Urge to Merge: A Global Phenomenon." *Global Equity Research (U.S.)*, New York, March 19.

Chapter 4

A History of the Future of Banking: Predictions and Outcomes

Maria Gloria Cobas, Larry R. Mote, and James A. Wilcox

INTRODUCTION

For decades, banking analysts have been predicting the coming of the cashless and checkless economy as more and more payments are made electronically. In the *American Banker*'s Century Edition, Marianovic (2000) wrote, "In 1963, Dale L. Reistad of the American Bankers Association said at the first ABA National Operations and Automation Conference that we would be a checkless society by 2000. Mr. Reistad, who went on to become a consultant and perhaps the most renowned payment-system futurist, never lived that misfire down, but it did not seem unreasonable at the time."

By the middle of the 1990s, Internet fever was rampant in the United States, and it intensified as the decade wore on. The dramatic actual growth in Internet-related, nonfinancial activity such as e-mail fueled predictions of dramatic future growth in Internet-based banking and payments. A 1995 *Business Week* cover story, "The Future of Money" (subtitled: E-cash Could Transform the World's Financial Life), cited predictions that the number of electronic purchases would grow more than sevenfold by the year 2000 and that, by 2005, nearly 20 percent of all purchases would be made electronically. Furst, Lang, and Nolle, (2001) reported that, at the end of the 1990s, Internet banking activity was widely predicted to grow very rapidly—on average, by more than 20 percent annually. Figure 4.1 plots the actual and predicted numbers of households to have online banking accounts for the years 1996–2000 and 2000–2004, respectively.

Some have tried to rein in optimism about how fast the world of payments and banking will change. Only a few pages earlier in the *American Banker*'s Century Edition, Teixeira (2000) wrote, "Technology penetrates over long periods of time. Yet legacy processes, concepts, and methods will always be with

Figure 4.1
Number of U.S. Households Banking Online, 1996–2004

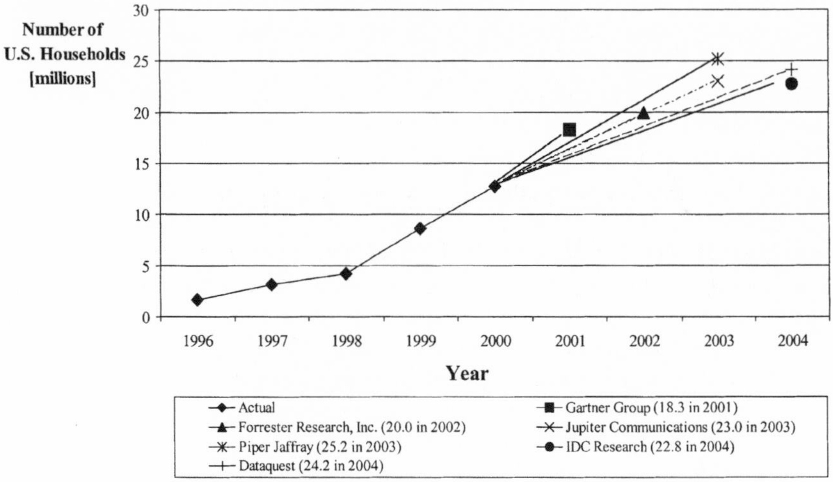

Source: Furst, Lang, and Nolle (2001).

us—and usually in much greater number than we realize. The usual predictions that such-and-such new technology will displace archaic processes are doomed to disappointment."

Forecasting is well known to carry reputation risk. Putting numbers with future dates requires courage; even moderate accuracy often requires luck and intellect. It is easy to find examples of predictions gone far awry. As World War II was ending, leading economists expected the U.S. economy to plunge back into a deep depression as a result of the likely cuts in military spending. In the 1970s, Henry Kaufman, the managing partner of Salomon Brothers, accurately predicted that interest rates would rise and in so doing made enormous profits for his company and earned both credibility and the appellation "Doctor Doom." When some of Kaufman's later predictions went awry, they cost Salomon Brothers a few hundred million dollars and cost Kaufman his aura of infallibility.

The difficulties of accurately predicting have led some analysts to be extremely cautious, or even cynical, in their approach to forecasting. One Fed economist, when asked how he forecasted, averred that he did so "only under duress." Others have quipped that predictions should be made for horizons far enough into the future that they would be forgotten by the time that future arrived.

Regardless of how accurate predictions have been, their great potential value for planning and decision making has sustained the demand for efforts to foretell the future, both in the private sector and in government. The most obvious examples are forecasts of near-term macroeconomic outcomes, such as those for interest rates or the growth rate of GDP over the next quarter or year. Predictions about banking are no different. Predicting difficulties in the banking system seems to have been neither easier nor harder than predicting downturns in the macroeconomy. There is also an ongoing demand for predictions of secular trends, particularly advances in technology and in analytics, which are in many cases less amenable to analysis using the economist's traditional toolbox of data and theoretical and empirical models.

As a consequence, many, and perhaps most, publicly available predictions that depend on judgment about such advances have been made not by economists but rather by journalists, business executives, practitioners, and consultants with extensive industry experience. Regional and national banking association meetings, which play an important role in helping bankers keep up with current developments, have provided a forum for many executives, banking analysts, and others to predict the future of banking. Unfortunately, many, and probably most, of the predictions about longer-term effects and outcomes are qualitative rather than quantitative, which makes them difficult to evaluate.

Here we present some predictions that were made a few decades ago about the rate of adoption of several key technological advances and their longer-term effects on banking. We also present some evidence on the degree to which actual outcomes matched those predictions. We selected three specific longer-term developments in banking as being representative of the kinds of changes that banking has seen, that bankers have suggested are important to the future of banking, and that are likely to continue into the future. These developments were deliberately chosen to include at least one that was largely driven by technology in the traditional sense of advances in electronics and mechanical devices (automated teller machines); one that was driven by the combined effects of technological change, regulation, and interindustry competition (the switch from paper-based to electronic-based payments); and one that, though facilitated by advances in computer technology and the desire to escape regulatory costs, was largely the product of financial engineering (securitization).

We then discuss the outcomes associated with these innovations and compare them with what had been predicted. We also note some of the common features of the deviations of actual from predicted outcomes. We then relate those observations to predictions and outcomes of the growth and structure of the banking industry as a whole.

AUTOMATED TELLER MACHINES

A History of ATMs

Here we examine the history of automated teller machines (ATMs), focusing particularly on early predictions about their use and deployment. In 1971, Seattle First National Bank installed what were considered to be the first ATMs in the

United States (*ABA Banking Journal*, 1979). Most early ATMs could be used only for cash withdrawal and to make deposits. Many were installed within or just outside bank branches and offered limited hours of operation. Different banks had different goals and expectations for their ATM programs, perhaps due to disparate assessments of the prospects for ATM technology.

What were the driving forces behind banks' decisions to install ATMs? Some analysts believe that changing economic conditions in the early 1970s, when rising inflation and interest rates made it more difficult for consumers to borrow, reduced consumers' loyalty to their local banks (Moore, 1984). These changes in economic conditions and consumer attitudes stimulated competition among financial institutions. For banks that could afford the investment, "ATMs represented an attractive strategy through which to distinguish themselves and achieve a competitive market advantage" (Moore, 1984). Thus, prior to 1975, the vast majority of banks that installed ATMs reported doing so to increase market share.

In the second half of the 1970s, more institutions began to install ATMs to enhance customer service and as a defensive measure against competition from other banks. Cost savings to banks were not a driving factor. Consumers used ATMs to access their accounts more frequently, so that the overall number of transactions increased. Moore (1984) made an analogy to the proliferation of convenience stores, which did not reduce use of supermarkets, but rather increased the frequency with which consumers make food and other purchases.

In the 1980s, other factors began to influence ATM installations. Because construction and operation of brick and mortar branches became increasingly expensive, some banks limited branch expansion or closed branches. ATMs provided a partial substitute for those lost branches. Also, banks began to face more competition from other financial services providers. Some of these other providers (e.g., Sears, Merrill Lynch) operated nationwide. Banks—which were still prohibited from branching across state lines—saw ATMs as a vehicle for competing across wider geographic areas (*Credit Union Magazine*, 1983).

A survey commissioned by the Board of Governors of the Federal Reserve System in the mid-1980s provides a snapshot of the demographic characteristics of ATM cardholders and users (Board of Governors, 1984). The survey findings indicated, among other things, that 42 percent of families had ATM cards, but only 30 percent of families had actually used the cards in the month before the survey. Ownership of ATM cards was "positively related to income and higher levels of education and inversely related to age. [. . .] Use of automated teller machines [was] also positively related to income and negatively related to age" (Avery et al., 1986). Thus, there was great potential for ATM usage to grow over the ensuing years.

Consumers now generally expect to be able to access their accounts in a much wider range of locations and times than they did 30 years ago. Initially, ATMs were installed only on bank premises. By 1998, according to a study by Dove Associates, over half of all supermarkets, gas/convenience stores, and malls in their survey had ATMs. Consumer acceptance has fueled this growth.

Predictions about ATMs

From the mid-1970s, most observers expected that ATMs would eventually be accepted and used by the general population. Early predictions reflected the belief that consumers would adopt even newer technologies—to the point of conducting their financial transactions from home. These predictions suggested that ATMs were likely to be displaced by banking from home.

Table 4.1 shows some of the key findings from a survey of consumer perceptions about ATMs conducted in 1976. Most respondents did not see a need for additional ATMs and, in fact, thought they would be infrequently used (Mears et al., 1978). At that time, only 5,000 ATMs had been installed in the United States. The researchers surmised that respondents preferred personal interaction with a teller to the convenience offered by ATMs. Many bank customers had not yet used ATMs, leading researchers to conclude that raising consumer acceptance and usage of ATMs would require a substantial educational campaign.

Respondents were asked whether or not they agreed with each statement as well as how strongly they agreed. The authors constructed an Agree Potency Index (API) to reflect the intensity of respondents' feelings regarding each statement. Although survey respondents did not anticipate the proliferation of ATMs, they believed that existing machines would be used for more than just withdrawing cash and making deposits. For example, more than half of those surveyed agreed with the statement that bank machines would allow users to make loan payments, including mortgage payments, and over 40 percent agreed with the statement that bank machines would offer cash advance loans.

By 1977, consumer acceptance was on the rise. The monthly rate of machine installations almost doubled in 1977, and there was "every indication that this higher rate will continue and perhaps quicken over the next several years" (Zimmer, 1978).

A 1980 article on the future of branch banking by Richard Rosenberg, then vice chairman of Wells Fargo Bank, began, "I trust that no one who reads this today will look me up in the year 2000 in the event that my predictions have been totally inaccurate. The best I can hope to do is to extrapolate some current and emerging trends in banking, technology, and social attitudes, and then generously season the results with imagination" (Rosenberg, 1980). He went on to predict that ATMs will be "obsolete by the year 2000" because most people will be using home-based devices to conduct personal business transactions. He

Table 4.1
Consumer Perceptions about ATMs

Agree Potency Index Rank	Percent Agree	Statement
1	89.9	Give me a printed statement describing my transactions.
2	88.9	Credit deposits immediately to my account.
3	86.5	Provide my current account balances.
4	82.4	Provide a telephone in case I need help.
5	79.1	Will be something I use most while my bank is closed.
6	81.4	Deduct withdrawals immediately from my account.
7	75.0	Be activated by a special card used only for the machine.
8	75.3	Have access to a live teller.
9	74.9	Have a two-way communication system.
10	68.2	Limit the amount of money I can receive from the machine.
11	72.3	Reduce trips made to the bank.
12	65.2	Provide privacy similar to a voting booth.
13	71.6	Be used at a bank while teller lines are long.
14	64.9	Be located in all major shopping centers.
15	67.6	Be the same as machines used by other banks.
16	68.9	Be near where I work.
17	64.2	Be used from my car.
18	61.1	Let me make mortgage payments.
19	57.8	Identify me by name.
20	61.0	Will be something I will have to get used to.
21	58.4	Be used to make loan repayments.
22	48.3	Handle most checking and savings transactions.
23	45.9	Will replace the need for cashing checks.
24	45.4	Be found in all major grocery stores.
25	43.2	Let me take out cash advance loans.
26	43.4	Be located at an information booth in a retail store.
27	40.9	Be installed at a few selected branches.
28	36.8	Be the way most banking will be done in the future.
29	22.3	Be used more often than bank tellers.

Source: Mears et al. (1978).

also expressed the belief that, because most transactions would be handled electronically, the number of bank branches would decrease and remaining branches would have "few, if any, support staff members." Rosenberg anticipated that technological advances would be such that households would have a comprehensive record of their finances in a home appliance that would be so reliable that taxpayers would be able to get a discount by allowing the government to tap into those devices when processing tax returns.

Without providing specific numbers, Rosenberg was predicting such widespread use and acceptance of new technologies that consumers would have little reason to visit either bank branches or ATMs. His remarks suggest, albeit implicitly, a sharp rise in the use and deployment of ATMs, followed by a quick decline as consumers switched to home banking by the end of the 1990s. Although his predictions may ultimately prove correct, it is clear that these shifts have not occurred as quickly as he suggested they would.

In the early 1980s, industry observers continued to predict growth in ATM use and deployment, possibly followed by a decline in favor of home banking. Here are a few examples of predictions about ATMs made during the early 1980s:

> ATM growth is not at maturity but at its beginning. There is a tremendous amount of growth still to take place. (Edwards, 1982)

> In 1980 a milestone was passed, with ATM shipments passing the 5,000 unit mark. 1981 was a record-smashing year, with 8,456 machines shipped, bringing the cumulative net installed base in the U.S. to 26,800. Forecasts for 1982 are even brighter, and it would come as no surprise if ATM shipments this year surpass 10,000 units. (Zimmer, 1982)

> By 1990, forecasters say, there will be 125,000 ATMs in place. Even if home banking catches on, ATMs will still be useful for on-the-spot cash needs. (*Credit Union Magazine*, 1983)

> During 1982, consumer usage of ATMs showed stunning growth. [. . .] Indeed, several estimates suggest that by 1985 the number of ATMs in the U.S. will reach the 84,000 level. (Duffy, 1983)

> Generally, the ATM may be viewed as a major success story for EFT [electronic funds transfer] in the 1970's, with impressive growth in installations adoption by consumers. [. . .] Indeed, the [adoption] pattern is similar to the demographic patterns of adoption of checking accounts in the early 1950's. (Murphy, 1983)

> This delivery system [self-service banking] will develop very quickly up until 1990 when it will start to slow down and eventually decline in favor of home banking. In the year 2000, home banking and self-service banking will compete for routine transactions. (Loviton, 1985)

Figure 4.2
Number of ATM Terminals, 1983–2001

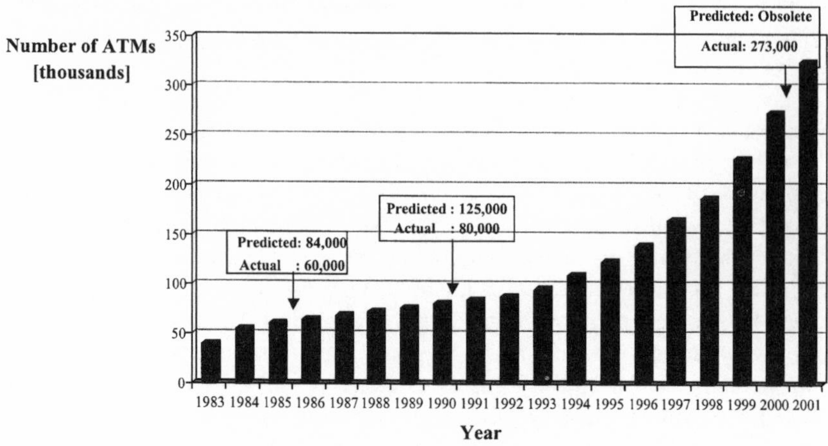

Sources: Rosenberg (1980); *Credit Union Magazine* (1983); Duffy (1983); *Bank Network News* (November 1995); *ATM & Debit News* (September 2001).

ATM Outcomes

In general, the predictions made in the 1980s were overly optimistic, as shown in Figure 4.2. This over-optimism is similar to predictions about home banking and about a cashless society. There were approximately 324,000 ATMs in the United States by early 2001. Tables 4.2 and 4.3 show that the number of ATMs in operation has grown steadily over the past three decades. The growth in ATMs was especially dramatic in the 1970s and early 1980s. For the 1973–1984 time period, for instance, ATMs grew at an annualized rate of about 36 percent. Similarly, the average number of transactions per ATM has increased almost every year since 1983 (*Bank Network News*, 1995; *ATM & Debit News*, 2001).

By 1994, although the availability of ATMs had increased tremendously, banks had yet to see cost reductions that many had anticipated. "[W]hile ATMs were successful in reducing the cost of each depositor transaction, depositors increased the number of transactions, leaving total costs relatively unchanged or slightly higher" (Humphrey, 1994). The advent of shared ATM networks in the early 1990s and the lifting of the ban on surcharging in 1996 spurred recent ATM growth. Not surprisingly, "[t]he ability of ATM owners to levy a fee on cardholders dramatically altered the economics of the business, leading to a surge in ATM placements" (Dove Associates, 1998). As banks and nonbank competitors such as Independent Sales Organizations (ISOs) and retailers continued to deploy more ATMs, the percent of ATMs on shared networks rose from 59 in 1985 to 100 by 1995 (*Bank Network News EFT Network Data Book*,

Table 4.2
ATMs Installed and in Operation

Year	Annual	Cumulative	Net Installed
1973	935	1,935	1,935
1974	965	2,900	2,900
1975	1,156	4,056	4,056
1976	1,249	5,305	5,305
1977	2,444	7,749	7,749
1978	2,001	9,750	9,750
1979	4,680	14,430*	13,800*
1980	5,428	19,858*	18,500*
1981	8,456	28,314*	25,790*
1982	11,035	39,349*	35,721*
1983	13,983	53,332*	48,118*
1984	12,352	65,684*	58,470*

* Cumulative shipments and net installed base began differing in 1979 due to warehousing, replacement, and scrapped machines.

Source: Zimmer (1985).

1995). While the number of ATMs grew at an annualized rate of 10.1 percent from 1983 through 1996, the growth rate rose to 18.4 percent over the 1996–2001 period. The monthly number of transactions per machine peaked at about 6,500 in 1995. Average monthly transactions per machine gradually declined to approximately 3,500 by March 2001.

Current Predictions about the Future of ATMs

Perhaps chastened by experience and suggestive of the wider range now warranted for confidence intervals, industry observers today are more likely to point out possibilities than to make predictions. They note that web-enabled ATMs, for example, might offer a wide range of services to consumers. Some machines already offer stamp sales, and now ATMs can dispense movie tickets, coupons, and maps. But cash dispensing is still thought to be the "killer-app" of ATMs (Newell, 2001). Large numbers of customers still rely on ATMs for cash, but few consistently use them for other services.

ELECTRONIC FUNDS TRANSFER

Paper checks have long had a larger market share (by number of retail transactions) in the United States than in Europe or in Japan. Payments in Europe

Table 4.3
ATMs in Operation and Monthly ATM Transactions

Year	Total ATMs	Transactions (millions)
1983	40,000	200.0
1984	55,000	261.0
1985	60,000	297.1
1986	64,000	302.1
1987	68,000	337.4
1988	72,492	373.4
1989	75,632	426.4
1990	80,156	479.3
1991	83,545	534.9
1992	87,330	600.5
1993	94,822	642.1
1994	109,080	704.5
1995	122,706	807.4
1996	139,134	890.3
1997	165,000	910.0
1998	187,000	930.0
1999	227,000	907.4
2000	273,000	1,070.0
2001	324,000	1,132.0

Sources: *ATM & Debit News*, September 13, 2001; *Bank Network News EFT Network Data Book*, November 24, 1995.

have long been more oriented toward smart cards and electronic payments; payments in Japan have long been more oriented toward cash.

By the 1970s, however, the ever-increasing volume and costs (due to the time lags in check processing and the associated amount of float) associated with paper currency and checks and the availability and falling costs of computer technology combined to stimulate the use of electronic funds transfer (EFT). Thus, individuals, banks, retailers, and governments greatly increased the proportion of their payments made electronically rather than via paper currency or checks. As making more payments via EFT seemed increasingly cost-effective, the prospects for even more EFTs in the future seemed likely during the 1970s. Credit cards issued by banks and retailers had already become quite popular and common. Debit cards were introduced in 1972 and transferred funds at point-of-sale (POS) terminals in retail stores. Although they were still rare in the

1990s, their usage continued to increase. EFT payments via automated clearinghouses (ACH) were displacing payroll and other checks for periodic payments of salaries, utility bills, insurance bills, and other direct deposits. Thus, the rising business and consumer acceptance of payment arrangements that had some electronic component and the falling relative costs of EFTs probably contributed to predictions that check usage would soon peak and that EFT volume would grow rapidly.

The Growth of Checks

A report prepared by Arthur D. Little, Inc. for the National Science Foundation estimated that the overall annual cost of the payments system in the mid-1970s was about $14 billion, with about $8 billion attributable to checks. Banks and government were concerned that the high costs associated with the rapid growth of paper-based payments volume would eventually make the payments system very inefficient. Banking analysts were perhaps influenced by the practice in the late 1960s of halting trading on the NYSE for one afternoon each week so that back offices could catch up on their backlog of paperwork. As a result, much attention and effort was devoted to EFT as a substitute for paper checks.

Predictions

Although there was much talk about checkless societies, nobody really expected checks to disappear. No matter how optimistic one's view about checks being displaced by EFT, the consensus was that checks would not be replaced as an important method of payment. Rather, predictions tended to suggest that checks would lose market share.

Mainstream predictions called for volume, measured by the number of checks cleared, to grow at 7 percent per year primarily due to growth in the macroeconomy and the number of check users. But some were even more optimistic about the development of EFT and more pessimistic about the future viability of the paper-based checking system. They foresaw a decline in the rate of growth of check volume for the remainder of the 1970s due to an expected rise in postage costs and clerical costs for check handling, a decline in the rate of productivity growth in check handling, and capacity constraints arising from the already high volume of checks being handled. As for the ability of EFT to attract some of the volume then handled by checks, many felt optimistic that per-unit costs of electronic data processing would decline as EFT volume rose.

Predictions were also made about the government's role in maintaining the checking system. In 1974, much discussion took place about the government's making social security payments by directly depositing the payments into individual accounts rather than by paper checks. In addition, the Federal Reserve's subsidy of paper-based check services (by charging nothing for them) was expected to end.

Figure 4.3
Number of Checks Cleared, 1970–1985

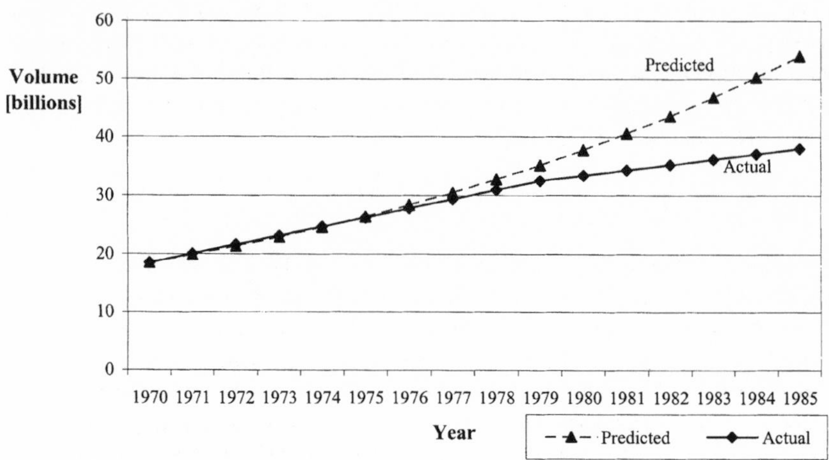

Sources: Sherrill (1971); Bucher (1973); Sheehan (1972); Department of the Treasury Financial Management Service (1990).

Outcomes

Figures 4.3 and 4.4 plot actual numbers of checks cleared during the 1970s and 1980s, along with predictions made about check volumes in the early 1970s and mid-1980s. Figure 4.3 shows that the predictions gleaned from statements made during the early 1970s by Federal Reserve officials and others in about the mid-1980s tended to overpredict ensuing check volumes (Bucher, 1973; Sheehan, 1972; Sherrill, 1971). For example, the estimated check volumes in 1980 predicted in 1974, 1975, and 1976 were 45 billion, 40 billion, and 37 billion, respectively. Actual volume in 1980 was about 33 billion. Naturally, predictions of check volume in 1980 were scaled back as time revealed that volumes were falling short of prior predictions.

During the 1980s, the opposite was true. Figure 4.4 shows that predictions made in the mid-1980s drastically underpredicted check volumes through the mid-1990s (Federal Reserve Bank of Atlanta, 1983; Lipis, Marschall, and Linker, 1985). By the mid-1990s, actual volume was more than 50 percent higher than had been predicted. Predictions of leveling and even declining check volumes were based on displacing checks with EFTs. Thus, underpredicting the former was tantamount to overpredicting payments made via ACH, to which we now turn.

Automated Clearing Houses

One element of the EFT system is the automated clearing house (ACH). An ACH is a paperless-entry facility that acts on behalf of local, regional, or na-

Figure 4.4
Number of Checks Cleared, 1985–1997

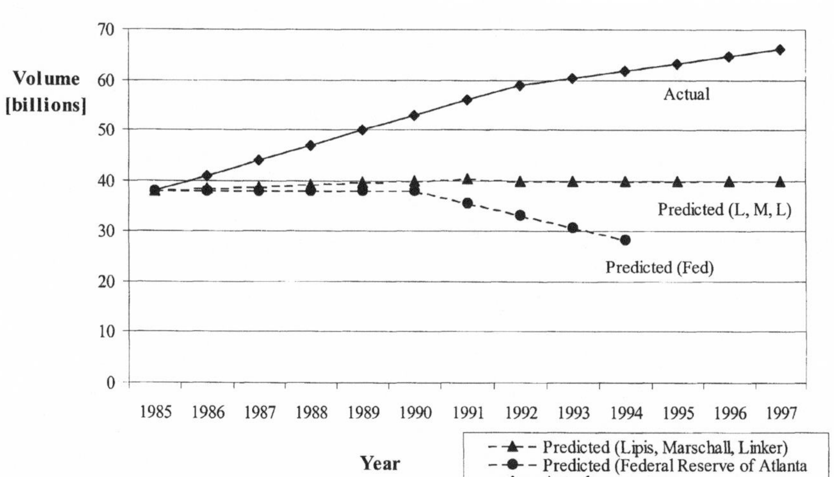

Sources: Department of the Treasury Financial Management Service (1990); Lipis, Marschall, and Linker (1985); Beckwith (1987); Bank for International Settlements (1999).

tional associations of commercial banks to make direct deposits and preauthorized payments. ACH is used for preauthorized payments of recurring bills, including car payments, utility bills, and mortgages. ACH is also used to make direct deposits of payroll and Social Security payments into recipients' accounts. ACH can replace checks and check-clearing facilities by transferring and processing the same information via tapes, discs, or e-messages between financial institutions. ACH was designed to replace checks as a means for making mortgage, insurance, utility, and other recurrent payments by consumers as well as wage, dividend, and other recurring payments to consumers. The first ACH was established in California in 1972. As local ACH associations expanded in number and size, the National Automated Clearing House Association (NACHA) was formed in 1974 with 18 charter member regional associations representing population centers in all 12 Federal Reserve Districts in order to facilitate the interregional exchange of ACH transactions on a national scale.

Although views on the development of ACH varied, many observers were hopeful that local and regional ACHs would eventually expand into an efficient, accessible, and widely used nationwide electronic payments clearing system. However, until banks faced and passed along to their customers more of the total costs of their check and currency processing services, incentives for customers to switch to the ACH remained muted.

Even as late as the mid-1970s, ACH volume was tiny. While over 25 billion checks were processed in 1976, for example, fewer than 0.1 billion ACH trans-

Figure 4.5
Number of ACH Transfers, 1976–1980

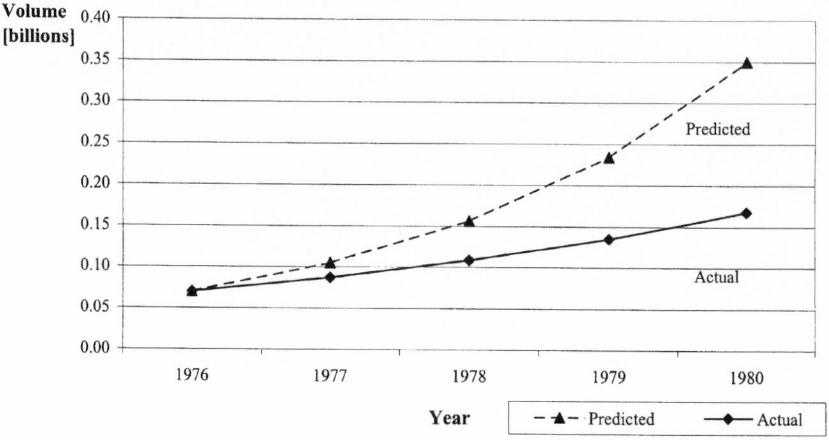

Sources: Nilson (1978); Bank for International Settlements (1980, 1989).

fers occurred. Of course, ACH volume was growing considerably in percentage terms, but from a very small base.

Predictions and Outcomes

In 1976, it was expected that the number of payments processed annually through the national ACH network would approximately quintuple by 1980, approaching 350 million (Nilson, 1979). Figure 4.5 plots the actual and predicted volumes of ACH transfers. By 1980, actual ACH volume was about half as large as had been predicted four years earlier.

In 1979, it was predicted that, by 1985, 15 percent of all check-type payments would be handled through direct deposits and preauthorized payments (Golson, 1980). Furthermore, preauthorized payments of industrial and commercial payrolls were anticipated to eliminate 3 billion checks annually. In addition, analysts foresaw consumer-initiated, or "GIRO," payments, such as those for telephone, electric utility, and department store charges, comprising a significant share of ACH volumes. In fact, George C. White Jr., a vice president of Chase Manhattan Bank, anticipated that the greatest growth in ACH volume would come from GIRO payments.

Figure 4.6 plots the actual and predicted volumes of ACH transfers for the years 1979–1985. Compared with the prediction that ACH volume would be 15 percent of check-type payments (and therefore nearly 7 billion transfers), ACH volume still hovered well below 1 billion transfers in 1985. Thus, electronic-based ACH transfers consistently fell far short of what was predicted for them during this period.

Figure 4.6
Number of ACH Transfers, 1979–1985

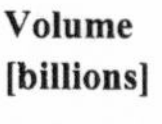

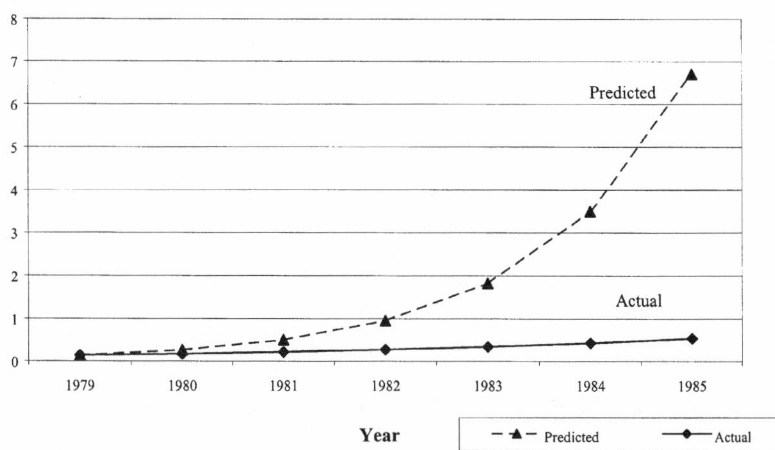

Sources: American Bankers' Association (1976); Golson (1980); Bank for International Settlements (1989).

Credit, Debit, and Smart Cards

By the 1970s, bank and nonbank credit cards were widely held and widely used. More than half of all banks provided credit card service by the early 1970s, and most banks belonged to one or more of the major bank credit card associations. In addition to banks, institutions such as travel companies, oil companies, retailers, and nonbank financial institutions issued credit cards for use in their own stores. These nonbank cards had developed decades before bank cards and were more widely held and used for many years after the development of the bank credit card. As late as 1978, the number of retail credit cards was almost three times that of bank credit cards.

Debit cards, unlike credit cards, are fed into a point-of-sale (POS) terminal that instantaneously deducts the amount of the purchase from the cardholder's account and credits it to the retailer's account, thereby eliminating float and credit risk. Although debit cards made their debut in the early 1970s, the volume of payments made with such cards constituted a very small share of total card volume until the 1990s. However, Figure 4.7 shows that from their minuscule volumes in the mid-1980s, debit card volumes were predicted to rise enormously (Osterberg, 1984).

More recently, advances in computing technology have permitted the development of "smart cards," which contain a computer chip sophisticated enough to carry vast amounts of data and permit a variety of transactions. So far, smart

Figure 4.7
Number of EFT/POS Transactions, 1985–1992

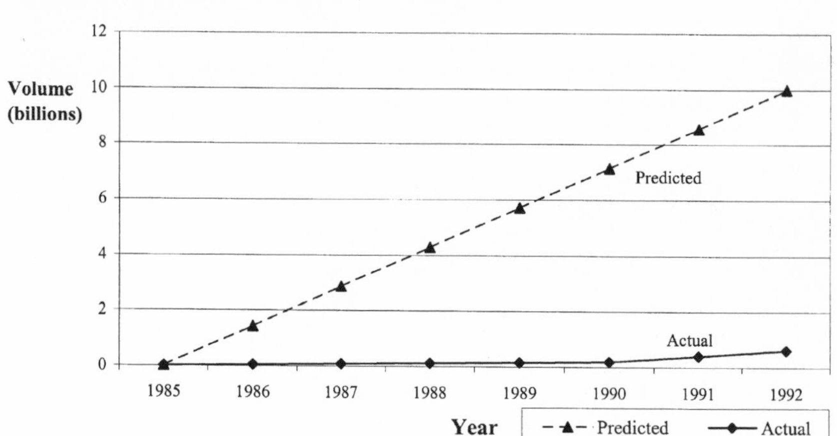

Sources: Osterberg (1984); *Bank Network News* (1999).

cards have achieved greater market penetration in Europe and in parts of Asia than they have in the United States. Because of their versatility and convenience, smart cards were predicted to grow extremely rapidly in the 1990s.

Predictions

Because of their convenience and extension of credit and float, credit cards have become very popular. With credit card accounts growing at about 30 percent each year, the future for both bank- and retailer-issued credit cards looked promising in the 1970s. Figure 4.8 plots the numbers of actual and predicted credit card transactions for the years 1978–1985.

Outcomes

The growth of credit card transactions over the period 1978–1985 tended to be overpredicted. Actual credit card transactions in 1985 were about 15 percent below what had been predicted in the late 1970s (Miller, 1979). Debit card volume was also greatly overpredicted. As late as 1992, EFT/POS volumes were only about one-tenth as large as they had been predicted only a few years earlier to become.

Figure 4.9 plots the actual and predicted percentages of U.S. households using smart cards for each of the years 1995 to 2000 (Ice, 1996). The pace of adoption of smart cards has been dramatically overpredicted. Although it was predicted six years earlier that roughly half of all households would be using smart cards by the year 2000, the actual proportion is close to 2 percent and has been growing rather slowly.

Thus, the history of the future of banking, in particular with regard to payment

Figure 4.8
Number of Credit Card Transactions, 1978–1985

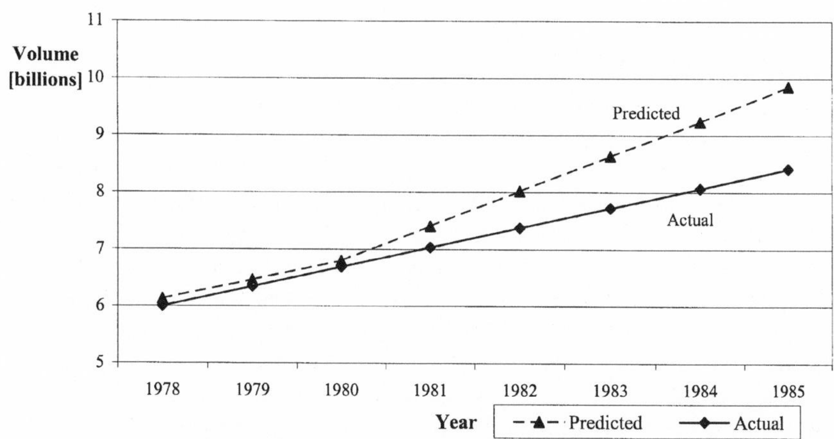

Sources: American Bankers' Association (1976); Miller (1979); Bank for International Settlements (1989).

Figure 4.9
Percent of Households with Smart Cards, 1995–2000

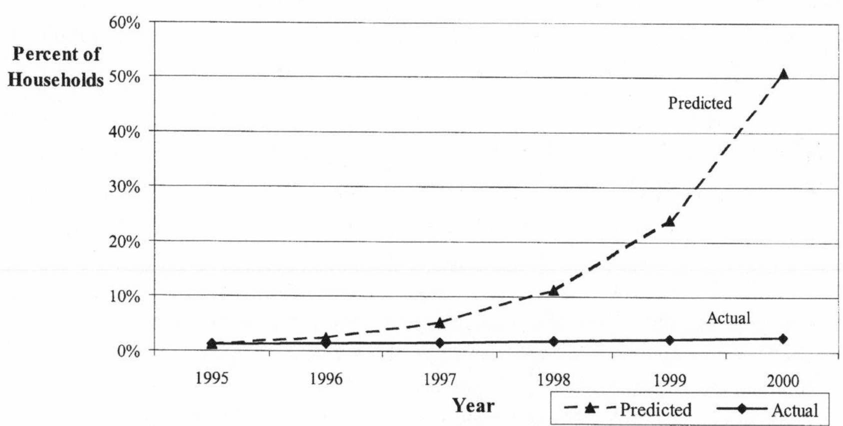

Sources: Ice (1996); Federal Reserve Bank of Philadelphia (2001).

instruments, is replete with examples where the market shares of newer instruments have grown far more slowly than predicted. It may be discouraging to some that the market has been so slow to loosen its embrace of older, less technically efficient payment instruments. The upside is that banks may be able to lower their predicted rate of technological obsolescence when calculating the cost of capital for payments operations. (A lower obsolescence rate is akin to a lower depreciation rate in that regard.) Thus, slower adoption of newer instruments reduces the effective cost of capital for existing instruments.

SECURITIZATION

Securitization has been defined narrowly by Pavel (1989) as "the pooling and repackaging of loans into securities." Although it can be argued that securitization in this sense occurred much earlier, it is generally regarded as having begun in 1970. At that time, the Government National Mortgage Association (GNMA) first issued "pass-through" securities that simply passed through the principal and interest payments from a pool of FHA-insured or VA-guaranteed one-to-four family mortgages. Since that time, the Federal National Mortgage Association (Fannie Mae) and Federal Home Loan Mortgage Corporation (Freddie Mac) have greatly expanded the volume and variety of mortgage-backed securities. More recently, large private sector financial institutions have gone into the business of securitizing both loans that they have underwritten themselves and loans originated by other lenders.

Securitization was a major step toward creating a true "secondary market" in mortgages. Prior to 1970, many thrifts and mortgage companies sold off some or all of the mortgage loans that they originated to institutional investors like insurance companies and pension funds. However, because of the difficulty of evaluating the credit quality of those loans, the purchasers generally held them to maturity; trading was virtually nonexistent. In contrast, there is an active market today for many issues of asset-backed securities.

Prerequisites for Securitization

Although the details differ greatly, depending on the type of loan or other asset that is securitized, at least three ingredients appear to be prerequisites to every successful securitization: pooling of assets, standardization, and credit enhancement in one form or another. Pooling of many individual loans into a portfolio is the most essential ingredient of securitization because it replaces a single risky asset—for example, an individual mortgage loan—with a portfolio of loans to borrowers in many locations and subject to many different economic circumstances, thereby achieving the benefits of diversification. To be sure, for any given issue of asset-based securities, the degree of diversification is limited by the need for some degree of standardization of the underlying assets.

Standardization of the assets underlying any given issue of asset-backed securities is important because it makes it easier for buyers of the securities to evaluate their collective credit risk. The mortgages underlying the first pass-through securities were relatively homogeneous because they were all required to meet the FHA's or VA's standards for issuing insurance or guarantees, as well as GNMA's standards for the purchase of mortgages. Thus, they were similar in terms of size, maturity, loan-to-value ratio, type of property, and default risk. It was only slightly more difficult to standardize credit card receivables, car loans, and other consumer loans for the purpose of securitization. Currently, the difficulty of standardizing small and middle-market business loans, let alone custom-tailored loans to large corporations, remains a significant barrier to the further growth of securitization (Feldman, 1995; Snyder, 1990). However, the ingenuity of market participations in solving what were initially viewed as insurmountable problems in the securitization of mortgage and consumer loans suggests that it is just a matter of time until securitization of business loans becomes commonplace (Feldman, 1995; Olson, 1986; Shapiro, 1985).

But pooling and standardization by themselves are rarely sufficient to overcome the reluctance of investors to purchase securities collateralized by assets whose default risk is difficult for anyone other than the originator to gauge. As a consequence, virtually all issuers of asset-backed securities offer some form of credit enhancement. In the case of GNMA's pass-through securities, this took the form of guarantees of repayment of the underlying mortgages by government agencies. Other types of credit enhancement that have been used include over-collateralization, the retention by the issuer of a subordinate interest in the securities, or a limited guarantee by the selling bank or an independent third party (Carney, 1989).

Benefits of Securitization

Although the rapid growth of securitization in recent decades creates a strong presumption that it is serving some well-defined human purposes, these purposes have not been evident to all observers. As Schwarcz (1994) asked, "[I]s the securitization process a zero-sum game or does it truly reduce net financing costs?" Schwarcz himself, and most other analysts who have looked closely at the market, have concluded that "securitization is an alchemy that really works." Like many other developments in finance in recent decades, securitization is a part of the ongoing "unbundling" process that breaks financial transactions into their constituent components, separating the loan origination and servicing functions from the bearing of credit and interest rate risk. By doing so, it is possible to achieve a closer match between the various components of the credit-granting process and the needs, desires, and abilities of those who participate in it.

Among the many benefits of securitization are reduced credit and interest rate risk for the banks and thrifts originating the securitized loans, many of which sell off their own securitized assets and then purchase asset-backed securities issued by other financial institutions to diversify their portfolios. To the extent that securitization results in a net shrinkage in depository institutions' balance sheets, it enables them to reduce or avoid several regulatory taxes, including capital requirements and reserve requirements. Investors benefit from having access to a highly liquid asset with risk-return characteristics that were previously not available. Finally, borrowers benefit from the increased supply of loans and reduced interest rates that result from broadening the range of investors willing and able to purchase the new class of asset-backed securities.

Predictions

Banking analysts offering predictions of the future of banking during the 1970s and early 1980s were aware of the developments in securitization. Nonetheless, they generally failed to predict either its rapid growth or its immense importance to banks. For example, in his excellent and widely praised book, *The Bankers*, Mayer (1974) devoted much attention to predicting the future of banking. However, he completely ignored the implications of securitization for the future of banking; indeed, the term does not even appear in the book. Similarly, there is no mention of securitization, or even of the secondary market for mortgages, in one of the most comprehensive and widely used textbooks on commercial bank management in the 1980s (Sinkey, 1986). We cite these examples not because they are outliers but because they are perceptive works that nevertheless, like most other analyses and assessments of the future of banking made at that time, overlooked a major development that was already underway.

One of the few analysts who did suggest that securitization would grow rapidly and have profound effects on the nature of banking was Sanford Rose, long a feature writer for *Fortune* magazine and later an associate editor of the *American Banker*. Rose proved to be extremely prescient in claiming that the secondary mortgage market would blossom and have important implications for banks. In 1982, he predicted that, "by the end of the decade, banks may make more money on the flow of assets through (and around) their balance sheets than on the stock of assets on those balance sheets" (Rose, March 23, 1982). This prediction referred not only to securitization; it also pertained to loan sales and a wide range of banks' off-balance-sheet activities. As it turned out, this was something of an overprediction, for noninterest income remains well below half of current income for all but a tiny minority of banks. Regardless, Rose was one of the few to foresee the magnitude of the coming wave of securitization.

Outcomes

Figure 4.10 shows the growth in the proportions of outstanding mortgage debt and consumer installment debt that are securitized for the years 1970 through 1999. Because consumer loans were not securitized until the late 1980s, there are no data for them before 1989. As can be seen, by 1999 nearly half of all mortgage debt and over 30 percent of consumer installment debt were securitized.

Just as most assessments of the future of banking made prior to the mid-1980s failed to foresee the enormous expansion of securitization, other analyses done a few years later exaggerated the negative impact of securitization on banks. Some predicted the demise or sharp retrenchment of banks as loans dis-

Figure 4.10
Mortgage and Consumer Installment Debt (Percents That Are Securitized), 1970–1999

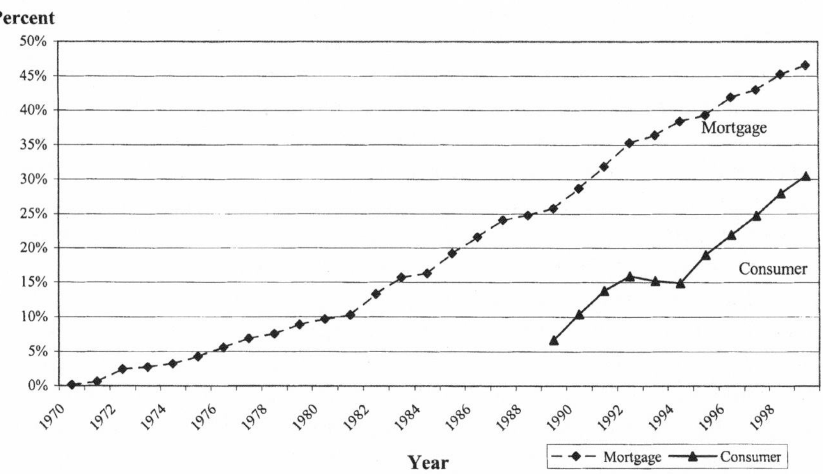

Sources: Board of Governors of the Federal Reserve System.

appeared from banks' balance sheets when they were sold or securitized in order to avoid regulatory taxes in the form of reserve and capital requirements, to reduce banks' concentration and interest rate risks, and to eliminate excess capacity from the industry (Moose, 1987). The next section discusses how an uncritical reading of faulty data led many to conclude that the role of banking in the financial system had declined much more than it actually had.

THE ALLEGED "DECLINE OF BANKING"

Predictions

A prediction often encountered in the popular press, banking publications, and even in several learned treatises in recent decades is that the commercial banking industry is in an incipient state of decline and that banks will soon lose their traditional role as the most important type of financial intermediary in the United States and perhaps in the rest of the world as well. Many of the trends in the data that led to such conclusions have become familiar to us all. The most striking trend is the decline in commercial banks' share of the total assets of all financial institutions in the United States from over 70 percent in 1860 to around 38 percent in 1960, followed by a precipitous drop from 35 percent in 1980 to 25 percent by 1993. Since then, banks' share of financial institution assets has declined much more gradually to just above 20 percent.

What is not clear from looking solely at these trends is that the meaning of the observed data changed significantly between the earlier part of the period and the most recent period. The general decline in banks' market share from 1860 until about 1960 probably reflected fairly accurately what was happening to banks' true relative importance in the financial system. Thus, the measured decline in commercial banks' share of financial institution assets from 1860 through the late 1920s appears to have been quite real, as the amount of assets was an accurate reflection of the volume of banking services, which continued to be dominated by traditional borrowing and lending activities.

Much of the decline in banks' market share from the end of World War II through about 1970 reflected the competitive handicaps that had been placed on banks by the Banking Acts of 1933 and 1935, enacted in response to the banking collapse of the early 1930s. These took the form of capital and reserve requirements, deposit interest rate ceilings, restrictions on bank investments, and the separation of commercial and investment banking. Although they were largely nonbinding until loan demand revived and market interest rates began to rise in the 1950s, these restrictions became more and more burdensome as the years passed. They were largely responsible for the advent in 1972 of money market mutual funds, whose share grew over the following decades to a level roughly comparable to that of total bank deposits.

Despite these handicaps, the renewed decline in banks' share of assets since about 1970 is largely illusory (Boyd and Gertler, 1994; Edmister, 1982; Kaufman and Mote, 1994). The reason is that, with the passage of time, the total of bank assets has become a progressively less satisfactory measure of banking activity and output. This, in turn, is due to the fact that the nature of banking activities has changed dramatically in recent decades. Probably the most important change has been the reduction in banks' role as a lender to nonfinancial corporations. Improvements in information technology have greatly increased the availability to investors of previously proprietary information on the creditworthiness of companies of all sizes, and more and more of the larger companies have found it economic to obtain short-term funding from the securities market rather than by borrowing from banks. Thus, the ratio of commercial paper outstanding to bank commercial and industrial loans, which was just over 10 percent in 1960, rose to about 30 percent in 1975 and to more than 100 percent by the early 1990s.

Nonetheless, banks remain a major source of credit for small and medium-sized businesses, as well as for households. Securitization of business and consumer loans, while in many cases resulting in the removal of assets from banks' balance sheets, does not eliminate them from the process. First of all, although the market has shown considerable ingenuity in securitizing assets that did not initially appear to lend themselves to that process, all of the assets that are easy to securitize have already been securitized. As efforts are made to extend the process to custom-tailored business loans, the difficulties will mount exponentially (Bryan, 1991). But even if these obstacles are overcome, it is likely to be a long time until small businesses can bypass banks and access the securities market directly. Until then, banks will retain a key role in the process as the originators of the loans to be securitized (Bennett, 1987).

Banks also offer a growing variety of services for fees, ranging from accounting and data processing to investment advising and the management of mutual funds. With the deregulation of deposit interest rates in the early 1980s eliminating the need to pay depositors for the use of their funds in the form of services provided free or at below-market prices, banks have also worked to increase fees on those services to market levels—an endeavor accompanied by considerable customer resistance and the loss of much institutional goodwill. Between 1984 and 1992, the aggregate ratio of noninterest income to total income for all commercial banks in the United States rose from 24.6 percent to 33.0 percent. In 1992, fee income, including service charges on deposit accounts, constituted at least 90.5 percent of total noninterest income, while the remaining 9.5 percent was divided between trading gains and fees from foreign exchange transactions, other foreign transactions, and assets held in trading accounts.

None of these so-called off-balance-sheet activities shows up in the Federal Reserve's *Flow of Funds* data from which the asset shares of banks and other financial institutions are typically calculated. Even if those data did not exclude such fee-based activities, total assets is a less than optimal measure of banking output because it does not capture important differences in the amount of risk-bearing and other ancillary services associated with loans, securities, and other earning assets of banks.

To overcome these shortcomings of the *Flow of Funds* data, one study used IRS data on total revenue and value added—which, in addition to including all types of noninterest income, do capture such differences—to calculate commercial banks' share of the output of the financial sector for every year from 1938 through 1989 (Kaufman and Mote, 1994). The results suggest that, aside from fluctuations of a few percentage points that persisted as long as five years to a decade, there has been almost no trend in banking's market share since the early 1960s. Not only has the output of the commercial banking increased in absolute terms in all but a few years over that 52-year period, but, after a brief decline in the late 1930s and early 1940s, value added in commercial banking as a percentage of gross domestic product has risen almost continuously ever since, more than tripling between 1943 and 1989. Similar conclusions were reached by Boyd and Gertler (1994) in the study mentioned earlier and by Levonian (1994 and 1995), based on the stock market's evaluation of future bank profitability. This is hardly the picture of a dying industry offered by some of the more sensationalistic journalism of the early 1990s.

Of course, there is no guarantee that the banking industry will do as well in the future as in the past. However, the recent health of the industry—as reflected in the sharp recovery of both its ROA and ROE from the depths of the recession of the early 1990s, capital ratios that are higher than at any other time in recent decades, and the relatively low delinquency rates for this stage of the business cycle—suggests that banking problems on the order of magnitude of those experienced between 1982 and 1992 are unlikely anytime in the near future. Most importantly, the dismantling over the past 20 years of the most burdensome of the regulations imposed in 1933, as well as geographic restrictions that go back to the turn of the century, culminated with the enactment of the Riegle-Neal Interstate Banking and Branching Efficiency Act of 1994 and the Gramm-Leach-Bliley Financial Institutions Modernization Act of 1999. Both should do much to enhance the competitiveness of U.S. commercial banks vis-à-vis other financial institutions, both domestic and foreign.

A LOOK BACK AT LOOKING AHEAD

Predictions about the market penetration of three important aspects of banking have generally been far off the mark. Starting at least three decades ago, industry analysts and bankers predicted that electronic payments would produce a checkless society within, at most, two decades. Over the past three decades, check volume has risen substantially. In contrast, the extent of home banking seems to have fallen far short of the typical predictions for it.

Similarly, the advent and rapid growth of automated teller machines (ATMs) gave rise to predictions that they were the vanguard of a major shift toward electronic banking. The shift toward using ATMs was envisioned to involve their providing many additional services, such as deposit-taking and acceptance of loan applications and displacing physical branches and paper-based payments. However, despite the continued rapid expansion in the number of ATMs, their use has overwhelmingly been confined to dispensing cash and occasionally providing account balances. Ironically, by bringing new security and convenience to getting cash, technological advances in ATMs probably retarded the adoption of electronic banking.

In contrast to the generally overoptimistic predictions about how quickly households would move to electronic payments and home banking, securitization grew far more rapidly and extensively than was generally predicted. However, many analysts then greatly overpredicted its effects on the role of banks.

It may be that adoption speeds were unexpectedly rapid in business-to-business technologies because the scale of operations made adoption profitable. Households' adoption of new technologies may have been hindered by unexpected lags in legal clarifications and protections for households.

It also may be that predictions about checkless payments, the disappearance of ATMs, the extent of home banking, and perhaps other aspects of retail banking erred primarily by overestimating adoption speeds for electronic banking by households. For many technology-based and other aspects of banking, however, timing is a crucial aspect of prediction. Accurate prediction of timing often dramatically influences the value and usefulness of predictions.

Prediction errors about the decline of banking stem, to some extent, from the tendency to cling to long-standing proxies for the amount of activity in banking. Historically, assets on the balance sheet were a good proxy. As securitization proliferated, however, less and less bank activity left its imprint in balance-sheet assets. Furthermore, banks' newer activities often produced few balance-sheet assets. Thus, the ratio of banking's balance-sheet assets to its value added declined more than banking itself declined.

The innovations that we focused on suggest that we may generally tend to overestimate the speeds at which retail banking evolves and underestimate the speed at which wholesale banking evolves. Our small sample makes for a very wide confidence interval around that generalization. The rate of adoption of new technologies seemed to be much slower in retail than in wholesale banking. If anything, it would make predicting retail banking developments easier. And differential adoption speeds alone would not explain why prediction errors about adoption speeds would differ so systematically. Thus, the differences between the prediction errors for retail banking and the prediction errors for wholesale banking merit further investigations.

NOTE

The opinions expressed here are not necessarily those of the U.S. Office of the Comptroller of the Currency or the Department of the Treasury. For their dedicated assistance, we thank Catherine Chen, Chian, Choo, Ellen Morse, Olayta Rigsby, and Maisy Wong. All errors are ours alone.

REFERENCES

ABA Banking Journal. "Progress Report on the Automated Teller Battle in Seattle," Vol. 71 (May 1979), p. 46.

American Bankers Association. *Selected EFTS Statistics*. Washington, D.C.: Author, 1976.

ATM & Debit News. "EFT Data Book," Vol. 1 (September 13, 2001), p. 3.

Avery, Robert B., Gregory E. Elliehausen, Arthur B. Kennickell, and Paul A. Spindt. "The Use of Cash and Transaction Accounts by American Families." *Federal Reserve Bulletin*, Vol. 72 (February 1986), pp. 87–106.

Bank for International Settlements. *Payment Systems in Eleven Developed Countries*. Basel, Switzerland: Author, 1980.

Bank for International Settlements. *Payment Systems in Eleven Developed Countries*. Basel, Switzerland: Author, 1989.

Bank for International Settlements. *Statistics on Payment Systems in the Group of Ten Countries*. Basel, Switzerland: Author, 1999.

Bank Network News. "EFT Network Data Book," 1996 ed., Vol. 14 (November 24, 1995), p. 3.

Beckwith, Burnham P. *The Future of Money and Banking*. Palo Alto, Calif.: B. P. Beckwith, 1987.

Bennett, Barbara. "Where Are Banks Going?" *FRBSF Weekly Letter*, Federal Reserve Bank of San Francisco (September 25, 1987).

Board of Governors of the Federal Reserve System. *Survey of Currency and Transaction Account Usage*. Washington, D.C.: Author, 1984.

Booth, James R. "The Securitization of Lending Markets." *FRBSF Weekly Letter*, Federal Reserve Bank of San Francisco (September 29, 1989).

Boyd, John H., and Mark Gertler. "Are Banks Dead? Or Are the Reports Greatly Exaggerated?" In *Proceedings of the 30th Conference on Bank Structure and Competition*. Chicago: Federal Reserve Bank of Chicago, 1994, pp. 85–117.

Bryan, Lowell L. *Bankrupt: Restoring the Health and Profitability of Our Banking System*. New York: HarperBusiness, 1991.

Bucher, Jeffrey. "The Check." Speech presented at the annual meeting of the Bank Stationer's Association, June 1973.

BusinessWeek. "The Future of Money." June 12, 1995, p. 70.

Carney, Owen. "Conceptual Overview: Securitization of Bank Assets." In "The American Banker Conference on Asset Securitization: An Intensive Briefing for the Senior Financial Decision Maker." Special Advertising Supplement, *American Banker*, May 30, 1989, pp. 1A–12A.

Credit Union Magazine. "ATMs Are Growing Up." March 1983, pp. 8–14.

Cumming, Christine M. "The Economics of Securitization." *Quarterly Review*, Federal Reserve Bank of New York (Autumn 1987), pp. 11–23.

Department of the Treasury Financial Management Service. *From Paper to Plastic: The Electronic Benefit Transfer Revolution*. Washington, D.C.,1990.

Dove Associates. *1999 ATM Deployer Study Executive Summary*. November 1998.

Duffy, Helen. "The ATM Movement." *Savings Bank Journal*, Vol. 64 (October 1983), pp. 31–39.

Edmister, Robert O. "Commercial Bank Market Share of the Financial Services Industry: A Value Added Approach." In *Proceedings of the 30th Conference on Bank Structure and Competition*. Chicago: Federal Reserve Bank of Chicago, 1982, pp. 97–115.

Edwards, Raoul D. "Tools and Technology: The Future of the ATM." *United States Banker*, Vol. 93 (February 1982), pp. 59–61.

Federal Reserve Bank of Atlanta. "Displacing the Check." *Economic Review*, Special Issue (August 1983).

Federal Reserve Bank of Philadelphia. *Business Review* (Third Quarter 2001).

Feldman, Ron. "Will the Securitization Revolution Spread?" *The Region*. Federal Reserve Bank of Minneapolis (September 1995), pp. 1–8.

Furst, Karen, William W. Lang, and Daniel E. Nolle. "Internet Banking in the United States: Landscape, Prospects, and Banking Industry Implications." *Journal of Financial Transformation*, 2nd ed. (Summer 2001).

Golson, James P. "ACH: Fewer Problems, More Opportunities." *ABA Banking Journal*, Vol. 72 (March 1980), pp. 105–110.

Humphrey, David B. "Delivering Deposit Services: ATMs versus Branches." *Economic Quarterly*, Federal Reserve Bank of Richmond, Vol. 80 (Spring 1994), pp. 59–81.

Ice, Thomas. *The Coming Cashless Society*. Eugene, Oreg.: Harvest House, 1996.

Kaufman, George G., and Larry R. Mote. "Is Banking a Declining Industry? A Historical Perspective." *Economic Perspectives*, Federal Reserve Bank of Chicago (May/June 1994), pp. 2–21.

Levonian, Mark E. "Why Banking Isn't Declining." *FRBSF Weekly Letter*, Federal Reserve Bank of San Francisco (January 20, 1995).

Levonian, Mark E. "Will Banking Be Profitable in the Long-Run." In *Proceedings of the 30th Conference on Bank Structure and Competition*. Federal Reserve Bank of Chicago. Chicago: Federal Reserve Bank of Chicago, 1994, pp. 118–129.

Lipis, Allen H., Thomas R. Marschall, and Jan H. Linker. *Electronic Banking*. New York: John Wiley & Sons, 1985.

Loviton, Christian. "ATMs at Home and Abroad: Today and Tomorrow." *Executive Magazine* (Fall 1985), pp. 35–38.

Marianovic, Steven. "Check It Out." *American Banker*, Century Edition (1999), pp. 113–114.

Mayer, Martin. *The Bankers*. New York: Weybright and Talley, 1974.

Mears, Peter, Daniel E. McCarty, and Robert Osborn. "An Empirical Investigation of Banking Customers' Perception of Bank Machines." *Journal of Bank Research*, Vol. 9 (Summer 1978), pp. 112–115.

Miller, Frederick W. "Checkless Society Gets Closer." *Infosystems* (March 1979).

Moore, James B. "Competition Remains Driving Force behind ATM Installations." *Bank Systems and Equipment*, Vol. 21 (January 1984), pp. 67–69.

Moose, Sandra O. "Securitization: Are the Banks Now Out in the Cold?" *Financial Executive* (February 1987), pp. 17–20.

Murphy, Neil B. "Determinants of ATM Activity: The Impact of Card Base, Location, Time in Place and System." *Journal of Bank Research*, Vol. 14 (Autumn 1983), pp. 231–233.

Newell, Amy, "ATMs: The New Role Models." *Bank Technology News* (September 2001). Available from: www.banktechnews.com/btn/articles/btnsep01-13.shtml.

Nilson, H. Spencer. "The Future of Credit Cards." *Banker's Magazine*, Vol. 162 (March–April 1979), pp. 54–60.

Olson, Wayne. "Securitization Comes to Other Assets: Technology Invented for Mortgages Enables the Sale of Other Loans." *Savings Institutions* (May 1986), pp. 81–85.

Osterberg, Roland. "POS Is on the Way." *Economic Review*, Federal Reserve Bank of Atlanta (July/August 1984).

Pavel, Christine A. *Securitization: The Analysis and Development of the Loan-Based/Asset-Backed Securities Markets*. Chicago: Probus Publishing, 1989.

Rose, Sanford. "The Future Competitive Environment: Strategic Planning for the 1990's." In *Proceedings of the 30th Conference on Bank Structure and Competition*. Chicago: Federal Reserve Bank of Chicago, 1982, pp. 22–26.

Rose, Sanford. "The Present and Future Shape of Banking." *American Banker* (March 23, 1982), p. 1.

Rosenberg, Richard, "Branch Banking in the Year 2000." *Long Range Planning*, Vol. 13 (October 1980), pp. 65–69.

Schwarcz, Steven L. "The Alchemy of Asset Securitization." *Stanford Journal of Law, Business, and Finance*, Vol. 1 (Fall 1994), pp. 146–151.

Shapiro, Harvey D. "The Securitization of Practically Everything." *Institutional Investor* (May 1985), pp. 197–202.

Sheehan, John. "Higher Productivity Demand Deposits." Paper presented at the ABA Automation Conference, May 1972.

Sherrill, William. "Banking at the Crossroads: The Outlook for Change over the Coming Twenty Years." Paper presented at the 1971 National Automation Conference, American Bankers Association, May 1971.

Sinkey, Joseph F., Jr. *Commercial Bank Financial Management.* 2nd ed. New York: Macmillan Publishing Company, 1986.

Snyder, Christopher L., Jr. *The Loan Asset Sales Market, What Lies Ahead?* A special report by the Loan Pricing Corporation, March 1990.

Teixeira, Diego. "Looking Back to Look Ahead." *American Banker*, Century Edition (1999), pp. 98–100.

Zimmer, Linda Fenner. "ATMs: Time to Fine-Tune and to Plan." *The Magazine of Bank Administration*, Vol. 58 (May 1982), pp. 20–30.

Zimmer, Linda Fenner. "ATMs and Electronic Banking: A Status Report." *The World of Banking* (July–August 1985).

Zimmer, Linda Fenner. "Cash Dispensers, Automated Tellers Come of Age." *The Magazine of Bank Administration*, Vol. 54 (May 1978), pp. 19–31.

Chapter 5

Financial Modernization under the Gramm-Leach-Bliley Act: Back to the Future

Bernard Shull

INTRODUCTION

The Gramm-Leach-Bliley Financial Modernization Act of 1999 (GLB) expands previous activity limits for banks in the United States by allowing financial holding companies (FHCs) and, to a lesser degree, financial subsidiaries of banks, to engage in an exhaustive set of financial activities, including dealing in securities, providing insurance, and merchant banking. It opens an important new avenue for activity expansion by authorizing the Board of Governors of the Federal Reserve System (the Board), in consultation with the Secretary of the Treasury (Treasury), to add to the list of permissible activities that they determine to be "financial in nature or incidental to a financial activity." For those banking organizations that qualify, the new "financial in nature or incidental" standard is superimposed on the "closely related to banking" standard introduced by the Bank Holding Company Act Amendments of 1970. GLB also permits FHCs to engage in a set of unspecified commercial activities determined by the Board to be "complementary to a financial activity."

One explicit intent of GLB is to intensify competition in financial markets by eliminating legal and regulatory barriers among different types of financial institution. At the same time, Congress also indicated an intent to sustain the traditional separation of banking and commerce. Over the course of more than a century, Congress has repeatedly defended separation against market-generated incentives that might otherwise have extinguished it.

The scope of banking firm activity, and the relationship of banking and financial firms with commercial firms, will, in the future, be determined by the expansion permitted under the new law. Two years after passage, the meaning of "financial in nature or incidental" has been at least partially revealed in specific proposals and rulings by the Board and the Treasury (collectively, "the Agencies").[1] On the basis of these early pronouncements and others, it is possible to infer the likely direction and potential reach of the new law, as well as its likely impact on banking in the future.[2]

This chapter reviews briefly the development and modification of bank activity limits in the United States; provides a description of relevant provisions of GLB; examines recent "financial in nature or incidental" proposals and rulings by the Agencies; evaluates the developing meaning of "financial in nature or incidental" and draws inferences with regard to the future scope of bank activity.

The Agencies' early interpretation of the new "financial in nature or incidental" standard suggests that it presents a slippery slope on which the Agencies are unlikely to find a clear boundary for meeting the congressional intention to sustain the separation of banking and commerce. Despite Board acceptance of this intention, and despite protestations in Congress to the contrary, GLB is likely, in progressive fashion, to promote integration. In historical context, it appears that, after a 70-year hiatus, the new law has put banking back on the road it had begun traveling in the days of J. P. Morgan.

ACTIVITY LIMITS BEFORE GLB

The policy of separating banking and commerce was initiated with the first chartered banks in the United States.[3] It has waxed and waned over the years, but when exceptions became pronounced, Congress typically responded by reestablishing a clear line. The policy has consistently differentiated banks in the United States from universal banks that developed in Germany, elsewhere on the European continent, and in Japan.

Early Restrictions on Bank Activities

The earliest commercial bank charters in the United States were modeled on the Bank of England. Because that Bank was not simply a private firm, but chartered to help finance the government (i.e., as a government agent), merchants argued that its activities should be limited. On their objection, it was prohibited from dealing in merchandise "to the intent that their Majesties subjects may not be oppressed by the said corporation by their monopolizing or engrossing any sort of goods, wares or merchandise." Though early banking law in the United States was not always specific in defining what banks could and could not do, the charters of the first banks typically prohibited them from dealing in "goods, wares or merchandise." Some restrictions, including those on real estate holdings, reflected concerns about bank safety as well as competition.

Beginning with bank charters in the mid-1820s in New York and, subsequently, in state legislation and in the National Banking Act (1863–1865), banking powers were defined as including, but limited to, certain financial transactions. These powers generally included the discounting of bills, notes, and other evidences of debt, receiving deposits, buying gold and silver bullion and foreign coins, buying and selling bills of exchange, and issuing bills, notes, and other evidences of debt. The National Banking Act also provided banks, as did legislation in New York and other states, "such incidental powers as necessary to carry on the business of banking."[4] In the years following passage of the National Banking Act, regulatory and judicial interpretation prohibited national banks from making mortgage loans, dealing in corporate stock as an investment, becoming a partner in a commercial enterprise in which they could incur unlimited liability; and operating a business, even if it had been acquired in satisfaction of a debt.[5]

Bank Affiliates and Holding Companies

In the latter part of the nineteenth century, large national banks began to undertake investment banking in their bond departments. When the Comptroller of the Currency informed banks, as early as 1903, that they were not permitted to purchase or deal in corporate stock, some organized securities affiliates, principally owned *pro rata* by bank stockholders and controlled by bank management.[6]

The early affiliates were organized under state banking laws, but later ones were simply incorporated and, thereby, permitted to engage in almost any kind of business. First Security Company, an affiliate of the First National Bank of New York, was organized in 1908. Its purpose, as explained in the circular sent to stockholders of First National, was to acquire and hold real estate, securities, stocks, and other property not permitted national banks. One of its principal holdings in its early years was the stock of Chase National Bank, which it controlled.

The bank affiliate system developed at the time when industry in the United States was in the process of a substantial change. Facilitated by prominent investment and commercial banking organizations, particularly by J. P. Morgan & Co, the restructuring evoked political concerns about concentration of power. The *Report* of a congressional committee established to investigate the "Concentration of Control of Money and Credit" (Pujo Committee) remains a compendium of issues raised ever since in debates on the dangers of combining commercial banking, investment banking, and commerce.[7] The *Report*, however, had little immediate impact on legislation and did not materially disturb the affiliate system that was developing and that grew through the 1920s.[8]

Although it had always been possible for national banks to invest in marketable debt, it was not until passage of the McFadden Act in 1927 that they were given explicit authority to trade in such obligations.[9] The Act gave the Office of the Comptroller of the Currency (OCC) the authority to further define the types of investment securities in which banks could deal. He (the comptroller) ruled that they could underwrite all debt securities and that their affiliates could underwrite both debt and equity securities.

Over these same first three decades of the twentieth century, bank holding companies also proved capable of combining commercial banking with other financial and commercial enterprises. Holding companies also grew rapidly in the 1920s, particularly in midwestern and western states where they served as a substitute for branch banking.[10]

Symbolic of the capacity of holding companies for integration of financial and commercial business was Transamerica, organized in 1928 to control the banking and nonbanking properties of A. P. Giannini. In 1952, in the course of an antitrust action brought by the Board, it was found that in addition to controlling banks in five western states, Transamerica also controlled insurance companies, engaged in real estate investment and management, the leasing and operation of agricultural, oil, gas, and mineral land, and in construction, as well as the operation of fisheries and fish processing plants, the manufacture of tractors, aircraft parts, and equipment, the production of metal, the operation of foundries, the production of diesel engines, oil burner equipment, and other machinery.[11] Years earlier, the Board had pointed out "(t)here is now no effective control over the expansion of bank holding companies either in banking or in any other field in which they may choose to expand."[12] With relatively unlimited possibilities for both activity and multiple-office expansion through bank affiliates and/or through holding companies, banking in the late 1920s seemed to have overcome the activity restrictions imposed by its limited-purpose charter.

The Glass-Steagall Act of 1933 and Bank Holding Company Act of 1956

The powers granted by the McFadden Act were effectively revoked by the Banking Act of 1933 (Glass-Steagall provisions).[13] Passed in the wake of the stock market crash of 1929, the failures of thousands of banks, and the slide of the U.S. economy into the worst depression in its history, Congress abandoned regulation for prohibition. It perceived the securities activities of some commercial banks as helping fuel the stock market speculation of the late 1920s, found improper securities activities and abuse of fiduciary responsibilities, and attributed bank failures to some of these faults. In recent years, some researchers, looking back at bank securities activities of banks in the 1920s, have found little evidence of improper activities and have concluded that passage of the Glass-Steagall Act was unjustified.[14] In historic perspective, however, the Glass-Steagall provisions were consistent with the long-existing policy of separating banking and commerce. For roughly 50 years thereafter, there was little commercial banking involvement in the securities business.

Other provisions of the Banking Act of 1933 imposed restrictions on bank holding companies. Corporations owning more than 50 percent of the stock of one or more Federal Reserve member banks were required to register with the Board in applying to secure permits to vote their stock. Such registration would submit the holding company and its affiliates to restrictions prescribed by the

Board aimed at maintaining their sound financial condition. Registered holding companies would also be required to divest themselves of securities affiliates within five years. Holding companies, however, found ways to control their affiliates without registering, and so the restrictions proved ineffective.

The growth of unregulated bank holding companies was ultimately terminated by the Bank Holding Company Act of 1956. The Act prohibited such holding companies (defined in the Act as organizations that controlled two or more banks) from engaging in almost all nonbanking activities, as well as effectively prohibiting, for about a quarter-of-a-century, their further expansion across state lines.[15]

The Bank Holding Company Act Amendments of 1970

Just as large banks had found, in the early 1900s, that they could overcome their limitations by owning state-chartered affiliates, so they found, in the late 1960s, comparable advantages in converting to one-bank holding companies.[16] On this occasion, however, a majority in Congress viewed the one-bank holding company conversions as a serious threat to competition and as likely to result in an unacceptable concentration of economic and financial power.[17] In 1970, Congress amended the Bank Holding Company Act to close the one-bank holding company "loophole." [18] At the same time, it authorized the Board to expand the scope of permissible nonbanking activities by implementing a new standard that allowed activities that were "so closely related to banking or managing or controlling banks as to be a proper incident thereto."[19]

The "closely related" phrase was elaborated in a Circuit Court decision in 1975.[20] The court found that the following kinds of connections could qualify: "(1) banks generally have, in fact, provided the proposed services; (2) banks generally provide services that are operationally or functionally so similar to the proposed services as to equip them particularly well to provide the proposed services; and (3) banks generally provide services that are so integrally related to the proposed services as to require their provision in a specialized form."[21]

The other part of the phrase, "a proper incident thereto," established a "net public benefits" test. The Board was to weigh the likely benefits and costs of at least a number of factors specified in the Act—that is, the benefits of increased competition, efficiency, and convenience against the likely costs of increased concentration, decreased or unfair competition, and diminished bank soundness.

A few years after passage of the 1970 Amendments, an Assistant General Counsel to the Board suggested that applying the "net public benefits" test generally to each newly proposed activity was appropriate because once it was determined to be "closely related to banking," *de novo* entry did not require prior Board approval. Therefore, at the same time that it found an activity to be "closely related," the Board should assure itself that "the balance of public benefits would normally be favorable."[22] Since passage of the 1970 Amendments, however, it has been the general practice of the Board to determine initially whether a newly proposed activity is "closely related to banking" and, if so, to apply the "net public benefits" test only to the specific facts of each holding company application requiring prior approval to engage in the activity.[23]

The 1970 Amendments also imposed constraints on tie-in and reciprocal agreements (Sec. 106). Representatives of business in which bank holding companies were likely to acquire affiliates complained about the dangers of having to compete with firms that could exert pressure on their customers through bank lending.[24] Despite the continued applicability of antitrust restraints, Congress enacted additional restrictions to "prevent coercive tie-ins and reciprocity."

From 1933 on, federal restraints had also imposed limits on interaffiliate transactions in order to safeguard banks from excessive payments to, and prevent subsidization of, nonbank affiliates. For the most part, interaffiliate transactions have been governed by Section 23A of the Federal Reserve Act.[25] Section 23B, added to the Federal Reserve Act in 1991, required that all such transactions be on an arms-length basis.

In the years following passage of the 1970 Amendments, constraints on bank and bank holding company activities evolved through legal changes, regulatory interpretation, and circumvention. Among other developments, banking companies expanded their securities and insurance activities.[26]

With expansion of bank activities, there also developed in the 1990s a conflict among the federal bank regulatory agencies as to how the expanding set of activities should be regulated and, in consequence, by whom. Since the 1970 Amendments, permissible bank activities had largely been a Board domain by virtue of its authority over bank holding companies. In 1996 the OCC adopted a new set of regulations, permitting national banks to engage in a variety of activities, otherwise not permitted, through operating subsidiaries.[27]

THE GRAMM-LEACH-BLILEY ACT

The Gramm-Leach-Bliley Act was enacted in November 1999, after about a decade of debate, in the context of expanding bank securities and insurance activities, and regulatory agency controversy.[28]

Purposes

The general purpose of GLB, as indicated in the *Conference Report* on the bill, was "to enhance competition in the financial services industry by providing a prudential framework for the affiliation of banks, securities firms, insurance companies, and other financial service providers."[29] The general expectation has been that GLB will intensify competition in financial markets by eliminating legal and regulatory barriers among different types of financial institution, facilitate the introduction of newly configured financial services made possible by changing technology, and level the "playing field" on which firms that provide financial services compete. Furthermore, a typical view expressed in Congress was that the restrictions on bank activities imposed in 1933 had become obsolete. New technologies and financial innovations had made them unnecessary, prevented useful diversification, and tended to increase bank risk.[30]

Although GLB explicitly permits entry into some commercial activities that are determined to be "complementary to financial activities," it is widely accepted that Congress intended to sustain the traditional separation of banking and commerce. The intention was made manifest in several ways, including the following:

1. A previous bill, which was not successful, included a provision permitting some financial holding companies to hold a limited amount of equities of commercial firms—a so-called market basket.[31] The "market basket" provision was eliminated from GLB.
2. In debate on the legislation, a substantial number of congressmen who supported the bill indicated that it was not their intention to have banking and commerce mixed.[32]
3. The Senate Report on the bill that became GLB, states: "The authority provides the Board with some flexibility to accommodate the affiliation of depository institutions with insurance companies, securities firms, and other financial service providers while continuing to be attentive not to allow the general mixing of banking and commerce in contravention of the purposes of this Act."[33]
4. GLB at least partially plugged a "loophole" that had permitted the integration of banking and commerce by imposing restrictions on unitary thrift holding companies.[34]
5. Congressman James Leach, a principal author of the Act, has repeatedly affirmed that GLB does not permit the integration of banking and commerce. For example:

   > Decision-makers came to understand the unhealthy social and competitive implications of the concentration of ownership that would be precipitated. . . . (T)he banking industry . . . became more skeptical as it became evident that financial firms would likely become takeover targets. . . . [of] new market dynamos such as AOL/Time Warner, Microsoft and Cisco, as well as older ones such as G.E. and BP/Amoco.[35]

6. The Board and the Treasury have explicitly acknowledged the congressional intention to maintain the separation of banking and commerce.[36]

Relevant Provisions

Most of the provisions[37] of GLB relevant to newly permissible activities for FHCs and financial subsidiaries can be found in Title I. They are as follows.[38]

Repeal of Glass-Steagall Act Provisions

GLB repeals Section 20 of the Glass-Steagall Act, prohibiting banks from having affiliates principally engaged in dealing in securities, and Section 32, prohibiting interlocks of directors and officers of securities firms and banks.[39] It does not repeal Section 16, which limits banks themselves to dealing in and underwriting securities. Nor does it repeal Section 21, which prohibits firms that deal in securities from accepting deposits. What remains of the Glass-Steagall Act, then, continues to prohibit the integration of the securities business into the operations of the bank itself. Rather, it is to be conducted in separate affiliates of holding companies or subsidiaries of banks, that is, in separate corporate entities.

Amendments to Bank Holding Company Act

GLB amends Section 4 of the Bank Holding Company Act, adding a series of new subsections that permit bank holding companies that qualify as FHCs to engage in a broad range of new activities.[40] Among the list of permissible financial activities in Title I are those engaged in by securities and insurance firms, and also merchant banking.[41] The Board is directed to define, "consistent with the purposes of this Act," certain general activities as "financial in nature or incidental to a financial activity." These statutorily listed financial activities include: (a) lending, exchanging, transferring, investing for others, or safeguarding money or securities; (b) providing any device or other instrumentality for transferring money or other financial assets; and (c) arranging, effecting, or facilitating financial transactions for the account of third parties.[42]

Structural Organization for Expanded Financial Activities

The new activities permitted by GLB may be undertaken in affiliates of a new type of bank holding company, termed an FHC. A bank holding company may become an FHC by notifying the Board of its intent and by meeting a number of regulatory qualifications.[43] With some exceptions, the new activities can also be undertaken by a new type of operating subsidiary of a national or state-chartered bank termed a financial subsidiary.[44] The Board is designated as "umbrella regulator" for FHCs, and continues in its traditional supervisory role with respect to other bank holding companies. It has general regulatory and supervisory authority over FHCs and may establish consolidated capital standards for all holding companies. However, Congress designated functional regulators for specific activities, including insurance and securities.

Regulatory Determinations of New Activities

The Board, with the Treasury, may determine a new activity to be "financial in nature or incidental" and therefore permissible for FHCs and financial subsidiaries. In general, an FHC need not obtain prior Board approval to engage in such activities.[45] The Board may also determine commercial activities to be "complementary to a financial activity" and, therefore, permissible for FHCs.[46]

GLB also permits FHCs to engage in "merchant banking" investments in any kind of company in any amount, without prior Board approval. These investments are perceived as temporary (though possibly long-term) passive investments in commercial enterprises. It is presumed that the Board and the Treasury, jointly responsible for issuing appropriate rules, can design restrictions that permit investments for purpose of appreciation and resale, while not, as a general matter, allowing FHCs to exercise control of the commercial firms in which they've invested.

Protections Against Adverse Effects

GLB extends the applicability of Sections 23A and B restrictions on inter-affiliate transactions to national banks and their financial subsidiaries. The Act prohibits cross-marketing between depository institutions and affiliated "commercial" businesses, including companies in which there is a merchant banking investment. Other cross-marketing arrangements are subject to regulations imposed by the federal banking agencies. The anti-tying provisions of Section 106 of the Bank Holding Company Act remain applicable to banks.[47] They are extended under GLB to the financial subsidiaries of banks.

In contrast to the evaluation of new activities under the 1970 Amendments to the Bank Holding Company Act, no "net public benefits" test is required for activities that are "financial in nature or incidental." Testing of specific applications, as discussed earlier, had been the general practice of the Board; such testing would not be applicable because, as noted, GLB provides for entry by FHCs without prior approval.

"Net public benefits" terminology does, however, appear in GLB in the authority granted the Board to impose restrictions on holding company affiliates, and on state member banks and their subsidiaries to prevent "other adverse effects such as undue concentration of resources, decreased or unfair competition, conflicts of interest, or unsound banking practices." Similar authority is granted the OCC with respect to national banks and their financial subsidiaries.[48]

THE REGULATORY DETERMINATION OF "FINANCIAL IN NATURE"

GLB provides some general guidelines for regulatory determinations under the new "financial in nature or incidental" standard. Several Agency proposals have provided regulatory clarification.

Legislative Guidelines

The Act lists four sets of factors that the Board/Treasury must consider in determining that an activity is "financial in nature or incidental": (1) "the purposes of this [Bank Holding Company] Act and the Gramm-Leach-Bliley Act"; (2) "changes or reasonably expected changes in the marketplace in which financial holding companies compete"; (3) "changes or reasonably expected changes in the technology for delivering financial services"; and (4) "whether such activity is necessary or appropriate to allow a financial holding company and the affiliates of a financial holding company to (i) compete effectively with any company seeking to provide financial services in the United States; (ii) efficiently deliver information and services that are financial in nature through the use of technological means, including any application necessary to protect the security or efficacy of systems for the transmission of data or financial transactions; and (iii) offer customers any available or emerging technological means for using financial services or for the document imaging of data."[49]

Agencies' Proposals and Rulings

The first several proposals and ruling by the Board, in consultation with the Treasury, are instructive as to how the legislative guidelines are to be applied and as to the likely reach of the new standard. The Board proposed in July 2000, and ruled in December 2000, that acting as a "finder" to bring together buyers and sellers of both financial and nonfinancial products is "incidental to a financial activity."[50] The Office of the Comptroller of the Currency had determined, a number of years earlier, that acting as a "finder" is permissible for national banks.[51]

The Board determined that acting as a "finder" was "necessary and appropriate," in accordance with the guidelines, to allow FHCs "to compete effectively" and "to efficiently deliver services that are financial in nature." It based its ruling on several factors: (1) new technology that now connects buyers and sellers, and the incentives to combine products, including financial products; (2) the fact that banks have experience in connecting buyers and sellers of nonfinancial products through customer mailings and referrals; and (3) the fact that banks now offer products, other than their own, on electronic web sites.[52]

The new "finder" activity for FHCs was, however, explicitly circumscribed by the Board; it indicated that acting as a "finder" is more limited than acting as an "agent," that is, as someone generally empowered to enter a business or legal relationship on behalf of a principal. The activity was also more limited than acting as a broker, that is, as someone who negotiates for a principal.[53] The ruling states that the new authority did not authorize FHCs to act as real estate agents or brokers.[54]

Shortly after this ruling, the Board and the Treasury jointly proposed rules that would establish real estate brokerage and real estate management services as "financial in nature or incidental."[55] It is noteworthy that these rules would overturn Board decisions in 1972, which held that neither was permissible under the "closely related" standard.[56]

The Agencies' approach in its "Brokerage Proposal" provides considerable detail as to the methodology the Agencies have developed in making determinations under the new standard. It is step-wise and can be summarized as follows: If the activity is determined to be "closely related to banking," it must fall within the set of activities that are "financial in nature or incidental." If it is not "closely related," but conforms to legislative guidelines (e.g., if it is "necessary or appropriate to allow a financial holding company . . . to compete effectively"), it will be "financial in nature or incidental." The guidelines notwithstanding, an activity may be "financial in nature or incidental" if it can be subsumed under one or more of the statutorily listed "financial activities" indicated earlier. Likely adverse effects are to be considered as a matter of course.

The Agencies' application of this approach in the "Brokerage Proposal" is discussed next. To avoid unnecessary duplication, the discussion focuses on the proposal that real estate brokerage be ruled a permissible activity, and not on real estate management services.

"Closely Related to Banking"

The "Proposal" indicates that "the Agencies believe that they should consider an activity to be financial in nature or incidental to a financial activity to the extent that it meets the old ["closely related"] standard."[57] With reference to earlier Board decisions finding that real estate brokerage and real estate management services were not "closely related," it states that "the financial services environment has changed significantly in the past 30 years, and what may have been an inappropriate activity for bank holding companies in the early 1970s may be appropriate for the diversified FHCs of the early 21st Century."[58]

The "Proposal" follows the court-determined approach for evaluating the extent to which the activity is "closely related to banking" by considering whether banks generally have provided the proposed service, generally provide services that are operationally or functionally similar, and generally provide services that are integrally related. It indicates that (1) some states permit their banks to act as real estate brokers; (2) the Office of Thrift Supervision (OTS) permits the service corporations of savings association to engage in real estate brokerage; (3) banks are involved in offering other real estate-related services, and in most aspects of real estate transaction; (4) banking companies engage in functionally and operationally similar brokerage activities, including securities, derivative, and insurance brokerage; (5) many elements of real estate brokerage are allowed under the new "finder authority" now permitted by the OCC and Board; (6) banking companies are authorized to engage in some activities engaged in by real estate brokers—for example, to help third parties obtain commercial real estate equity financing for others; and (7) national banks are authorized to assist in a variety of ways in the purchase or sale of real estate.[59]

"Necessary and Appropriate"

In applying the new legislative Guidelines for determining whether an activity is "financial in nature or incidental," the "Proposal" articulates a key reason why the new standard provides for a broader set of permissible activities than the old:

> Before passage [of GLB] . . . the law directed the Board to consider whether banks engaged in the activity, but did not explicitly authorize the Board to consider whether other financial service providers engaged in the activity. . . . This change . . . represents a significant expansion of the Board's capacity to consider . . . competitive realities . . . in determining the permissibility of activities for FHCs.[60]

The Agencies find that a number of diversified financial companies, some of which may still operate thrifts under "unitary thrift holding company" powers, have added real estate brokerage to their services. The "Proposal" notes that the American Bankers Association (ABA) has argued that "buyers and sellers of real estate are increasingly looking to a single company to provide all their real estate-related needs,"[61] and has pointed out that nonbank financial companies, such as GMAC, Prudential Insurance Co., Cendant Corporation, and Long & Foster, provide real estate brokerage services.[62]

Statutorily Listed Financial Activities

In support of including real estate brokerage under one or more of the statutorily listed activities, the "Proposal" restates arguments made by the ABA to the effect that real estate itself is a financial asset and that real estate transactions are financial transactions. Real estate is a financial asset, the ABA argues, because (1) the home is the largest asset for many individuals; (2) real estate services are the underpinnings for mortgage-backed securities; and (3) real estate serves as a means of wealth creation and providing tax benefits.

The "Proposal" notes that if real estate is a financial asset, its purchase and sale would be included under the statutorily listed financial activity of "lending, exchanging . . . safeguarding financial assets other than money or securities."[63] It acknowledges "that real estate does have certain important attributes of a financial asset, namely, that individuals often purchase real estate, at least in part, for investment purposes and with a view toward financial benefit of the transaction."[64] But financial assets are generally thought to be intangible property, and real estate is tangible. Furthermore, many nonfinancial assets are purchased for investment purposes, including stamps and art. In addition, there are many tangible assets, with substantial value, that are used as collateral but that are generally considered to be nonfinancial. And real estate may be held for noninvestment purposes as well.[65]

The ABA has further argued that the purchase, sale, or lease of real estate is a financial transaction because it is the most important, complex, and financially difficult transaction most individuals undertake. Real estate brokerage should therefore be subsumed under the statutorily listed activity of "[a]rranging, . . . facilitating financial transactions for the accounts of third parties."[66]

The Agencies do not accept the size, complexity, and difficulty of a transaction as determining whether the it is "financial in nature or incidental." However, they do recognize that real estate transactions are often for purposes of investment and, to that extent, have some aspects of a financial transaction.[67]

Adverse Effects

As noted, GLB does not explicitly include the "net public benefits test" introduced by the Bank Holding Company Act Amendments of 1970. The Agencies do, however, consider the likelihood of adverse effects in the "Brokerage Proposal." The "Proposal" points out that, because real estate brokerage does not involve any "principal risk," it does not seem to present any significant safety risks to banking companies or their depository subsidiaries.[68] Moreover, existing law and regulation, including those mentioned earlier, generally preclude likely anticompetitive effects.[69] Finally, it notes that the Board and the OCC are authorized under GLB to impose, if necessary, additional restrictions on transactions and relationships between depository institutions and their subsidiaries or affiliates to further safeguard against adverse effects.[70]

THE MEANING OF "FINANCIAL IN NATURE"

The term "financial in nature or incidental to a financial activity," like the term "closely related to banking," has no "clear meaning." In the 1975 *Courier* case, the court asked whether "closely related" was "an intentionally vague phrase by which Congress very largely left it up to the Board to decide what kinds and degrees of relationships are sufficiently close? Or is there some more specific connection?" It concluded that "[un]fortunately, no clear answers emerge from the legislative history."[71] The court, then, provided the criteria indicated earlier.

Again, it appears that, pending court intervention, imprecision in the term "financial in nature or incidental" provides the Agencies with considerable discretion. The Agency premise that "closely related" activities are a subset of those that are "financial in nature or incidental" means that well-established criteria remain relevant. Notably, these criteria do not involve the "closeness" of current bank services to those of nonbanking firms with respect to consumer demand, conceptually measurable by cross-elasticity or some variant. Rather, they are, supply-side factors of "product" and "production process" comparable to those that underlie the industry groupings of Bureau of the Census' "Standard Industrial Classification."

The services banks currently provide, and therefore their supply-side "closeness" to services not currently permissible, are invariably the product of earlier legal and regulatory decisions. It is not, therefore, surprising that almost all the examples in the "Brokerage Proposal" of banks providing brokerage services, or services that are "functionally similar" or "integrally related," derived from earlier decisions, some relatively recent, by federal and state agencies. It is also not surprising, given the substantial number of separate legal and regulatory domains in banking, that there would be examples of some banks that are permitted to provide a particular service, and/or services that are similar, or related to a proposed service that is currently impermissible.

It is an unavoidable fact of banking life, then, that "closely related" activities today are inextricably tied to earlier legal and regulatory decisions. This fact suggests the potential, under GLB, for regulatory bootstrapping to expand the scope of permissible activities. Nowhere are the possibilities more dramatically illustrated than in the Agencies' argument that real estate brokerage is functionally similar to acting as a "finder," an activity ruled permissible for FHCs less than two weeks prior to its "Brokerage Proposal."

"Closeness" to banking on the supply-side notwithstanding, the Agencies have made clear in their "Brokerage Proposal" that an activity may be "financial in nature or incidental" under GLB if there is "closeness" on the demand side, that is, if it is "necessary and appropriate" for FHCs to compete effectively. The competitive issues raised in the "Proposal" involve rivalries between banking and nonbanking firms, some of which, like GMAC are financial affiliates of commercial companies. If, as the "Proposal" observes, there are nonbanking firms that offer mortgage lending, insurance, *and* real estate brokerage, the question remains as to whether this combination of services injures banking companies that cannot offer brokerage. The ABA assertion that customers place value on one-stop real estate shopping, which presumably includes real estate lending, insurance, and brokerage, is, as yet, unsupported empirically. It remains to be seen what kinds of empirical support the Agencies will themselves undertake and/or require of proponents.

In considering competitive relationships, the "Brokerage Proposal" refers to services that enter into real estate transactions that FHCs and bank subsidiaries are not permitted to offer but that nonbanking firms can provide. It makes no reference to services that enter into real estate transactions that banking companies provide exclusively (i.e., depository services). How is the balance of competitive advantage to be established among banking and nonbanking companies that offer diverse sets of services? The "Proposal" does not elaborate, though it does solicit comments. Judging by the information provided, interindustry competitive analysis is at a rudimentary stage.

The third avenue to a "financial in nature or incidental" determination is to subsume a proposed activity under one of the statutorily listed financial activities. The Agencies' acknowledgment that the arguments of proponents for subsuming real estate brokerage have some merit raises questions as to how such decisions are likely to be made. The "Proposal" suggests an approach that identifies "financial attributes" of assets and "financial aspects"of transactions. It describes the financial attributes of real estate as an asset that is purchased "at least in part, for investment purposes and with a view toward the financial benefits of the transaction"; and a financial aspect of real estate transactions as "often entered into, at least in part, for investment purposes."[72]

Assets purchased as an investment, with a view toward financial benefit, and transactions entered into for investment purposes, appear common, however, to most, if not all, business assets and transactions.[73] More generally, even if "attributes" were well specified as "financial" and "nonfinancial," some method of aggregation and of measuring their relative importance would have to be developed.

The "Proposal" does refer to the conventional economic distinction that "financial assets are generally thought to include money, loans, securities, and other intangible properties, while real estate is a tangible, physical asset."[74] If a tangible/intangible distinction could be sustained, it would draw a clear line between potentially permissible and impermissible activities. But it is not clear, at this point, that the Agencies intend to adopt this distinction. The analysis, again, appears to be at an early stage.

On the likely impact of adverse effects, the "Brokerage Proposal" leaves few unanswered questions. Safety and soundness issues will be considered carefully in the initial evaluation of a newly proposed activity. Competitive issues, the "Proposal" implies, have been resolved by protections offered under existing law and regulation. There is little reason to believe, then, that any new proposals would be rejected on competitive grounds. Furthermore, once an activity is ruled permissible, competitive factors will no longer play any role in evaluating entry by FHCs or bank subsidiaries. Under GLB, once an activity is determined to be "financial in nature or incidental," prior approval is no longer necessary. In the interests of regulatory simplification, only post-entry notice is required.

There remains the possibility for regulatory interventions to prevent adverse effects. It is conceivable that intervention might be undertaken to prevent unsound banking practices, though GLB authority appears redundant. Intervention to prevent adverse anticompetitive effects, such as undue concentration of resources, decreased or unfair competition, and/or conflicts of interest seems less likely. The specific conditions that might invoke post-entry intervention by the Board or the OCC, for example, to forestall an "undue concentration of resources" are difficult to imagine.

THE FUTURE OF BANKING

The Agencies' analysis of the new "financial in nature or incidental" standard strongly suggests a substantial expansion of permissible activities. The supply-side characteristics that satisfy the "closely related to banking" standard have now been augmented by demand-side factors that underlie the new "financial in nature or incidental" standard. The combination suggests the possibility for a dynamic expansion in which regulatory decisions expand the scope of activities that are "closely related" and simultaneously expose banks to new rivals whose "production processes" may be substantially different, but whose "products" become substitutes or necessary complements for "products" offered by banks.

As suggested, what is not "closely related" today can become so tomorrow through a progressive enlargement of permissible activities based on earlier Agency decisions. If, for example, the Agencies determine that real estate brokerage and real estate management services are "closely related to banking" (and, therefore, "financial in nature or incidental"), it is plausible that additional activities might, then, become "closely related" because they have become "functionally or operationally similar" or "integrally related." So, for example, it might be argued that the combination of real estate brokerage, management services, and construction lending involves banks in many of the same functions that characterize real estate development. Alternatively, it might be argued that real estate development is "financial in nature or incidental" because many rival real estate firms not only provide brokerage and management services, but also develop real estate, thus making development authority "necessary and appropriate" for competitive reasons.[75]

If real estate development were to be ruled "financial in nature or incidental," it would be a short step to ruling that other real estate-intensive activities were also "financial in nature or incidental," or "complementary" to a financial activity. There is, after all, little qualitative difference between developing real estate through the construction of housing or commercial buildings and the use of real estate for agricultural, mining, and oil exploration.

The extent of such progressive expansion may seem fanciful. Construction, agriculture, mining, and oil exploration are not generally viewed today as financial or financially related activities. But real estate development was an activity in which many savings and loans were extensively engaged in the 1980s. And construction, agriculture, mining, and oil exploration are precisely the types of activities in which Transamerica, the most prominent bank holding company of the pre-Bank Holding Company Act era, engaged.

The potential for such activity expansion under GLB has not escaped the notice of banking groups. The ABA's contention, reported in the "Brokerage Proposal," that real estate itself is a financial asset is suggestive. The possibilities are explicitly portrayed in an assertion by FHCs, reported by Governor Lawrence Meyer of the Board, that "anything done by a financial holding company or anything that includes processing a payment is intrinsically financial."[76] Governor Meyer has also recognized the possibility that the Agencies will, through their determinations, expand the scope of "banking" at the expense of "commerce": "[T]he structure [of GLB], of course, has some obvious tensions that, themselves, reflect some difficult compromises. These tensions . . . mean that both the regulators and the regulated face no bright lines on the commerce and banking front."[77] He goes on to comment on the wide discretion GLB has afforded the Agencies:

> The Congress specifically rejected commerce and banking in GLB but empowered the Federal Reserve and the Treasury to add to the permissible activities list any activity that is either "financial," without much guidance as to what that means, or is "complementary" to financial activities, with no guidance. . . . GLB grants the agencies authority to move toward mixing banking and commerce at the margin as markets and technology begin to dim the already less than bright line between them.[78]

Within the dynamically permissive framework of GLB, the Board, and probably the Treasury, appear prepared to facilitate FHC entry into new "financial in nature or incidental" activities currently perceived as "commercial." Combined with commercial activities ruled permissible because they are "complementary," the expansion over the next decade is likely to be extensive. There is, in fact, no obvious limit. As a result, the congressional intent to maintain the traditional separation of banking and commerce has become unusually muddled.

In perspective, GLB has placed commercial banking organizations, particularly large ones, back on the road they had begun to travel before the Glass-Steagall Act of 1933 and the Bank Holding Company Act of 1956 terminated the movement toward an American form of universal banking. The future of American banking, then, can be seen as a continuation of the course that had emerged prior to 1933 and that had been arrested for nearly 70 years.

CONCLUSIONS

From the earliest days of banking in the United States, legislators have imposed activity limits on banking firms by crafting legal phrases intended to describe what banks could and could not do. Even before these limits were aimed at the prevention of excessive risk-taking, they were seen as promoting competition in a free market economy.

In passing GLB, Congress clearly intended to permit a wider range of banking activities than permitted under earlier legislation. The new Act provides for activity expansion that is reminiscent in scope of the expansion that developed, largely outside legislative limits, in the first 30 years of the twentieth century. Not only are all "financial" activities allowed, including merchant banking, but also some commercial activities. At the same time, Congress also expressed an intention to sustain the traditional separation of banking and commerce.

A principal avenue for activity expansion under GLB is the new powers it grants financial holding companies and financial subsidiaries to engage in activities that are "financial in nature or incidental to a financial activity." The early regulatory decisions of the Federal Reserve Board, in consultation with the Treasury Department, have helped clarify the likely impact of the new standard. Examination of recent proposals and determinations suggests a regulatory approach that will potentially accommodate a progressive expansion of permissible new activities into areas that are currently perceived as "commercial."

The intention of Congress to sustain the traditional separation of banking and commerce notwithstanding, early pronouncements by the Federal Reserve Board and the Treasury suggest that GLB provides no obvious limits to activity expansion. Although the regulatory process of making the law operational is still at an early stage, it appears that, after a 70-year hiatus, GLB has created an opportunity for the bank-centered financial organizations to expand significantly into areas that today are perceived as commercial.

NOTES

1. Early proposals and rulings with regard to the new "financial in nature or incidental" standard have included: Board of Governors of the Federal Reserve System, July 31, 2000, "Proposed Rule" (hereinafter "Finder Proposal"); Board of Governors of the Fed-

eral Reserve System, December 19, 2000, "Final Rule" (hereinafter "Finder Rule"); and Board of Governors of the Federal Reserve System and Department of the Treasury, December 22, 2000, "Proposed Rule" (hereinafter "Brokerage Proposal").

2. The Board has also determined several activities to be "complementary to a financial activity." See Board of Governors of the Federal Reserve System, December 13, 2000, "Proposed Rule." The Board and Treasury have also issued interim and, then, final rules for merchant banking. See Board of Governors of the Federal Reserve System and Treasury Department, March 17, 2000, "Interim Rule on Merchant Banking Activities;" and February 15, 2001, "Final Rule on Merchant Banking Activities."

3. This section draws on Shull (1994).

4. In 1857, the New York Court of Appeals acknowledged that the state's banking act did not list all authorized powers; and it indicated that the unlisted powers were not necessarily limited to the implicit powers needed to exercise powers that were listed. In particular, it decided that banks had the right to borrow money by issuing bonds, though this power was not specified in the New York law. *Curtis v. Leavitt*, 15 N.Y. 2 (1857).

5. *Harvard Law Review* (1920).

6. See the Office of the Comptroller of the Currency, 1915, pp. 35–39. See also Peach (1941), 46–47; and Redlich (1968), Vol. II, 390 ff. George Baker, Chairman of the Board of First National Bank of New York, testified in 1913 that the First Security Company was organized "(f)or doing business that was not specially authorized by the banking act. We held some securities that in the early days were considered perfectly proper, but under some later decisions of the courts the holding of bank stock or other stock was prohibited; at any rate the comptroller prohibited it." U.S. House, 1913, Hearings, 1424, 1432.

7. See U.S. House, 1913, *Report*. For example, the *Report* argues, among other things, that bank funds were likely to be used to finance speculative operations (155), that the mistakes of affiliates were likely to impact the bank (155), and that the relationships between banks and the industrial and railway companies they financed would compromise the interests of creditworthy borrowers (159–60).

8. The *Report*'s criticism did result in limited restrictions of interlocking directorates. Section 8 of the Clayton Act (1914) prohibited interlocks in cases in which individuals served as directors or officers of two or more competing companies, where the elimination of competition between the companies would be a violation of the law. Section 11 of the Act gave enforcement authority with respect to commercial banks to the newly created Federal Reserve Board. The Board appears not to have vigorously implemented the restrictions. See Willis (1923), 192–193. On the growth of the affiliate system, see Peach (1941, 18, 51, 54).

9. Peach (1941, 40 ff.).

10. For information on the development of bank holding companies, see Fischer (1961), Ch. 1.

11. Transamerica Corporation (1952, 369–370).

12. Board of Governors (1943, 37).

13. In general terms, the restrictions were as follows: Section 16 limited bank dealing and underwriting to specified types of securities, that is, obligations of the United States and general obligations of states and political subdivisions; banks are permitted to provide brokerage services to customers. Section 20 prohibited banks from having affiliates principally engaged in dealing in securities. Section 21 prohibited any business that deals in

securities from being in the business of receiving deposits. Section 32 prohibited interlocks of directors and officers of securities firms and banks.

14. See, for example, Benston (1990).

15. Under the law, permissible activities were to be "of a financial, fiduciary, or insurance nature" and "so closely related to the business of banking or managing or controlling banks as to be a proper incident thereto." The Board narrowly interpreted the term "the business of banking" to mean a relationship between the customers of specific banks and their nonbanking affiliates.

16. The exemption of one-bank holding companies under the 1956 Act had permitted some large commercial and industrial firms, including W. R. Grace, R. H. Macy, and Corn Products Refining, to own small banks, principally to accommodate employees. Until the late 1960s, however, the one-bank holding company was, for the most part, a small firm controlling a small bank in a unit banking state. Board of Governors (1972).

17. See, for example, the statement of President Richard Nixon reprinted in U.S. House, 1970, Conference Report, 11, 12; and Richard W. McLaren in U.S. House, 1970, Hearings, 238 ff.

18. The "purposes" of the Amendments of 1970 are spelled out in a discussion of the factors leading to the legislation in congressional reports. See U.S. House, 1970 Conference Report; U.S. Senate, 1970, Report, 1–4; and U.S. House, 1969, Report, 2–3.

19. See U.S. House, 1969, Hearings, 15–16. By eliminating the term "the business of" from the phrase "so closely related to the business of banking," Congress made clear that new activities need only be related to banking in general, and not to the business of specific banks.

20. *National Courier Association* v. *Board of Governors of the Federal Reserve System*, 516 F.2d 1229 (1975).

21. Ibid., 1237.

22. See Heller (1976, 230–231 n.3).

23. On occasion, the "net public benefits" test has been applied more generally, independently of any specific application. In 1977, the Board found that the operation of a savings and loan association was not a permissible activity, even though it was "closely related to banking," because the savings and loan business was not "a proper incident thereto." See *D.H. Baldwin & Co.*, 63 *Fed. Res. Bul.* 280 (1977).

24. Testimony can be found in U.S. House, 1969, Hearings; and in U.S. Senate, 1970, Hearings.

25. Section 23A was enacted in 1933. In 1956, it was superseded by Section 6 of the Bank Holding Company Act which imposed more severe restrictions. Section 6 was repealed in 1966, and Section 23A again became binding. With certain exceptions, Section 23A imposes a maximum of 10 percent of capital stock and surplus on loans by a bank to any one affiliate and a 20 percent maximum for loans to all affiliates. The extension of credit is to be collateralized by securities having a market value at least equivalent to the credit extended. Amendments in 1982 substantially liberalized transactions among the bank subsidiaries of holding companies.

26. On the development of expanded securities powers for bank holding companies and state-chartered nonmember banks, see Shull and White (1998), 455–458. In the 1990s, Court rulings expanded the insurance powers of national banks. See *NationsBank* v. *Variable Annuity Life Insurance Co.*, 115 S.Ct. 810 (1995); and *Barnett Bank of Marion County N.A.* v. *Nelson*, 517 U.S. 25 (1996).

27. 12 C.F.R. Part 5.

28. A summary of the legislative background of this Act can be found in U.S. Senate, 1999, Report, 3,4.

29. U.S. House, 1999, *Conference Report*, 151.

30. See, for example, U.S. Senate (1999, 4 ff.).

31. H.R. 10, as passed by the House of Representatives on May 13, 1998, permitted certain holding companies to derive up to 15 percent of their consolidated annual gross revenues from commercial activities.

32. See the "Additional Views" of Senators Sarbanes et al. in U.S. Senate (1999, 70–76).

33. U.S. Senate (1999, 21).

34. GLB prohibits new charters for unitary thrift holding companies and also prohibits the sale of existing companies to commercial firms. Nevertheless, it grandfathers holding companies that existed on or before May 4, 1999, or that came into existence as the result of an application that had been pending as of that date. These are not, however, permitted to transfer their grandfathered status through acquisition or merger. It further limits their expansion by providing that no unitary thrift company can acquire control of a savings association after May 4, 1999, unless its activities conform to those currently authorized for multiple thrift holding companies or for FHCs.

35. Leach (2000, 1, 2).

36. See, for example, Board of Governors and Treasury, 2000, "Interim Rules for Merchant Banking," 8, 9.

37. For a more detailed review of these provisions, see Shull (2000).

38. GLB is divided into seven Titles. Title II and III deal with "functional regulation" of bank securities and insurance activities, respectively; Title IV deals with unitary thrift holding companies, and Title V with consumer privacy issues; Title VI modifies the operations of the Federal Home Loan Bank System; and Title VII covers a number of miscellaneous issues, including ATM fees and Community Reinvestment Act matters, and clarifies the "source of strength doctrine" long associated with Board policy. On the "source of strength doctrine," see *Harvard Law Review* (1994). GLB also mandated several studies, including a study by the Board and the Treasury on the effectiveness of subordinated debentures in providing for market discipline, and by the Treasury on the effectiveness of the Community Reinvestment Act.

39. Title I, Section 101.

40. Title I, Section 102.

41. These activities are included in a new Section 4(k) added to Section 4 of the Bank Holding Company Act in Title I, Sec. 103 of GLB.

42. Section 4(k)(5).

43. All subsidiary banks must be "well capitalized" and "well managed," as defined by regulation. All insured depository institution subsidiaries must have a satisfactory or better Community Reinvestment Act (CRA) rating on its most recent examination. Failure of a subsidiary bank to have a satisfactory rating after becoming a FHC will result in a prohibition against any new activities, but not divestiture or limits on activities already undertaken.

44. Title I, Subtitle C. As in the case of FHCs, national banks must be "well-capitalized," "well-managed," and have a satisfactory CRA rating to operate financial subsidiaries. Explicitly prohibited are: insurance or annuity underwriting, with an exception for underwriting permitted prior to January 1, 1999; insurance company portfolio investments; real estate investment and development, with some exceptions authorized

by law; and merchant banking. But after five years, based on experience and other relevant facts, the Agencies may jointly adopt rules permitting financial subsidiaries to engage in merchant banking. Similar provisions hold for financial subsidiaries of state banks.

45. The Board must be notified no later than 30 days *after* beginning the activity or acquiring the firm.

46. The Board must consider whether a proposed "complementary" activity poses a substantial risk to the safety and soundness of insured depository institutions or the financial system. FHCs are required to notify the Board at least 60 days before engaging in any complementary activity.

47. In 1997, the Board rescinded its previous extension of Section 106 restrictions to holding companies themselves and their nonbanking affiliates. See Board of Governors (1997).

48. Title I, Section 114(a) and (b).

49. Title I, Section 103.

50. "Finder Proposal" and "Finder Rule."

51. "Finder Proposal," 6.

52. Ibid., 4–6.

53. Ibid., 5; and "Finder Rule," 10.

54. "Finder Rule," 11.

55. "Brokerage Proposal." The American Bankers Association (ABA), Fremont National Bank & Trust Company, and two additional banking associations requested that these activities be made permissible.

56. In *Boatmen's Bancshares, Inc.*, 58 *Fed. Res. Bul.* 427, 428 (1972), the Board stated that "real estate brokerage is not an activity that the Board has determined to be so closely related to banking or managing or controlling banks as to be a proper incident thereto." In "Bank Holding Companies: Property Management Services," 58 *Fed. Res. Bul.* 652 (1972), the Board stated that "property management services [are not] a permissible activity for bank holding companies under Section 4(c)(8)."

57. "Brokerage Proposal," 5. The Agencies' position is based on a statement in the Conference Report that "permitting banks to affiliate with firms engaged in financial activities represents a significant expansion from the current requirement that bank affiliates may only be engaged in activities that are closely related to banking." U.S. House, 1999, *Conference Report*, 153.

58. "Brokerage Proposal," 16.

59. Ibid., 8–11.

60. Ibid., 11.

61. Ibid., 12.

62. Ibid.

63. Ibid., 14.

64. Ibid.

65. Ibid., 14, 15.

66. Ibid., 15.

67. Ibid., 15.

68. Ibid., 13, 14; and for management services, 19.

69. "Brokerage Proposal," 12, 13. Also cited are provisions of the Real Estate Settlement Procedures Act aimed at protecting customers.

70. "Brokerage Proposal,"13 n.28.

71. 516 F.2d 1229 at 1236.
72. "Brokerage Proposal," 14, 15.
73. Moreover, some financial assets may be "purchased" for financial benefit, but not, in the conventional sense, as investments (e.g., liquid assets held for precautionary and/or transactions purposes); and some financial transactions are not, in the conventional sense, entered into for "investment purposes" (e.g., cashing checks).
74. "Brokerage Proposal," 15.
75. In 1987, the Board seriously considered authorizing bank holding companies to engage in real estate investment. See "Brokerage Proposal," 6, 7 n.8.
76. Meyer (2001, 12).
77. Ibid., 3.
78. Ibid., 11, 12.

REFERENCES

Benston, George J. 1990. *The Separation of Commercial and Investment Banking*. New York: Oxford University Press.

Board of Governors of the Federal Reserve System. 1943. *Annual Report*. Washington, D.C.

Board of Governors of the Federal Reserve System. 1972. "One Bank Holding Companies before the 1970 Amendments." *Federal Reserve Bulletin*, 58: 999–1008.

Board of Governors of the Federal Reserve System. February 20, 1997. "Press Release on Revisions to Regulation Y."

Board of Governors of the Federal Reserve System. July 31, 2000. "Proposed Rule" (Finder Authority), 12 CFR Part 225, Reg. Y; Docket No. R-1078. (Under "Press Release," July 31.) (Cited as "Finder Proposal.")

Board of Governors of the Federal Reserve System. December 13, 2000. "Proposed Rules with Request for Public Comment" (Complementary Activities, etc.), Reg. Y; Docket No. R-1092. (Under Press Release, December 13, 2000.)

Board of Governors of the Federal Reserve System. December 19, 2000. "Final Rule" (Finder Authority), 12 CFR Part 225, Reg. Y; Docket No. R-1078. (Under "Press Release," December 19, 2000.) (Cited as "Finder Rule.")

Board of Governors of the Federal Reserve System and Department of the Treasury. March 17, 2000. "Interim Rule on Merchant Banking Activities." Federal Reserve System 12 CFR Part 225, Reg. Y; Docket No. R-1065; Department of the Treasury, 12 CFR 1500. (Under Joint Press Release, "Federal Reserve and Treasury Announce Rules on Merchant Banking Activities," March 17, 2000.)

Board of Governors of the Federal Reserve System and Department of the Treasury. December 22, 2000. "Proposed Rule with Request for Public Comments" (Real Estate Brokerage and Real Estate Management Services), 12 CFR 225, Reg. Y; Docket No. R-1091 and 12 CFR 1501; RIN 1505-AA84. (Under "Press Release," December 27, 2000.) (Cited as "Brokerage Proposal.")

Board of Governors of the Federal Reserve System and Department of the Treasury. February 15, 2001. "Final Rule on Merchant Banking Activities." Federal Reserve System, 12 CFR Part 225; Docket No. R-1065; Department of the Treasury, 12 CFR Part 1500; RIN 1505-AA78. (Under Joint Press Release "Federal Reserve and Treasury Department Announce Final Rule on Merchant Banking Activities," January 10, 2001.)

Dewey, D. R. 1910. *State Banking before the Civil War*. Washington, D.C.: National Monetary Commission.

Federal Deposit Insurance Corporation. 1987. *Mandate for Change*. Washington D.C., October.

Fischer, Gerald C. 1961. *Bank Holding Companies*. New York: Columbia University Press.

Harvard Law Review. 1920. "Powers of National Banks to Acquire Various Kinds of Property." 33, No. 5, 718–721.

Harvard Law Review. 1994. "The Expanding Obligations of Financial Holding Companies." 107, 507.

Heller, Pauline B. 1976. *Handbook of Federal Bank Holding Company Law*. New York: Law Journal Press.

Leach, James A. 2000. "Excerpts of Remarks before ABA Leadership Council." Pentagon City Ritz-Carlton Hotel, March 28.

Meyer, Lawrence. 2001. "Implementing the Gramm-Leach-Bliley Act: One Year Later." Remarks before the American Law Institute and American Bar Association, Washington, D.C., February 15.

Office of the Comptroller of the Currency. 1915. *Annual Report*, Vol. I. Washington, D.C.

Peach, W. Nelson. 1941. *The Security Affiliates of National Banks*. Baltimore, Md.: Johns Hopkins University Press.

Redlich, Fritz. 1968. *The Molding of American Banking*. Vols. I and II. New York: Johnson Reprint Corp.

Sarbanes, P. et al. April 28, 1999. "Additional Views." In U.S. Senate. *Financial Services Modernization Act of 1999*. Report of the Committee on Banking, Housing and Urban Affairs, S.R. No. 106–44, Washington, D.C., 54–76.

Shull, Bernard. January 1994. "Banking and Commerce in the United States." *Journal of Banking and Finance*, 18, 255–270.

Shull, Bernard. 2000. "Financial Modernization in the United States: Background and Implications." *Discussion Paper Series*, United Nations Conference on Trade and Development.

Shull, Bernard, and Lawrence J. White. May 1998. "The Right Corporate Stucture for Expanded Bank Activities." *The Banking Law Journal*, 115, No. 5, 455–458.

Transamerica Corporation. April 1952. "Findings as to the Facts, Conclusions and Order." *Federal Reserve Bulletin*, 38, 368.

U.S. House. 1913. Hearings, *Concentration of Control of Money and Credit*. Before a Subcommittee of the Committee on Banking and Currency. Parts 19, 20. Washington, D.C.

U.S. House. February 18, 1913. *Report of the Committee to Investigate the Concentration of Control of Money and Credit*. H.R. No. 1593, 52d Cong., 3d Sess. Washington, D.C.

U.S. House. July 1969. Report, *Bank Holding Companies*. Committee on Banking & Currency, H.R. No. 91–387. Washington, D.C.

U.S. House. 1970. Conference Report, *Bank Holding Company Act Amendments*, To Accompany H.R. 6778. H.R. No. 1747, 91st Cong., 2d Sess., Washington, D.C.

U.S. House. 1970. Hearings, "One Bank Holding Company Legislation of 1970." Before the Committee on Banking and Currency. 91st Cong., 2d Sess., Washington, D.C., pp. 238 ff.

U.S. House. November 2, 1999. *Conference Report on Gramm-Leach-Bliley Act* to Accompany S. 900, H.R. 106–434. 106th Cong., 1st Sess., Washington, D.C.

U.S. Senate. May 1970. Hearings, *One-Bank Holding Company Legislation of 1970*, Before the Committee on Banking and Currency. U.S. Senate, 91st Cong., 2d Sess., Parts 1, 2. Washington, D.C.

U.S. Senate. August 1970. Report, *Bank Holding Company Act Amendments of 1970.* Committee on Banking & Currency, S.R. No. 91–1084, 91st Cong., 2d Sess., Washington, D.C.

U.S. Senate. April 28, 1999. Report, *Financial Services Modernization Act of 1999.* Committee on Banking, Housing and Urban Affairs, S.R. No. 106–44, Washington, D.C.

Willis, H. Parker. 1923. *The Federal Reserve System.* New York: Ronald Press.

Chapter 6

Restructuring the Federal Safety Net after Gramm-Leach-Bliley

Arthur E. Wilmarth, Jr.

INTRODUCTION

The structure of the U.S. financial services industry has been transformed during the past two decades. Between 1980 and 1999, the combined forces of new technologies, deregulation, and increased competition produced a steady erosion of the legal and market barriers that separated banks from securities firms and insurance companies. For example, sophisticated computer systems and new financial instruments (e.g., commercial paper, junk bonds, and asset-backed securities) made it feasible to "securitize" many types of business and consumer debt. As a result, many business firms and consumers who previously relied on bank loans gained access to credit from nonbank sources, including finance companies, mortgage companies, and the markets for publicly traded and privately placed debt. At the same time, securities brokers, credit card banks, and mutual fund companies offered low-cost cash management and investment management services to the general public. In response to these innovations, consumers shifted a rapidly growing share of their investment funds from traditional bank deposits and life insurance policies into mutual funds, variable annuities, and other investment vehicles linked to the capital markets.

In combination, these developments caused a dramatic increase in competition and a narrowing of profit margins in the markets traditionally served by banks, securities firms, and life insurance companies. Large banks, securities broker-dealers, and life insurers responded to these trends by pursuing a twofold consolidation strategy. First, to defend existing markets, leading institutions in each sector tried to enhance their pricing power by acquiring traditional competitors. Second, to capture new sources of revenue, market leaders diversified their activities by acquiring firms in other sectors.[1]

These consolidation efforts triggered a wave of mergers within and across the banking, securities and insurance sectors. Consolidation in the banking industry was also spurred by (1) new state and federal laws that removed longstanding barriers to geographic expansion, and (2) more lenient antitrust policies adopted by federal bank regulators and the Justice Department. Between 1980 and 1999, the number of banking organizations fell by nearly half, and the market share held by the 10 largest banks more than doubled.[2] Three huge bank mergers were announced in 1998, and four additional mergers of comparable magnitude were agreed to during 1999–2001.[3] As a result of this rapid consolidation, the U.S. banking industry is developing a two-tiered structure. Within the next decade, it seems likely that a small group of 10 to 15 very large banks will control most of the industry's assets, and the remaining competitors will primarily be community-based institutions or specialized niche providers. Similar patterns of consolidation have occurred within the securities and insurance sectors.

Cross-industry acquisitions also became important during the 1990s, due to favorable rulings issued by federal bank regulators and the courts. By 1999, all of the 25 largest U.S. bank holding companies owned securities broker-dealers, and banks had made significant inroads into the insurance business. At the same time, several large securities firms and insurance companies established conglomerates that competed with each other and with banks across a wide range of financial businesses. In 1998, the Federal Reserve Board (FRB) gave a major impetus to cross-industry consolidation by approving the merger between Citicorp and Travelers. This merger created a huge diversified holding company called "Citigroup," which currently ranks as the world's largest financial services organization.[4] Proponents of financial modernization hailed Citigroup as the first modern American "universal bank" because it was the first U.S. banking organization since 1933 that could offer comprehensive banking, securities, and insurance services to its customers.[5]

The Gramm-Leach-Bliley Act of 1999 (GLB Act) effectively ratified the Citigroup merger and removed all remaining legal barriers to affiliations among banks, securities firms, and life insurers.[6] The GLB Act thus encouraged further cross-industry consolidation. During 2000 alone, two large foreign banks acquired major U.S. securities firms, another leading foreign bank purchased a large U.S. insurance company, and Charles Schwab and MetLife acquired banks.[7]

Advocates of universal banking have predicted that the new financial conglomerates will generate the following significant benefits: (1) higher efficiency and profitability, as a result of favorable economies of scale and scope, (2) increased safety and soundness, due to a broader diversification of business lines, and (3) greater convenience and cost savings for customers, based on the concept of "one-stop shopping."[8] Part I of this chapter discusses several reasons for doubting whether these optimistic forecasts will be achieved. In particular, Part I argues that financial conglomeration has intensified the problem of systemic risk in the financial markets. Over the past two decades, major banks, securities firms, and life insurers have significantly expanded their involvement in high-risk activities that are closely tied to the capital markets, thereby increasing their vulnerability to market fluctuations. In addition, the growing concentration of credit and market risk within a small group of huge financial institutions has increased the likelihood that the failure of a leading institution will have serious "spillover" effects. As a result, financial conglomeration has created greater pressures on regulators to approve "too big to fail" (TBTF) bailouts for major banks and their nonbank affiliates.

As discussed in Part II, domestic and foreign regulators have responded to the growing risks of financial holding companies by trying to improve the effectiveness of capital requirements and by seeking to enhance supervisory and market discipline over large financial conglomerates. However, Part II contends that these regulatory initiatives will not solve the underlying problems of supervisory forbearance and moral hazard, which are the inevitable corollaries of the current TBTF policy.

Part III proposes a new plan for bank regulation and deposit insurance that is designed to counteract the perverse effects of the TBTF doctrine. Under this plan, financial conglomerates would be allowed to accept FDIC-insured deposits only within narrow banks, and those banks would be barred from making transfers of funds or credit to affiliates (except for lawful dividends out of profits). The FDIC would be strictly prohibited from paying any uninsured claims when banks fail, and the deposit insurance funds would be completely insulated from the cost of TBTF bailouts. Drawing on its emergency powers as "lender of last resort" (LOLR), the FRB would bear primary responsibility for dealing with financial failures involving systemic risk. The FRB would recover the cost of TBTF rescues from financial conglomerates, which are, after all, the principal beneficiaries of the TBTF doctrine. Additional reforms would enhance both regulatory and market-based controls over the risk-taking incentives of universal banks.

PART I: FINANCIAL CONGLOMERATES ARE UNLIKELY TO ACHIEVE THEIR EXPECTED BENEFITS AND WILL INCREASE SYSTEMIC RISK

Empirical studies over the past two decades have generally failed to verify the existence of global economies of scale or scope in large diversified banks, full-service securities firms, or multiple-line insurance companies. Most researchers have found that the biggest and most diversified firms in each sector are less profitable and less efficient than their smaller or more specialized competitors.

Studies questioning the existence of economies of "super-scale" are supported by the poor track record of large U.S. bank mergers during the 1980s and 1990s. Two-thirds of those mergers failed to produce the expected synergies and instead resulted in profit shortfalls and long-term losses in shareholder wealth. Several of the biggest mergers during 1996–1998 proved to be costly disappointments or outright failures (e.g., Bank One's mergers with First Chicago NBD and First USA, First Union's acquisitions of CoreStates and Money Store, NationsBank's mergers with Barnett Banks and Bank of America, and Wells Fargo's hostile acquisition of First Interstate).[9] In addition, most big, consolidated banks did not deliver on their promises to provide better service and lower prices to customers.[10]

Large financial conglomerates similarly achieved little success during the past two decades. The "financial supermarkets" created during the 1980s by American Express, GE, Kemper, Prudential, and Sears were all dismantled after generating poor returns. Since 1990, AXA, Bankers Trust, Barclays, ING, NatWest, and Security Pacific have either agreed to forced acquisitions or abandoned the capital markets business after their expansion plans produced negative results. Bank of America's acquisition of Montgomery Securities was an expensive failure, while Conseco absorbed crippling losses from its purchase of Green Tree. The most spectacular disaster, resulting in a $20 billion bailout by the French government, occurred at Credit Lyonnais, which made huge, ill-advised investments in a wide range of European and overseas enterprises.

Five big international banks—J. P. Morgan Chase, Citigroup, Credit Suisse, Deutsche Bank, and UBS—continue to pursue a universal banking strategy. However, all five banks have incurred significant losses from capital markets activities at various times in recent years, and even Citigroup cannot yet be declared a long-term success. During the first nine months of 2001, a general slump in the world's equity markets caused sharp declines in earnings from investment banking operations at all five banks and the "big three" securities firms (Goldman Sachs, Merrill Lynch, and Morgan Stanley). In September, the terrorist attack on the World Trade Center inflicted substantial losses on insurance companies (including Citigroup) and further depressed investment banking revenues. Thus, the diversification strategies pursued by universal banks have exposed them to material risks during disruptions in the financial markets.[11]

The most troubling aspect of financial consolidation is its effect on "systemic risk" (i.e., the risk that the failure of a major financial institution will severely disrupt the financial system and have adverse "spillover" effects on the general economy). Over the past three decades, large U.S. banks have consistently adopted more aggressive strategies as they have grown in size and complexity. Throughout this period, in comparison with smaller banks, big U.S. banks have operated with greater leverage, less liquidity, and a more risky asset—liability mix. The correlation between growth and risk is *not* a uniquely American phenomenon. A recent study concluded that the largest banks in 21 developed nations (including the United States) engaged in more risky activities and faced a greater probability of insolvency during 1988–1998.[12]

The "too big to fail" (TBTF) doctrine—that is, the policy of protecting uninsured depositors and other payments system creditors at large failing banks—provides the most likely explanation for the inclination of big banks to assume greater risks. Studies have shown that the TBTF policy confers a significant implicit subsidy on big U.S. banks because (1) it allows them to pay below-average rates to depositors and other creditors, and (2) it shields them from effective market discipline, despite their below-average capitalization and above-average risks.[13] A recent study found a similar link between TBTF status and perverse risk incentives among large European banks.[14]

Many observers believe that U.S. bank consolidation has substantially increased the risk that a major bank failure could bankrupt the FDIC's deposit insurance fund.[15] Similarly, a recent "Group of Ten" report acknowledged that the growth of large complex banking organizations (LCBOs) has probably aggravated systemic risk. As the report pointed out, the consolidation of financial assets within LCBOs has (1) increased the complexity of major financial institutions, making it harder for regulators and market participants to understand the risks inherent in LCBOs, (2) produced a higher concentration and correlation of credit and market risks among the largest financial institutions, due to their growing domination of the markets for interbank loans, over-the-counter (OTC) derivatives and investment banking services, and (3) created close linkages between banking and nonbanking subsidiaries of financial holding companies, thereby complicating the problem of resolving the failure of a large bank in isolation from its nonbank affiliates.[16]

Regulators and investors recognize that LCBOs are highly integrated enterprises, despite the corporate veils between their various subsidiaries. Most financial holding companies are centrally managed and closely coordinate the activities of their nonbank subsidiaries with operations of their lead banks (e.g., by combining securities underwriting with syndicated lending for the same corporate clients). LCBOs have also increased their reputational stake in nonbank affiliates by promoting unitary "brand names" covering the entire holding company. Financial conglomeration has therefore increased the pressure on bank regulators to protect nonbank affiliates of LCBOs.[17] The financial markets fully expect that regulators will bring entire financial holding companies within the federal "safety net" for banks.[18]

For example, a senior official at Moody's Investors Services recently declared that federal regulators *must* support these conglomerates during "times of extreme financial stress." In his view, the TBTF status of big financial holding companies is undeniable—it is "like the elephant at the picnic—everyone is aware of it, but no one wants to mention it."[19] Other analysts agree that regulators would probably rescue a failing nonbank affiliate of an LCBO during a severe economic disruption because (1) the affiliate's default could trigger a contagious "run" by all of the holding company's investors and creditors, and (2) the holding company's collapse could set off a systemic "flight to safety" in the financial markets.[20] As discussed in Part II, this de facto extension of the safety net greatly reduces the chances that regulators or investors will impose meaningful limits on risk-taking by LCBOs.

By authorizing unlimited mergers between banks and securities firms, the

GLB Act has also effectively removed the "shock absorbers" that the U.S. financial system contained prior to 1999. The FRB mobilized leading U.S. banks to counteract serious disruptions in the capital markets during the Penn Central commercial paper crisis of 1970, the Hunt Brothers silver crisis of 1980, the stock market crash of 1987, and the Russian debt crisis of 1998. In each case, major banks provided emergency credit that enabled large nonbank firms to avoid bankruptcy or severe distress. Banks were able to serve as standby sources of liquidity and credit on each occasion because their capital markets activities represented a relatively small portion of their overall operations and did not expose them to devastating losses. Conversely, the securities industry provided an alternative financing channel for U.S. business firms during the recession and banking crisis of 1990–1992, because securities firms were not crippled by the lending problems that plagued major banks at that time. Thus, the legal barriers separating banks and securities firms prior to 1999 reduced systemic risk in the U.S. economy by (1) insulating each sector to a substantial degree from the other's problems, and (2) allowing each sector to act as an alternative source of financing while the other recovered from serious financial losses.[21]

As an instructive comparison, consider the record of Japan during the 1990s. In 1990, the Japanese banking system had massive exposures to *both* the real estate market *and* the stock market. Japanese banks had made huge amounts of loans secured by real estate and securities, and they also held extensive portfolios of corporate stocks due to cross-shareholding relationships within their keiretsu corporate groups. Beginning in 1990, the Japanese real estate and stock markets both collapsed, with prices in each sector falling by two-thirds or more. Two large Japanese banks failed, and several other leading banks were driven to the brink of insolvency. Two major securities firms and three large insurance companies also failed. Notwithstanding a decade of hugely expensive government spending programs, Japan has not revived its economy or restored its financial system. Because Japanese banks remain hobbled by nonperforming loans and depreciated stock portfolios, they cannot provide the credit needed by business firms.[22]

Many observers have blamed Japan's failure to resolve its problems on the unwillingness of its political and business leaders to undertake a fundamental restructuring of Japan's financial system and general economy.[23] Resistance to change undoubtedly accounts for a significant portion of Japan's difficulties. However, the role of Japanese banks as dominant providers of business finance, and their exposure to *both* credit risk in the real estate market *and* investment risk in the securities market, help to explain the severity and protracted nature of the Japanese crisis. Given the banks' dual risk exposures, the collapse of Japan's real estate and stock markets crippled the banks and left no substantial alternative source of financing for Japanese businesses. The Japanese experience provides a clear warning signal about the potential for systemic risk that may already exist within U.S. and European LCBOs.[24]

PART II: CURRENT REGULATORY EFFORTS ARE INADEQUATE TO CONTROL THE RISK-TAKING INCENTIVES OF FINANCIAL CONGLOMERATES

Pursuant to congressional mandates in the GLB Act, federal regulators are implementing a four-part strategy to control the risks of LCBOs. First, financial holding companies must conduct securities, insurance, and merchant banking activities in separate nonbank subsidiaries that are insulated by regulatory "firewalls" from their affiliated banks.[25] Second, all banks in a financial holding company must be "well capitalized," and regulators must apply "prompt corrective action" (PCA) to any bank that fails to meet prescribed capital standards.[26] Third, all banks in a financial holding company must be "well managed," and regulators have instituted new supervisory procedures for evaluating the effectiveness of each LCBO's management.[27] Fourth, regulators are exploring ways to encourage greater market discipline of LCBOs.[28]

This regulatory philosophy is consistent with a new capital adequacy proposal issued in January 2001 by the Basel Committee on Banking Supervision. The Basel Committee's 2001 proposal recommends a new regulatory framework based on "three pillars"—capital adequacy, supervisory review, and market discipline.[29] The Basel Committee's proposal includes two new approaches that have been adopted by U.S. bank regulators: (1) applying capital requirements on a consolidated basis to the entire financial holding company (including nonbank subsidiaries), and (2) establishing capital requirements for each LCBO in accordance with internal risk ratings developed by the LCBO's managers and reviewed by bank regulators.[30]

Unfortunately, all four elements of this supervisory program have exhibited serious shortcomings in the past. This approach is therefore unlikely to prevent LCBOs from taking excessive risks at the expense of the federal safety net.

The Ineffectiveness of Corporate Separation as a Risk Control Device

Supervisory requirements based on the concept of corporate separation are in fundamental conflict with the actual behavior of financial holding companies. As noted above, most LCBOs operate as highly integrated enterprises, based on centralized management policies that disregard structural divisions between corporate subsidiaries. On many occasions, financial holding companies have rescued nonbank affiliates or their customers in order to protect the reputation of the parent holding company and its regulated financial institutions. In the most serious cases, holding company managers have deliberately breached regulatory firewalls by exceeding the legal limits on financial support that banks or other regulated financial institutions may provide to troubled affiliates.[31]

The GLB Act relies on Sections 23A and 23B of the Federal Reserve Act to prevent abusive transactions between banks and their nonbank affiliates within the new financial holding company structure.[32] However, regulators and analysts have acknowledged that (1) the affiliate transaction rules under Sections 23A and 23B are complicated and difficult to enforce, and (2) managerial evasions of those provisions are often subtle and hard to detect. As a result, when a financial holding company or its subsidiaries are under severe financial stress, regulators may fail to discover and prevent a transfer of bank funds or bank credit that violates regulatory limits.[33] Moreover, to avert a systemic financial crisis, regulators may decide to waive affiliate transaction rules so that banks can help their troubled affiliates. In September 2001, the FRB reportedly suspended Section 23A and urged banks to transfer funds to their securities affiliates to head off a threatened liquidity crunch following the terrorist attack on the World Trade Center.[34]

Federal bank regulators currently appear to give little weight to the theory of corporate separation as an effective risk control device. Regulators are now stressing the importance of supervising financial holding companies in a *consolidated* manner that cuts across corporate divisions among banks' subsidiaries and their nonbank affiliates.[35] Given the banking agencies' current adherence to the concept of consolidated supervision, did regulators and lobbyists for the financial services industry actually believe in the virtues of corporate separation during the 1990s? Or did they simply use the "firewall" argument to help persuade Congress to enact the GLB Act?[36]

Shortcomings in Capital Regulation

The Basel Committee issued an international risk-based capital accord in 1988 (the 1988 Accord). The 1988 Accord establishes capital requirements for banks by assigning loans and off-balance-sheet commitments to four risk-weighted categories based on perceived credit risk. Many commentators have criticized the four "risk buckets" of the 1988 Accord because they are too broad and imprecise to distinguish among similar types of assets with different degrees of credit risk. For example, a loan to a "blue chip" corporation with a triple-A credit rating carries the same 100 percent risk weight under the 1988 Accord as a loan to a speculative company with a below-investment grade rating.[37] The 1988 Accord's unsophisticated treatment of credit risk has enabled LCBOs to engage in "capital arbitrage" by (1) using complex derivatives, whose embedded risks are difficult to value, as substitutes for conventional financing arrangements, and (2) structuring securitizations that transfer low-risk assets out of the bank while retaining more risky assets (including residual interests in securitizations).[38]

The 1988 Basel Accord did not take account of the market risk of derivatives, securities, and other trading assets held by banks. In response to rapid increases in trading activity at large banks during the 1990s, the Basel Committee promulgated supplemental capital rules for market risk in early 1996. Those rules allow qualifying banks to determine their capital requirements for market risk based on internal models that measure their "value at risk" (VaR). The Basel Committee's 2001 proposal would extend this policy of reliance on internal risk management by allowing qualifying banks to use internal risk ratings in calculating their capital requirements for credit risk and operational risk.[39]

Past banking crises have shown that capital is a lagging indicator of bank problems because declines in capital are frequently not recognized or reported until banks have already become seriously troubled. One reason for this time lag is that many assets held by banks (e.g., commercial loans, OTC derivatives, and residual interests in securitizations) are not traded on any organized market and are therefore very difficult for regulators and outside investors to evaluate. Accordingly, outsiders frequently do not identify problems of asset depreciation until a significant reduction in capital has already occurred. Another reason is that managers of a troubled bank often postpone any writedowns of assets and capital, hoping that the bank's situation will improve before its next supervisory examination or required public disclosure to investors.[40]

PCA seeks to strengthen the effectiveness of capital regulation by forcing regulators to impose progressively more stringent enforcement measures if a bank falls below the "adequately capitalized" standard or below two lower capital thresholds.[41] However, federal regulators weakened the effectiveness of PCA by choosing a lenient capital adequacy test. Virtually all banks met this standard when the PCA rules took effect in 1992, even though the banking industry was just emerging from a major crisis.[42] Studies have shown that PCA's "adequately capitalized" test would *not* have identified most troubled banks during the 1980s, and that the standard was also too low to capture most problem banks during the mid-1990s.[43]

The regulators' selection of a lenient capital threshold for PCA creates serious doubts about whether they would return to a policy of supervisory forbearance if they were confronted with a systemic crisis involving the potential failure of several large banks. The recent failure of Superior Bank raises additional questions about the effectiveness of PCA because regulators failed to recognize or respond to the severity of the bank's problems until its capital was already deeply impaired by losses resulting from risky subprime lending and securitization activities.[44] Two recent studies provide additional evidence that regulatory capital requirements *failed* to eliminate high-risk bank strategies during the early 1990s, especially among larger banks.[45]

The Basel Committee and federal regulators believe that capital supervision for LCBOs can be improved by shifting from uniform rules to an individualized approach based on internal risk management policies developed by each LCBO.[46] However, this effort to base capital requirements on LCBOs' internal risk models is a highly problematic move. Automated bank credit scoring models failed to anticipate the surge in consumer defaults on credit card loans that occurred during 1996–1997. Similarly, VaR models developed by J. P. Morgan and other leading banks did not predict the severe trading losses that occurred during the global financial market disruption triggered by Russia's debt default in 1998.[47] Studies have shown that the most widely used bank models for estimating market risk and credit risk are unreliable because (1) they are based on faulty assumptions and insufficient data, and (2) they permit banks to pursue strategies that may prove to be disastrous, because they tolerate a low-percentage risk of catastrophic losses.[48]

A further problem is that regulators may not possess sufficient expertise to understand and critique the internal risk management systems developed by LCBOs. Regulators generally cannot compete with major financial institutions in hiring highly paid financial "rocket scientists" to design and analyze complex derivatives and other sophisticated risk management tools. Accordingly, regulators may not be able to verify, with a high degree of confidence, the internal risk models and ratings developed by LCBOs.[49]

Bank regulators and bankers also have sharply conflicting motivations in establishing capital standards. Regulators want conservative capital rules that discourage imprudent risk-taking and protect the federal safety net, even at the expense of constraining bank profits. In contrast, bankers want liberal capital rules that permit higher leverage and a greater ability to exploit the federal safety net subsidy because those circumstances create the potential for higher shareholder returns. Bankers therefore have strong incentives to manipulate their internal risk rating systems to reduce their effective capital requirements.[50] Unfortunately, the Basel Committee's 2001 proposal does not suggest any reliable mechanism for deterring LCBOs from using aggressive internal risk models to engage in a new form of capital arbitrage.

Current Limitations on Supervisory and Market Discipline

Bank supervision and market discipline share a common goal of discouraging banks from taking excessive risks. Recent studies have shown that regulators and market participants play complementary roles in restraining risk-taking by banks. It appears that differing oversight methods used by regulators and market observers enable each group to discover proprietary information about banks that is not readily available to the other group.[51]

Nevertheless, both bank regulators and the securities markets have often failed to identify problems at major financial institutions until those institutions were already seriously or fatally injured. For example, federal regulators, credit rating agencies, and investors did not recognize severe weaknesses at many large banks during the 1980s (including Continental Illinois and Bank of New England) until those banks were dangerously close to failure.[52] Federal regulators also failed in 1998 to perceive the grave threat that Long-Term Capital Management (LTCM) posed to leading banks and securities firms, as well as the financial markets generally, until the hedge fund revealed its perilous condition to the Federal Reserve Bank of New York. In the international arena, the IMF, bank regulators, credit rating agencies, and investors all failed to anticipate the onset, severity, and contagious effects of the Mexican peso crisis of 1994–1995 and the Asian and Russian crises of 1997–1998.[53]

Two major factors help to explain these repeated failures in supervisory and market discipline of LCBOs. First, major banks have become more complex and more difficult to evaluate by regulators and the financial markets over the past three decades. Second, market discipline is frequently *ineffective* in predicting the onset of financial crises, and it can be *indiscriminate* in punishing firms *after* a financial crisis begins. As a consequence, regulators have consistently followed market stabilization policies that blunt the impact of market discipline, thereby encouraging investors to reduce their scrutiny of large financial firms.

The Growing Complexity and Opacity of Financial Conglomerates

Major banks have increased their opacity to regulators and the securities markets by expanding their dealing and trading activities involving securities and OTC derivatives. Like bank loans, OTC derivatives are privately negotiated, customized financial instruments whose terms and potential financial impact are largely unknown to outsiders. OTC derivatives and complex, option-based securities enable banks (1) to place highly leveraged bets on the direction of interest rates, currency rates, and market prices for commodities, bonds, and stocks, and (2) to make rapid changes in their risk exposures. As a consequence, it is very hard for regulators and market participants to evaluate the financial condition of major banks in a timely manner. In addition, financial conglomerates are creating new correlations among interest rate risk, credit risk, and market risk as they combine traditional lending operations with investment banking and insurance activities. Neither regulators nor market participants are well positioned to assess the potential dangers of these new risk correlations.[54]

Two recent studies demonstrate the relative opacity of major banks to the financial markets. The first study found that investors did not anticipate either dividend cuts or regulatory enforcement actions at 17 big "money center" banks during 1975–1992. Public disclosures of these events caused sharp, immediate declines in the stock prices of the subject banks and significantly negative contagious effects on the stock prices of other money center and regional banks.[55]

The second study determined that, during 1983–1993, Moody's and Standard & Poor's had greater disagreements in their bond ratings for banks and insurance companies than for any other type of firm. Moreover, the rating agencies' disagreements over bond ratings for banks *increased* after 1986, despite the efforts of Congress and bank regulators to restrict the scope of the TBTF policy. Donald Morgan, the study's author, concluded that the largest banks became *less* transparent to credit rating agencies after 1986, due to the banks' increased focus on trading in securities, OTC derivatives, and other financial instruments. The rating agencies apparently found it difficult to assess the risks inherent in bank trading positions that changed rapidly and without timely notice to market participants.[56]

Limitations on the Effectiveness of Market Discipline as a Risk Control Device for Universal Banks

Financial markets often seem to be *ineffective* in predicting the onset of economic crises and *indiscriminate* in punishing risky firms *after* crises occur. Recent studies have shown that market discipline fluctuates in its intensity, with more relaxed monitoring in good times and more stringent oversight during periods of financial stress. The varying intensity of market discipline is exemplified by the tendency of investors to act with excessive optimism during an expansionary "bubble" and to panic when the "bubble" bursts. For example, during the mid-1990s, financial institutions and other investors from developed nations disregarded potential warning signs and made huge investments in Latin America, Asia, and Russia. However, when subsequent events revealed the full risks of those investments, investors engaged in frenzied "flights to safety" that had a devastating impact on developing economies. The crises of the 1990s, like earlier "boom-and-bust cycles" in domestic and foreign economies since 1970, show how difficult it is for market participants and regulators to avoid an excessive expansion of credit and speculative activities during the "bubble" phase of an economic boom, and to prevent a liquidity crisis in the financial markets and a sharp contraction in credit after the "bubble" bursts.[57]

Thus, market discipline does *not* exert a consistent restraining force on managerial risk-taking. Investors are vulnerable to periodic cycles of euphoria and panic, due in part to their uncertainty about the direction of the economy and the soundness of financial intermediaries.[58] Cycles of investor sentiment are evident in the banking industry as well as the general economy. Studies of recent banking crises in the United States and Latin America have shown that investors and depositors (1) failed to restrain risk-taking by bank managers until a financial crisis revealed that some banks had already suffered severe harm, (2) typically reacted to a crisis in the short term by punishing *all* banks exposed to the crisis, with only a limited degree of discrimination among banks with differing risk exposures, and (3) applied a more effective and discriminating form of discipline only *after* the crisis had passed.[59] Benton Gup has summarized the historical record of market discipline as a risk control device as follows:

> [B]ank regulators hope that market discipline will aid them in their task of bank supervision. . . . The track record of market discipline . . . suggests that it usually occurs after a significant incident, and that it does little to prevent misbehavior. . . . If market discipline means survival of the fittest, it works. If market discipline means controlling behavior, it does not appear to be effective.[60]

Bank regulators recognize the potentially harsh effects of market discipline during financial crises.[61] For that reason, they have shown little enthusiasm for any "strong" form of market oversight, despite their recent expressions of support for better monitoring by investors.

For example, during the banking crisis of 1989–1991 regulators lamented many of the adverse effects of market discipline (e.g., bank failures, the difficulty of raising new capital, and the "credit crunch" resulting from the inability of capital-constrained banks to make new loans).[62] Regulators also did their best to weaken the restrictions on supervisory forbearance established by the PCA regime.[63] During the mid-1990s, regulators joined the banking industry in trying to block changes in accounting rules that required banks to adopt market-value accounting principles for assets held in trading accounts. These new accounting rules were designed to improve market discipline by making the financial operations of banks more transparent to investors. Nevertheless, regulators argued that the new rules would have a destabilizing effect by creating more volatility in the reported earnings of banks.[64]

The most recent evidence of regulatory opposition to strict market discipline can be seen in the decision by the FRB and the Treasury Department to *reject* a mandatory subordinated debt program for LCBOs. The agencies acknowledged that a mandatory subordinated debt policy would increase market discipline. However, they argued that a rule penalizing LCBOs if they could not issue qualifying debt would disrupt credit flows and increase systemic risk during economic crises.[65] A prominent analyst declared that the FRB-Treasury report had "dump[ed] buckets and buckets of cold water on the idea of using subordinated debt as a tool for market discipline."[66]

The opposition of federal regulators to any strong form of market discipline is consistent with their faithful adherence to the TBTF doctrine whenever they have determined that the failure of a large financial institution could destabilize the financial system. TBTF bank rescues appear to be part of a broader, unstated federal policy of maintaining stability within the financial markets. This implicit policy has grown out of the recognition that major banks increasingly depend on the health of the securities and derivatives markets, due to their leading role in those markets, and that investments tied to the capital markets (including OTC derivatives, mutual funds, annuities, and variable life insurance) account for a rapidly growing percentage of the financial assets and risk management tools of businesses and consumers. The regulators' rescues of TBTF banks (from Franklin National Bank in 1974 to Bank of New England in 1991) and the FRB's repeated interventions in the financial markets (from the Penn Central crisis of 1970 to the rescue of LTCM in 1998) provide strong evidence of the regulators' commitment to market stabilization as a key policy objective.[67]

In July 2001, FRB Chairman Alan Greenspan informed Congress that the FRB was aggressively cutting interest rates in response to a sharp downturn in the high-technology sector, which had weakened the general economy and produced a significant decline in equity market prices. In his remarks, Chairman Greenspan revealed the FRB's underlying policy goal of stabilizing the financial markets: "[O]ur only realistic response to a speculative bubble is to lean against the economic pressures that may accompany a rise in asset prices, bubble or not, and *address forcefully the consequences of a sharp deflation in asset prices should they occur.*"[68]

In response to the terrorist attack on the World Trade Center in September 2001, the FRB flooded the financial markets with liquidity by purchasing more than $150 billion in government securities. The FRB prevented a prolonged liquidity crunch in the markets, just as it had done during the 1987 stock market crash. The FRB also reportedly suspended Section 23A's limitations on affiliate transactions and urged major banks to transfer funds to their securities affiliates. Gerald Corrigan, who was president of the Federal Reserve Bank of New York during the 1987 crash, defended the FRB's conduct in September 2001 in the following terms: "This whole thing is a confidence game, and you better damn well think carefully of anything that can shake . . . public confidence in the financial markets, and in particular, the stock market."[69]

Few would question the FRB's wisdom in cutting interest rates to counteract a serious economic downturn or in providing emergency liquidity through open-market operations during a stock market crash. However, the FRB's key role in organizing the rescue of LTCM in 1998, and its waiver of affiliate transaction rules for LCBOs in 2001, strongly indicate that the FRB views the survival of major financial conglomerates as an indispensable element of its broader mission to preserve market stability. Investors therefore have every reason to be confident that the TBTF policy remains a centerpiece of U.S. financial regulation.

The TBTF policy is the great unresolved problem of bank supervision, because it undermines the effectiveness of both regulatory oversight and market discipline over LCBOs.[70] A recent article in the *American Banker* summed up the current situation in the following words:

> [A] lingering impression that the government will bail out any large institution that gets into trouble has encouraged the markets to give financial institutions less scrutiny than other businesses. "Until the market has a credible expectation that discipline is required," market discipline is "a long way off."[71]

PART III: A NEW REGULATORY REGIME IS NEEDED TO COUNTERACT THE RISK-TAKING INCENTIVES OF FINANCIAL CONGLOMERATES

Given the shortcomings of current approaches, a new regulatory program must be designed to counteract the risk-taking incentives of LCBOs. The following proposed program has three major elements: (1) protecting the deposit insurance system from the expense of TBTF bailouts, (2) requiring financial conglomerates to bear primary responsibility for the financial costs of such bailouts, and (3) adopting further reforms to improve supervisory oversight and market discipline.

Insulating the Deposit Insurance System from TBTF Bailouts

The most effective way to protect the deposit insurance system from the cost of TBTF rescues is to create a two-tiered structure of bank regulation and deposit insurance.[72] The first tier would consist of "traditional" banking organizations that limit their activities (including the activities of all holding company affiliates) to lines of business that meet the "closely related to banking" test in Section 4(c)(8) of the Bank Holding Company Act. For example, this first tier of traditional banks could take deposits, make loans, and offer fiduciary services. They could act as *agents* in selling securities, mutual funds, and insurance products underwritten by *nonaffiliated* firms. They could underwrite, purchase, and deal in "bank-eligible" securities that national banks are permitted to underwrite or deal in directly. They could use derivatives for bona fide hedging transactions that qualify for hedging treatment under FAS 133.[73] Most first-tier banks would probably be smaller, community-based banks because those banks do not have any comparative advantage—and therefore have not shown any substantial interest—in engaging *as principal* in insurance underwriting, securities underwriting, derivatives dealing, or other capital markets activities. These community banks are well positioned to continue their traditional business of attracting core deposits, providing relationship loans to consumers and firms, and offering wealth management services through their fiduciary operations.

In order to provide reasonable flexibility for this first tier of traditional banks, Congress should amend Section 4(c)(8) of the BHC Act by allowing the FRB to expand the list of approved "closely related" activities for holding company affiliates of traditional banks.[74] Traditional banks and their holding companies would continue to operate under their current supervisory arrangements, and all of the banks' deposits (up to the statutory limit) would be covered by deposit insurance.

In contrast, depository institutions and their affiliates would be placed in the second tier of "nontraditional" banking organizations if they engage in underwriting or trading in "bank-ineligible" securities; underwriting insurance (except for credit insurance); dealing or trading in derivatives (except for bona fide hedging transactions under FAS 133); or merchant banking. These second-tier, nontraditional banking organizations would include financial holding companies under the GLB Act; holding companies owning grandfathered "nonbank banks"; and grandfathered "unitary thrift" holding companies.[75] Second-tier holding companies would therefore encompass all of the largest banking organizations, which are heavily engaged in capital markets activities, together with other financial conglomerates that control FDIC-insured depository institutions.

Under this proposal, FDIC-insured depository institutions that are subsidiaries of second-tier holding companies must adopt a "narrow bank" structure. These narrow banks would hold all of their assets in the form of cash and highly marketable debt obligations, such as qualifying government securities, highly rated commercial paper, and other debt instruments eligible for investment by money market mutual funds (MMMFs) under rules of the Securities and Exchange Commission. Narrow banks could not accept any *uninsured* deposits. Narrow banks would present a very small risk to the FDIC's deposit insurance funds because (1) each narrow bank's assets would be "marked to market" on a daily basis, and the FDIC could therefore quickly determine whether a narrow bank was threatened with insolvency, and (2) the FDIC could quickly convert a narrow bank's assets into cash if the FDIC decided to liquidate the bank to pay off the claims of its insured depositors.[76]

The foregoing asset restrictions would effectively protect the FDIC from loss if a narrow bank failed. In addition, three rules would prevent nontraditional holding companies and their *nonbanking* subsidiaries from receiving any subsidy from the narrow bank's deposit insurance. First, the narrow bank could not make (or receive) any transfer of funds or credit to (or from) its affiliates, *except* for the bank's payment of dividends out of profits to its parent holding company; and the bank's receipt of capital infusions from its parent holding company. Second, if a narrow bank failed, the FDIC would be strictly prohibited from making payments to anyone who was not an *insured* depositor of the bank. Third, the "systemic risk" exception currently included in the Federal Deposit Insurance Act (FDI Act) would be abolished. As a result, the FDIC would be required to follow the least costly resolution procedure for *all* failed banks, and the FDIC could no longer rely on the TBTF policy as a justification for protecting *uninsured* creditors of a failed bank or its nonbank affiliates.[77] As discussed below, the FRB would undertake primary responsibility for TBTF problems under its LOLR powers.

Insulating the FDIC's deposit insurance funds from the possibility of TBTF bailouts would have several major benefits. It would make clear to the financial markets that the FDIC's deposit insurance funds could *only* be used to protect *insured* depositors of failed banks. *Uninsured* creditors of a financial holding company—regardless of its size—would no longer have any reasonable expectation of being protected by the FDIC if the holding company or any of its banking or nonbanking subsidiaries failed. Shareholders and creditors of the holding company would therefore have greater incentives to monitor its financial condition. Moreover, the narrow bank format would eliminate the ability of financial conglomerates to exploit the deposit insurance subsidy by orchestrating transfers of funds or credit from their insured depository subsidiaries to nonbank affiliates.

A further benefit of my proposal is that traditional banks (which are likely to be smaller banks) would no longer bear any part of the cost of rescuing *uninsured* creditors of TBTF banks. Under current law, all FDIC-insured banks must pay a special assessment (allocated in proportion to their total assets) to reimburse the FDIC for the cost of protecting uninsured claimants in a "systemic risk" bailout. The FDIC has noted the unfairness of expecting smaller banks—which could *never* be the subject of a TBTF rescue—to help pay for "systemic risk" bailouts. The FDIC has suggested that the way to correct this inequity is "to remove the systemic risk exception from the [FDI Act],"[78] as proposed here.

Critics have raised two major objections to the narrow bank concept. First, critics point out that the asset restrictions imposed on narrow banks would prevent them from acting as intermediaries of funds between depositors and borrowers. Most narrow bank proposals would require such banks to invest their deposits in safe, highly marketable assets such as those permitted for MMMFs. Narrow banks would therefore be largely or entirely barred from making commercial loans. As a result, a banking system composed *exclusively* of narrow banks could not provide credit to small and midsized firms that lack access to the securities markets.[79]

However, the two-tiered proposal presented here should greatly reduce any disruption of the traditional role of banks in acting as intermediaries between depositors and bank-dependent firms. This proposal would permit first-tier banks (primarily community banks) to continue making commercial loans that are funded by deposits. As shown elsewhere, community banks make most of their commercial loans in the form of longer-term "relationship" loans to small and midsized firms. Community banks have significant advantages in making such loans, because (1) their main offices are located in the communities where they make most of their commercial loans, and their employees are therefore well informed about the character, reputation, and skills of local business owners; (2) they maintain greater continuity in their branch managers and loan officers, thereby allowing those employees to build stronger relationships with local business owners; and (3) they typically provide greater flexibility to their loan officers and loan customers. Under this proposal, community banks could carry on their deposit-taking and lending activities without any change from current law, and their primary commercial lending customers would continue to be smaller, bank-dependent firms.

In contrast to community banks, most big banks do not make a substantial number of relationship loans to small firms. Instead, big banks provide credit to smaller firms primarily through automated "transaction-based" programs that (1) disburse loans in relatively small amounts (usually under $100,000), (2) use centralized, impersonal approval methods based on credit scoring, and (3) enable loans to be securitized into asset-backed securities sold to investors in the capital markets. Under the present proposal, most large banks would become second-tier organizations. Those second-tier holding companies would conduct their business lending programs through nonbank finance subsidiaries that are funded by commercial paper and other debt instruments sold to investors in the capital markets. This lending structure should not create a substantial disincentive for the small business lending programs currently offered by big banks because a major portion of those programs is already financed by the capital markets through securitization. In short, this two-tier proposal should not cause a significant reduction in bank loans to bank-dependent firms because big banks have already moved away from traditional relationship-based lending funded by deposits.[80]

The second major criticism of narrow bank proposals is that they lack credibility because federal regulators would retain the inherent authority (whether explicit or implicit) to organize bailouts of major financial firms during periods of severe economic distress. Accordingly, critics maintain, the narrow bank concept simply shifts the TBTF problem from the insured bank to its nonbank affiliates.[81] The following section answers this criticism, and it is proposed that the responsibility for administering TBTF rescues—with important new restrictions—be transferred to the FRB.

Assigning the FRB with Responsibility over TBTF Institutions

Given its role as "umbrella regulator" for financial holding companies, as well as its responsibility for monetary policy and the payments system, the FRB is best suited to deal with large financial conglomerates whose failure might create a systemic crisis.[82] In addition, as LOLR, the FRB has authority to provide emergency discount window advances to a major financial institution or its affiliates.[83] Under the proposal presented here, the FRB could use its LOLR powers to support financial conglomerates in situations involving systemic risk.

However, three restrictions should be imposed to prevent the FRB from encouraging moral hazard among large financial conglomerates. First, the FRB must obtain the Treasury Department's concurrence before making any discount window advances for the purpose of protecting uninsured creditors of a failing financial institution or its affiliates. Second, the FRB must recover the unpaid balance of any emergency advance by imposing a special assessment on other holding companies of the same class as the entity that received the advance.[84] This reform would require the FRB to charge *all* second-tier holding companies, in proportion to their total assets, for the unpaid balance of any discount window loan extended to a second-tier holding company.[85]

Potential liability for FRB special assessments would give each nontraditional holding company a strong incentive to monitor other second-tier organizations and to alert the FRB if the holding company became aware of circumstances indicating that a competitor was taking excessive risks or was otherwise exposed to losses that might threaten its solvency. A system of joint liability and mutual discipline could be formalized by organizing second-tier holding companies into one or more self-regulating clearing houses. Such clearing houses could attract members based on a common geographic location or similar product offerings. A clearing house structure would allow its members to establish rules for (1) monitoring the financial condition of each member, (2) settling obligations between members, and (3) providing assistance to weakened members during market disruptions. Each clearing house could also organize a self-insurance system by requiring its members to make contributions to a reserve fund, which could be used to help members during financial emergencies or pay FRB special assessments for unpaid discount window loans to members.[86]

Under the third restriction on its LOLR powers, the FRB could not make emergency advances to protect uninsured creditors of a financial conglomerate unless a mandatory "haircut" was assessed against all uninsured claims. Requiring about a 10 percent "haircut" would appear reasonable, for it would encourage uninsured creditors to exercise greater discipline over financial holding companies but would probably not be so great as to trigger contagious "runs" by large depositors, holders of commercial paper, and other uninsured short-term creditors. The FRB could be given discretion to waive this mandatory "haircut" during an exceptionally severe economic crisis. However, as an appropriate disincentive, the FRB should be obligated to use its own reserves to pay for the cost of such waivers.

Adopting Further Reforms to Improve Supervisory Oversight and Market Discipline

The proposals outlined here would significantly reduce the TBTF subsidy currently enjoyed by large financial conglomerates. However, further reforms are urgently needed to correct existing flaws in supervisory oversight and market discipline. First, federal regulators should promptly implement "Pillar 3" of the proposed new Basel accord, which would require LCBOs to provide more extensive and timely disclosures to investors about their risk exposures and risk management systems. Second, regulators should require LCBOs to issue publicly traded senior or subordinated debt securities on a frequent basis. Regulators should be permitted to experiment with publicly traded debt requirements over a period of five years and then report to Congress on the prospects for adopting a more formalized system of market-based discipline (e.g., a program requiring LCBOs to issue qualifying subordinated debt on a continuous basis, with mandatory PCA sanctions for institutions unable to do so).

Third, regulators should revise their monitoring systems to incorporate signals from the capital markets. Recent studies have shown that regulatory oversight would be more effective if supervisors frequently reviewed market signals such as equity securities prices; yield spreads and ratings on senior and subordinated debt securities; and interest rates paid on uninsured deposits and interbank loans. Although market discipline is unlikely to replace supervisory oversight within the foreseeable future, market-based signals would provide regulators with helpful tools for analyzing the financial condition and potential risks of large, publicly traded financial institutions.[87]

CONCLUSION

The U.S. financial services industry has been fundamentally restructured over the past two decades, culminating in the emergence of big universal banks and other large financial diversified institutions. The GLB Act effectively ratified this ongoing consolidation of the financial services industry. Unfortunately, regulatory policies have not kept pace with the challenges of supervising financial conglomerates. These giant institutions present formidable risks to the federal safety net and are largely insulated from both market discipline and supervisory oversight.

International and domestic regulators have tinkered with supervisory policies in the vain hope that revised capital rules, better oversight procedures, and increased disclosures to investors will induce financial conglomerates to adopt prudent risk management policies. However, the unmistakable lesson of the past three decades is that regulators will protect major financial firms against failure whenever such action is deemed necessary to preserve the stability of the capital markets. As a consequence, financial institutions understand that they can increase their leverage and pursue more risky activities as they grow in size and complexity. Without a comprehensive reform of the current regulatory structure, LCBOs will continue to exploit the subsidies provided under the TBTF policy and other components of the federal safety net.

This chapter proposes a new regulatory regime for financial conglomerates. Under the plan outlined here, diversified banking organizations would be allowed to accept insured deposits only through narrow banks. Strict limitations on affiliate transactions would prevent narrow banks from transferring their deposit insurance subsidy to nonbank affiliates. The FDIC's deposit insurance funds would be used *solely* to pay insured depositor claims and would be completely insulated from the potential cost of TBTF bailouts. The FRB would be primarily responsible for dealing with financial failures involving systemic risk, and the cost of TBTF rescues would be borne *entirely* by the TBTF policy's potential beneficiaries—viz., large financial conglomerates. Additional measures would improve supervisory oversight and market discipline over universal banks. In combination, these reforms should significantly reduce the incentives for excessive risk-taking that currently exist in our financial system.

NOTES

1. For discussions of these industry trends, see, for example, Charles W. Calomiris, *U.S. Bank Deregulation in Historical Perspective* 334–349 (Cambridge: Cambridge University Press, 2000); Arthur E. Wilmarth, Jr., "The Transformation of the U.S. Financial Services Industry, 1975–2000: Competition, Consolidation and Increased Risk," 2002 *University of Illinois Law Review* Issue 2 (forthcoming) [hereinafter cited as Wilmarth, "Transformation"].

2. Wilmarth, "Transformation," supra note 1 (reporting that (1) the number of independent U.S. banking organizations declined from 12,500 to 6,800 during 1979–1999, and (2) the percentage of banking industry assets held by the 10 largest banks grew from 23 percent to 49 percent during 1984–1999).

3. Id. (discussing (1) mergers in 1998 involving NationsBank and BankAmerica, Bank One and First Chicago NBD, and Norwest and Wells Fargo, (2) a 1999 merger

between Fleet and BankBoston, and (3) mergers in 2000 involving J. P. Morgan and Chase, and FirstStar and U.S. Bancorp); R. Christian Bruce, "Fed Clears First Union, Wachovia Deal," 77 *BNA's Banking Report* 315 (2001).

4. R. Christian Bruce, "Fed Approves Citicorp-Travelers Merger Creating World's Largest Bank Company," 71 *BNA's Banking Report* 449 (1998). By the second quarter of 2001, Citigroup had total assets of $940 billion and ranked first in the world in terms of both assets and market capitalization. Niamh Ring, "Citi Surpasses Deutsche As No. 1 in Asset Size," *American Banker*, July 6, 2001, at 2; "The Business Week Global 1000," *Business Week*, July 9, 2001, at 75 (tbl.).

5. Michael Siconolfi, "Big Umbrella: Travelers and Citicorp Agree to Join Forces in $83 Billion Merger," *Wall Street Journal*, April 7, 1998, at A1. Based on an exemption in Section 4(a)(2) of the federal Bank Holding Company Act (BHC Act), the FRB allowed Citigroup to offer securities and insurance services beyond the scope of the BHC Act for up to five years after the Citicorp–Travelers merger. In practical effect, the FRB gave Citigroup a five-year license to operate as a universal bank and did not require Citigroup to divest any of its nonconforming securities or insurance activities. See Travelers Group, Inc., 84 *Federal Reserve Bulletin* 985 (1998). As used herein, the term *universal bank* refers to a single organization that can engage, either directly or indirectly, in all aspects of the banking, securities, and life insurance businesses.

6. For general descriptions of the GLB Act, see, for example, Michael P. Malloy, "Banking in the Twenty-First Century," 26 *Journal of Corporation Law* 787, 793–819 (2000); Michael K. O'Neal, "Summary and Analysis of the Gramm-Leach-Bliley Act," 28 *Securities Regulation Law Journal* 95 (2000).

7. John Tagliabue, "Acquisition Highlights Swiss Flair for Managing Expansion," *New York Times*, August 31, 2000, at C20 (discussing Credit Suisse's acquisition of Donaldson, Lufkin & Jenrette and UBS's acquisition of PaineWebber); Amy L. Anderson, "Sales at Banks a Key Prize in ING Deal for ReliaStar," *American Banker*, May 2, 2000, at 1; Pui-Wing Tam and Randall Smith, "Schwab, Going for High-End Clients, Sets $2.9 Billion Stock Accord for U.S. Trust," *Wall Street Journal*, January 14, 2000, at C1; Lee Ann Gjertsen, "MetLife Has Big Plans for One-Branch Bank," *American Banker*, August 17, 2000, at 1.

8. See, for example, Senate Report No. 44, 106th Cong., 1st Sess. 4–6 (1999); James R. Barth, R. Dan Brumbaugh, Jr., and James A. Wilcox, "The Repeal of Glass-Steagall and the Advent of Broad Banking," 14 *Journal of Economic Perspectives* 191, 198–199 (2000); Joao A. C. Santos, "Commercial Banks in the Securities Business: A Review," 14 *Journal of Financial Services Research* 35, 37–41 (1998).

9. For discussion of the results of bank mergers and cross-industry consolidation during the 1980s and 1990s, see Wilmarth, "Transformation," supra note 1.

10. Arthur E. Wilmarth, Jr., "Too Good to Be True? The Unfulfilled Promises Behind Big Bank Mergers," 2 *Stanford Journal of Law, Business & Finance* 1 (1995) [hereinafter cited as Wilmarth, "Big Bank Mergers"], at 4–5, 31–41, 87 (big bank mergers resulted in inferior service and higher prices for consumers and small businesses); Gerald A. Hanweck and Bernard Shull, "The Bank Merger Movement: Efficiency, Stability and Competitive Policy Concerns," 44 *Antitrust Bulletin* 251, 258–259, 265–281 (1999) (same); Timothy H. Hannan, "Retail Fees of Depository Institutions," 1994–1999, 87 *Federal Reserve Bulletin* 1, 8–11 (2001) (compared with smaller banks, multistate banks and larger banks charged significantly higher fees on deposit accounts).

11. Wilmarth, "Transformation," supra note 1; Kenneth N. Gilpin and Elizabeth Olson,

"Market Place: Credit Suisse Is Taking Hits on Wall Street and at Home," *New York Times*, October 10, 2001, at C1; Jathon Sapsford et al., "Citigroup, J. P. Morgan Chase and FleetBoston See Earnings Slump," *Wall Street Journal*, October 18, 2001, at A4; Emily Thornton, "Wall Street: The Big Chill," *Business Week*, October 22, 2001, at 120; Marcus Walker, "Slowdown Grips Deutsche Bank: Profit Falls 49%," *Wall Street Journal*, August 2, 2001, at A10.

12. Henry Kaufman, *On Money and Markets: A Wall Street Memoir* (New York: McGraw-Hill, 2000) [hereinafter cited as Kaufman, *On Money and Markets*], at 223–231, 242–246, 259–268, 278–286, 306–307; Gianni De Nicolo, "Size, Charter Value and Risk in Banking: An International Perspective," Working Paper, April 2001; Wilmarth, "Transformation," supra note 1.

13. Edward J. Kane, "Incentives for Banking Megamergers: What Motives Might Regulators Infer from Event-Study Evidence?," 32 *Journal of Money, Credit & Banking* 672, 673–674, 691–694 (2000); Kaufman, *On Money and Markets*, supra note 12, at 207–210, 226–230, 259–268, 278–286; Wilmarth, "Transformation," supra note 1.

For recent studies documenting the implicit subsidy provided to big U.S. banks by the TBTF policy, see, for example, Craig H. Furfine, "Banks as Monitors of Other Banks: Evidence from the Overnight Federal Funds Market," 74 *Journal of Business* 33, 36–40, 47 (2001) (in 1998, banks with more than $10 billion of assets paid significantly lower interest rates on overnight loans than those paid by smaller banks); Hanweck and Shull, supra note 10, at 274–276 (in 1997, big banks paid much lower interest rates on deposits and operated with substantially lower equity capital ratios, compared to smaller banks); Donald P. Morgan and Kevin J. Stiroh, "Bond Market Discipline of Banks," in *The Changing Financial Industry Structure and Regulation*, at 494, 504–506 (Fed. Res. Bank of Chicago, 36th Annual Conference on Bank Structure & Competition, 2000) (during 1993–1998: (1) public bond markets applied much less stringent discipline to banks with assets of more than $85 billion, and (2) weaker bond market discipline was especially evident among the 11 big banks that were publicly identified as TBTF in 1984).

14. Reint Gropp and Jukka M. Vesala, "Deposit Insurance and Moral Hazard: Does the Counterfactual Matter?," *European Central Bank Working Paper* No. 47, July 2001.

15. See, for example, Robert Oshinsky, "Effects of Bank Consolidation on the Bank Insurance Fund," *FDIC Working Paper* No. 99–3; William M. Isaac, "Financial Reform's *Unfinished* Agenda," 14 Region No. 1 (Fed. Res. Bank of Minneapolis, Minn.), March 2000, at 34, 37; Kaufman, *On Money and Markets*, supra note 12, at 226–230, 237–238, 329–337.

16. See Group of Ten, Report on Consolidation in the Financial Sector, January 2001, at 125–146. See also Gianni De Nicolo and Myron L. Kwast, "Systemic Risk and Financial Consolidation: Are They Related?," Board of Governors of Federal Reserve System, Finance & Economics Discussion Series, Working Paper 2001–2033, June 19, 2001 (concluding that the rapid growth of LCBOs probably increased systemic risk in the United States during 1988–1999).

17. See, for example, Mark J. Flannery, "Modernizing Financial Regulation: The Relation Between Interbank Transactions and Supervisory Reform," 16 *Journal of Financial Services Research* 101, 103–109 (1999); Lisa M. DeFerrari and David E. Palmer, "Supervision of Large Complex Banking Organizations," 87 *Federal Reserve Bulletin* 47, 51–53 (2001); Anthony Santomero and David L. Eckles, "The Determinants of Success in the New Financial Services Environment," 6 *Economic Policy Review* No. 4 (Fed. Res. Bank of N.Y.), October 2000, at 11, 15, 18–19; U.S. General Accounting Office,

"Risk-Focused Bank Examinations: Regulators of Large Banking Organizations Face Challenges," GAO/GGD-00–48, January 2000 [hereinafter cited as GAO LCBO Study], at 5, 15, 24, 28–30. For example, Citigroup recently decided to market all of its global corporate and investment banking services under the unified brand name of Citigroup Corporate and Investment Bank. Paul Beckett, "So Long, Poker Players: Salomon Is History," *Wall Street Journal*, May 23, 2001, at C18.

18. Wilmarth, "Transformation," supra note 1. The federal "safety net" for banks consists of deposit insurance, protection of uninsured depositors, and payments system creditors of major banks under the TBTF policy, discount window advances provided by the FRB as LOLR, and the FRB's guarantee of interbank payments made on Fedwire. George G. Kaufman and Peter J. Wallison, "The New Safety Net," 24 *Regulation* No. 2, Summer 2001, at 28.

19. Christopher P. Mahoney, "Commentary," 6 *Economic Policy Review* No. 4 (Fed. Res. Bank of N.Y.), October 2000, at 55, 57–58. Similarly, Alan Blinder, a former FRB vice chairman, recently stated that "[e]verybody knows that there are institutions that are so large and so interlinked with others that it is out of the question to let them fail." Quoted in Rob Blackwell, " 'Too Big to Fail' Deniers Have a Tough Audience," *American Banker*, June 4, 2001, at 1.

20. Thomas M. Hoenig, "Financial Industry Megamergers and Policy Challenges," 84 *Economic Review* No. 3 (Fed. Res. Bank of K.C., Mo.), 3d Qtr. 1999, at 7–8, 10–13; Kaufman, *On Money and Markets*, supra note 12, at 207, 237–238; Remarks by FRB Governor Laurence H. Meyer before a National Bureau of Economic Research Conference, January 14, 2000 [hereinafter cited as 2000 Meyer NBER Speech], at 1–2; Frederic S. Mishkin, "Financial Consolidation: Dangers and Opportunities," 23 *Journal of Banking & Finance* 675, 680–681 (1999); Santomero and Eckles, supra note 17, at 15, 18–19; Gary H. Stern, "Thoughts on Designing Credible Policies after Financial Modernization," 14 Region No. 3 (Fed. Res. Bank of Minneapolis, Minn.), September 2000, at 4–5, 24–25.

21. Remarks by FRB Chairman Alan Greenspan before the World Bank Group and the IMF Program of Seminars, September 27, 1999 [hereinafter cited as 1999 Greenspan IMF Speech], at 1–3; George G. Kaufman, "Designing the New Architecture for U.S. Banking," in Benton E. Gup, ed., *The New Financial Architecture: Banking Regulation in the 21st Century* (Westport, Conn.: Quorum Books, 2001) [hereinafter cited as Gup, *New Financial Architecture*], at 39 [hereinafter cited as Kaufman, "Banking Architecture"], at 44; Wilmarth, "Transformation," supra note 1.

22. See, for example, Franklin Allen and Douglas Gale, "Bubbles and Crises," 110 *Economic Journal* 236, 236–238, 252–254 (2000); Valentine V. Craig, "Japanese Banking: A Time of Crisis," 11 *FDIC Banking Review* No. 2, at 9, 12–17 (1998); Curtis J. Milhaupt, "Japan's Experience with Deposit Insurance and Failing Banks: Implications for Financial Regulatory Design?," 77 *Washington University Law Quarterly* 399, 408–424 (1999); Joe Peek and Eric S. Rosengren, "Japanese Banking Problems: Implications for Lending in the United States," *New England Economic Review* (Fed. Res. Bank of Boston, Mass.), January/February 1999, at 25 [hereinafter cited as Peek and Rosengren, "Japanese Banking Problems"], at 25–31; Wilmarth, "Big Bank Mergers," supra note 10, at 62–69; "Japan's Economy: Chronic Sickness," *Economist*, June 2, 2001, at 71; "Japan's Banks: Out for the count," *Economist*, October 11, 2001.

23. See, for example, Craig, supra note 22, at 14–17; Milhaupt, supra note 22, at 408–424; Michael Williams et al., "Day of Reckoning: Wall Street Intensifies Japan's Woes,

But They All Trace Back to Home," *Wall Street Journal*, March 16, 2001, at A1; Neil A. Martin, "Will Japan's Koizumi Soon Be Ex-Prime Minister?," *Barron's*, September 10, 2001, at MW10.

24. Craig, supra note 22, at 9–14; 1999 Greenspan IMF Speech, supra note 21, at 2; Peek and Rosengren, "Japanese Banking Problems," supra note 22, at 26–31; Wilmarth, "Big Bank Mergers," supra note 10, at 62–63, 69 n.319; Jacob Schlesinger and Peter Landers, "Parallel Woes: Is the U.S. Economy at Risk of Emulating Japan's Long Swoon?," *Wall Street Journal*, November 7, 2001, at A1.

25. Senate Report No. 44, supra note 8, at 7–8; O'Neal, supra note 6, at 100–112.

26. O'Neal, supra note 6, at 104–105, 108, 112; George J. Benston and George G. Kaufman, "FDICIA after Five Years," 11 *Journal of Economic Perspectives* 139, 144–149 (1997); U.S. General Accounting Office, "Bank and Thrift Regulation: Implementation of FDICIA's Prompt Regulatory Action Provisions," GAO/GGD-97–18, November 1996 [hereinafter cited as GAO PCA Study], at 14–21, 25–27.

27. O'Neal, supra note 6, at 104–105, 108, 112 (discussing the GLB Act). For descriptions of the new supervisory procedures for LCBOs, see generally DeFerrari and Palmer, supra note 17; 2000 Meyer NBER Speech, supra note 20; Remarks by Governor Laurence H. Meyer at the International Banking Conference of the Federal Financial Institutions Examination Council, May 31, 2000 [hereinafter cited as 2000 Meyer FFIEC Speech]; GAO LCBO Study, supra note 17.

28. O'Neal, supra note 6, at 109 (under the GLB Act, a national bank must have at least one issue of outstanding debt securities with a qualified credit rating if the bank plans to establish a financial subsidiary and is one of the 50 largest U.S. banks); Meyer NBER Speech, supra note 20, at 2–6 (explaining measures designed to encourage greater market discipline).

29. Basel Committee on Banking Supervision, "Overview of the New Basel Capital Accord," January 2001 [hereinafter cited as "2001 Basel Capital Proposal Overview"], at 1, 7, 12–36. In June 2001, responding to widespread criticism of its January proposal, the Basel Committee extended its timetable for adopting and implementing its new capital accord. However, the Committee stressed that "it remains strongly committed to the three pillars architecture of the new Accord." Basel Committee on Bank Supervision, "Update on the New Basel Capital Accord," June 25, 2001.

30. Under the Basel Committee's proposal, only large, sophisticated banks that establish satisfactory internal risk management systems would be permitted to use internal risk ratings to calculate their capital requirements. Smaller banks would continue to comply with uniform, standardized capital rules established by the Basel Committee. See "2001 Basel Capital Proposal Overview," supra note 29, at 1–2, 7–8, 11–17; 2000 Meyer NBER Speech, supra note 20, at 1–3.

31. Helen A. Garten, "Subtle Hazards, Financial Risks, and Diversified Banks: An Essay on the Perils of Regulatory Reform," 49 *Maryland Law Review* 314 (1990) [hereinafter cited as Garten, "Subtle Hazards"], at 352–354 describing how (1) Hamilton National Bank failed in the mid-1970s after its parent holding company caused the bank to disregard affiliate transaction rules and purchase large amounts of low-quality mortgages from its troubled mortgage banking affiliate; and (2) Continental Bank ignored legal lending limits by extending credit to rescue its options trading subsidiary during the October 1987 stock market crash; William S. Haraf, "The Collapse of Drexel Burnham Lambert: Lessons for the Bank Regulators," *Regulation* (Winter 1991), at 22, 23. (When Drexel Burnham was threatened with failure in early 1990, it withdrew capital

from its regulated securities subsidiaries in excess of regulatory limits until the SEC intervened to prevent further capital transfers.)

32. Board of Governors of the Federal Reserve System, "Transactions Between Banks and Their Affiliates: Notice of Proposed Rulemaking," 66 *Federal Register* 24,186–187 (2001) (discussing restrictions on affiliate transactions under Sections 23A and 23B).

33. Garten, "Subtle Hazards," supra note 31, at 380–381 (stating that the "[FRB] has admitted that restrictions on interaffiliate funds transfers frequently have been violated or interpreted creatively by management in times of stress"); "GAO Says Banks May Pass Net Subsidy to Their Affiliates," 16 *Banking Policy Report* No. 18, September 15, 1997, at 7, 8–9 (reprinting letter from GAO Chief Economist James Bothwell to Rep. Richard Baker).

34. Anita Raghavan et al., "Team Effort: Banks and Regulators Drew Together to Calm Markets after Attack," *Wall Street Journal*, October 18, 2001, at A1.

35. DeFerrari and Palmer, supra note 17, at 51–53; GAO LCBO Study, supra note 17, at 5, 7, 14–18, 24–30; Meyer FFIEC Speech, supra note 27, at 5–8.

36. See, for example, House of Representatives Report No. 74, 106th Cong., 1st Sess,. 99–102 (citing statements by regulators and industry representatives claiming that corporate separation and regulatory "firewalls" would insulate FDIC-insured banks from the potential risks of their nonbank affiliates). See also Flannery, supra note 17, at 112 n.10 (stating that "many proponents of broad financial conglomerate powers insist that legal separateness will effectively insulate banking activities, without explicitly addressing the question of de facto integration. This omission is particularly noteworthy when it is accompanied by an assertion that regulation should permit conglomerates to take maximum advantage of scope economies among the various product lines—which seems to contradict the promise of de facto separateness!").

37. For example, Allen N. Berger, Richard J. Herring, and Giorgio P. Szegö, "The Role of Capital in Financial Institutions," 19 *Journal of Banking and Finance* 393, 414–415 (1995).

38. For example, Robert C. Merton, "Financial Innovation and the Management and Regulation of Financial Institutions," 19 *Journal of Banking and Finance* 461, 468–470 (1995); Wilmarth, "Transformation," supra note 1.

39. See U.S. General Accounting Office, "Risk-Based Capital: Regulatory and Industry Approaches to Capital and Risk," GAO/GGD-98–153, July 1998 [hereinafter cited as "GAO Risk-Based Capital Study"], at 49–53; "2001 Basel Capital Proposal Overview," supra note 29, at 7–10, 17–29; D. Johannes Jüttner, "Message to Basle: Risk Reduction Rather Than Management," in Gup, *New Financial Architecture*, supra note 21, at 207, 208–209, 217–218.

40. See, for example, Berger, Herring and Szegö, supra note 37, at 411–416, 425; Jeffrey W. Gunther and Robert R. Moore, "Financial Statements and Reality: Do Troubled Banks Tell All?," *Economic and Financial Review* (Fed. Res. Bank of Dallas, Tex.), 3d Qtr. 2000, at 30; Joe Peek and Eric S. Rosengren, "The Use of Capital Ratios to Trigger Intervention in Problem Banks: Too Little, Too Late," *New England Economic Review* (Fed. Res. Bank of Boston, Mass.), September/October 1996, at 49 [hereinafter cited as Peek and Rosengren, Capital Ratios] at 50–57.

41. Benston and Kaufman, supra note 26, at 144–148; GAO PCA Study, supra note 26, at 14–21.

42. GAO PCA Study, supra note 26, at 26–28 (more than 98% of all banks and thrifts satisfied the "adequately capitalized" standard at the end of 1992); Benston and Kaufman,

supra note 26, at 146–148 (federal regulators set the "adequately capitalized" threshold too low under their PCA rules); Peek and Rosengren, "Capital Ratios," supra note 40, at 57 (same).

43. David S. Jones and Kathleen K. King, "The Implementation of Prompt Corrective Action: An Assessment," 19 *Journal of Banking & Finance* 491, 493, 498–499, 508 (1995); Peek and Rosengren, "Capital Ratios," supra note 40, at 52–56; GAO PCA Study, supra note 26, at 45 and Table 3.1.

44. Benston and Kaufman, supra note 26, at 146–149, 152–156; GAO PCA Study, supra note 26, at 5–7, 25–29, 41–49, 55–56; Statement of FDIC Director John Reich on the Failure of Superior Bank, FSB, submitted to the Senate Committee on Banking, Housing and Urban Affairs, September 11, 2001 (Superior Bank's failure "illustrates the limits of [PCA] tools given to regulators," particularly with regard to institutions holding securitization residuals and other exotic assets whose worth depends on "complex, assumption-driven" valuation models).

45. See Tina M. Galloway, Winson B. Lee, and Dianne M. Roden, "Banks' Changing Incentives and Opportunities for Risk Taking," 21 *Journal of Banking & Finance* 509 (1997); Armen Hovakimian and Edward J. Kane, "Effectiveness of Capital Regulation at U.S. Commercial Banks, 1985 to 1994," 55 *Journal of Finance* 451 (2000).

46. The Basel Committee's proposal would allow each qualifying bank, in determining its capital requirements for credit risk, to use internal risk models to estimate (1) the probability of default by borrowers and (2) the bank's exposure to loss in the event of default. "2001 Basel Capital Proposal Overview," supra note 29, at 8, 17–23; Speech by FRB Governor Laurence H. Meyer before the Institute of International Bankers, May 5, 2001, at 4–5, 7–8.

47. See Jeremy Berkowitz and James O'Brien, "How Accurate Are Value-at-Risk Models at Commercial Banks?," Board of Governors of Federal Reserve System, Finance & Economics Discussion Series Working Paper 2001, July 31, 2001, at 3–5; Wilmarth, "Transformation," supra note 1.

48. See Wilmarth, "Transformation," supra note 1 (discussing flaws in bank models for market risk); Patricia Jackson and William Perraudin, "Regulatory Implications of Credit Risk Modelling," 24 *Journal of Banking & Finance* 1 (2000) (discussing problems with bank models for credit risk); Robert A. Jarrow and Stuart M. Turnbull, "The Intersection of Market and Credit Risk," 24 *Journal of Banking and Finance*. 271, 272–278 (2000) (same); Jüttner, supra note 39, at 208–222 (same).

Two studies conclude that current capital rules for market risk create a perverse incentive for banks. Those rules penalize a bank whose trading losses exceed its specified VAR on more than 1 percent of trading days during a 250-day period. However, the rules do not assess any additional penalties based on the magnitude of losses that a bank may incur during those "outlier" days. Because the rules focus on the *frequency* rather than the *magnitude* of trading losses, profit-maximizing banks are encouraged to construct risky asset portfolios that may produce larger gains but also tolerate a low-percentage risk of catastrophic losses. See Gordon J. Alexander and Alexandre M. Baptista, "A VaR-Constrained Mean-Variance Model: Implications for Portfolio Selection and the Basle Capital Accord," Working Paper, July 16, 2001; Suleyman Basak and Alexander Shapiro, "Value-at-Risk-Based Management: Optimal Policies and Asset Prices," 14 *Review of financial Studies*, 371, 372–380, 385, 398–399 (2001).

49. Kaufman, *On Money and Markets*, supra note 12, at 225–229; GAO LCBO Study, supra note 17, at 7, 48; "GAO Risk-Based Capital Study," supra note 39, at 98–99.

50. GAO LCBO Study, supra note 17, at 41–42; "GAO Risk-Based Capital Study," supra note 39, at 94.

51. For example, Allen N. Berger, Sally M. Davies, and Mark J. Flannery, "Comparing Market and Supervisory Assessments of Bank Performance: Who Knows What When?," 32 *Journal of Money, Credit & Banking* 641 (2000); Robert DeYoung et al., "The Information Content of Bank Exam Ratings and Subordinated Debt Prices," 33 *Journal of Money, Credit & Banking* 900 (2001); Board of Governors of the Federal Reserve System, Staff Study 172, "Using Subordinated Debt as an Instrument of Market Discipline," December 1999 [hereinafter cited as "FRB Staff Subordinated Debt Study"], at 5, 12–15.

52. Benton E. Gup, "Market Discipline and the Corporate Governance of Banks: Theory vs. Evidence," in Gup, *New Financial Architecture*, supra note 21, at 187 [hereinafter cited as Gup, "Market Discipline"], at 195–199; Richard E. Randall, "Can the Market Evaluate Asset Quality Exposure in Banks?," *New England Economic Review* (Fed. Res. Bank of Boston, Mass.), July/August 1989, at 3.

53. See, for example, Jeffrey E. Garten, "Lessons for the Next Financial Crisis," 78 *Foreign Affairs* No. 2, March/April 1999, at 76, 76–83; Gup, "Market Discipline," supra note 52, at 199–201; Jüttner, supra note 39, at 215–217; Kaufman, *On Money and Markets*, supra note 12, at 281–286; Wilmarth, "Transformation," supra note 1.

54. Flannery, supra note 17, at 101–103, 105–109; Kaufman, *On Money and Markets*, supra note 12, at 71–83, 281–286, 329–337; Meyer FFIEC Speech, supra note 27, at 1, 5–6; Santomero and Eckles, supra note 38, at 15, 18; Alfred Steinherr, *Derivatives: The Wild Beast of Finance* 252–265, 274–284 (New York: John Wiley & Sons, 1998).

55. Myron B. Slovin, Marie E. Slushka, and John A. Polonchek, "An Anlysis of Contagion and Competitive Effects at Commercial Banks," 54 *Journal of Financial Economics* 197 (1999).

56. Donald P. Morgan, "Rating Banks: Risk and Uncertainty in an Opaque Industry," Fed. Res. Bank of N.Y., Staff Reports No. 105, May 2000.

57. See, for example, Allen and Gale, supra note 22, at 236–240, 247–254; Ben Bernanke and Mark Gertler, "Monetary Policy and Asset Price Volatility," 84 *Economic Review* No. 4 (Fed. Res. Bank of K.C., Mo.), 4th Qtr. 1999, at 17, 17–21; Roberto Chang and Andres Velasco, "A Model of Financial Crises in Emerging Markets," 116 *Quarterly Journal of Economics* 489 (2001); Kaufman, "Banking Architecture," supra note 21, at 46–47; Kaufman, *On Money and Markets*, supra note 12, at 68–83, 201–225, 270–325; Robert J. Shiller, *Irrational Exuberance* 96–132, 203–233 (Princeton, N.J.: Princeton University Press, 2000).

58. For recent discussions of psychological factors that may contribute to investor euphoria and panic, see, for example, David Hirshleifer, "Investor Psychology and Asset Pricing," 56 *Journal of Finance* 1533 (2001); Shiller, supra note 57, at 135–232.

59. Randall, supra note 52, at 4, 7–18; John S. Jordan, "Insiders' Assessments of the Stock Market's Pricing of New England Bank Stocks, 1988 to 1991," *New England Economic Review* (Fed. Res. Bank of Boston, Mass.), July/August 1997, at 3; Maria S. M. Peria and Sergio L. Schmukler, "Do Depositors Punish Banks for Bad Behavior? Market Discipline, Deposit Insurance, and Banking Crises," 56 *Journal of Finance* 1029, 1030–1031, 1048–1050 (2001).

60. Gup, "Market Discipline," supra note 52, at 202.

61. For example, 1999 Greenspan IMF Speech, supra note 24, at 1–3; 2000 Meyer NBER Speech, supra note 20, at 1–4.

62. See Helen A. Garten, "Whatever Happened to Market Discipline of Banks?," 1991 *Annual Survey of American Law* 749, 750–754, 776–783.

63. Benston and Kaufman, supra note 26, at 146–49; GAO PCA Study, supra note 26, at 20–21, 36–40, 49–52.

64. The FRB joined the banking industry in opposing the decision of the Financial Accounting Standards Board (FASB) to adopt Statement of Financial Accounting Standards (FAS) 115 in 1993. FAS 115 requires banks to "mark to market" all investment securities except for those properly designated as "held to maturity." David Siegel, "Capital: FASB Votes to Adopt Mark-to-Market Rule," *American Banker*, April 14, 1993, at 1; Barbara A. Rehm, "Rising Rates Put Banks in Double Bind," *American Banker*, May 13, 1994, at 1.

The FRB also echoed the banking industry's strong objection to FASB's decision to adopt FAS 133 in 1998. FAS 133 requires banks to give market-value treatment to all derivatives except for those qualifying as hedges. Elizabeth McDonald, "Greenspan Urges FASB to Drop Plan on Adjusting Earnings for Derivatives," *Wall Street Journal*, August 7, 1997, at B2; Aaron Elstein, "Banks Decry Plan to Make Them Report Derivatives' Market Value," *American Banker*, November 19, 1996, at A1.

65. "FRB Staff Subordinated Debt Study," supra note 51, at 53–56.

66. Rob Garver, "Skepticism Rising on Market as Regulator," *American Banker*, January 22, 2001, at 1 [hereinafter cited as Garver, "Market as Regulator"] (quoting Bert Ely).

67. Henry T.C. Hu, "Faith and Magic: Investor Beliefs and Government Neutrality," 78 *Texas Law Review* 777, 780, 865–872 (2000); Kaufman, *On Money and Markets*, supra note 12, at 208–221, 257–259, 310–312; Mahoney, supra note 19, at 56–58; Steinherr, supra note 54, at 53–61, 274–276, 282–283; Wilmarth, "Transformation," supra note 1.

68. Testimony of FRB Chairman Alan Greenspan before the House Committee on Financial Services, July 18, 2001, reprinted in 87 *Federal Reserve Bulletin* 588 (2001) (quote at 592) (emphasis added). See also James C. Cooper and Kathleen Madigan, "Business Outlook: The Data Will Be Grim—But Give the Fed a Chance," *Business Week*, October 15, 2001, at 37 (stating that the FRB's interest rate cuts during 2001 were "the most aggressive easing [of monetary policy] in the postwar era").

69. See Raghavan et al., supra note 34 (quoting Mr. Corrigan and reporting on the FRB's waiver of Section 23A); supra notes 32–33 and accompanying text (discussing restrictions on affiliate transactions under Section 23A).

70. See Robert T. Parry, "Financial Services in the New Century," *FRBSF Economic Letter* No. 98–15 (Fed. Res. Bank of S.F., Calif.), May 8, 1998, at 2; Hoenig, supra note 20, at 10–13; Stern, supra note 20, at 4–5, 24–26.

71. Garver, "Market as Regulator," supra note 137 (quoting analyst Karen Shaw Petrou).

72. For a previous description of this proposal for a two-tiered structure of bank regulation and deposit insurance, see Wilmarth, "Big Bank Mergers," supra note 10, at 77–87. As indicated in that article, I am indebted to Robert Litan for many of the concepts incorporated in my two-tiered proposal. See Robert E. Litan, "What Should Banks Do?" 164–189 (Brookings, 1987).

73. See 12 U.S.C. § 24(Seventh) (defining securities eligible for underwriting and dealing by national banks); supra note 64 (discussing FASB's adoption of FAS 133).

74. Unfortunately, the GLB Act prohibits the FRB from approving any new "closely

related" activities for bank holding companies under Section 4(c)(8) of the BHC Act. See Malloy, supra note 6, at 801 (stating that the GLB Act "freezes in place," as of November 12, 1999, the list of permissible activities under Section 4(c)(8)). Congress should revise Section 4(c)(8) by authorizing the FRB to approve a limited range of new activities that are "closely related" to the traditional banking functions of accepting deposits, extending credit, discounting negotiable instruments, and providing fiduciary services. See Wilmarth, "Big Bank Mergers," supra note 10, at 80 n.365, 84 n.378.

75. See Wilmarth, "Transformation," supra note 1 (explaining that (1) during the 1980s and 1990s, many securities firms, life insurers, and industrial firms used the "nonbank bank" loophole or the "unitary thrift" loophole to acquire FDIC-insured institutions, and (2) those loopholes were closed to new acquisitions by a 1987 statute and the GLB Act, respectively).

76. See Wilmarth, "Big Bank Mergers," supra note 10, at 79–82.

77. See Wilmarth, "Transformation," supra note 1 (describing the FDI Act's general rule requiring the FDIC to choose the least costly method for resolving failed banks, and the "systemic risk" exception in 12 U.S.C. § 1823(c)(4)(G), which allows the FDIC, with the concurrence of the FRB and the Treasury Department, to protect uninsured creditors while resolving a TBTF bank).

78. Federal Deposit Ins. Corp., Options Paper, August 2000 [hereinafter cited as 2000 FDIC Options Paper], at 33 (explaining that the FDI Act requires the FDIC to recover the cost of a "systemic risk" bailout by imposing a special assessment on all FDIC-insured banks in proportion to their total assets).

79. See, for example, Neil Wallace, "Narrow Banking Meets the Diamond-Dybvig Model," 20 *Quarterly Review* No. 1 (Fed. Res. Bank of Minneapolis, Minn.), Winter 1996, at 3. See also Wilmarth, "Big Bank Mergers," supra note 10, at 79–81 (explaining that narrow banks would be prohibited from making commercial loans, except perhaps for a limited basket of loans based on a fraction of their equity capital).

80. For discussions of the important differences between the small business lending patterns of community banks and larger banks, see, for example, Allen N. Berger and Gregory F. Udell, "Small Business Credit Availability and Relationship Lending: The Importance of Bank Organizational Structure," *Economic Journal* (2002) (forthcoming); Wilmarth, "Transformation," supra note 1.

81. For example, Mishkin, supra note 20, at 689–690; Stern, supra note 20, at 25–26.

82. See O'Neal, supra note 6, at 104–106 (observing that the GLB Act designates the FRB as the "umbrella regulator" for financial holding companies); Heidi Mandanis Schooner, "Regulating Risk Not Function," 66 *University of Cincinnati Law Review* 441, 478–486 (1998) (contending that the FRB is best situated to act as "systemic risk regulator" for financial conglomerates).

83. The FRB provides discount window loans to banks under 12 U.S.C. §§ 347, 347a, & 347b. In addition, under 12 U.S.C. § 343, the FRB may extend discount window loans to nonbank entities in "unusual and exigent circumstances." Thus, Section 343 permits the FRB to provide emergency liquidity support to securities firms and other nonbank firms after a major economic shock similar to the 1987 stock market crash. See Walker F. Todd, "FDICIA's Emergency Liquidity Provisions," 29 *Economic Review* No. 3 (Fed. Res. Bank of Cleve., Ohio), 3d Qtr. 1993, at 16, 19–22.

84. These two conditions would be similar to provisions currently embodied in the FDIC's "systemic risk" authority under the FDI Act. See 2000 FDIC Options Paper, supra note 78 (explaining that the FDIC must obtain the concurrence of the FRB and

the Treasury Department before protecting any uninsured creditors of a TBTF bank, and make a special ex post assessment on the banking industry to recover the cost of any such bailout).

85. As already explained, this second-tier category would include (1) financial holding companies under the GLB Act, (2) holding companies owning grandfathered "nonbank banks," and (3) grandfathered "unitary thrift" holding companies. If the FRB provided an emergency discount window advance to protect the creditors of a failing securities firm or a failing insurance company that was *not* affiliated with an insured depository institution, the FRB would recover the unpaid balance of that advance by imposing a special assessment on *nonaffiliated* securities firms or insurance companies.

86. For descriptions of the monitoring, liquidity, and self-insurance services provided by private bank clearing houses to their members prior to the creation of the FRB and the FDIC, see, for example, Calomiris, supra note 1, at 8–10, 60, 71; David G. Oedel, "Private Interbank Discipline," 16 *Harvard Journal of Law & Public Policy* 327, 344–360 (1993).

87. See, for example, Berger, Davies and Flannery, supra note 51; DeYoung et al., supra note 51; Ron Feldman and Mark Levonian, "Market Data and Bank Supervision: The Transition to Practical Use," 15 *Region* No. 3 (Fed. Res. Bank of Minneapolis, Minn.), September 2001, at 11; Jeffery W. Gunther, Mark E. Levonian, and Robert R. Moore, "Can the Stock Market Tell Bank Supervisors Anything They Don't Already Know?," *Economic & Financial Review* (Fed. Res. Bank of Dallas, Tex.), 2d Qtr. 2001, at 2.

Chapter 7

Electronic Banking

Benton E. Gup

INTRODUCTION

Electronic banking is one of the first things that comes to mind when one thinks about the future of banking. It is generally assumed that electronic banking is new and that it will replace or supplement many channels of delivery of retail banking services. The term *electronic banking* as used here refers to any banking activity accessed by electronic means.[1] It includes automated teller machines (ATMs), automated call centers, digital cash, Internet banking, screen telephones, and so on. These channels of delivery can be used for presenting and paying bills, buying and selling securities, transferring funds, and providing other financial products and services.

Electronic banking can be used for retail banking and business-to-business (B2B) transactions, as well as for facilitating large-dollar transfers. Equally important, electronic banking is a worldwide phenomenon. As the term is used here, it involves transactions. Some institutions only offer web sites that provide information about services offered but do not allow for transactions. These would not be covered under the definition of electronic banking. However, web sites that are transactional are considered electronic banking.

Electronic banking and the Internet in general are forcing a shift in the way banks and other businesses organize and the way they think of themselves. A shift is taking place from vertical integration to virtual integration.[2] Banks and other financial intermediaries must realize that they are in the financial information industry. The Internet makes it possible to bring both customers and suppliers together to share critical business information. For example, Identrus Global Trust Services helps banks and their customers carry out secure payments online and to deal with other risk management systems.[3] The roles of asymmetric information, adverse selection, and moral hazard have been examined extensively in the literature in connection with lending.[4] Today, a substantial amount of lending is done over the Internet.[5]

HISTORY

Electronic banking is not a new phenomenon. It began in 1871, when the Western Union Telegraph Company, headquartered in Rochester, New York, began to offer a nationwide money-transfer service (Ridgway, 2000). The Fedwire began as a telegraph system in 1918. SWIFT and CHIPs payments systems began in the 1970s. In 2000, Western Union, which is now owned by First Data Corporation, offered its services over the Internet.

About 80 years later there was another major innovation that did not receive as much attention from the public. It was the 1950 development of magnetic ink character recognition (MICR) used in connection with reading and sorting checks by both humans and machines. Without MICR, it would not have been possible for our paper-based system to process about 70 billion checks used in the early twenty-first century.

In 1951, the first credit card was issued by Franklin National Bank (New York), and in the early 1970s, the first ATM machines came into operation at City National Bank of Columbus, Ohio, the predecessor of Bank One (Power and Senior, 1999). In 2000, there were about 285,000 ATMs in operation in the United States (Spong, 2000) and about 592,000 worldwide ("Mastercard International Fact Sheet," 2001).

In 1993, the Office of Thrift Supervision chartered Security First Network Bank (SFNB) in Atlanta, Georgia, and it opened for business in October 1995. SFNB was the first fully transactional Internet thrift institution. In 1998, it was acquired by the Royal Bank Financial Group (Canada), which had assets of $180 billion and 9.5 million customers. The first national charter for an Internet bank was for Houston, Texas-based CompuBank N.A. in 1997. Since then, other Internet banks have been formed. For example, Nexity Bank only has an Internet presence.[6] In 1999, only 20 percent of the largest national banks in the United States offered Internet banking services. However, they accounted for 90 percent of the national banking system assets (Furst, Lang, and Nolle, 2000). Stated otherwise, a few very large banks were the most active in offering Internet services. These banks served a small but growing number of their customers. Furst, Lang, and Nolle (2000) conclude that the low percentage of customers and the modest cost of setting up an Internet banking web site make it unlikely that Internet banking is having a major influence on the profitability of most institutions, with the exception of the largest ones. This may help to explain why some small banks, particularly *de novo* banks, are unprofitable. Those banks that rely primarily on Internet banking must absorb the full cost, making that cost disproportionately large when compared to that of the large banks.

Internet banks may or may not be affiliated with brick and mortar banks or other financial institutions. For example, Telebanc Financial Group was acquired by E-Trade Group Inc., an online brokerage firm.[7] This was the first merger of an online broker with an online thrift institution. In addition, Bank One established an Internet bank—WingspanBank.com—that is separate from the brick and mortar Bank One. Internet-only banks are sometimes called virtual banks.

Electronic banking is not limited to the United States. Banco Bilbbao Vizcaya Argenatria (BBVA), Spain's largest bank, Telefónica, an international telecommunications company, and Terra Networks, an Internet provider, established Uno-e-com, an online bank (Burns, 2000; Harris, 2000). It will operate in Argentina, Brazil, France, Germany, Italy, Mexico, Portugal, Spain, and elsewhere. Germany's Deutsche Bank offers "moneyshelf," an online financial portal that provides various financial services including financial planning, aggregation of bank accounts, purchase of mutual funds, and insurance policies ("Moneyshelf.de," 2000).[8]

FASTER, BETTER, CHEAPER

Although virtual banks can provide a wide range of financial services, they are at a disadvantage compared with brick and mortar banks when it comes to customers making deposits and withdrawing cash—which raises the issue of convenience. Nevertheless, advocates of Internet banking claim that it is *faster*, *better*, and *cheaper* than brick and mortar. Faster/better/cheaper has become the mantra of electronic commerce, whereas anything, anytime, anywhere has become the mantra of consumers.

Roger Ferguson, Jr. (2000), vice chairman of the Board of Governors of the Federal Reserve, claims that three other words—convenience, confidence, and complexity—are going to help shape the future of electronic commerce and banking.

Convenience refers to the capital, labor, time, and other resources that are needed to make transactions. Customers with computer modems can access banks by using banking software installed on their personal computers, local area networks, or mainframe computers that connect to the bank (U.S. General Accounting Office, January 15, 1998). Others may use Internet service providers in order to access banks through their web sites. Banks may operate their online systems in-house, or they may use third-party vendors.

Experience with strictly online banking services has been mixed. Morgan Online, J. P. Morgan's Internet-only private banking service, found that high net worth customers preferred a combination of Internet-based tools as well as a close relationship with a personal banker (Labate, 2001). Similarly, Bank of America's CEO, Hugh McColl, reported that its most sophisticated Internet customers used all avenues of banking and visited a branch banking center at least once a month (Bennett, 2000). Finally, Charles Schwab, a leading online broker, reports that about 70 percent of its new accounts are opened at branch offices rather than online (Bekier, Flur, and Singham, 2000). Schwab plans to open more branch offices. This suggests that online banking complements brick and mortar banking rather than being a substitute.

Confidence refers to the trust that the parties have in the transactions that generate risks. The risks, which include operational, security, and legal risks, affect both the users and providers of such services. For example, the use of electronic check presentment (ECP) may increase a paying bank's risk of check fraud (U.S. General Accounting Office, January 15, 1998; July 14, 1998). Trust also includes privacy issues.

Finally, *complexity* refers to the ease of making the transactions. To some extent there are tradeoffs among these three factors. Greater convenience may increase security risks, and greater complexity may reduce convenience.

We can look at this issue in another way. The financial services industry, including banking, securities, and insurance, is an information industry that makes extensive use of electronic banking. Richard M. Kovacevich, president and chief executive officer of Wells Fargo & Co., has said that the "winners in this industry will be those who master the management of information and use it to give their customers what they want, and when and where they want it" (Kovacevich, 2000). However, the winners may be software companies rather than banks.

As financial services become unbundled and outsourced, and there is a growing use of open standards (e.g., Open Financial Exchange, OFX) for exchanging account and transaction information over the Internet, software providers such as Intuit and Microsoft may become intermediaries between customers and financial institutions.[9] Another aspect of unbundling and outsourcing is illustrated by firms such as LendingTree.com which advertise to prospective customers that more than 100 banks and lenders will compete to offer mortgage, home equity, and car loans.[10] The challenge for banks is to create value and to retain control over their customers.

Control over the payments, though not mentioned by Ferguson, is another factor that will affect Internet banking (Mantel, 2000). Control includes the ability to review bills, initiate payments, talk to a person, and other factors. It ranked as one of the most important considerations by consumers in their use of electronic bill paying services. In addition, use of checks instead of electronic payments gives some control over "float" and "controlled disbursement" which are designed to speed collections but slow disbursements (McAndrews and Roberds, 2000). In addition, online customers may not understand the implications of certain financial transactions. For example, those shopping for the lowest cost mortgages online may not know the difference between fixed-rate mortgages and adjustable rate mortgages, or the implication of paying "points" up front. Similarly, those shopping for credit cards online may not be aware of the different methods used to compute monthly interest charges.[11] Thus, the mere existence of a new high-tech delivery channel alone may not be sufficient for many customers to change their banking habits. This may be one reason why the online mortgage service, Mortgage.com, failed (Mullaney, 2001).

Profitability depends in part on the quality of products and services that banks offer and in part on costs. The transaction cost of Internet banking is substantially less than that of the other channels of distribution. The estimated transaction cost at a branch was $1, mail-in was $0.70, phone $0.55, ATM $0.28, and the Internet a few cents ("Branching Out," 2000). The fact that some costs are lower does not guarantee profits. The noninterest expenses of Internet banks tend to be higher than those of brick and mortar banks. Moreover, pure Internet banks have not proved to be very profitable, and as a result, many banks are retrenching and combining their Internet banks with their brick and mortar banks (DeYoung, First Quarter, 2001 and September 2001; Mackintosh, 2000). This may help to explain why some banks, such as ABN Amro (Dutch), Vontobel (Swiss), and Lloyds TSB (UK) have scrapped their plans and sell their products on the Internet (Croft, 2001).

RETAIL INTERNET FINANCIAL PRODUCTS AND SERVICES

A July 2000 survey of Internet banking by the Office of the Comptroller of the Currency (OCC) found that more than 90 percent of all national banks with assets of greater than $500 million had web sites ("More National Banks," 2000). In contrast, only 46 percent of banks with assets of less than $100 million had them. The largest banks, those with assets of $10 billion or more, offered the widest range of services and products. Various Internet products and services are listed in Figure 7.1. Although the use of Internet banking is growing, there is still strong demand for physical banks. The number of bank branches in the United States increased from 64,334 in 1985 to 75,166 in 1999.[12]

Although banks have been quick to embrace the Internet, insurers have not been eager users (Healy, 2001). Some insurance products are too complicated to sell online, and customers need the services of an agent. Nevertheless, other products, such as term insurance and long-term care insurance, are expected to do well on the Internet. A study by Brown and Goolsbee (2000) revealed that use of the Internet reduced the cost of term life insurance policies by 8 to 15 percent.

The *aggregation* business—the collection of an individual's financial data from multiple accounts into a single Internet site—is becoming an increasingly important online customer service. Customers provide the aggregators with their security passwords and personal identification numbers so that they can access the accounts.[13] This service can be provided by banks, such as Citibank's www.myciti.com, and by Charles Schwab, Merrill Lynch, Yahoo Finance, America Online, and other firms that offer competing services (Altman, Simon, Bhandari, and Hyatt-Shaw, 2001).

Figure 7.1
Selected Internet Financial Products and Services

Personal Products

- Certificates of deposit
- Checking accounts
- Savings accounts
- Commercial loans
- Consumer loans
- Credit cards
- Home equity loans
- Residential mortgages

Personal Services

- Balance inquiry on deposit accounts
- Balance inquiry on non-deposit retail products
- Bill payment for retail customers
- Bill presentment for retail customers
- Brokerage
- Customer electronic mail
- Fiduciary
- Funds transfer between bank-controlled accounts
- Funds transfer outside of the bank
- Insurance
- New account setup

Business Products and Services

- Cash management
- Checking accounts
- Cash transfer
- Credit products
- Payroll direct deposits
- Savings accounts

Sources: "More National Banks" (2000); Furst, Lang, and Nolle (2000).

RETAIL PAYMENTS SYSTEM

Electronic payments exceeded paper-based payments in the industrialized nations of the world for the first time in 2000 (Teixera, 2000).[14] According to Mester (2001), by 1998, 86 percent of households used some form of electronic payment, with ATMs and direct deposits being the most widely used. Growth of retail electronic payments in the United States is being driven by the increased use of credit cards, debit cards, and automatic clearing house (ACH) transactions (Weiner, 1999). Credit and debit cards provide fee and interest income to the issuers who encourage their use, which is growing. Nevertheless, a survey reported by Mester (2000) found that cash is still the most widely used means of point-of-sale payment, through its share of payments slipped from 79 percent in 1992 to 53 percent in 1997.[15]

Of the noncash transactions (checks, credit cards, debit cards, smart cards, ACH, and wire transfers), checks were the most popular means of payment, followed by credit cards. In 1997, 66 billion checks were written in the United States. The aggregate value of the checks was $77.8 trillion, or about $1,177 per check (McAndrews and Roberds, 2000). That amounts to each U.S. resident writing 250 checks annually.

A study by Mantel (2000) revealed that checks accounted for 59 percent of all noncash transactions in 1997, while a study reported by Weiner (1999) and McAndrews and Roberds (2000) revealed that checks accounted for 72 to 73 percent of all noncash transactions in that same year. The Weiner and McAndrews and Roberds studies did not include ATMs, debit at point-of-sale, or electronic funds transfer, so it may overstate checks' share of noncash transactions. Nevertheless, checks may not be as widely used in other countries. Checks accounted for 42 percent of noncash transactions in France, 36 percent in Canada, 31 percent, in the United Kingdom, 8 percent in Belgium, 6 percent in Germany, and 3 percent in the Netherlands (Weiner, 1999). In contrast, Humphrey (2000) and Palva (2000) found that the use of checks in Norway and Finland declined, whereas in recent years the use of electronic payments increased in both countries. Thus, there may be less resistance and lower costs to establishing electronic payments in those countries than in the United States. However, Mantel's (2000) survey of consumers revealed important differences between nonusers, low users, and high users of electronic bill payment services. The high users tended to have higher incomes and valued convenience more than those who used it less. Mantel also noted significantly different results depending on the types of bill (credit card, insurance, mortgage, telephone, etc.) and control factors, such as when the bill is paid and receipts for payment.

Although consumers are using checks, organizations involved in the payments system are converting paper checks to electronic transactions that are cleared through the ACH system (Mantel, 2001). For example, TeleCheck Electronic Check Acceptance® Service allows firms that receive checks to electronically present the transaction to the check writer's bank for settlement, and the funds are automatically deposited in the firm's account.[16] Along this line, Citigroup has agreements with Microsoft's online money transfer service that allows funds to be sent via e-mail.[17] The National Clearing House Association (NACHA) Electronic Check Council (ECC) is examining payments services that will enable the conversion of paper checks to electronic entries.[18]

Credit cards are the second most popular means of noncash payments, accounting for 18 percent of the total (Weiner, 1999). In 1998, 68 percent of all U.S. families surveyed by the Federal Reserve had credit cards, compared to 16 percent in 1970 (Durkin, 2000). However, they are the most popular means of payment for transactions on the Internet (Teixera, 2000). Internet transactions are a small but growing percentage of overall payments.

According to Mester (2000), the average size of cash payments in 1997 was $20, personal checks $76, credit cards $55, and debit cards $35.[19] In 1998, Mann (2001) reported another study showing that the average credit card transaction was $76. Based on this finding, we can conclude that the average transaction size for each means of payment varied widely.

Retail payments systems are not limited to financial institutions. The U.S. Postal Service has established USPS eBillPay to receive and make retail payments online.[20] The payments made by the USPS can be debited against checking accounts. As an historical note, the United States had an active postal savings system until 1996 (Kuwayama, 1999). Postal savings systems still play an important role in Europe and Japan and are involved in GIRO (payment) services. Online payments systems are the latest method of making person-to-person retail payments; such systems are offered by Citibank, Western Union, and others. Almost anyone with an e-mail address can use person-to-person (or P2P) for sending or receiving funds.[21] P2P requires the use of financial institutions where accounts can be credited or debited.

Finally, new payments mechanisms are being created by wireless technologies.[22] Robert Selander, president and CEO of MasterCard International, sees a strong competitive threat from telecom companies that let consumers in some countries buy goods by using their wireless phones and charging the cost of those goods to their phone bills (Fickenscher, 2000).

INTERNATIONAL WHOLESALE PAYMENTS ISSUES

The Society for Worldwide Interbank Financial Telecommunications (SWIFT) is a financial industry cooperative that dominates the market for messages concerning secure international money transfers and settlement between banks. However, increasing Internet competition is coming from Reuters PLC, Equant NV, J. P. Morgan Chase & Co., and others. As the Internet drives the cost of sending messages down to near zero, SWIFT's prior competitive advantages are disappearing as use of the Internet to send secure messages becomes more widespread.[23]

PRIVACY

The efficient flow of information about customers is at the heart of the financial services industry. As previously noted, the winners in the information-based financial service industry will be those firms that master the management of information and use it to give their customers what they want, when and where they want it. However, Title V of the Gramm-Leach-Bliley Act (GLB) of 1999 and other laws[24] restrict the use and transfer of nonpublic personal information about customers from financial service companies to nonaffiliated third parties.[25] Nonpublic personal information, in general, is "personally identifiable information" that is not "publicly available." Such information includes account balance information, whether the individual is or has been a customer, information collected through an Internet "cookie," information from applications, consumer reports, and so on.

In order to protect consumers, financial institutions are required to provide privacy notices "at the time of establishing a customer relationship" and annually thereafter. The privacy notices contain the type of information that may be collected and how it may be used. Consumers can "opt out" of having the information disclosed by the financial institution.

Financial service providers argue that the cost of restricting the use of consumer information reduces the quality of services that can be provided to them, including slower responses for loans, and affects the ability of firms to offer products and services that are most suitable for the consumer.

BUSINESS-TO-BUSINESS

Although most of the hype about electronic banking focuses on retail banking activities, the greatest dollar volume is on the wholesale side. Trading activity in foreign exchange, for example, is estimated to be $1.5 trillion per day, making it the largest financial market in the world. Most of the trading is handled by bank-sponsored alliances (e.g., Atriax, and FXall.com).[26] Business-to-business (B2B) domestic payments and wire transfers also account for large dollar amounts.[27] Thus, with regard to B2B banks will likely provide bill presentment and payments systems that are faster, cheaper, and better than the current paper-based system.[28] However, companies are not rushing to the new Internet, billing, presentation, and payments (IBPP). Many large companies currently use Financial Electronic Data Interchange, (FEDI, sometimes called EDI), which has some of the features available on IBPP.[29]

REGULATORY ISSUES

Financial Institutions

A recent General Accounting Office Study, "Electronic Banking" (August 1999), found that none of the five financial institution regulatory agencies (Federal Deposit Insurance Corporation, Federal Reserve, National Credit Union Administration, Office of the Comptroller of the Currency, and the Office of Thrift Supervision) had consistent policies for supervising banks, thrifts, and credit unions to mitigate the risks associated with Internet banking. The risks included lack of polices to deal with security issues and standard operating procedures, and insufficient audits. The report also stated that third-party firms providing Internet banking services add to the regulatory challenge. The report recommended that the regulators share information on examining Internet banks.[30]

At the beginning of the twenty-first century, the burden of dealing with electronic banking has fallen mainly on the Federal Reserve, which is charged with regulating banks' role in the payments system. The Electronic Fund Transfer Act (1978) gave the Federal Reserve (Regulation E) limited powers to protect consumers when using electronic banking and payments (Spong, 1994). However, the safety and soundness of nonbank participants in the payments system are not subject to the Fed's scrutiny. This raises some questions about the stability and integrity of the payments system.

The issue becomes more complex when viewed on a global scale. In 1998, the European Central Bank, expressing concerns over monetary policy, the smooth functioning of the payments system, the protection of customers and merchants, and the stability of financial markets, recommended that all issuers of electronic money be subject to prudential regulation (European Central Bank, 1998).

In 2000, the Basel Committee on Banking Supervision produced the Electronic Banking Group Initiatives and White Papers and reported that

> electronic delivery channels raise prudential issues that must be viewed in a new light by supervisors. These include the oversight of outsourcing and partnership arrangements, and the oversight of security and data integrity controls and safeguards, especially when the supporting operations are located in another jurisdiction.

The problem is further complicated by defining what constitutes "banking services" that will affect what institutions are "banks" and subject to licensing and supervision. The key feature of the supervisory approach to dealing with these issues is to "develop supervisory guidance for prudent risk management of e-banking activities." This is consistent with the Federal Reserve's view that the "focus must be on the quality of internal systems and processes for identifying, measuring, monitoring and controlling risk" (Spillenkothen, 1999). The Federal Reserve also hopes that market discipline will be effective. Gup (2000) found that market discipline usually occurs after a significant incident, and it does little to prevent misbehavior.

Electronic Money—Déjà Vu

Money is defined in terms of its functions, which include a generally accepted means of exchange in terms of a defined unit of account. It also acts as a store

Figure 7.2
European Union Definitions of Electronic Money

According to the "Report on Electronic Money," published by the European Central Bank in August 1998, "Electronic Money is broadly defined as an electronic store of monetary value on a technical device that may be widely used for making payments to undertakings other than the issuer without necessarily involving bank accounts in the transaction, but acting as a prepaid bearer instrument."

According to Article 1 of the European Parliament and Council Directive 2000/46/EC, "Electronic money shall mean monetary value as represented by a claim on the issuer which is: (i) stored on an electronic device; (ii) issued on receipt of funds of an amount not less in value than the monetary value issued; (iii) accepted as a means of payment by undertakings other than the issuer."

Source: "Issues Arising from the Emergence of Electronic Money," European Central Bank, *ECB Monthly Bulletin*, November 2000, 49–60.

of value. Historically, four major innovations have influenced how people have paid for things with money: metallic coins, checks, paper money, and payment cards. Now a fifth innovation—electronic money—can be added to the list. Regulating electronic money raises separate but related issues. In general terms, electronic money refers to the variety of ways that electronic and other payment systems can be used as a means of exchange. It includes privately issued credit cards, debit cards, stored value cards, digital cash (also known as ecash, cybercash, Flooz, etc.), and other electronic forms (McAndrews, 1997; Schreft, 1997).[31] (Definitions of electronic money used by the European Union are presented in Figure 7.2.)

Privately issued money—currency that is not backed by the government—in the United States dates back to colonial times. Travelers checks issued by American Express, Cook's, and Visa, as well as stored value cards, are current examples of private money.[32]

There are advantages and disadvantages to each form of money. According to Harvey Rosenblum of the Federal Reserve Bank of Dallas, the major advantage of the current paper system is that it works—it's cheap, it's reliable, and we trust it (Sheenhan, 1998). The disadvantages are that paper currency can be lost or stolen, and there are no records of cash transactions. Furthermore, you can't send cash to someone over a phone line. Electronic money such as Mondex electronic cash can be sent over telephone lines without delay.[33] To date, electronic cash systems have found very limited acceptance in the United States.

If the privately issued electronic money were to become widely accepted, it could threaten the safety, uniformity, and stability of U.S. currency. Privately issued currencies could produce different values of exchange due to lack of acceptance or the risk of default, and the increased risk of fraudulent electronic currencies.

Privately issued money is not legal tender. Stated otherwise, unlike U.S. currency, electronic money it is not suitable for payment of all debts, public and private.[34] Moreover, electronic money is not backed by the U.S. government.

Similar issues arose in the free banking era of the early 1800s in the United States.[35] In New York, notes from 200 different banks circulated. Each issue had had six denominations, resulting in 1,200 different bills (Teixiera, 1999). Because of the problems caused by private money, Abraham Lincoln observed in 1839 that no duty was more imperative on the government than the duty it owed to its people to furnish them with a sound and uniform currency.[36] During this period, some banks closed when they were unable to redeem the currencies that they issued. These problems were not resolved until passage of the National Currency Act in 1864 and its revision as the National Bank Act in 1864. Under these acts, national banks could issue notes that were backed by U.S. bonds deposited with the Comptroller of the Currency. In addition, they were required to hold reserves against their notes and deposits in the form of cash or deposits at national banks in selected cities. Congress passed a 10 percent tax on state bank notes in 1865, which was the beginning of the end of state banks issuing profitable notes. Thus, the National Bank Act helped to establish a uniform currency that was accepted nationwide at par (Spong, 1994).[37]

U.S. and foreign regulators today are faced with the choice of letting the market regulate itself or of limiting who can issue electronic money and stating the conditions under which it can be done. However, a very strong case can be made for some regulation. One rationale for bank regulation is to achieve certain social goals, such as protecting consumers. That same rationale may apply here. For example, who is liable in the event an issuer of electronic money fails?

Another legal issue has to do with the lack of any generally accepted way on the Internet for a merchant to verify the identity of customers making transactions. As a result, the liabilities of the parties are unclear in the event that a transaction is repudiated by the customer who allegedly authorized it using a digital signature (McAndrews, 1997).

Another issue is that *seigniorage*, which can be thought of as the interest saved by the Treasury from having currency that is noninterest-bearing debt circulating as a medium of exchange. To the extent that electronic money replaces currency, there is a cost to the Treasury and to taxpayers. A study in the late 1990s by the Congressional Budget Office estimated that if electronic money were to replace 10 percent of the coin and currency denominations under $10, the government would lose about $370 million per year (Litan and Rauch, 1997). It is also estimated that the Treasury will lose about $20 billion per year if electronic money replaces physical notes and coins (Castle, 1996).The greater the use of electronic money, the greater the loss to the government. In the G-10 countries (Belgium, Canada, Germany, Italy, Japan, Netherlands, Sweden, Switzerland, United Kingdom, and the United States), the effects of seigniorage due to electronic money are estimated to account for 0.7 percent of the gross domestic product (Boeschoten and Hebbink, 1996).

Finally, there is the issue of the cost of operating a checking system. McAndrews and Roberds (2000) argue that the cost of relying on checks is between $60 million and $100 billion per year and that electronic payments would reduce this cost.

Finally, although electronic money is not regulated in the United States, it is subject to regulation in the EU. The Eurosystem's requirements and objectives for electronic money are as follows:[38]

1. Issuers are subject to prudential supervision.
2. Electronic money schemes must have solid and transparent legal arrangements.
3. Electronic money schemes must maintain adequate technical, organizational, and procedural safeguards to prevent, contain, and detect threats to security, particularly counterfeits.
4. Protection against criminal abuses must be taken into account in the design and implementation of electronic money schemes.
5. Electronic money schemes must supply the European Central Bank with whatever information it needs for purposes of monetary policy.
6. Issuers of electronic money must be legally obligated to redeem it at par value.
7. The European Central Bank may impose reserve requirements on all issuers of electronic money.

It is also desirable that electronic money schemes be *interoperable* and adopt an adequate guarantee, insurance, or loss-sharing plan. Interoperable means that the payments belonging to one payments system can be used in other systems.

SECURITY ISSUES

International Frauds

The European Union Bank was chartered as an Internet bank in 1994 in Antigua as an offshore subsidiary of Menatap, a Russian bank whose sole shareholder was in a U.S. prison (Farah, 1996). Banks in Antigua are not well regulated or transparent to law enforcement officials. The newly chartered bank solicited business in the United States. In August 1997, the Russian directors and the depositor's money disappeared.

In 2001, the FBI issued warnings that Russian and Ukrainian hacker rings were breaking into computers of U.S. firms (e.g., Western Union, Creditcards.com; CD Universe) and stealing credit card information on hundreds of thousands of customers (Gomes and Bridis, 2001; Hopper, 2001).[39] The hackers make demands and ask for ransom money, and if it is not paid, the credit card numbers are posted online.

Domestic Frauds

The Common Law of the Republic of Arizona solicited CDs for the Freedom Star National Bank ("Phony Banks," 1997). The CDs paid up to 30 percent per annum on deposits of $5,000 or more and were guaranteed by the Shangri-La Mining and Development Company of Alaska and Arizona. The term *common law* is frequently associated with militia groups. In this case, it was a fraud.

Netware International Bank, an Internet bank, had a North Carolina address, but according to the OCC, no bank charter was ever issued for that bank in North Carolina (OCC Alert, 97–14). Similarly, Citicorp Financial Services (California) is not associated with Citibank; Midland Credit & Guarantee Bank Ltd. (New York) is not associated with Midland Bank (OCC Alert 97–13); and Chase (Trust) Bank is not associated with Chase Manhattan Bank (OCC Alert 2001–1).

According to Castle (1996), concern was expressed in congressional hearings about breaking into stored value cards, such as a Mondex card, without reference to an institution. A hacker could produce the "ultimate" counterfeit by creating value indistinguishable from the original digital cash. It could be replicated millions of times and sent around the world. One consequence would be the potential collapse of a currency.

Computer Attacks

In 1995, Vladimir Levin, a computer operator for a trading company in St. Petersburg, Russia, used a personal computer to try to steal $10 million from Citibank's money transfer system (Hansel, 1995). Citibank, which transfers half a trillion dollars per day, lost only $400,000 to this hacker, but, there are other hackers waiting for their chance. A General Accounting Office study, "Information Security" (1996), revealed that informal hacker groups, such as Legions of Doom and the 2600 Club, share information on the Internet. On the other side of the issue, Microsoft, Unisys Corporation, and Baltimore Technology have announced a deal to provide banks with software that will make their Internet transactions ultrasecure ("Microsoft," 2001).

A U.S. General Accounting Office survey of 33 banks implementing online banking services revealed that 30 percent had security problems (U.S. General Accounting Office, "Electronic Banking," 1998). The most common problem was unauthorized access. The FBI was not able to determine the number of successful unauthorized access attempts.

CONCLUSION

In 2000, a survey of online finance by the *Economist* concluded that "Within a few years, the internet will become the instrument of choice for managing our finances" ("The Digital Future," 2000). The article also stated that the boundaries between banks and other financial service providers will blur, and that bricks and clicks complement each other. As a result, banks will require less of a physical presence than they now have, and the Internet and related technologies may bypass many banks in the payments system. For example, large companies, including Bear Stearns, Dow Chemical, DaimlerChrysler, and Ford, have turned to the Internet to auction their debt instruments, thereby bypassing the traditional financial institutions (Barr, 2000).

Like any new endeavor, only the fittest firms will survive. The European Internet bank First-e was not a survivor (First-e Bank, 2001). First-e operated from Ireland under a banking license from Banque d'Escompte in France. It has about 200,000 customers and 1 billion Euros on deposit; it will close its operations in the UK and Germany but will continue operating in France.

Against this background, the survivors in the market are likely to be those institutions with strong brand identity that can attract profitable customers. Among them will be individual institutions as well as strategic alliances that blend together financial services and technology. The players in the various markets will change. For example, as a result of Freddie Mac's "automated-underwriting" system used by mortgage brokers, the bank's leading role in the home mortgage market is being eroded. Banks may be squeezed out of the mortgage market altogether if and when Freddie Mac and Fannie Mae become lenders (Barta, 2001).

NOTES

1. The definition used here is from the U.S. General Accounting Office, "Payments, Clearance, and Settlements," 1997, p. 183. Furst, Lang, and Nolle (2000) define the term *Internet banking* as a remote delivery channel used for banking services. Internet banking is part of electronic banking as defined here. In addition, ATMs are a mechanical/electronic mechanism used for the delivery of cash. Some ATMs are being integrated into point-of-sale networks to improve the use of online debit cards (Ferguson, 2000).
2. For further discussion of this subject, see Dell (1998).
3. See www.identrus.com.
4. The role of information in financial markets is discussed in Mishkin and Eakins (2000, ch. 14).
5. Examples of retail and small business loans that can be made online can be found at www.bankrate.com and www.lendingtree.com.
6. See www.nexitybank.com.
7. See Couch and Parker (2000).
8. For additional information, see www.moneyshelf.de or visit the web site for Deutsche Bank, http://public.deutsche-bank.de.
9. For further discussion of this point, see "Payments, the Battle Banks Must Win" (2000).
10. See www.lendingtree.com.
11. Online loans are offered at www.quickenloans.quicken.com, www.lendingtree.com, www.priceline.com, and other sites.

12. U.S. Census Bureau, (2001).

13. The aggregators consolidate account information through "screen scraping," which involves the culling of data from other institutions' web sites, often without their knowledge. This may create some security and operational problems (Electronic Banking Group Iniatives, 2000).

14. The Federal Reserve Bank of Chicago's Payment Systems Resource Center is an excellent online source of information about payments systems, electronic banking, e-commerce, and so on. For further information, see www.chicagofed.org/paymentsystem/index/cfm.

15. The figure reported by Mester (2000) are consistent with survey data reported in U.S. Census Bureau, *Statistical Abstract of the United States, 2000*, No. 818, Washington, D.C., 2001.

16. See www.telecheck.com.

17. Beckett (2000).

18. See http://ecc.nacha.org.

19. Mester (2000) also reported transaction sizes for other forms of payment, including certified checks, food stamps, and money orders.

20. For more information about the U.S. Postal System's payment service, see www.usps.gov.

21. See "Now Arriving by E-Mail" (2001).

22. For an excellent discussion of electronic payments mechanisms, see Ganesan (2000).

23. Delaney (2001).

24. The GLBA is Public Law 106–102, and Section 501 deals with privacy. Other related federal laws include the Fair Credit Reporting Act (15 U.S.C. 1681 et seq.); the Electronic Fund Transfer Act (15 U.S.C. 1693 et seq.); the Right to Financial Privacy Act (15 U.S.C. 3401 et seq.); the Children's Online Privacy Protection Act (15 U.S.C. 6501 et seq.); and the Federal Trade Commission Act (15 U.S.C. 41 et seq.).

25. The details of the privacy rules under the GLBA are beyond the scope of this chapter. Nevertheless, it should be noted that customers are consumers, but not all consumers are customers. Anyone who applies for a loan is a consumer. If the loan is denied, that individual will not be a customer of the lender. Being a customer implies a continuing relationship with a financial institution.

26. See "Banks Form Exchange Site" (2000); Condon (2000); Marlin (2001).

27. A U.S. General Accounting Office study ("Retail Payment Issues," 1998) revealed that electronic check presentment (ECP) accounted for 14 percent of the 16 billion total checks collected. However, the GAO did not report the dollar values represented by ECP.

28. See Wenninger (2000) for a discussion of the bank's role in e-commerce.

29. "Internet Billing Gets Its Due" (2001, 30).

30. There were similar recommendations from the Basel Committee on Banking Supervision's "Electronic Banking Group Initiatives (2000)," dealing with cross-border electronic banking.

31. Electronic data capture (EDC) is a point-of-sale terminal that captures information from credit and debit cards and electronically authorizes transactions. By using an encryption standard known as secured electronic transactions (SET) and other means, credit cards can be used for secure transactions over the Internet.

32. See Good (1998) for a discussion of local currency and local electronic trading systems in the United States.

33. Mondex International Ltd. is a subsidiary of MasterCard International. For further information about Mondex, see www.mondex.com.

34. For a discussion of legal tender, see Gup (1994).

35. For a discussion of the free banking era and these issues, see Schreft (1997).

36. *Federal Reserve Bank of Cleveland, 1995 Annual Report*, 1996.

37. Osterberg and Thomson (1998) point out that establishing a uniform currency in the 1800s resulted in forfeiting an elastic money supply.

38. "Issues Arising" (2000).

39. For current information about online attacks, frauds, and warnings, see the National Infrastructure Protection Center (NIPC) web site, www.nipc.gov. The NIPC is the government's focal point for dealing with threats to the U.S. infrastructure, including telecommunications, banking, and other areas. Also see the National Consumer League's National Fraud Information Center at www.fraud.org.

REFERENCES

Altman, Larry, 'Anju Simon, Ami Bhandari, and Zaki Hyatt-Shaw. "Run for the Money: The Battle for Online Aggregation Business." Booz Allen & Hamilton, Developments in Strategy + Business, January 15, 2001, www.strategy-business.com/enews/022501/enews022501.html (visited 1/22/01).

"Banks Form Exchange Site." CNNfn, June 6, 2000 (visited 6/7/00).

Barr, Stephen. "Bond Auctions Go Live." *CFO*, October 2000, 30.

Barta, Patrick. "Why Lenders Fear Mortgage Giants Will Steal Their Turf." *Wall Street Journal*, April 5, 2001, A1, A10.

Beckett, Paul. "Citigroup, Microsoft Sign Pact Allowing MSN Users to Make Web Money Transfers." *Wall Street Journal*, May 1, 2001, B6.

Bekier, Matthias M., Dorlisa K. Flur, and Seelan J. Singham. "A Future for Bricks and Mortar." *U.S. Banker*, October 2000, 76.

Bennett, Robert A. "McColl Sees the Future." *U.S. Banker, e-banking*, September 2000, www.us-banker.com/usb/articles/usbsep00-cs1.shtml (visited 1/16/01).

Boeschoten, W. C., and G. E. Hebbink. *Electronic Money, Currency Demand and Seigniorage Loss in the G-10 Countries*. DNB-Staff Reports, De Nederlandsche Bank NV, Amsterdam, The Netherlands, 1996.

"Branching Out." On Line Finance Survey, *Economist*, May 20, 2000, 19–20.

Brown, Jeffry, and Austan Goolsbee. "Does the Internet Make Markets More Competitive? Evidence from the Life Insurance Industry." John F. Kennedy School of Government, Harvard University, Faculty Research Working Paper, October 2000.

Burns, Tom. "BBVA Launches Online Bank." FT.com, *Financial Times*, February 14, 2000 (visited 3/6/00).

Castle, Michael N. Remarks by the Honorable Michael N. Castle, Chairman, Subcommittee on Domestic and International Monetary Policy, presented at "Toward Electronic Money & Banking: The Role of Government," U.S. Department of Treasury, Washington, D.C., September 19–20, 1996.

Condon, Tom. "Dueling Forex Titans." *U.S. Banker*, December 2000, 55–60.

Couch, Karen, and Donna Parker. " 'Net Interest' Grows as Banks Rush Online." Federal Reserve Bank of Dallas, *Southwest Economy*, March/April 2000, 1–5.

Croft, Jane. "ABN Amro Abandons Plans to Sell on the Internet." FT.com, *Financial Times*, March 16, 2001 (visited 3/16/01).

Delaney, Kevin J. "Swift, Global Banking's Messenger, Is Less Fleet-Footed." *Wall Street Journal*, June 12, 2001, A17.

Dell, Michael. "The Virtual Firm." *The World in 1999, Economist*, 1998, 96.

DeYoung, Robert. "The Financial Performance of Pure Play Internet Banks." Federal Reserve Bank of Chicago, *Economic Perspective*, First Quarter 2001, 60–75.

DeYoung, Robert. "Learning-by-Doing, Scale Efficiencies, and Financial Performance at Internet-Only Banks." Federal Reserve Bank of Chicago, Working Paper Series (WP-01-06), September 2001.

"The Digital Future." Survey of Online Finance, *Economist*, May 20, 2000, 52.

Durkin, Thomas A. "Credit Cards: Use and Consumer Attitudes 1970–2000." *Federal Reserve Bulletin*, September 2000, 623–634.

"Electronic Banking Group Initiatives and White Papers." Bank for International Settlements, Basel Committee for Banking Supervision, October 2000.

European Central Bank. "Report on Electronic Money." August 1998, www.ecb.int/pub/pdf/emoney.pdf (visited 12/23/00).

Farah, Douglas. "Russian Crime Finds a Haven in Caribbean." *Washington Post*, October 7, 1996, A15.

Federal Register, Rules and Regulations. Vol. 65, No. 106 (12, CFR 40, 216, 332, 573), June 1, 2000, 35162–35236.

Federal Reserve Bank of Cleveland 1995 Annual Report. Cleveland, Ohio: Author, 1996.

Ferguson, Roger W., Jr. "Electronic Commerce, Banking, and Payments." Remarks by Roger W. Ferguson, Jr., Vice Chairman, Board of Governors of the Federal Reserve System, before the 36th Annual Conference on Bank Structure and Competition, Federal Reserve Bank of Chicago, May 4, 2000.

Fickenscher, Lisa. "Card Banks Told to Make Telecoms Partners, or Have Them as Rivals." *American Banker*, April 7, 2000, 1, 9.

"First-e Bank to Close in UK and Germany." *BBC News*, September 7, 2001, http://news.bbc.co.uk (visited 9/9/01).

Furst, Karen, William W. Lang, and Daniel E. Nolle. "Internet Banking: Developments and Prospects." Office of the Comptroller of the Currency, Working Paper 2009, September 2000.

Furst, Karen, William W. Lang, and Daniel E. Nolle. "Who Offers Internet Banking." Office of the Comptroller of the Currency, *Quarterly Journal*, Vol. 19, No. 9, June 2000, 29–48.

Ganesan, Ravi. "Electronic Bill Payment." In *Promoting the Use of Electronic Payments: Assessing Future Requirements*, Federal Reserve Bank of Chicago, 2000, 64–78.

Gomes, Lee, and Ted Bridis. "FBI Warns of Russian Hackers Stealing Credit-Card Data from U.S. Computers." *Wall Street Journal*, March 8, 2001, A4.

Good, Barbara A. "Private Money: Everything Old Is New Again." Federal Reserve Bank of Cleveland, *Economic Commentary*, April 1, 1998.

Gup, Benton E. "The Changing Role of Legal Tender: An Historical Perspective." In *Marketing Exchange Relationships, Transactions, and Their Media*, Franklin S. Houston, ed. Westport, Conn.: Quorum Books, 1994, 239–246.

Gup, Benton E. "Market Discipline and the Corporate Governance of Banks: Theory vs. Evidence." In *The New Financial Architecture: Banking Regulation in the 21st Century*, Benton E. Gup, ed. Westport, Conn.: Quorum Books, 2000, 187–206.

Hansel, Saul. "A $10 Million Lesson in the Risks of Electronic Banking." *New York Times News Service*, August 19, 1995.

Harris, Clay. "First-e, Uno-e Combine, Form First Global Online Bank." FT.com, *Financial Times*, March 6, 2000 (visited 3/6/00).

Healy, Beth. "Insurers Slow to Hop on Boat of Internet Services." *Tuscaloosa News*, March 4, 2001, 13J.

Hopper, D. Ian. "Credit Card Hacker Issued Warning." www.washingtonpost.com, March 9, 2001 (visited 3/9/01).

Humphrey, David. "International Comparisons: Lessons Learned." In *Promoting the Use of Electronic Payments: Assessing Future Requirements*, Federal Reserve Bank of Chicago, 2000, 11–19.

"Internet Billing Gets Its Due." *CFO*, February 2001, 30.

"Issues Arising from the Emergence of Electronic Money." European Central Bank, *ECB Monthly Bulletin*, November 2000, 49–60.

Kovacevich, Richard M. "*Privacy* and the *Promise* of Financial Modernization." Federal Reserve Bank of Minneapolis, *The Region*, March 2000, 27–29.

Kuwayama, Patricia Hagan. "Postal Banking in the United States and Japan: A Comparative Analysis." Bank of Japan, *IMES Discussion Paper Series*, No. 99-E-18, June 1999.

Labate, John. "Ameritrade to Cut Workforce." FT.com, *Financial Times*, January 8, 2001 (visited 1/9/01).

Litan, Robert E., and Jonathan Rauch. *American Finance for the 21st Century*, U.S. Department of the Treasury, November 17, 1997.

Mackintosh, James. "How Banking on the Internet Has Become a Fallen Icon." FT.com, *Financial Times*, October 27, 2000 (visited 3/15/01).

Mann, Ronald J. "Card-Based Payment Systems in the United States and Japan." Bank of Japan Institute for Monetary and Economic Studies. *IMES Discussion Paper Series*, No. 2001-E-2, February 2001.

Mantel, Brian. "E-money and E-commerce: Two Alternative View of Future Innovation." Federal Reserve Bank of Chicago, *Chicago Fed Letter*, March 2001.

Mantel, Brian. "Why Do Consumers Pay Bills Electronically? An Empirical Analysis." Federal Reserve Bank of Chicago, *Economic Perspectives*, Fourth Quarter 2000, 32–47.

Marlin, Steven. "50 Leading Banks Kick Off Online FX Venture." *Bank Systems and Technology*, Issue 3801, January 1, 2001, www.banktech.com (visited 1/11/01).

"Mastercard International Fact Sheet." www.mastercard.com (visited 1/18/01).

McAndrews, James J. "Making Payments on the Internet." Federal Reserve Bank of Philadelphia, *Business Review*, January–February 1997, 3–14.

McAndrews, James J., and William Roberds. "The Economics of Check Float." Federal Reserve Bank of Atlanta, *Economic Review*, Fourth Quarter 2000, 17–27.

Mester, Loretta J. "The Changing Nature of the Payments System: Should New Players Mean New Rules?" Federal Reserve Bank of Philadelphia, *Business Review*, April 2000, 3–26.

"Microsoft Strikes Banking Deal." Washingtonpost.com, May 7, 2001, www.washingtonpost.com (visited 5/9/01).

Mishkin, Frederic S., and Stanley G. Eakins. *Financial Markets and Institutions*, 3rd ed. Reading, Mass.: Addison-Wesley, 2000.

"Moneyshelf.de—One-click Optimization of Personal Finances." Deutsche Bank, *Cur-*

rent Issues, August 30, 2000. http://public-deutsche-bank/de/global (visited 12/18/00).

"More National Banks Offer Internet Services, But Active On-Line Customers Are Few." Office of the Comptroller of the Currency, *News Release*, NR 2000–84, October 27, 2000.

Mullaney, Timothy J. "Gone But Not Forgotten." *Business Week*, January 22, 2001, EB14-EB16.

"Now Arriving by E-Mail . . . Money." *FDIC Consumer News*, Summer 2001, 3.

"OCC Alert 97–13." Office of the Comptroller of the Currency, June 20, 1997.

"OCC Alert 97–14." Office of the Comptroller of the Currency, June 24 1997.

"OCC Alert 2001–1." Office of the Comptroller of the Currency, February 21, 2001.

Osterberg, William P., and James B. Thomson. "Bank Notes and Stored-Value Cards: Stepping Lightly into the Past." Federal Reserve Bank of Cleveland, *Economic Commentary*, September 1, 1998.

Palva, Marianne. "International Comparisons: Lessons Learned." In *Promoting the Use of Electronic Payments: Assessing Future Requirements*, Federal Reserve Bank of Chicago, 2000, 31–40.

Payments, the Battle Banks Must Win." Booz-Allen & Hamilton, Banking and Capital Market Group, 2000, www.bah.com (visited 1/18/01).

"Phony Banks Multiply on the Internet." *Future Banker*, August 1997, 21.

Power, Carol, and Adriana Senior. "Small Steps, Giant Leaps." *American Banker*, Century Edition, December 1999, 102–106.

Promoting the Use of Electronic Payments: Assessing Future Requirements. Federal Reserve Bank of Chicago, 2000.

Ridgway, Nichole. "Down to the Wire." *Forbes*, November 13, 2000, 222–228.

Schreft, Stacey L. "Looking Forward: The Role of Government in Regulating Electronic Cash." Federal Reserve Bank of Kansas City, *Economic Review*, Fourth Quarter 1997, 59–84.

Sheenhan, Kevin P. "Electronic Cash." Federal Deposit Insurance Corporation, *FDIC Banking Review*, Vol. 11, No. 2, 1998, 1–8.

Spillenkothen, Richard. "Remarks by Richard Spillenkothen, Director, Division of Supervision and Regulation, Federal Reserve Board, at the New York State Banking Department," October 25, 1999.

Spong, Kenneth. *Banking Regulation: Its Purposes, Implementation, and Effects*, 4th ed. Federal Reserve Bank of Kansas City, 1994.

Spong, Kenneth. *Banking Regulation: Its Purposes, Implementation, and Effects*, 5th ed. Federal Reserve Bank of Kansas City, 2000.

Teixeira, Diogo. "Keynote Address." In *Promoting the Use of Electronic Payments: Assessing Future Requirements*. Federal Reserve Bank of Chicago, 2000, 48, 57.

Teixeira, Diogo. "Looking Back to Look Ahead." *American Banker*, Century Edition, December 1999, 98–100.

U.S. Census Bureau. *Statistical Abstract of the United States, 2000*. No. 798, Washington, D.C., 2001.

U.S. General Accounting Office. "Electronic Banking—Experiences Reported by Banks Implementing On-Line Banking." GAO/GGD-98–34, January 15, 1998.

U.S. General Accounting Office. "Electronic Banking: Enhancing Federal Oversight of Internet Banking Activities." Statement of Richard J. Hillman, Associate Director Financial Institutions and Markets Issues General Government Division before the Subcommittee on Domestic and International Monetary Policy, Committee on Banking and Financial Services, House of Representatives, GAO/GGD-99–152, August 3, 1999.

U.S. General Accounting Office. "Information Security." GAO/AIMD 96–84, May 1996.

U.S. General Accounting Office, "Payments, Clearance, and Settlement." GAO/GGD-97–73, June 1997.

U.S. General Accounting Office. "Retail Payment Issues: Experience with Electronic Check Presentment." GAO/GGD-98–145, July 14, 1998.

Weiner, Stuart E. "Electronic Payments in the U.S. Economy: An Overview." Federal Reserve Bank of Kansas City, *Economic Review*, Fourth Quarter 1999, 53–64.

Wenninger, John. "The Emerging Role of Banks in E-Commerce." Federal Reserve Bank of New York, *Current Issues*, Vol. 6, No. 3, March 2000.

Chapter 8

The New Institutional Structure of Banking: A Framework for Survival in the Digital Age

Susan Hine and Ronnie J. Phillips

INTRODUCTION

Banking has been undergoing dramatic changes over the past two decades. International competition and global banking, increased demand for information technology, the start of e-commerce, and a continued push for cost efficiencies through consolidations are some of the major factors that have contributed to these changes. What is perhaps most interesting, however, is the driver behind these factors of change: *the consumer*. Although this may appear to be a simplistic and rather obvious fact, consumer-driven products and services are a relatively new concept to business in general and banking specifically. In fact, it is only recently that banks have even seemed ready to recognize the importance of treating the industry as a "business," thus *inheriting* a new institutional structure for banking as a whole. Retaining the customer who, as a result of technology, now has options other than those provided by the traditional brick and mortar bank has led to the creation of new customer service models and a new way of doing business. This chapter will look at this new institutional structure and its implications for the future survival of commercial banks in the United States.

BANKING AS A BUSINESS

The Consumer

In the 1920s, General Motors (GM) developed the prototype of a good business profitability model that was product driven; GM simply developed an automobile that the public would buy. It is important to remember that at this time in U.S. history, prices had been relatively constant and competition was seen mainly as a domestic concern. In fact, from the mid-1920s to well into the 1960s, a firm could realistically set a long-range target of return on profit with fairly certain production volume due to a regime of relatively stable prices (Nagle and Holden, 1995). Given this scenario, it seemed appropriate to view pricing decisions from a long-term perspective. Banks were no exception to this rule. A bank had to be very poorly managed in order to suffer a loss. In addition, banking customers had very few product choices, which primarily consisted of checking or passbook savings accounts. The system was completely product driven with little concern placed on customer value.

The 1960s were followed by a decade that included two recessions, double-digit inflation, stagflation, and the start of what would become dramatic technological advances. A significant outcome of these technological changes was the shortening of product life cycles, with the result that firms could no longer rely on long-term pricing strategies. Yet both banks and other industry firms were slow to recognize the change in the traditional model of doing business, a model that embraced a product-driven orientation focused on products that were cost efficient.

Cost-Based Pricing:
Product→ Cost→ Price→ Value→ Customer

(Nagle and Holden, 1995)

Things were brought to a head, however, in the U.S. automobile industry. In the 1970s, increased fuel prices found consumers looking for the more fuel-efficient and often better-made cars offered by the Japanese automakers. Fat and happy U.S. auto manufacturers were left in a lurch totally unprepared for the fact that consumers would not continue to buy whatever cars they manufactured. As a result, the first break from the traditional model occured when Lee Iacocca (of the Ford Industry) chose to venture out into new territory through production of the Mustang.

Rather than take the traditional approach of building a car that fit within the cost structure of the producer and assuming that consumers would purchase it, Iacocca and the team at Ford discovered through their research that there was a market "out there" waiting for an inexpensive sports car. The result was the Mustang, which was an instant success with record sales in the first year (Iacocca, 1984). Iacocca had introduced a new model for business that had totally reinvented the old one by reversing the directional flow of information; the consumer was now directing how product and service should be delivered:

Value-Based Pricing:
Customers→ Value → Price→ Cost→ Product

(Nagle and Holden, 1995)

This model is applicable to the banking industry as well. It is no longer possible to deliver a product and assume that the customer will want it, for banks no longer enjoy a monopoly with respect to both payments and lending products. Rather, banks (as is the case with other industries) must offer a product that delivers value to the customer. Banks can no longer rely on providing products that customers like today; rather, it has become important to be more proactive and less defensive by determining what is going to be the value product/service that the customer will demand tomorrow. As part of this process, it is important for banks:

- To deliver effective and efficient technology
- To provide products and distribution options
- To acquire and manipulate ever-greater amounts of customer data (Gandy, 2000)

Currently, banks are struggling not only to gain a new customer base but also to retain that base once it is in place. With the traditional brick and mortar banks of the past, customer retention was not such a difficult task, but with the many new products and services currently afforded the consumers today, banks need to be more conscious of the value-based model. Customers have wireless banking, electronic banking, electronic cash, and ATMs (to name but a few innovations) at their disposal, and even though they may have a primary bank where they do business, this does not negate the use of other facilities. Customers are no longer loyal to one bank. A survey of 459 bank consumers conducted by O'Neil Associates (Vandeveire, 1997) showed that 41 percent would switch banks if they found something better. Thus, customers will go where they can receive the highest return, and they have many options from a supply-side perspective, as depicted by Thomas Monahan's (2000) new Paradox of Primacy in Figure 8.1. As shown in the figure, only 2 percent of consumers actually did their borrowing with their primary banker and only 10 percent had a majority of their deposits with this bank.

This trend will continue as the industry and technology continue to change. Some of the major trends identified by Karmarkar (2000) include the following:

- Consumers who are more familiar with computers and online access
- Increasing simplicity in methods for accessing online resources
- High penetration of online access and of broad-bank services to the home
- Increasing levels of transaction automation (e.g., voice response)
- Higher customer expectations for integrated services with easy access
- Increasing comfort levels with the use of electronic payment methods
- Higher transaction volumes due to easy access and lower transaction costs

Figure 8.1
Primary Provider

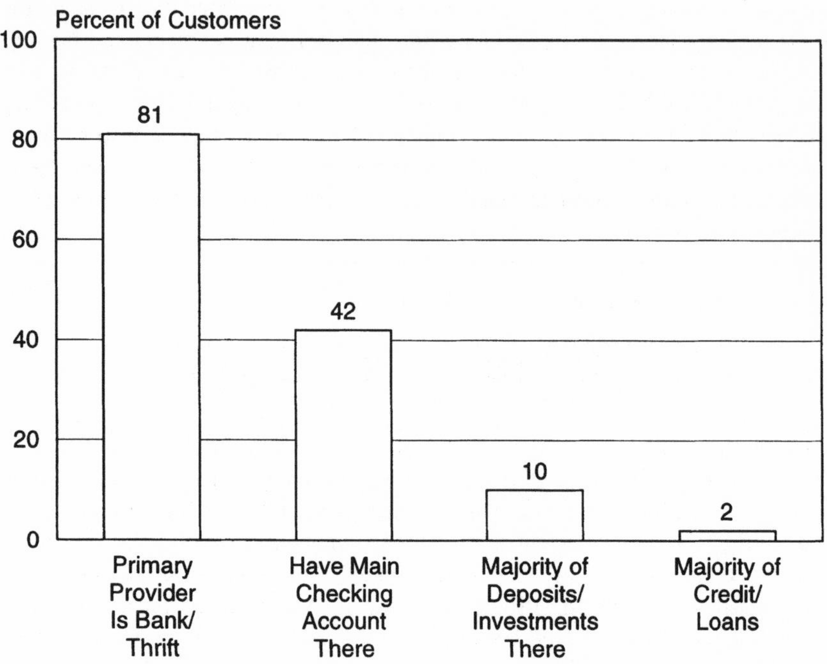

Source: Author, based on BAI National Payment System Symposium and Monahan (2000).

Customers now have greater access to the capital markets and can more easily find and change to new providers given their comfort with the web. Where it used to take five hours to shop for a CD rate, consumers can now hop on the web and locate rates in less than one minute (Monahan, 2000). Basically, this advance has dictated the end of an oligopoly era for bankers. Until the 1980s, nearly 75 percent of business was completed with the primary provider; that level is now less than 20 percent. The buying power of the average banking customer fits nicely into Michael Porter's model of key determinants of buyer power as shown in Table 8.1.

The oligopoly era of banking is over, and the customer will continue to demand new and better products, will switch to new providers quickly, will find information more easily, and may even do more and more of the "legwork" personally. All of these factors mean more buying power for the consumer.

> Institutions are beginning to integrate non-proprietary products into their relationship management platform providing choice among competing product sets and establishing themselves as navigators among complex offerings. This activity, which began in the mutual fund business, is rapidly moving to incorporate mortgage lending, credit cards, insurance, and other products. (Monahan, 2000, 102)

Table 8.1
Buying Power of the Consumer

Key Determinant	**Impact on Banking Customer**
Relative Choice of Products	Rising
Buyer Switching Costs	Falling
Buyer Information	Rising
Ability to Backward Integrate (do work him/herself)	Rising

Source: Porter (1985).

By understanding this change in their institutional structure, banks can begin working to properly segment their target markets while keeping in mind the new buying power of their customers. An understanding of this new business structure that is powered by consumer-driven product/service offerings also means understanding how information technology has impacted the industry as a whole.

INFORMATION TECHNOLOGY

> [A] man honored for fifty years of service to a Virginia bank, who was asked at the party the bank gave to celebrate him what he thought had been "the most important thing, the most important change that you have seen in banking in this half-century of service." The man paused for a few minutes, finally got up before the microphone, and said, "Air conditioning." (Mayer, 1997, 16)

Although this anecdote is humorous, we tend to forget about some of the basic technological improvements that are now taken for granted. The first digital form of technology that helped to revolutionize how business was conducted in the United States was the telegraph. "The telegraph made enormous contributions to productivity growth in many industries, especially railroads and the financial sector" (Phillips, 2000, 278). In order to maintain security, banks needed telegraphic code books enabling "technological" transfer of financial information over the telegraph lines. In addition, only 80 years ago, record-keeping in banks was a paper-based process limited to the use of a typewriter and adding machine and was all a part of backroom operations. In essence, however, all of this was the precursor of what would become the technology center of the bank in the future. In the 1960s, the emerging technology wave began to increase the operational needs of the bank with the advent of credit cards, followed later by ATM networks, money market mutual funds, direct deposit, and home equity lines. With the addition of the Internet, these services now range from electronic cash payments and wireless transactions to E-signatures and automated decision-making processes.

Yet, in spite of these changes, technology is sometimes still relegated to back-room operations, although most banks (and other financial institutions) give these operations the more sophisticated name of information technology (IT). In the beginning of this technological transformation, it was (and in some cases still is) common for the small IT department to be responsible for the day-to-day operations of the bank, leaving this group very little time to be on the forefront of the revolutionary change that was occurring with increasing intensity (McGilloway, 2000).

The spur for these most recent changes had its seeds in the 1980s with the start of deregulation, which in turn spawned securitization in the financial services sector.[1] Combining these two phenomena with the newly arrived Internet technology, the new forms of e-business were created and now exist throughout the world. This "disruptive technology," as it is called by many, has had a tremendous impact on the bank's institutional form, forcing it not only to accept the value-added business model as discussed in the previous section, but also to restructure its traditional banking organization. "Technology is not a part of the strategy—often it is the strategy. As a bank needs knowledge of its customers to succeed, so it also needs knowledge of technology, its future and its applications, to intercept market opportunities" (Gandy, 2000, 163).

Thus, the IT unit should no longer just be the place where bank operations are conducted but a place that can serve as the necessary catalyst for change as banks move to a greater business and customer orientation. This means that the group also has the important job of communicating its ideas to individuals who may not see the need for the value model of business, further emphasizing the need for IT to be part of the strategic planning process. The adoption of the radio serves as one of the classic examples portraying this necessary integration: " 'The wireless music box has no imaginable commercial value. Who would pay for a message sent to nobody in particular?' David Sarnoff's associates in response to his urgings for investment in the radio in the 1920s" (Gandy, 2000, 19).

With increased worldwide competition, banks need to be competitive and aggressive in their approach to business in order to keep their customer base. This means integrating the IT unit with the strategic decision-making individuals of the bank and not leaving IT to backroom operations. Tables 8.2 and 8.3 show how dramatically this *institutional* change has affected banking.

The move from the traditional vertical institution to the horizontal market structure has meant that the list of the traditional vertically oriented processes conducted by banks in the past has been *disintermediated*, leading to the development of new niche products. These products tend to start with higher margins, low liquidity, and higher risks, for they are new and unknown to the public in general, but this quickly changes as the product becomes "commoditized" or more widely accepted. This is particularly striking with the change in commer-

Table 8.2
Changing Institutional Structure of the Banking Industry

The Old "Vertical" Institution	The New "Horizontal" Institution
Defined geographic domain	Global, borderless, ill-defined
Scheduled operational hours	Continuous operations
Regulated/protected	De-, re-, and unregulated
Narrowly focused products/services	Broad, integrated solutions
Long product cycles	Accelerated life cycles
Lifetime employment	Career "resets" every 3 to 4 years
Self-contained operating model	Open, permeable model
Proprietary infrastructure	Standardized, common infrastructure
Central administration	Distributed and networked
Balance Sheet/Fixed Asset	Capital Market/Virtual Assets
Hierarchical mentality	Matrix management; alliances

Source: Author, based on McGilloway (2000).

Table 8.3
Commoditization of New Banking Products

	Niche	Mature	Commodity
Market	Complex, new	Maturing	Well understood
Example	Structured credit	Corporate bonds	U.S. governments
Liquidity	Low	Medium/high	High
Margins	High	Medium	Low
Commercial/Residential Mortgages	> 15%	0–15%	Declining
Information Technology Emphasis	Speed, flexibility	Control	Efficiency

Source: Author, based on McGilloway (2000).

cial/residential mortgages, which had traditionally been associated only with savings and loan institutions and commercial banks.

Another important fact associated with IT is the cost. There is a natural perception that technology reduces costs of products, goods, and services, and in many cases this perception is true. Banks, however, are finding that this is

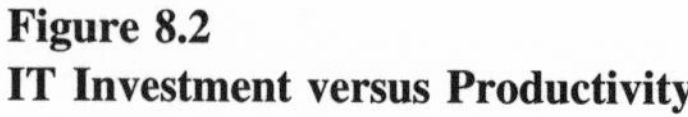

Figure 8.2
IT Investment versus Productivity

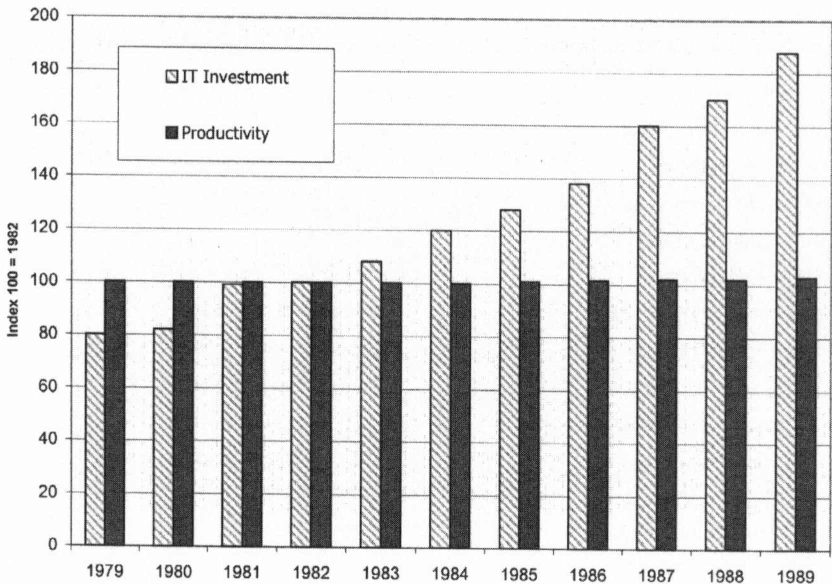

Source: Gandy (2000).

generally not the case. For example, although the cost of computers has been falling with increasing speed over the past decade, the cost of implementing an entire computer system is rising dramatically. Trying to maintain "a hotchpotch of systems with 30,000 end-users in 100 different departments and 500 different functions" is very expensive indeed (Gandy, 2000, 34). It has been estimated that the cost of owning a personal computer in a corporate environment is approximately $8,179 and of that total only $2000 represents the actual purchase price (Gandy, 2000). According to Sullivan (2000), Internet banks do have higher noninterest expenses, which includes the cost of web site development and promotion, data processing costs, and employee training. Although these increased expenses do not necessarily equate with lower profits, an interesting paradox has nonetheless occurred. Although investment in IT has increased dramatically over the past two decades, productivity has not changed much at all (see Figure 8.2).

Part of the explanation for this poor increase in productivity is that banks have doubled the amount of money they have spent on technology since 1987 and "unfortunately, capital has not been effectively replacing the labor component of bank expenses" (Cutler, 2000, 466). The number of commercial bank employees is down about 3 percent, but banks are spending 16 percent more on technology and labor combined (Cutler, 2000). This is not to say that technology

Figure 8.3
Old and New Models for Bank Organization

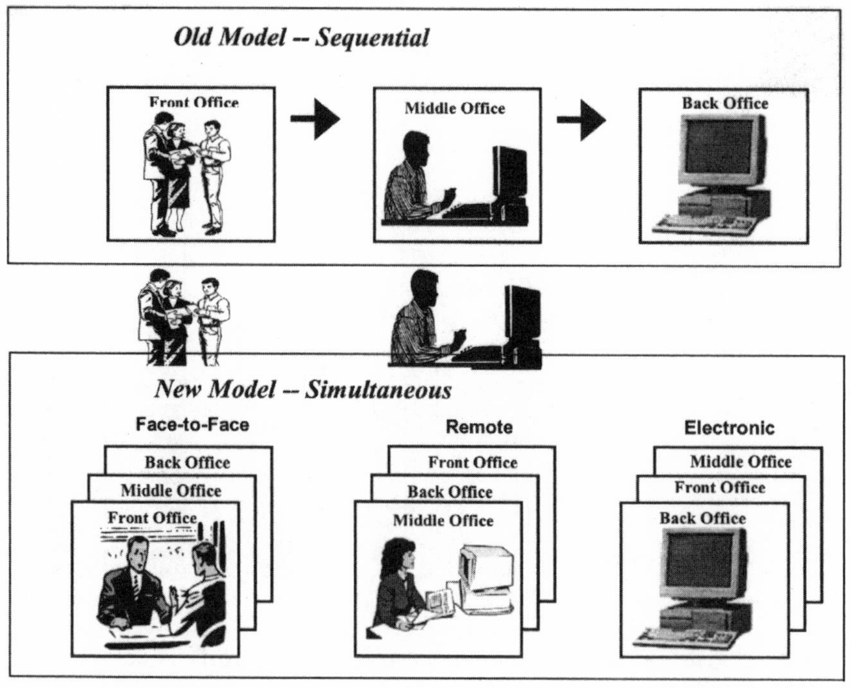

Source: Author, based on Cutler (2000).

is too expensive and should not be undertaken. That is simply not an option for banks if they wish to remain competitive. It is just important to remember that technology is not equivalent with cost savings; rather, it is usually a high-cost expense because it requires the hiring of knowledgeable and well-educated individuals to manage the technology unit. This cost needs to be added to the bank's operations, and that is why it should be undertaken as part of a strategic decision-making process. This policy change in turn leads to a new paradigm of simultaneous business design, as shown in Figure 8.3. This new structure dictates the need for banks to operate on all fronts simultaneously if they are to be competitive in the new IT environment. This requires sound planning and incorporating IT in the strategic decision-making process in order to keep costs manageable while allowing for an improvement in productivity and profits—important goals for most banking institutions.

The Internet

The increased importance of the Internet as a part of IT warrants special attention here. The rise of the Internet has been characterized as one of those

Figure 8.4
Banks Using Web Sites

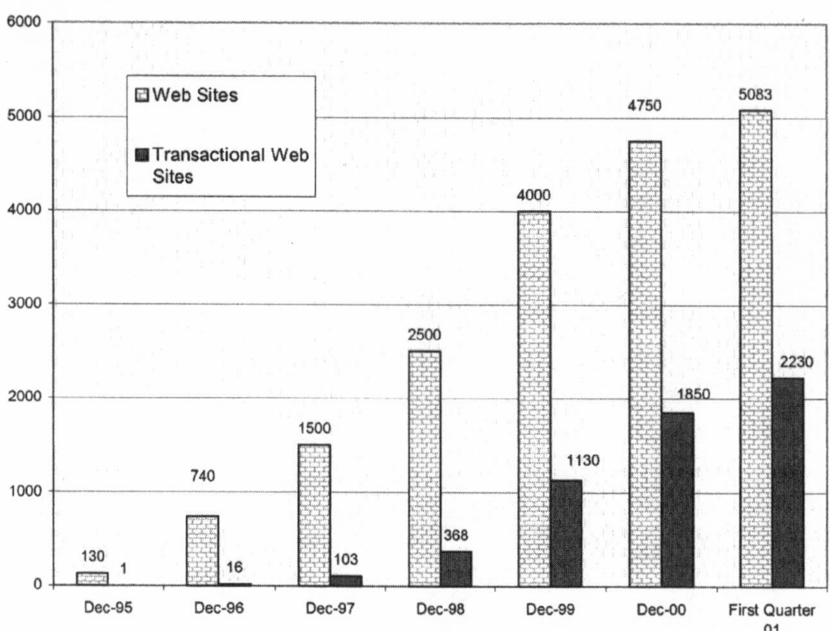

Source: Call Report data and informal off-site monitoring (Bonnette, 2001).

revolutionary technologies that has dramatically changed the way people work and live, much as the telephone, personal computers, and television have done in the past. Although adoption rates for new technology may vary across countries and cultures with respect to the impact of electronic (e) banking, this adoption has been gradual but steady within the United States and is slowly gaining a foothold worldwide. Thus, given that the banking industry is about the exchange of information (payments-related information in this case), it is not surprising that banking has been particularly impacted by what the Internet offers the customer.

As of the first quarter of 2001, 51 percent of all banks and thrifts had a web site, with 23 percent having a transactional web site (Bonnette, 2001). Most of the largest national banks do offer Internet banking, with smaller banks accounting for a much lower amount of transactions (Furst, Lang, and Nolle, 2000). The need for banks to have web sites, however, will only continue to grow, for it is estimated that by 2003, about 23 million households will be using Internet banking. As Figure 8.4 shows, during the first quarter of 2001, 51 percent of all banks and thrifts had a web site and 23 percent had a transactional web site. Figure 8.5 also shows the importance of how consumer and customer retention serves as a primary motivator for Internet banking drivers.

Figure 8.5
Internet Banking Drivers

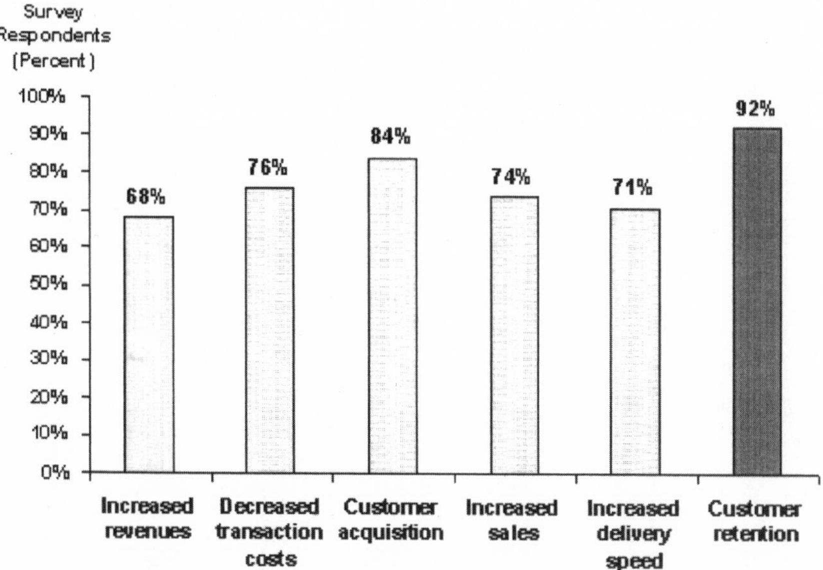

Source: Bonnette (2001).

Four basic characteristics are quite unique to e-banking and help to explain why it has become such an important part of the banking strategic planning process. First, the customer has anonymity when making transactions over the Internet, forcing banks to find methods to authenticate who the users are. Speed of transactions, access to global markets, and strong reliance on third parties to develop and maintain the technology-based systems are the other important components of e-banking's popularity and success. In addition, e-banking is made up of a broad category of systems and devices, including one of its first and perhaps most common forms—credit and debit card development (Bonnette, 2001). In addition to the debit and credit cards, terms that have now become very familiar include PC banking, Internet banking, wireless banking, and electronic data interchange (EDI).[2]

As already discussed, it is expected that adoption of technology will in and of itself reduce costs for firms using it, and this expectation extends to e-banking. Courchane, Nickerson, and Sullivan (2001) examine and empirically test how sunk investment costs in e-banking can endogenously create alternative forms of competition between banks in a game-theoretic framework. However, not only has cost reduction not occurred, but bank costs are actually increasing in many cases. Banks expected that technology adoption would reduce general and administrative (G&A) expenses since electronic transactions are by definition cheaper than delivery by physical channels (see Figure 8.6). Unfortunately, how-

Figure 8.6
Percentage of U.S. Households Using Delivery Channels

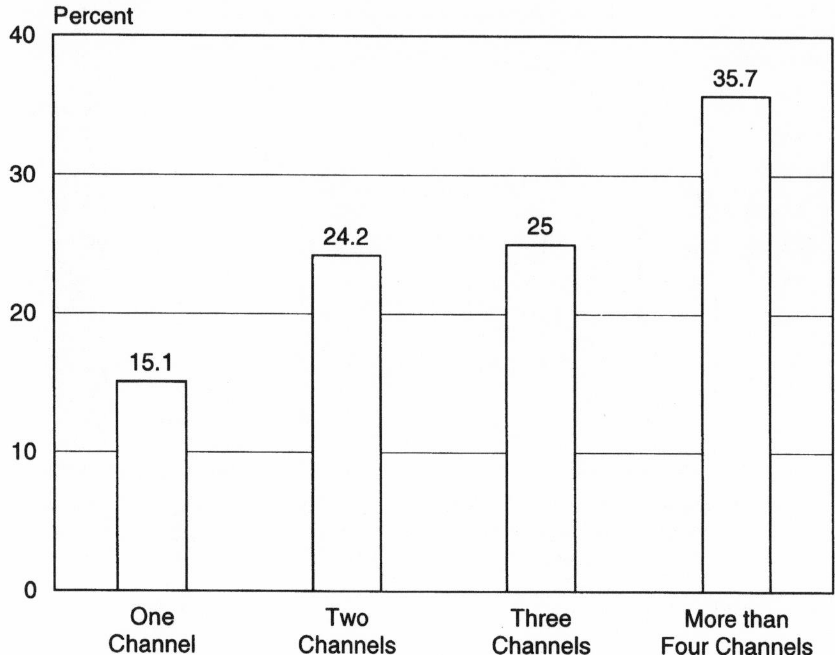

Source: Author, based on Frei and Harker (2000).

ever, most customers do not want to totally relinquish use of the branch and phone. Thus, banks have been unable to close as many branches as they had originally anticipated. Added to this is the cost of hiring technologically astute personnel capable of running the more advanced operating systems, not to mention the need for additional advertising promoting the Internet banking system, (Bonnette, 2001). In essence, customers want both the clicks and the bricks.

E-banking first evolved from a purely informational web site to one with increasingly interactive capabilities, next moving to one with more transactional offerings, and finally on to a site that provides more sophisticated and complex products (see Figure 8.7). Depending on the customer base (retail or commercial), Internet offerings have varied, with some banks providing unique services for each category. Some banks have even used the strategy of offering a complex system of products from the very onset of Internet services (Bonnette, 2001).

Who Are the Players?

The banks that are engaged in these e-banking activities can be categorized into three main types. *Bricks and clicks*, the first type, are traditional banks that

Figure 8.7
Web Site Functionality

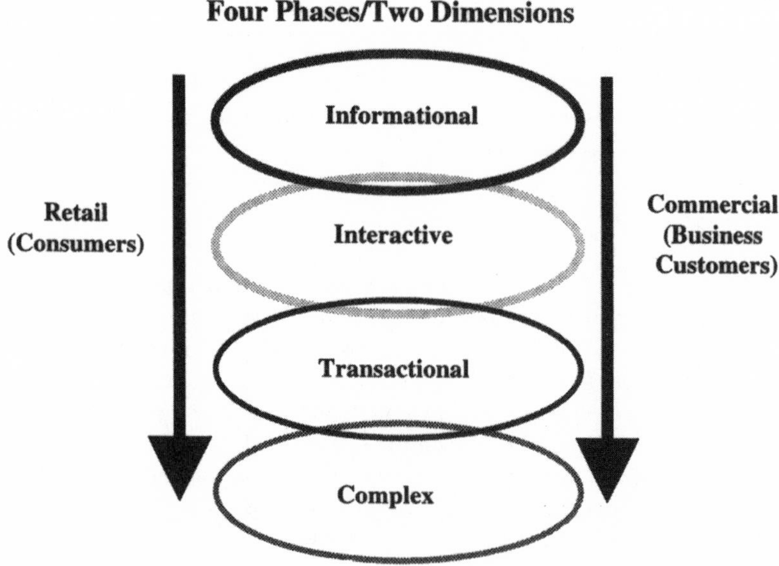

Source: Bonnette (2001).

have both mortar offices and Internet banking delivery for their customers. This group includes 97 percent of the 1,850 banks (including such large banks as Citibank, Wells Fargo, and First Union). The second type is the *Internet-primary* bank, which refers to a small number of banks that just started business in the past few years. There are approximately 22 Internet-primary banks. These banks operate primarily on the web and are sometimes referred to as cyber banks (DeYoung, 2001). At their inception, it was felt that the savings achieved through closing branches would be high. Unfortunately, the high costs associated with "acquiring and retaining customers and with updating and improving their technology infrastructure" have offset any anticipated savings (Garver 2000, 2).

To make matters worse, most of these banks have been compelled to offer some form of physical delivery channel such as an ATM or a kiosk in order to be competitive. Again, customers prefer to have a physical place where they can transact business even if it's only for occasional use. Instead of attracting the basic core client that would build a long-term relationship with the bank, however, the Internet bank is getting "hot" money.[3] Thus, Internet banks actually refer to the bank's primary business strategy and not to the fact that they only offer Internet services (Bonnette, 2001). Although the total number of banks in the United States has declined by close to 5,000 over the past 10 years, branches such as those associated with the cyber banks have increased by 33 percent (Cutler, 2000).

Table 8.4
Emerging Technology Trends

- **Automated Decision Making**
- **Risk Modeling Technologies**
- **Intranets, Extranets, and Remote Access for Bank Employees**
- **Imaging and Electronic Record Keeping**

Source: Bonnette (2001).

There is one very positive aspect of the Internet or cyber bank, however, and this is its assistance to the rural or agricultural community. As of 1999, 47 percent of the United States' 1.9 million farms had computers, and 29 percent had Internet access. The Web allows access to financial services that many rural communities simply did not have in the past, and with the advent of more online loan processing, this could be a boon to both the banks and the farmers as they shop for loans on the Internet. This is a very reasonable assumption, for farmers currently shop for everything from "tractors to bull sperm at sites such as Farmbid.com and Breednet.com" (Wonker, 2000, 6A).

The third form of Internet banks includes institutions that offer Internet banking under a distinctive trade name. These *Internet-branded* banks try to create a new identity in order to target a different customer group. The Internet-branded bank can be seen as a cross between the traditional bricks and clicks bank and the Internet-primary bank, for in this case, the traditional bank has simply created a unique name for its web operations and runs it like a separate branch. One concern associated with the Internet-branded type of bank, however, is that customers may not know the legal identity of the bank. Thus, they could unknowingly be investing in only one bank and would be underinsured if they exceeded the $100,000 insurance limit (Bonnette, 2000).

There are yet more evolving bank technologies on the horizon. The hope is that as the cost and complexity of technologies decrease, banks will be more likely to begin using them. As noted earlier, however, this will not necessarily decrease overall costs for the banks, as long as customers require a physical presence for their business transactions.

Perhaps the most interesting new technology noted in Table 8.4 is automated decision making, which provides for credit scoring, online advice, and pricing models that provide more and better tools for bank clients. Risk modeling technologies allow the customer to use online tools to estimate their potential portfolio risk or loss exposure. Finally, imaging technology allows the bank to create electronic images of the actual paper documents and records used in ordinary banking transactions.

Before leaving our discussion of e-banking, we need to address a topic associated with the new risks inherent in the system. Although the Internet does allow for a more level playing field in which more banks can offer innovative products, "a bank that adopts Internet banking must develop different methods of conducting business, methods that may introduce new risks to the bank" (Sullivan, 2000, 1). The FDIC has identified at least seven risks (Bonnette, 2001). The first risk (1) is strategic, which refers to the business risk associated with any decision; for example, when should the bank introduce a new wireless service? Is the bank acting in a knee-jerk defensive manner to retain a customer base, or is this new service part of an overall strategic plan that has been well thought out?

Operational risk (2) includes some of the obvious concerns: online fraud (anonymity of user), system abuse, or system failure. The cost of maintaining these systems can be high, for knowledgeable personnel are needed to cope with potential problems involving security, availability/accessibility, or system integrity, all problems which could expose banks to unrecoverable losses. This type of system requires strong internal controls, effective policies, and strong management oversight.

Credit risk (3) will be a factor to those banks using online loan applications as fraud or other problems could arise through remote access. Related to this same issue is liquidity risk (4) associated with online deposits, which by definition are more volatile.

A bank could even be subject to different legal and compliance risks (5)—defining jurisdictions with cross-border Internet access complicates the law. Another interesting factor is that of reputation (6). People can be very unforgiving if a web system goes down or experiences security problems. The bank may have initiated a web-based operation in the hopes of retaining its customers, but if it develops and launches one too soon, its reputation could be permanently damaged. Finally, systemic risk (7) increases if there are industrywide security problems or even if a general loss of confidence develops in Internet banking as a whole (Bonnette, 2001).

CONSOLIDATION

There were over 500 bank mergers in the 1990s, most of which were driven by "technological progress, desire for improvements in financial condition, excess capacity or financial distress in the industry or market, international consolidation of markets, and deregulation of geographical or product restrictions" (Berger, Demsetz, and Strahan 1999, 136). The common thread tying the vast majority of these mergers was the need to improve cost efficiencies as well as the need for stronger information technology and for maximizing shareholder wealth. In the United States, both the cost-driven retail model and the need for improved technology continue to be major forces. "Fleet Boston's Brian Moynihan foresees a continuation of the merger trend with the strategic goal of slashing the expense base," and Chase Manhattan's Walter Shipley feels that "IT will dramatically change the game" (Davis, 2000, 115).

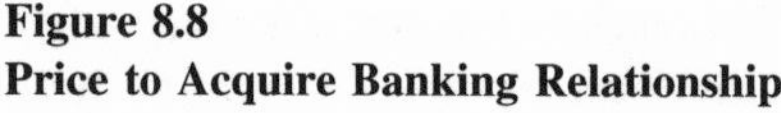

Figure 8.8
Price to Acquire Banking Relationship

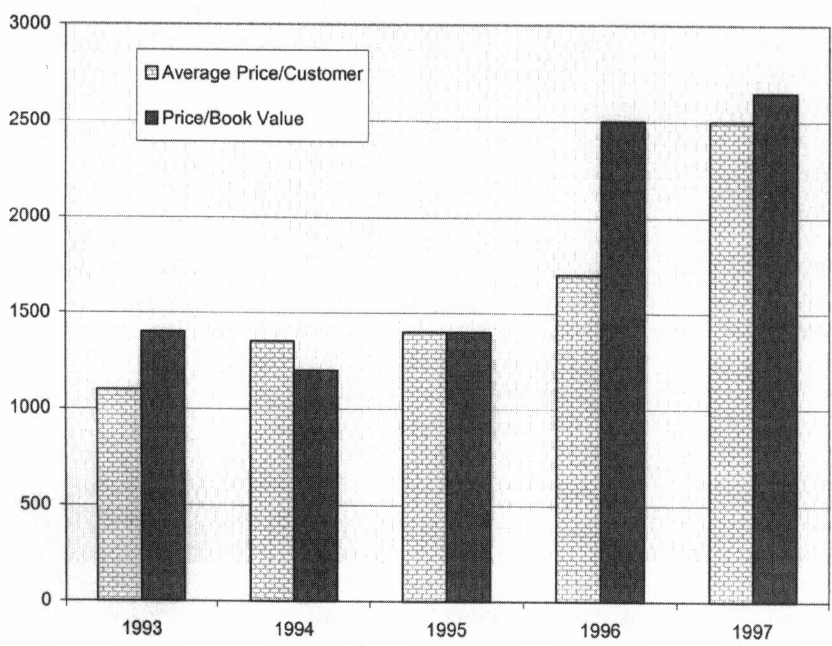

Source: Boston Consulting Group 1998—Author, based on Gandy (2000).

Perhaps the most interesting aspect of the entire merger phenomenon, however, is that it, too, is a reflection of the changing structure of the banking industry. Just as the traditional product-driven model of banking is no longer applicable, so perhaps is the traditional merger a thing of the past. For the large number of mergers occurring during the 1990s, gains have been "either small or nonexistent" according to the Stern School of Business (Davis, 2000). The Federal Reserve Bank of New York has also been unable to find that in-market mergers ever lead to significant improved efficiency (Davis, 2000). Part of this small return may be due to the fact that banks are not aware of all the costs associated with present-day mergers, not the least of which is associated with the impact of the Internet and IT, and "the growing risk and cost of execution failure, and the period of time needed for organizational change to bear fruit" (Davis, 2000, 136).

Interestingly, two of the primary reasons noted as reasons for mergers—cost efficiency and the need for technology information—are actually part of the reason that the mergers are often unsuccessful. IT costs tend to rise just after a merger has occurred because often two separate systems are in place and are being used concurrently. Even though sharing these economies of scale associated with the new technology could improve costs, some institutions still main-

Figure 8.9
Return Required on Acquisitions Made at $2,500 Customer

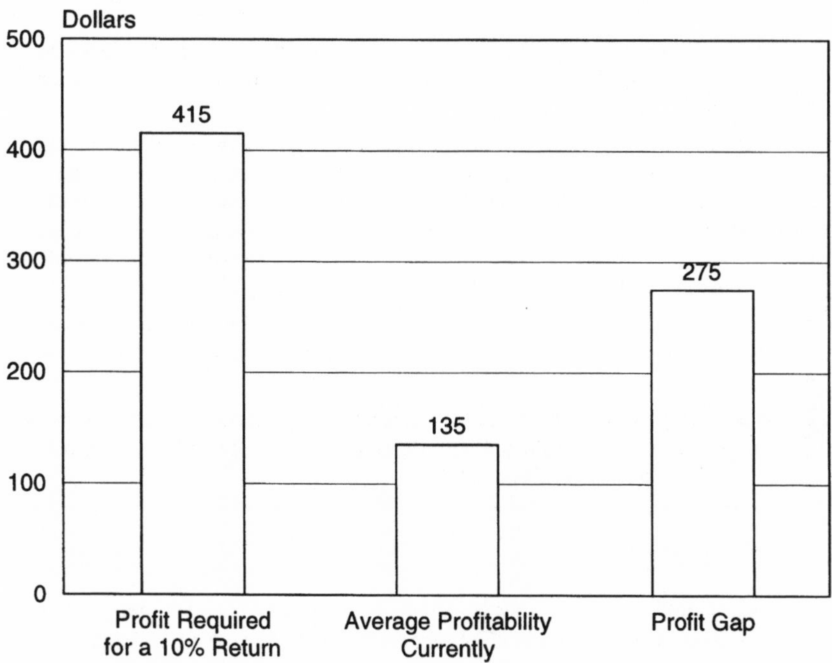

Source: Boston Consulting Group—Hine, based on Gandy (2000).

tain their own information and back-office operations to improve their future ability to expand yet again (Thackor, 1999).

For those wishing to merge systems, however, it is important to find the most competent form. Boston Consulting Group showed that the price to acquire a banking relationship doubled during the 1990s (Figure 8.8), with the return required on acquisitions not providing the necessary profits to cover acquisition costs (Gandy, 2000). Most studies indicate that there were no significant scale efficiencies gained and "possibly some slight scale efficiency losses to be suffered from M&As involving large banks" (Berger, Demsetz, and Strahan, 1999, 155). This trend is changing somewhat with the innovative techniques afforded by technology and regulatory changes. The point remains, however, that consolidation does not guarantee improved efficiencies.

Coupled with the increased costs associated with a bank merger (see Figure 8.9) is the fact that very few cost savings have been implied from consolidating the outputs of various banks (Berger, Demesetz, and Strahan 1999). Thus, it might be prudent to start thinking about new alternative models for evaluating mergers; valuation models that focus on issues other than just cost savings or efficiencies. With the still unknown full impact of the Internet, global cross-

Table 8.5
Banking Merger Model

- ***Leadership*: Is there a clear leader (or possibly leaders) with a track record of success in piloting similar mergers? If not, a significant discount could be applied to projected merger gains.**
- ***Strategic Positioning*: Will the merger simply add together two (or more) organizations, or is there a likelihood that two and two will equal five—through cross-selling, achieving market dominance, building the skills base, or improving competitive positioning? Such a question is particularly relevant for cross-border or so-called complementary mergers. As the consolidation wave continues, inevitably a significant number of deals will be those jammed together for defensive reasons or simply to create size.**
- ***Execution Skills*: Do the banks have a track record of successful merger execution, and is it likely they will execute efficiently? What is the likely cost and duration of integrating IT systems?**
- ***Financial Synergies*: Have the indicated synergies been appropriately discounted to take into consideration the downside risks of market share loss, an extended merger period, poor due diligence and loss of key staff?**

Source: Davis (2000).

border transactions, and greater risk of merger failures, a newer perspective is warranted. The model shown in Table 8.5 is just one alternative for banks today. It addresses the necessary leadership skills, strategic positioning, ability to execute a merger, and the financial synergies that banks would hope to accomplish.

Given this alternative model for bank mergers, what are some of the strategies that could evolve in the future? Ironically, according to Davis (2000), there could actually be more de-consolidation owing to the need for more structural diversity with respect to investment banking, fund managements, or retail banking. This has already occurred with e-commerce businesses in U.S. banks. Yet another strategy postulated might be centered around the cross-selling of retail products through various *distribution channels*. Finally, another strategy could find the bank connected with the global product specialist. This includes the "Schwab in discount brokerage, GE Capital in equipment finance and credit cards, and Fidelity and Alliance Capital in fund management" (Davies, 2000, 139). Such strategies have worked for other businesses, which brings the bank back full circle to the original concept first laid out in this chapter: in order to survive in the future, banks will have to act like and become a business focused on the customer, who is now in the driver's seat.

CONCLUSION

The dramatic advances in technology are indeed astounding and are affecting banking in some very fundamental ways, but this change is only one factor behind this new banking structure—a true revolution has occurred in the way that banks now need to conduct business. The traditional institutional oligopoly structure of the bank has changed dramatically over the past 20 years, with the traditional brick and mortar institution definitely a thing of the past. The customer is now sovereign and is exerting a considerable amount of buying power over financial institutions. Customers will continue to expect competitive services and products from their bankers. In order to meet these needs, it will be essential for banks to think of themselves as a business structure and to form alliances accordingly—alliances that are based on sound strategic plans that work hand in hand with the information technology center.

The future of banking, like any industry in today's technological advanced society, will continue to be dynamic and fraught with uncertainty, and perhaps the only certainty will rest in the fact that change will continue. This is best expressed by the nineteenth-century metaphysicist, Marcel Proust:

> We do not succeed in changing things according to our desire, but gradually our desire changes. The situation we hoped to change because it was intolerable becomes unimportant. We have not managed to surmount the obstacle, as we were absolutely determined to do, but life has taken us round it, led us past it, and then if we turn round to gaze at the remote past, we can barely catch sight of it, so imperceptible has it become. (McGilloway, 2000, 265)

NOTES

1. Securitization is the act of repackaging assets on the balance sheets into new financial instruments that trade easily in the marketplace.
2. PC banking uses a dial-up connection separate from the Internet. Internet banking allows banking access via the world wide web, wireless banking enables banking access via a wireless telephone or other device, and EDI allows for e-business to occur between two businesses using standardized electronic formats.
3. "Hot" money is deposited by individuals who shop for the highest rates and pull money out once rates are lowered. The money leaves the bank very quickly, and it is difficult for banks to depend on this money.

REFERENCES

Berger, Allen N., Rebecca S. Demsetz, and Philip E. Strahan. "The Consolidation of the Financial Services Industry: Causes, Consequences, and Implications for the Future." *Journal of Banking and Finance*, Vol. 23, Nos. 2–4, 1999: 135–194.

Bonnette, Cindy. "E-Banking Overview." Presentation to the FDIC Bank Technology Group. Kansas City, Mo., 2001.

Courchane, Marsha, David Nickerson, and Richard Sullivan. "Strategic Real Options and Endogenous Market Structure in Internet Banking: Theory and Empirical Tests." Manuscript, Colorado State University, August 2001.

Cutler, Wayne. "Bank Productivity: Promises Unrealized." In Edward L. Melnick, Praveen R. Nayyar, Michael L. Pinedo, and Sridhar Seshardri, eds., *Creating Value in Financial Services*. Boston: Kluwer Academic Publishers, 2000.

Davis, Steven I. *Bank Mergers: Lessons for the Future*. New York: St. Martin's Press, 2000.

DeYoung, Robert. "The Financial Performance of Pure Play Internet Banks." *Economic Perspectives*, Federal Reserve Bank of Chicago, 2001.

Frei, Frances X., and Patrick T. Harker. "Value Creation and Process Management: Evidence from Retail Banking." In Edward L. Melnick, Praveen R. Nayyar, Michael L. Pinedo, and Sridhar Seshardri, eds., *Creating Value in Financial Services*. Boston: Kluwer Academic Publishers, 2000.

Furst, Karen, William W. Lang, and Daniel E. Nolle. "Internet Banking: Developments and Prospects." *Economics and Policy Analysis*. Working Paper, 2000–9, September 2000.

Gandy, Anthony. *Banking Strategies and Beyond 2000*. Chicago: Glenlake Publishing Company, 2000.

Garver, Rob. "OTS Finding Web Banks a Regulatory Handful." *American Banker*, Vol. 165, No. 182, September 21, 2000.

Iacocca, L. *Iacocca: An Autobiography*. New York: Bantam Books, 1984.

Karmarkar, Uday S. "Financial Service Networks: Access, Cost Structure and Competition." In Edward L. Melnick, Praveen R. Nayyar, Michael L. Pinedo, and Sridhar Seshardri, eds., *Creating Value in Financial Services*. Boston: Kluwer Academic Publishers, 2000.

Mayer, Martin. *The Bankers: The Next Generation*. New York: Truman Talley Books/Dutton, 1997.

McGilloway, Kevin. "Impending Revolution in Corporate Information Technology Departments." In Edward L. Melnick, Praveen R. Nayyar, Michael L. Pinedo, and Sridhar Seshardri, eds., *Creating Value in Financial Services*. Boston: Kluwer Academic Publishers, 2000.

Monahan, Thomas L., III. "Redefining Customer Relationships in the Age of the Ascendant Customer." In Edward L. Melnick, Praveen R. Nayyar, Michael L. Pinedo, and Sridhar Seshardri, eds., *Creating Value in Financial Services*. Boston: Kluwer Academic Publishers, 2000.

Nagle, T. T., and R. K. Holden. *The Strategy and Tactics of Pricing*, 2nd ed. Englewood Cliffs, N.J.: Prentice Hall, 1995.

Phillips, Ronnie J. "Digital Technology and Institutional Change from the Gilded Age to Modern Times: The Impact of the Telegraph and the Internet." *Journal of Economic Issues*, Vol. 34, No. 2, June 2000: 267–289.

Porter, Michael E. *Competitive Advantage*. New York: Free Press, 1985.

Sullivan, Richard J. "How Has the Adoption of Internet Banking Affected Performance and Risk in Banks? A Look at Internet Banking in the Tenth Federal Reserve District." *Financial Industry Perspectives*, Federal Reserve Bank of Kansas City, 2000.

Thackor, A. V. "Information Technology and Financial Services Consolidation." *Journal of Banking and Finance*, 1999: 23.

Vandeveire, M. "Survey: Major Banks Lack Customer Loyalty." *The Business Journal*, Vol. 18, No. 9, December 26, 1997: 1–2.

Wonker, Craig. "Agriculture: Shopping Online for Tractors—and Mortgages." *American Banker*, August 24, 2000, 6A.

Chapter 9

Deregulation, the Internet, and the Competitive Viability of Large Banks and Community Banks

Robert DeYoung and William C. Hunter

INTRODUCTION

Over the past decade we have witnessed tremendous changes in how banks are regulated, how banks use technology to produce financial services, and how banks compete with each other. At first glance, these developments—for example, reduced barriers to geographic entry and expansion, increased competition from banks in other countries and nonbanks in other industries, less expensive and more rapid movement of financial information—would appear to favor large domestic and international banks at the expense of small local banks. But upon further reflection, it seems that well-managed community banks should be able to turn these competitive threats into opportunities. For example, Hunter (2001) has argued that progressive community banks might combine Internet distribution, strategic acquisitions, and alliances with other financial institutions to better exploit the existing informational advantages of their local branching networks. In this chapter, we argue that the banking industry will continue to feature both large global banks and small local banks into the foreseeable future.[1]

We set the stage for our arguments by first examining how changes in banking regulations, developments in financial markets, and advances in communications technology over the past two decades have fundamentally changed the landscape of the U.S. commercial banking industry. We then analyze the strategic implications of these changes, using a simple competitive strategy framework introduced by DeYoung (2000). We use this framework to argue that deregulation and new financial technologies have driven a wedge between large banks and small banks, resulting in an industry equilibrium with two very different—but both potentially profitable—competitive strategies. Finally, we consider how widespread implementation of Internet banking will affect this new strategic equilibrium.

We conclude that the Internet has the potential to add value for both large banks and small banks. For large banks, the Internet naturally complements their large-scale operations, cost advantages, and marketing presence, and if used effectively could help large banks carve away at community banks' traditional "relationship" markets. For community banks, the Internet naturally complements the high-service quality that they provide to their existing relationship customers, and if used judiciously could partially reduce their cost disadvantages vis-à-vis large banks. In the end, mature Internet strategies could make large and small banks more alike in retail banking markets, reversing the trends of the past two decades.

Although we conclude that the community banking strategy will remain viable in the future, we also believe that the number of small banks in the United States will almost certainly continue to decline. The implementation of the Internet is likely to increase competitive pressures further, and while many community banks will survive and prosper, the less progressive and poorly managed community banks will not. Although our empirical analyses are based solely on U.S. banking data, we believe our conclusions also apply outside the United States where banks face similar forces of change. Just as deregulation has allowed U.S. banks to expand across state borders, similar deregulatory acts passed in the European Union have allowed banks there to expand across national borders. Similarly, the communications and financial technologies that are transforming the operations of U.S. banks are freely available to banks in other countries.

GEOGRAPHIC DEREGULATION AND CHANGES IN BANKING INDUSTRY STRUCTURE

Even if the stock of technology had remained constant over the past 20 years, the liberalization of U.S. banking laws alone would have resulted in drastic changes in the structure of the U.S. banking industry. The relaxation and eventual repeal of federal and state banking regulations during the 1980s and 1990s eliminated the barriers to geographic mobility which had artificially limited the size of U.S. banks.[2] Many U.S. banks took advantage of the new laws and grew substantially larger in a relatively short period of time, typically via in-market and out-of-market mergers and acquisitions. The accumulated effect of these mergers greatly increased the size of the participating banks and also substantially changed the overall structure of the banking industry. For example, in 1990 the largest U.S. commercial bank held about $150 billion in assets, and the average bank held about $275 million in assets. One decade and over 9,000 bank mergers later, the largest U.S. bank now holds about $600 billion in assets, and the average bank now holds about $750 million in assets. In addition, a

Figure 9.1
U.S. Bank Mergers, 1985–1999

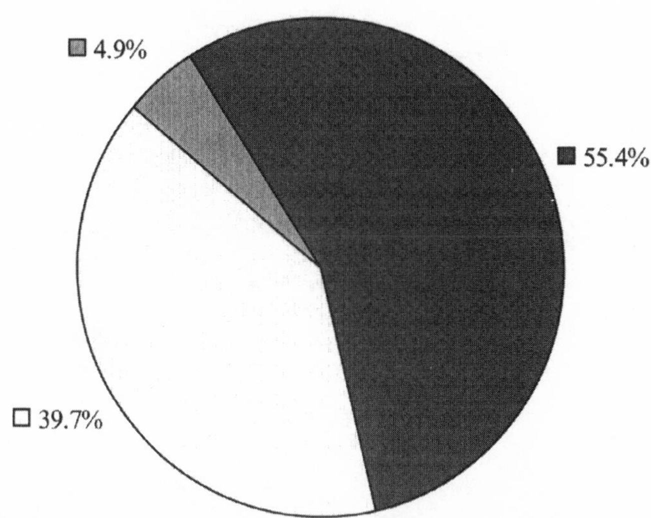

Acquirer is large or mid-sized, target is large or mid-sized (4.9%).
Acquirer is a community bank, target is a community bank (55.4%).
Acquirer is large or mid-sized, target is a community bank (39.7%).

Notes: Large banks have more than $10 billion in assets. Mid-sized banks have between $1 billion and $10 billion in assets. Community banks have less then $1 billion in assets. Assets are in 1999 dollars.

Source: FDIC.

growing number of large U.S. banks are becoming global players by making acquisitions across international borders.

Figures 9.1 and 9.2 further illustrate the dramatic changes in the size distribution of U.S. banks. The most visible bank mergers are the "megamergers" between two very large and well-known institutions, like the 1998 merger of Bank of America and NationsBank, which arguably created the first nationwide U.S. retail banking franchise. But since 1980 only 1 in 20 U.S. bank mergers has been a megamerger. Most bank mergers have combined two community banks (assets less than $1 billion), and in many acquisitions the target bank is a community bank. As a result, between 1980 and 2000 the number of large and midsized banks (over $1 billion) remained relatively constant, as did the number of large community banks (between $500 million and $1 billion). But the number of small community banks (less than $500 million) has been nearly cut in half, declining from about 11,000 banks to less than 6,000.

Banks have a variety of motivations for making acquisitions. Benefits from increased scale are the most obvious, including but not limited to reduced unit

Figure 9.2
Number of U.S. Commercial Banks, 1980–1999

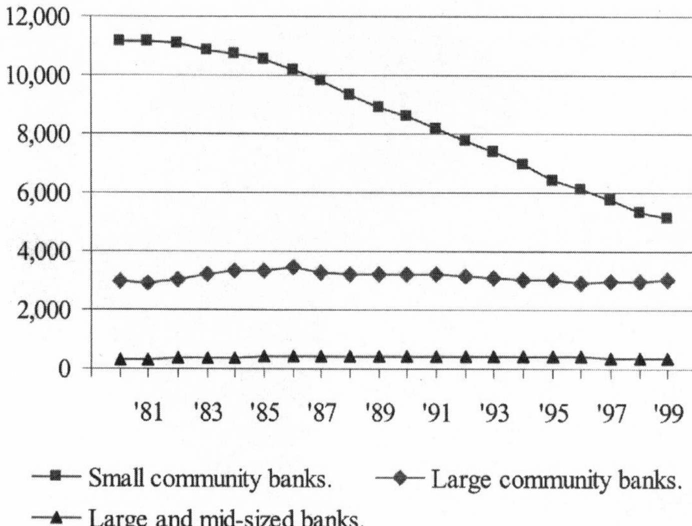

Notes: Large banks have more than $10 billion in assets. Mid-sized banks have between $1 billion and $10 billion in assets. Large community banks have between $500 and $1 billion in assets. Small community banks have less then $500 million in assets. Assets are in 1999 dollars.

Source: FDIC.

costs; higher per unit revenues; improved access to capital markets; the ability to make larger loans or offer broader product lines; the ability to attract and retain high-quality managers; reduced portfolio risk from diversifying into new geographic markets; and network benefits from integrating systems of branches and ATMs that cover different geographic areas.[3] For banks that use traditional bank distribution channels, acquiring existing banks is simply faster and easier than growing internally by building new physical capacity. (As discussed later, acquiring physical branches may become a less important motivation for bank mergers as banking products and services are increasingly delivered over electronic banking channels.) Other motivations do not enhance efficiency. Banks operating in the same local or regional banking markets might merge in order to acquire market power. Bank managers might pursue mergers because managing a large bank tends to be related to high salaries.[4] And banks might pursue absolute size in order to become "too-big-to-fail," a strategy which, if effective, reduces the bank's cost of long-term debt financing by eliminating any default risk premium.[5]

INCREASED COMPETITION IN BANKING MARKETS

The impact of geographic deregulation can be thought of as a two-sided coin. One side of the coin is the increased geographic mobility and growth opportunities for banks; the other side is increased competition for incumbent banks located in the target markets. How has the merger wave of the 1980s and 1990s affected concentration and competition in U.S. banking markets?

Since the mid-1980s, the geographic reach of the typical U.S. bank holding company has more than doubled. For example, the average holding company affiliate with more than $100 million in assets was located about 160 miles from its holding company headquarters in 1985; by 1998, this distance had increased to about 300 miles.[6] This increase in the geographic reach of banking companies has substantially changed the overall structure of the U.S. banking industry, but it has had little effect on the structure of local markets. The share of the national market held by the 10 largest U.S. banks doubled from about 20 percent to about 40 percent over the past two decades, while the Herfindahl Index—a standard measure of market concentration—in the average urban banking market during this time period fluctuated between 1,950 and 2,050 with no clear upward trend. These data reflect the fact that most large bank mergers have been market extension mergers, in which a target bank is purchased by a bank from outside the local market.[7]

Even though local Herfindahl indices have remained stable during the bank merger wave, competition in local banking markets has probably grown more intense. A number of recent studies have found that local banks tend to operate at higher levels of efficiency after one of their local competitors is acquired by an out-of-market bank.[8] There are a number of explanations for this phenomenon, all of which begin with a post-merger change in the behavior of the acquired bank. The new owners of the bank often replace underperforming managers, reallocate assets to higher yielding investments, slash expenses, introduce new products and services, cut fees, raise deposit rates, or make numerous other changes that intensify competitive rivalry in the local market. Local banks either respond in kind or they lose market share.

By making repeated market extension mergers, large banks find themselves competing in hundreds of different local markets. Not only are these superregional banks substantially larger than the community banks they face in these local banks, but their business strategies tend to diverge from those of community banks. These shifts in large bank business strategies can create important profit opportunities for community banks. For example, when a large out-of-state bank acquires a small local bank, the acquired bank often reduces its commitment to small local businesses. These "abandoned" small business customers provide a growth opportunity for other local banks, or provide a critical mass of business for new start-up banks to enter.[9]

ADVANCES IN FINANCIAL MARKETS AND INFORMATION TECHNOLOGY

An explosion in the growth of new financial instruments and institutions over the past two decades has placed increased competitive pressures on commercial banks. Bank depositors now have access to a vast array of mutual funds as an alternative vehicle for savings and liquidity. Bank borrowers now have access to a greater set of financing vehicles, like commercial paper for the most creditworthy firms and junk bond financing for riskier firms. To be sure, the banking sector has grown more slowly as a result of these new financial instruments and institutions. But the loss of market share has been limited, in part because banks have responded with new financial technologies to create entirely new business strategies. In many cases, these changes have fundamentally changed the way that banks do business.

For example, by securitizing their loans (rather than holding them in portfolios) banks have economized on increasingly scarce sources of funds. Similarly, by reorienting their business mix toward off-balance-sheet activities like backup lines of credit, banks have continued to earn revenues from business customers that switch from loan financing to, say, commercial paper financing. And banks have made themselves relatively more attractive to depositors by offering increased convenience (e.g., ATM machines) and a broader array of investment options (e.g., proprietary or third-party mutual funds).

These changes have greatly affected the composition of bank revenues, particularly at large banks. A bank with a securitized lending strategy collects little interest income because the loans it underwrites are not held for long on the books, but it collects lots of noninterest income (e.g., loan origination fees) because the volume of loans it underwrites increases. Similarly, a bank that writes backup lines of credit (rather than writing loans) receives a fee for this service, but receives interest income only in the rare case that the client draws on the credit line. And a bank with a large ATM network will receive fee income from third-party access fees, as well as disproportionate amounts of fee income from its own customers, who arguably chose the bank because of its large ATM network and are presumably willing to pay for this convenience.

Figure 9.3 shows that noninterest income has increased more quickly and to higher levels over time at large banks than at small banks. This is consistent with different fundamental business strategies at large banks and small banks. Large banks are more likely to originate large volumes of standardized loans that can be securitized (e.g., auto loans, credit card loans), more likely to charge high fees to retail depositors, and more likely to operate widespread ATM networks that generate fee income. In contrast, community banks are more likely to make relationship loans to small businesses that generate interest income year after year and are more likely to offer low-fee deposit accounts.[10]

As large banks have embraced new financial technologies, new opportunities have been created for community banks. One case in point concerns the market

Figure 9.3
Noninterest Income-to-Net Revenue—Annual Averages for Various Sizes of U.S. Commercial Banks, 1985–2000

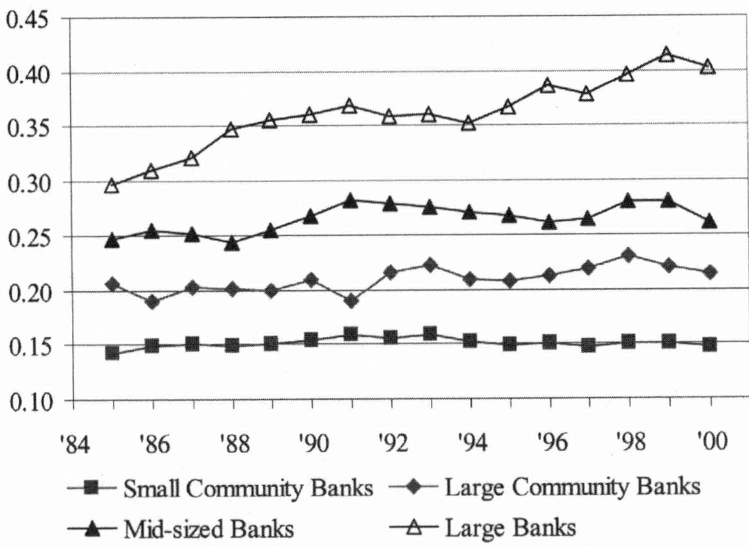

Notes: Large banks have more than $10 billion in assets. Mid-sized banks have between $1 billion and $10 billion in assets. Large community banks have between $500 and $1 billion in assets. Small community banks have less then $500 million in assets. Assets are in 1999 dollars.

Source: Authors' calculations using data from the Reports of Condition and Income (FDIC).

for small business loans, a prime product line for small community banks.[11] Although some large banks (most notably Wells Fargo) have launched efforts to credit score and securitize small business loans, the idiosyncratic nature of small business relationship lending is in many ways inconsistent with automated lending technology. Thus, shifts in large bank strategies toward automated lending may create a business opportunity for traditional community banks. Similarly, the movement of large banks toward charging explicit (and often higher) fees for separate depositor services may provide an opportunity for community banks to attract relationship-based retail customers who prefer bundled pricing.

Innovations in financial technology have also created new challenges for community banks. Mutual funds, online brokerage accounts, and sweep accounts have provided more attractive investment options for retail and small business depositors. As a result, core deposit funding has declined for all size classes of banks, but this decline has been proportionately smaller for community banks.[12] Small banks have fewer nondeposit funding options than large banks (for example, small banks typically do not have access to bond financing), so this probably indicates that small banks are paying more to attract and retain core deposits (some combination of higher deposit rates and/or lower fees on deposit accounts).[13] This puts pressure on small-bank profit margins and could constrain growth at these banks.

Developments in communications and information technologies may also help improve the efficiency of large banking firms. Repeated rounds of market extension acquisitions have left many large banking companies with numerous branches, subsidiaries, and affiliates located far away from the headquarters. It can be difficult to monitor activities at these far-flung installations, and this can result in increased "agency" costs for banks that have to combat shirking and/or cost-preference behaviors by managers at locations far away from the headquarters. Faster and less expensive communications technologies will likely make it easier to effectively monitor these managers. There is some evidence that large multibank holding companies were more successful in controlling the operations of their affiliate banks during the 1990s than during the 1980s.[14]

TECHNOLOGY AND DEREGULATION DRIVE A STATIC WEDGE BETWEEN LARGE AND SMALL BANKS

The foregoing discussion described a myriad of ways that deregulation and technological change have affected the competitive environment in banking. At the risk of oversimplification, we will boil down these changes to just three parameters: unit costs, product differentiation, and bank size. Following DeYoung (2000), we use these three parameters to construct the strategic maps in Figures 9.4 and 9.5. The vertical dimension in these maps measures the unit costs of producing retail and small business banking services. The horizontal dimension measures the degree to which banks differentiate their products and services from those of their closest competitors. This could be either actual product differentiation (e.g., customized products or person-to-person service) or perceived differentiation (e.g., brand image). In this framework, banks select their business strategies by combining a high or low level of unit costs with a high or low degree of product differentiation. The positions of the circles indicate the business strategies selected by banks, and the relative sizes of the circles indicate the relative sizes of the banks.

The banking industry prior to deregulation and technological advances is illustrated in Figure 9.4. Banks were clustered near the northeast corner of the strategy space. The production, distribution, and quality of retail and small business banking products were fairly similar across banks of all sizes. Small banks tended to offer a higher degree of person-to-person interaction, but this wasn't so much a strategic consideration as it was an indication that delivering high-touch personal service becomes more difficult as an organization grows larger. Large banks tended to service larger commercial accounts, but in many cases differences in bank size were predetermined by the economic size of the local market and the restrictiveness of local branching rules.

But deregulation, increased competition, and new financial technologies created incentives for large banks and small banks to become less alike. Bank size

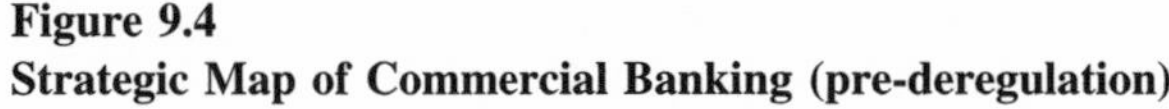

Figure 9.4
Strategic Map of Commercial Banking (pre-deregulation)

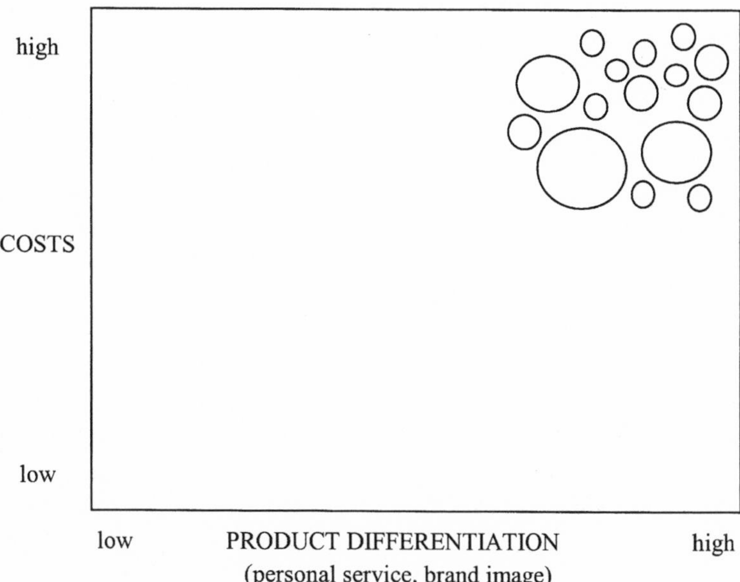

Source: DeYoung (2000).

began to increase, at first as a result of modest within-market mergers, and then more rapidly following market extension megamergers. These increases in bank size yielded economies of scale, and so unit costs fell. Increased scale also gave these growing banks access to the new production technologies discussed earlier (e.g., automated underwriting, securitization, widespread ATM networks), which reduced unit costs further but more importantly changed the nature of their retail business to a high-volume, low-cost, impersonal "financial commodity" strategy.[15]

The combined effect of these changes effectively drove a strategic wedge between the large and growing banks on one hand and the smaller community banks on the other hand. The result is shown in Figure 9.5. Large banks have moved in a southwest direction on the map, sacrificing personalized service for size and producing high volumes of standardized products at low unit costs. This allowed large banks to charge low prices and still earn a satisfactory rate of return. Although many community banks have also grown larger via mergers, they have continued to occupy the same strategic ground, providing differentiated products and personalized service. This allows small banks to charge a high enough price to earn a satisfactory rate of return, despite low volumes and unexploited scale economies.[16]

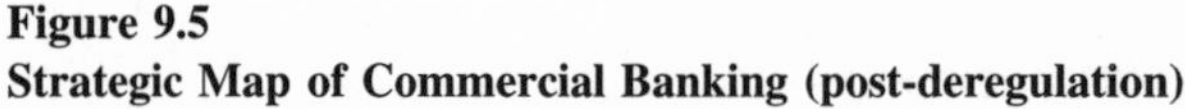

Figure 9.5
Strategic Map of Commercial Banking (post-deregulation)

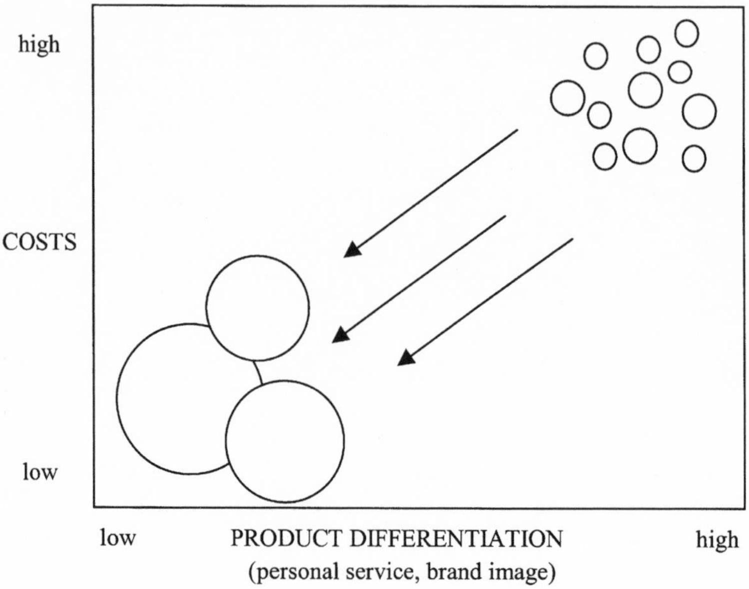

Source: DeYoung (2000).

THE INTRODUCTION OF THE INTERNET

As social pundits and industry analysts are fond of reminding us, the Internet "changes everything." In banking, the Internet is changing the strategic landscape in two fundamental ways. First, it reduces the importance of geography in the production of financial services and the maintenance of financial relationships. Second, the Internet greatly reduces the cost of delivering most financial services. From the standpoint of our strategic map (Figures 9.4 and 9.5), this raises two compelling questions: Can community banks use the Internet to reduce unit costs while still providing personalized services to their customers? Can large banks use the Internet to deliver customized financial services without abandoning their high-volume, low-cost strategies?

The Internet and Bank Distribution Channels

At its most basic level, the Internet is simply an alternative distribution channel, so clues to how a bank will use the Internet can be gleaned from how it uses its more traditional distribution channels. Figure 9.6 shows how the mix of bank distribution channels has evolved in the United States over the past decade; in general, the point of purchase is gradually moving further from the

Figure 9.6
Distribution Channels for U.S. Commercial Banks, 1991–2000

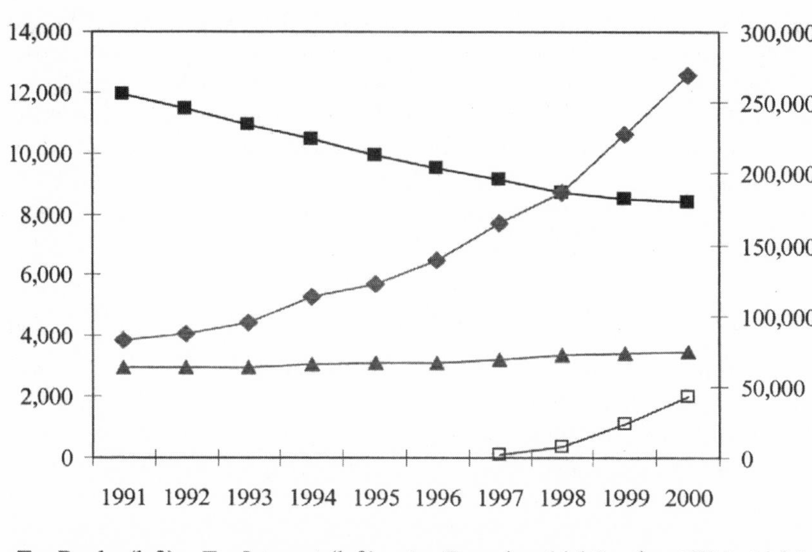

Note: Internet includes only fully transactional web sites.

Source: DeYoung (2000).

bank and closer to the customer. The number of bank branches has increased steadily—from around 60,000 branches in 1990 to more than 70,000 branches in 2000—while at the same time the number of U.S. banks has declined substantially. Although some of the new branches offer only a limited range of services (e.g., supermarket branches), all of them offer person-to-person service. Thus, bank branches are consistent with the high-touch, highly personalized business strategies of community banks.

The number of ATM locations has increased even faster than the number of branches. ATMs deliver a more limited array of services, but they do so at increased convenience because they are located close to the customer—a convenience for which many customers are willing pay fees. Although ATMs cost the bank less per transaction than brick and mortar branches, they accomplish this chiefly by replacing human tellers with automated tellers, and as such they cannot provide personalized service. Thus, an expanded network of ATMs is more consistent with the arms-length, high-volume, commodity-like business strategies of large banks.

It is not yet clear whether Internet distribution is more consistent with large-bank strategies or with small-bank strategies. Internet web sites offer bank customers increased convenience: banking transactions can be performed at home, and pairing ATMs with hardwired computer terminals at public kiosks allows customers to perform Internet transactions while also making cash withdrawals or deposits. Thus, the Internet distribution channel naturally extends the large-bank retail strategy. But the Internet also fits well with community bank business practices. Because providing and processing an Internet transaction costs banks just pennies compared to transactions made at its branches, banks can substantially reduce their costs by encouraging their retail and business customers to migrate (at least partially) from branch banking to Internet banking. Thus, the Internet distribution channel naturally complements a community bank's business strategy by simultaneously reducing its high expenses and providing its computer-savvy (read: high-value) customers with additional options.

The Internet and Switching Costs

Historically, both large banks and community banks have felt that they owned their deposit customers. Banks provided a limited range of financial services to deposit customers, including primary checking and savings accounts, credit cards, and access to settlement and clearing procedures. Customers had only to choose a bank, deposit money, and draw on those funds at some future date. To a large extent these customers were captive—that is, there was little threat that they would move their deposits to a different bank because the costs of switching banks generally exceeded the benefits of switching. There were often few competitors (due to geographic and product market restrictions); competing banks could not compete freely on prices (due to Regulation Q); and most banking transactions required visits to physical bank offices (because ATMs, telephone banking, and Internet banking had not yet been introduced). Most deposit customers simply selected the bank that was located closest to their homes or workplaces and as a result had inelastic demand curves that allowed banks to charge high prices for financial services. It simply didn't pay for depositors to switch banks.

Today, however, customers have a wider range of choices. In the days when a customer had to be physically present to engage in most banking activities, proximity to the bank branch was important. A bank's best customers—that is, the customers with the most inelastic demand—were those who lived closest to the branch. But as lower communications costs and near universal access to the Internet have greatly expanded the geographic area within any given bank's reach, the geographic distance between a bank and its deposit customers has become less important. Deposit accounts can now be opened over the Internet without ever visiting a bank or branch office. As a result, customer switching costs are declining substantially, depositors have become more price sensitive, and this reduction in demand elasticity has sharply reduced bank pricing power. At the same time, deregulation (which allowed market entry by other banks) and financial market innovations (such as checkable money market mutual funds) have increased the number of financial institutions to which depositors can switch. Banks are having to rethink their deposit and retail banking business, and relearn how to exploit their increasingly tenuous deposit relationships to create rents for the bank.

There is a great deal of inertia among deposit customers, however. Many customers still prefer to use bank branches for depositing checks, despite the fact that ATM machines can produce records just as well as tellers in manned branches. Similarly, customers who are perfectly willing to use ATMs are often unwilling to conduct basic banking transactions over the Internet. This hesitancy to use new banking technologies will undoubtedly fade as time passes, as the cost of contacting and switching to competing financial institutions continues to fall, and as local bank customers move up the technological learning curve. Until that happens, however, depositor inertia may provide a window of opportunity for banks to impose *new* switching costs on these depositors.

The Internet and Cross-Selling Financial Services

One way to increase the switching costs of local deposit customers is to embed them even *more* firmly in the local branch network. Banks can do this by cross-selling an array of products to these customers, with the goal of making the branch network the customer's primary gateway to financial services. This is advantageous for the bank because the cost of switching to a different bank increases with the number of services the customer accesses through the bank. Providing personal advisory services for these customers is an excellent, albeit costly, way to do this because it builds human bonds that are hard to break. Another approach is to offer a variety of services in a manner that makes them appear seamless. For example, a bank can link a home equity loan, a credit card, an overdraft facility, direct payroll deposits, insurance services, and perhaps even automated payment services to these customers' deposit accounts, and present a consolidated statement to the customer at the end of every month.

Once these relationships have been solidified—that is, once the switching costs of local branch depositors have been increased by binding these customers even more closely to the bank—the bank can safely begin to wean these customers from the branches and migrate them to Internet distribution. This approach has three benefits for the bank. First, Internet transactions are less expensive to produce than branch transactions. Second, once customers begin to use the Internet, the bank can widen the gateway further by linking customers to even more cross-selling opportunities. Third, the specialized computer software required for the customer to gain access (which the customer must install, initialize, and learn to use) acts as yet another switching cost.

Cross-selling a vast array of financial services can require a bank to operate at a large scale and/or have a high degree of financial expertise. So this raises the interesting question: Should community and regional banks offer access to more than their own in-house products and services? The answer is: They should, and not simply because the bank will become more attractive as an access point if it offers the best services. By offering other firms' services, banks also make a commitment to customers that they will not be overcharged, ripped off, or gouged later if they lock themselves into their banks. (Economists call this technique "second sourcing.") Moreover, the banks are in a position to extract rents from the other services providers, not vice versa, because it is the banks that control the unique assets: captive customers and the access gateway.

This approach has been followed successfully by the discount brokerage firm Charles Schwab. With its mutual fund OneSource product, Schwab allows customers access to over 1,100 mutual funds from over 100 fund families. Schwab consolidates all fund statements into one statement for the customer. Fidelity's decision to withdraw most of its popular mutual funds from OneSource suggests that Schwab has the market power because it controls access to the customer.

The Internet and Electronic Payments

Payments services have always been a primary service provided by banks, and access to the payments system is central to the value of a banking franchise. The Internet will eventually cause a sea change in the production of payments services—away from physical checks, toward electronic impulses—and this change could have a potentially large and negative strategic impact on community banks.

Most analysts agree that payments provision is a high fixed cost/low variable cost business. In high fixed cost industries, service providers have an incentive to acquire a large share of the market because this allows them to spread their high fixed costs over a larger base of customers. In addition, gaining a dominant market share in payments might allow a firm to establish industry standards for hardware or software (a good example from the computer industry is Microsoft Windows), giving it a competitive advantage over new entrants who must adopt these standards in order to access the system. Being a dominant firm in payments may also allow the firm to exploit scope economies (for example, if the payments infrastructure could also be used to collect useful demographic or financial data) or economies of sequencing (for example, if the payments infrastructure can be integrated with the bank's other data systems) that give it cost advantages over competitors in other product markets.

If electronic payments provision does become concentrated in a handful of the large financial institutions, standard economic theory suggests that these firms will be able to exploit monopoly power. Dominant firms will not face much competition because entry is unlikely: a failed attempt at entering the business will saddle the prospective entrant with large sunk costs. In addition, financial institutions with large market shares—and thus low unit costs—in this segment may be able to exploit their positions by engaging in limit pricing that further reduces the chance of competitive entry. Thus, small banks may be at a disadvantage in offering electronic payments to their customers. Being too small to economically produce the service themselves, they may have to pay high prices to dominant firms in order to purchase electronic payments on behalf of their deposit customers. Furthermore, the dominant providers may be able to extend their monopoly power in payments services into more traditional banking services.

The Internet and Overarching Bank Strategies

If banks use the Internet mainly as a substitute for, or as a complement to, more traditional distribution channels, then the current strategic banking environment will not materially change. If anything, deploying the Internet in this way might drive the strategic wedge illustrated in Figure 9.5 even deeper. Large banks could expand their customer base without having to acquire other banks and without having to operate their expensive branch networks. This would hasten the ongoing process of increased size, lower unit costs, and greater product commoditization at large banks, and would carry them even further to the southwest in the strategy space. In this scenario, large banks would be even less attractive for the high-value, relationship-based target customers of community banks. Community banks would be able to maintain their profit margins without cutting their costs. As a result, they could simply use the Internet as a complement to their existing branch networks, offering only a limited array of convenience services at their websites. Community banks would remain pinned in the northeast corner of the strategy space, producing high-cost, customized services for local customers.

If banks deploy the Internet more thoughtfully, however, they may be able to move closer to the highly profitable southeast corner of the strategy space, as shown in Figure 9.7. The southeast corner dominates all other strategic positions because banks that locate there can charge high prices for differentiated products and can produce those products at a low unit cost. So we reiterate the two questions we asked at the beginning of this section: Can community banks use the Internet to reduce unit costs while still providing personalized services to their customers? Can large banks use the Internet to deliver customized financial services without abandoning their high-volume, low-cost strategies?

COMMUNITY BANK STRATEGY

The massive reduction in the number of U.S. community banks since 1980 does not signal a lack of viability for the community bank business model. Primarily, it indicates that a history of regulatory entry barriers left the United States with too many community banks. Thousands of poorly managed banks were protected from competitive pressure, and when barriers to geographic and product market entry were lifted, the least viable community banks (the poorly managed, the poorly located, or the otherwise just plain unlucky) exited the market, while well-managed community banks flourished.

Thousands of U.S. community banks are indeed prospering. Figure 9.8 displays the annual average profitability between 1985 and 2000 for best-practices community banks. (We define "best-practices" endogenously, as banks that earn

Figure 9.7
Strategic Map of Commercial Banking (post-Internet)

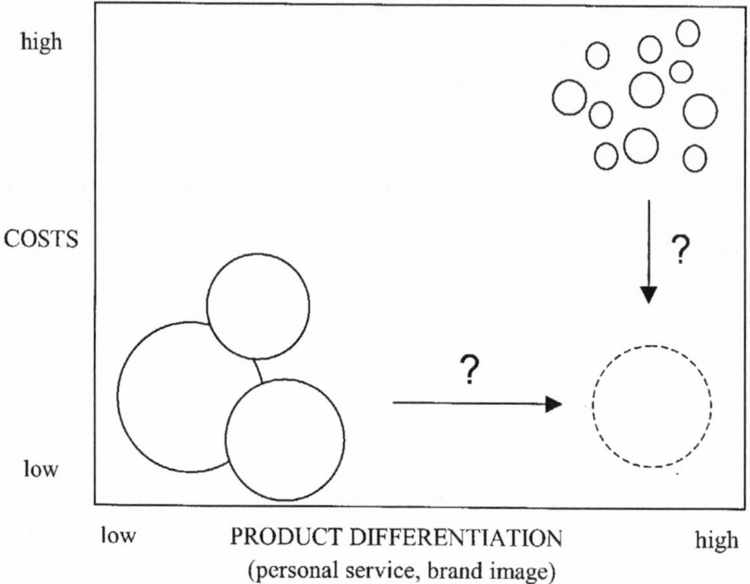

Source: DeYoung (2000).

return-on-assets equal to the 75th percentile for their size group.) Large best-practice community banks have consistently earned returns equal to or exceeding those of the typical large commercial bank over each of the past 10 years.[17] Small best-practices community banks have earned slightly lower returns—evidence that scale economies exist for community banks—but still have been quite competitive with returns at the typical large commercial bank. So despite the problems that face community banks—the increasing competitive pressure, the declining bank numbers, the small scale of operations, and the problems retaining core depositors—there is plentiful evidence that the community banking strategy can be a profitable one.

Table 9.1 investigates the sources of high and low profitability at large banks and community banks over the past five years. On average, the data suggest that poor performance at community banks is attributable to inefficient operations and not to any fundamental weakness in the community bank business model. On one hand, both highly profitable community banks (represented by banks above the median) and moderately profitable community banks (represented by all banks) tended to use high amounts of core deposit funding and to generate low levels of noninterest income—two of the items identified above with the technology-based wedge between large bank business strategies and community bank business strategies. On the other hand, highly profitable community banks

Figure 9.8
Return-on-Equity: Best-Practices Community Bank Averages versus Large Bank Averages

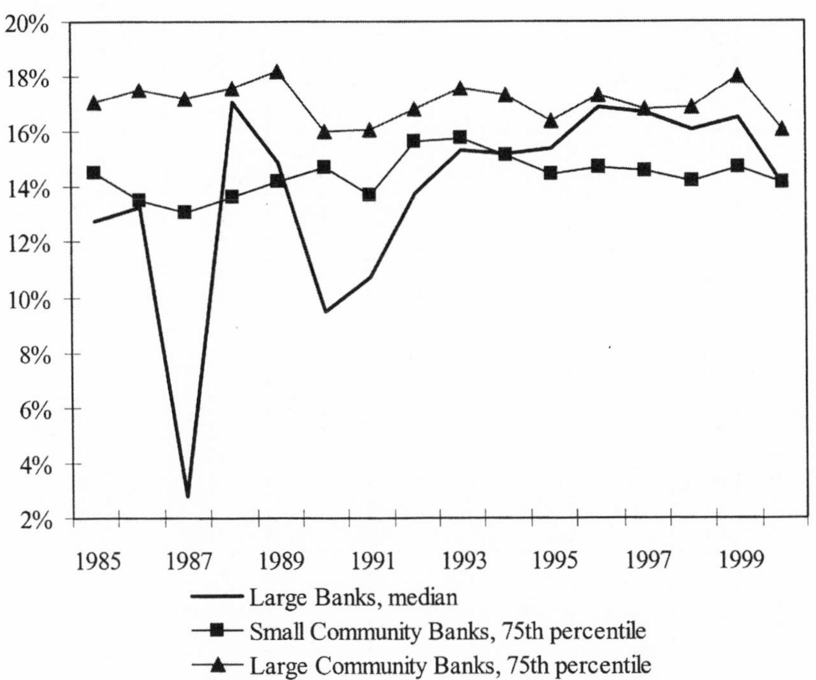

Notes: Large banks have more than $10 billion in assets. Mid-sized banks have between $1 billion and $10 billion in assets. Large community banks have between $500 and $1 billion in assets. Small community banks have less than $500 million in assets. Assets are in 1999 dollars.

Source: Authors' calculations using data from the Reports of Condition and Income (FDIC).

were more likely to have high loans-to-asset ratios and low noninterest expense ratios—two measures typically associated with efficient bank operations. Thus, the data are consistent with recent research on managerial efficiency at U.S. banks, which consistently finds that the potential benefits from eliminating cost, revenue, and production inefficiencies at poorly run banks can outweigh the potential benefits from increasing the size of small banks.[18]

These historical data bode favorably for the competitive viability of community banks. But community banks may face even greater challenges in the future. The structural fallout from geographic deregulation is not yet complete, and consolidation will likely continue to reduce the number of community banks in the United States. As with past mergers, most future mergers will likely combine community banks with each other and will generate efficiencies not only by eliminating poorly performing target banks but also by increasing the

Table 9.1
Community Banks versus Large Banks (selected financial ratios, mean values over 1996–2000 period)

	Large banks	Small community banks		Large community banks	
		All	Above median ROE	All	Above median ROE
Return-on-Equity	0.1653	0.1267 ***	0.1748 **	0.1431 ***	0.1832 ***
Loans-to-Assets	0.6469	0.6207 ***	0.6426	0.6304 *	0.6342
Noninterest Expense-to-Net Revenue	0.6013	0.6133	0.5646 ***	0.6040	0.5776 ***
Core Deposits-to-Assets	0.4749	0.7286 ***	0.7387 ***	0.6785 ***	0.7258 ***
Noninterest Income-to-Net Revenue	0.3967	0.1684 ***	0.1800 ***	0.2192 ***	0.2229 ***

Notes: Large banks have more than $10 billion in assets. Large community banks have between $500 and $1 billion in assets. Small community banks have less then $500 million in assets. Assets are in 1999 dollars. The asterisks ***, **, or * (HHH, HH, or H) indicate that the community bank mean is significantly higher (significantly lower) than the large bank mean at the 1 percent, 5 percent, or 10 percent levels.

Source: Authors' calculations using data from the Reports of Condition and Income (FDIC).

scale of the combined banks. This increase in scale *within* the community bank population may prove to be more important than in the past, as academic studies have found that minimum efficient bank size tends to increase with technological change.[19] Further advances and wider implementation of the Internet and other communications technologies will continue to reduce switching costs, making it increasingly difficult for community banks to hold on to their best customers.

How can well-managed community banks best respond to these challenges? They should not abandon their core strategy of delivering high-value-added, relationship-based services. Rather, they should adjust this core strategy to make it work better under the new technological, competitive, and financial conditions.

More Centralized Decision Making

For most banks, the optimal organizational structure combines some degree of centralized decision-making authority with some degree of decentralized decision-making authority.[20] Decentralized authority gives the operations side of the bank the flexibility to exploit local market information advantages, while centralized authority allows the product side of the bank to exploit opportunities for product synergies, scale economies, and innovation. Banks at the very extremes of the strategic map may not find such a combined strategy useful: a very large and geographically dispersed bank that sells completely standardized financial products has little need for local information gathering or decision making (e.g., a credit card bank), while a very small community bank that personalizes all of its retail and small business relationships has little need for centralized command and control type decision making. But banks that wish to migrate from these extreme corners of the strategic map toward the more profitable southeast corner will likely benefit from a mix of centralized and decentralized decision making.

As a first approximation, decentralized decision making is a good fit for community banks because it keeps bank decision makers in close proximity with the customer and with local information. To be sure, decentralized decision making also has some potential disadvantages: branch office managers can misuse the autonomy granted to them by senior management, and maintaining a decentralized approach may mean foregoing opportunities for scale or scope economies in certain product processes. But these types of problems are less severe for community banks in the first place because small banks are less likely to have internal information and management control (agency) issues and because they have relatively limited access to economies of scale and scope.

As we move into a more integrated electronic and Internet banking world in which geographic location is less important for defining a bank's customer base, maintaining a decentralized decision-making approach may become less important for community banks. For banks that possess special localized knowledge about their markets—but recognize that retail customers in an Internet banking world will have fairly low switching costs—a combined strategy of decentralized operational decision making and centralized product decision making may make more sense.

Outsourcing and Affiliations

Because they lack significant scale, community banks will always be at a cost disadvantage relative to large banks. Some small banks have attempted to mitigate their lack of scale by outsourcing back-office operations to large-scale vendors (to reduce unit costs) or by affiliating with large-scale providers of nonbank financial services (to provide their customers with broader access). However, when attempting to circumvent the weaknesses of their small-scale and decentralized strategy, community banks must be careful. Outsourcing must be done without sharing a substantial portion of their profits with the outsourcing vendors and without having a substantial portion of their customers captured by the access providers. More fundamentally, focusing too closely on scale can be a strategic mistake for community banks because—as illustrated in the strategic map analyses—large-scale operations can be antithetical to relationship-based services, and community banks overreaching for scale can easily lose their core strategic advantage.

Internet Implementation

The Internet can be both an opportunity and a threat for community banks. On one hand, community banks are unlikely to successfully use the Internet to acquire new customers because small banks cannot afford the high advertising expenditures necessary to support a web-based marketing campaign. (One of the ironies of e-commerce is that advertising in the print media and on television is often needed to attract customers to a new web site.) On the other hand, it is absolutely crucial for community banks to offer transactional web sites in order to retain their existing high-value customers, who are willing to pay high prices for differentiated, highly personalized products and services, but who also want the flexibility and convenience of performing some of their financial transactions over the Internet.

In some ways, the Internet may level the playing field between large banks and small banks. The expense of setting up a basic transactional web site is relatively low, which allows small banks to offer their basic retail customers a web channel that is competitive with those offered by larger banks. Once the web site is in place, community banks could reduce their unit costs by eliminating *some* of their expensive brick and mortar branches' locations. This must be carefully done because overdoing this cost-cutting strategy could diminish the branch-based, person-to-person contact on which the community banking strategy is based. In other words, community banks cannot run the risk of getting too far out in front of the migration of captive, inertial local branch depositors to the Internet. As time passes, however, the Internet should allow community banks to stay in close touch with their high-value customers while selectively pruning their physical plant and personnel overhead.

LARGE BANK STRATEGY

The continuing movement of large banks from the northeast corner to the southwest corner of the strategic map is to some extent a self-fulfilling prophecy. These banks have grown large via merger, and achieving scale economies is typically among the announced objectives of these mergers. Indeed, this is backed up by recent studies that find opportunities for significant economies of scale at regional, super-regional, and global banks.[21] Larger banks also tend to sell a nontraditional mix of services, using production and distribution techniques that give them access to deep scale savings but that require higher operating leverage (lower per unit expenses but higher fixed expenses).[22] The most extreme cases of this are "mono-line" banks that employ new financial technologies to specialize in a single standardized product (e.g., credit card banks, mortgage banking) which enjoy scale economies out to very large sizes.[23] But standardized (i.e., undifferentiated) products do not command high prices. Thus, for large banks the path to higher profits requires continued growth to capture additional scale-related savings.

Another reason that the profit margins of large banks rely so much on cost reductions is the plentiful competition among large banks in most retail and wholesale markets. Scale and scope economies typically have important implications for the structure of an industry. If such economies are substantial, an industry will tend to be relatively concentrated and entry will be difficult. But despite the large cost savings apparently available from increased size in banking, there is currently little evidence of market power for large banks in U.S. banking markets. As long as industry consolidation does not devolve into a tight oligopoly and pricing power—and currently there is little reason to expect this, given continued entry by large domestic banks, large foreign banks, and de novo banks—there should continue to be pricing pressure on large and small banks alike. In such a world, a bank cannot raise its prices unless the products they are selling are differentiated from their competitors' products.

Limits to Scale

Like all physical phenomena, there are limits to scale-related gains: at some point, the unit cost curve must stop declining. But interpersonal phenomena may be more limiting than physical phenomena in this regard. As discussed earlier, when business units move further away from headquarters, it becomes more difficult to control their activities.[24] This could be one of the reasons why researchers simultaneously find significant *potential* gains from increased bank size, but that most large banks do not fully exploit that potential.[25] These difficulties are amplified at cross-border banks: in addition to the problems of managing a geographically diverse company, cross-border banks must overcome differences in language, culture, currencies, regulations, and local business practices that could drive up costs, depress revenues, or hamper growth.[26]

As time passes, improved technology is likely to partially mitigate the operational and managerial problems of distance. For example, there is evidence that improved communications technology has allowed banking customers to move farther away from their banks, challenging the idea that local proximity—and thus small bank size—is necessary for a strong banker–borrower relationship.[27] There is also evidence that advances in communications technology are allowing banks to better control the operations of their affiliates as these offices move farther away from the headquarters.[28]

Imposing centralized decision-making authority may also help mitigate the agency costs found in large, geographically dispersed banks. In many ways, a centralized management model goes hand-in-hand with the ongoing movement of large banks from the northeast corner to the southwest corner on the strategic map. Centralization is consistent with standardized products and services; centralization seems like a natural way to limit agency costs as an organization grows in size; and centralization may become easier to implement as new technologies allow headquarters managers to better communicate in real time with branch managers. Barnett Bank and Bank One are two examples of U.S. banking companies that switched from very decentralized strategies to more centralized strategies as they grew larger: separately chartered bank affiliates were converted into branch offices, and decision-making authority was moved from local managers to headquarters management.

Less Centralized Decision Making

Although centralization has its merits, a *completely* centralized organizational strategy is unlikely to be optimal for large banking companies.[29] Complete centralization works well for a company like McDonald's, which never customizes its products to fit individual consumer needs, but it can be costly in the banking industry where gathering and processing unique customer information is a core competency. Maintaining at least some degree of decentralized decision-making authority would seem to be essential for banks because creating and capturing new profit opportunities in banking frequently depends on keeping bankers in close (and fast) touch with local customers and local information.

Furthermore, ongoing reductions in customer switching costs are likely to lessen the future effectiveness of centralized decision making. With customers that can switch easily among multiple financial service providers, it will become increasingly difficult for banks to make significant profits by selling traditional banking products on a commodity basis. In other words, the southwest corner of the strategy space becomes less attractive. In such a world, retaining high-value customers requires more personalized products and services (a movement toward the southeast corner of the strategy space), which in turn requires more decentralized decision-making authority within the bank. A potentially profitable strategy for large banks may be to offer all customers a choice of a wide menu of standardized products and services (which emerge from a centralized product and services strategy) but to also offer personalized financial service and advice, along with customized pricing, for certain products and customers deemed to be high value-added (this emerges from a decentralized operations strategy).

Innovation

As large banks exhaust all the potential gains from increased scale—or after they grow so large or so geographically diverse that their agency problems become unmanageable—large banks will have to change course and concentrate on strategic advantages that are not directly related to size. Instead, a change in strategy aimed at the potentially profitable southeast corner will be in order. How might large banks maintain their low-cost advantages while simultaneously providing more personalized products and services that yield higher prices?

Innovation is one potential path. However, most product innovations on the retail side are easily imitated and quickly replicated by competitors, so any first-mover advantages are likely to be fleeting. Unless the innovation is proprietary, or unless it can be linked to a strategic behavior that discourages rival firms from competing against the innovating firm, the innovation must be continuous, which is both expensive and unpredictable.

One potentially long-lasting innovation is to identify areas of high transaction cost and to reduce those costs by *internalizing* the transactions. To the extent that there are first-mover advantages in this approach, the bank can build a long-term franchise. For example, Citibank has recognized that there are still very high costs in making cross-border payments. By setting up a global network of branches and developing tremendous expertise in foreign exchange transactions, it has internalized cross-border payments. The savings in transactions costs coupled with the very high volume of transactions make this a very profitable franchise. Moreover, other banks are unlikely to challenge this franchise because of the high costs of setting up a competing network and the formidable position now occupied by Citibank.

Another possibility is to use innovation to build a captive customer base. This is, in a sense, what Charles Schwab has done. Charles Schwab was one of the first brokerages to allow customers to trade electronically. In the process, it cross-sold a variety of products, including information services and mutual funds services that locked the electronic customer into a relationship with Schwab. At the same time, these customers gave Schwab the scale to pursue further innovation.

Internet Implementation

The current conventional wisdom is that both large banks and community banks will combine the Internet channel with their traditional brick and mortar branches, using a "click and mortar" distribution strategy.[30] An alternative approach is the Internet-only, or "virtual bank," distribution strategy that eschews brick and mortar branches altogether. Only a few Internet-only banks are operating in the United States, and to date these banks have not performed well. But Internet-only banks are using a very new business model, and it is possible that both these banks and their customers are only just learning how to efficiently use this model and that financial performance will improve in the future.[31] If the Internet-only delivery model ultimately proves profitable, it would seem to be well-suited for banks that have the capacity to offer large volumes of low-cost, standardized products and services.

THE FUTURE: A NEW COMPETITIVE ENVIRONMENT

At some point in the near future, the bank merger wave will finally subside. When it is over, the market structure of the banking industry will no longer reflect the historical restrictions on geographic and product market mobility. At that point, the banking industry will more closely resemble nonbanking industries in an important strategic dimension: growth by internal expansion will become a viable strategic alternative for banks because in the new industry equilibrium there will be fewer easy opportunities to grow by acquisition. Under these more "normal" industry conditions, the Internet will play an expanded and more complicated strategic role. Internal growth strategies typically require increased advertising and marketing expenditures, and this is an area where deep-pocketed large banks have a clear advantage over small community banks. When large banks exhaust their opportunities to grow *via* inexpensive acquisitions, their strategic growth objective will switch from wholesale acquisition of other banks to acquisition of individual customers of other banks.

Large banks will have two sources of customers. At one extreme, the large banks will compete for each other's customers in a kind of zero sum game, consuming any cost or productivity gains by reducing prices. In this scenario, large banks remain mired in the southwest corner of the strategy space, selling commodity-like services at low margins and relying on innovation and increased scale to drive down unit costs. Community banks will have uncontested access to the highly profitable southeast corner, although they may or may not be able to occupy it. At the other extreme, the large banks will compete for the customers of the community banks, perhaps using the informational potential of the Internet to target high-value community bank customers and offering them customized or semicustomized financial services at relatively low prices. In this scenario, large banks will migrate toward the more profitable southeast corner of the strategy space, and the market share of community banks will shrink.

Continued technological change in the banking and financial services industry and in electronic or Internet banking are inevitable. The degree to which large banks are successful—and hence the amount of profitable market share ultimately retained by community banks—may depend on how well both sets of bankers can harness the benefits of new technology in an increasingly competitive and fully deregulated environment. These changes pose great challenges and offer potential opportunities for community banks, regional banks, and large banks alike. Is new banking technology more likely to allow large banks to personalize their product offerings while maintaining the cost advantages of large-scale production? Or is new banking technology more likely to allow community banks to overcome the cost disadvantages of small-scale production while maintaining their traditional, personalized approach to banking? The data and analysis presented here suggest a future with far fewer community banks than exist today, but they also suggest a future competitive equilibrium in which a relatively large number of community banks remain viable alongside a relatively small number of increasingly large banks.

NOTES

1. The views expressed in this chapter are those of the authors and do not necessarily reflect the views of the Federal Reserve Bank of Chicago or the Federal Reserve System.
2. The Riegle-Neal Act of 1994 eliminated virtually all prohibitions against interstate banking in the United States. This Act followed 25 years of *ad hoc* deregulatory acts by state governments, which had gradually permitted banking companies to expand across state borders. The European Union passed similar legislation at roughly the same time. The Single Europe Act of 1986 eliminated all barriers to cross-border resource movements, paving the way for a single uninterrupted economic marketplace in the EU. The Second Banking Directive of 1989 (implemented in 1993), together with several sister acts, created a "single passport" for financial firms in the EU and harmonized banking regulations across its member states.
3. For an in-depth review of scale economies in banking, see Berger, Demsetz, and Strahan (1999).
4. Bliss and Rosen (1999) find evidence of this "managerial hubris" explanation for bank mergers.
5. See Kane (2000) and Penas and Unal (2001) for recent studies that attempt to find explicit evidence of the too-big-to-fail phenomenon. See Benston, Hunter, and Wall (1995) for evidence of the portfolio, or earnings diversification, motivation for bank mergers.
6. See Berger and DeYoung (2001b).
7. DeYoung (1999) reports that about two-thirds of bank megamergers in the United States since 1980 have been market extension mergers.
8. See DeYoung, Hasan, and Kirchhoff (1998), Evanoff and Ors (2001), and Whalen (2001).
9. For evidence of this phenomenon, see Berger, Bonime, Goldberg, and White (1999) and Keeton (2000).
10. Federal Reserve System (1997, 1998, 1999).
11. See Strahan and Weston (1998), Peek and Rosengren (1998), and DeYoung, Goldberg, and White (2000) for details on small business lending and the consolidation of the banking industry.
12. See Genay (2000) for details. Core deposits are typically defined as funds in transactions accounts plus funds in savings accounts under $100,000.

13. There is evidence consistent with this in the Federal Reserve's Survey of Retail Pricing and Fees (1997, 1998, 1999), which reports that small banks tend to charge lower fees on deposit accounts.

14. Berger and DeYoung (2001b).

15. There is an extensive literature on scale and scope economies in the commercial banking industry. See Hunter, Timme, and Yang (1990), Hunter and Timme (1991), Evanoff and Israilevich (1991), Berger and Mester (1997), and Hughes, Lang, Mester, and Moon (2001) for evidence. This evidence suggests that scale economies are quite modest for community banks under $1 billion, but that larger banks produce a different output mix using a different production technology that yields more substantial economies of scale.

16. Note that large banks personalize some of their financial services—for example, investment banking or merger finance to large wholesale clients—but that their retail and small business strategies tend to be commodity-like compared to those delivered by small community banks.

17. The returns displayed in Figure 9.7 are book returns, and are not adjusted for risk. It is not possible to compare risk-adjusted earnings because the stocks of most community banks do not trade publicly. However, the intertemporal variability in the Figure 9.7 data suggests that community bank earnings are less risky than large bank earnings. Hence, on a risk-adjusted basis, Figure 9.7 may understate community bank returns relative to large banks. DeYoung and Roland (2001) provide evidence that large bank business strategies (e.g., increases in fee-based activities) reduce earnings stability.

18. See Berger, Hunter, and Timme (1993) and Berger and Humphrey (1997) for reviews of this literature.

19. See Hunter and Timme (1986, 1991) for a discussion of technological change and minimum efficient bank size.

20. See Hunter (1995) for an examination of the importance of centralized versus decentralized decision making in large and small banks.

21. See Berger and Mester (1997) and Hughes, Lang, Mester, and Moon (2001) for evidence.

22. Hunter, Timme, and Yang (1990) and Hunter and Timme (1991) provide evidence that large and small banks use entirely different production functions; their research suggests that efficient scale for community banks is well below efficient scale for large banks. DeYoung and Roland (2001) discuss in detail the implications of operating leverage at commercial banks.

23. See Rossi (1998) for evidence of mono-line scale economies in mortgage banking. See Jones, Lang, and Nigro (2001) for evidence of recent consolidation in the loan syndication business.

24. See Berger and DeYoung (2001a).

25. See Hughes, Lang, Mester, and Moon (2000) and Demsetz and Strahan (1997).

26. Berger, DeYoung, Genay, and Udell (2000) provide evidence that banks tend to do poorly when operating abroad.

27. See Petersen and Rajan (2002) and Cyrnak and Hannan (2000).

28. See Berger and DeYoung (2001b).

29. See Hunter (1995) for evidence on the general efficiency of centralized and decentralized organizational forms in banking.

30. Furst, Lang, and Nolle (2000) find evidence that click and mortar banks are more

profitable than traditional brick and mortar banks. Sullivan (2000) concludes that click and mortar banks are no less profitable than traditional banks.

31. DeYoung (2001a, 2001b) finds that new Internet-only banks perform poorly relative to other new banks, but he also finds some evidence in support of the proposition that Internet-only banks are moving up a steep learning curve.

REFERENCES

Benston, George J., William C. Hunter, and Larry D. Wall. 1995. "Motivations for Bank Mergers and Acquisitions: Enhancing the Deposit Insurance Put Option versus Earnings Diversification." *Journal of Money, Credit, and Banking* 27 (August): 777–798.

Berger, Allen N., Seth D. Bonime, Lawrence G. Goldberg, and Lawrence J. White. 1999. "The Dynamics of Market Entry: The Effects of Mergers and Acquisitions on De Novo Entry and Small Business Lending in the Banking Industry." Washington, D.C.: Board of Governors of the Federal Reserve System.

Berger, Allen N., Rebecca S. Demsetz, and Philip E. Strahan. 1999. "The Consolidation of the Financial Services Industry: Causes, Consequences, and Implications for the Future." *Journal of Banking and Finance* 23 (February): 135–194.

Berger, Allen N., and Robert DeYoung. 2001a. "The Effects of Geographic Expansion on Bank Efficiency." *Journal of Financial Services Research* 19: 163–184.

Berger, Allen N., and Robert DeYoung. 2001b. "Technological Progress and the Geographic Expansion of the Banking Industry." Chicago: Federal Reserve Bank of Chicago, manuscript.

Berger, Allen N., Robert DeYoung, Hesna Genay, and Gregory F. Udell. 2000. "The Globalization of Financial Institutions: Evidence from Cross-Border Banking Performance." In *Brookings-Wharton Papers on Financial Services*, Robert Litan and Anthony Santomero, eds., vol. 3, pp. 23–125.

Berger, Allen N., and David B. Humphrey. 1997. "Efficiency of Financial Institutions: International Survey and Directions for Future Research." *European Journal of Operational Research* 98: 175–212.

Berger, Allen N., William C. Hunter, and Stephen G. Timme. 1993. "The Efficiency of Financial Institutions: A Review and Preview of Research Past, Present, and Future." *Journal of Banking and Finance* 17: 221–249.

Berger, Allen N., and Loretta J. Mester. 1997. "Inside the Black Box: What Explains Differences in Efficiency of Financial Institutions?" *Journal of Banking and Finance* 21: 895–947.

Bliss, Richard T., and Richard J. Rosen. 1999. "CEO Compensation and Bank Mergers." Federal Reserve Bank of Chicago, Conference on Bank Structure and Competition, *Proceedings*: 516–532.

Cyrnak, Anthony, and Timothy Hannan. 2000. "Non-Local Lending to Small Businesses." Washington, D.C.: Federal Reserve Board of Governors, manuscript.

Demsetz, Rebecca S., and Phillip E. Strahan. 1997. "Diversification, Size, and Risk at Bank Holding Companies." *Journal of Money, Credit, and Banking* 29 (August): 300–313.

DeYoung, Robert. 1999. "Mergers and the Changing Landscape of Commercial Banking (Part I)." Federal Reserve Bank of Chicago, *Chicago Fed Letter*, No. 145, September.

DeYoung, Robert. 2000. "Mergers and the Changing Landscape of Commercial Banking (Part II)." Federal Reserve Bank of Chicago, *Chicago Fed Letter*, No. 150, February.

DeYoung, Robert. 2001a. "The Financial Performance of Pure Play Internet Banks." Federal Reserve Bank of Chicago, *Economic Perspectives*, First Quarter: 60–75.

DeYoung, Robert. 2001b. "Learning-by-Doing, Scale Efficiencies, and Financial Performance at Internet-Only Banks." Federal Reserve Bank of Chicago, manuscript.

DeYoung, Robert, Lawrence G. Goldberg, and Lawrence J. White. 2000. "Youth, Adolescence, and Maturity of Banks: Credit Availability to Small Business in an Era of Banking Consolidation." *Journal of Banking and Finance* 23 (February): 463–492.

DeYoung, Robert, Iftekhar Hasan, and Bruce Kirchhoff. 1998. "The Impact of Out-of-State Entry on the Efficiency of Local Banks." *Journal of Economics and Business* 50: 191–204.

DeYoung, Robert, and Karin P. Roland. 2001. "Product Mix and Earnings Volatility at Commercial Banks: Evidence from a Degree of Leverage Model." *Journal of Financial Intermediation* 10 (January): 54–84.

Evanoff, Douglas D., and Philip R. Israilevich. 1991. "Productive Efficiency in Banking: Econometric and Linear Programming Evidence." Federal Reserve Bank of Chicago, *Economic Perspectives* 15 (July): 11–32.

Evanoff, Douglas D., and Evren Ors. 2001. "Local Market Consolidation and Bank Productive Efficiency." Federal Reserve Bank of Chicago, manuscript.

Federal Reserve Board of Governors. 1997, 1998, 1999. *Annual Report to Congress on Retail Fees and Services of Depositories*. Washington, D.C.: Author.

Furst, Karen, William W. Lang, and Daniel E. Nolle. 2000. "Internet Banking: Developments and Prospects." Office of the Comptroller of the Currency, Working Paper 2000–9.

Genay, Hesna. 2000. "Recent Trends in Deposit and Loan Growth: Implications for Small and Large Banks," Federal Reserve Bank of Chicago, *Chicago Fed Letter*, No. 160, December.

Hughes, Joseph P., William Lang, Loretta J. Mester, and Choon-Geol Moon. 1996. "Efficient Banking under Interstate Branching." *Journal of Money, Credit, and Banking* 28: 1043–1071.

Hughes, Joseph P., William Lang, Loretta J. Mester, and Choon-Geol Moon. 2000. "Are Scale Economies Elusive or Illusive?" Federal Reserve Bank of Philadelphia, manuscript.

Hughes, Joseph P., William Lang, Loretta J. Mester, and Choon-Geol Moon. 2001. "Recovering Risky Technologies Using the Almost Ideal Demand System: An Application to U.S. Banking." *Journal of Financial Services Research.*

Hunter, William C. 1995. "Internal Organization and Economic Performance: The Case of Large U.S. Commercial Banks." Federal Reserve Bank of Chicago, *Economic Perspectives* (September/October): 10–20.

Hunter, William C. 2001. "The Internet and the Commercial Banking Industry: Strategic Implications from a U.S. Perspective." In *Financial Intermediation in the 21st Century*, Zuhayr Mikdashi, ed. New York: Palgrave.

Hunter, William C., and Stephen Timme. 1986. "Technical Change, Organizational Form and the Structure of Bank Production." *Journal of Money, Credit and Banking* 18 (May): 152–166.

Hunter, William C., and Stephen Timme. 1991. "Technological Change in Large U.S. Commercial Banks." *Journal of Business* 64: 206–245.

Hunter, William C., Stephen G. Timme, and Won Keun Yang. 1990. "An Examination of Cost Subadditivity and Multiproduct Production in Large U.S. Banks." *Journal of Money, Credit, and Banking* 22: 504–525.

Jones, Jonathan, William W. Lang, and Peter J. Nigro. 2001. "Recent Trends in Loan Syndications: Evidence for 1995 to 1999." Office of the Comptroller of the Currency, manuscript.

Kane, Edward J. 2000. "Incentives for Banking MegaMergers: What Motives Might Regulators Infer from Event-Study Analysis?" Boston College, manuscript.

Keeton, William R. 2000. "Are Mergers Responsible for the Surge in New Bank Charters?" Federal Reserve Bank of Kansas City, *Economic Review*, pp. 21–41.

Peek, Joe, and Eric S. Rosengren. 1998. "Bank Consolidation and Small Business Lending: It's Not Just Bank Size That Matters." *Journal of Banking and Finance* 22 (August): 799–819.

Penas, Maria F., and Haluk Unal. 2001. "Too-Big-To-Fail Gains in Bank Mergers: Evidence from the Bond Market." University of Maryland, Working Paper.

Petersen, Mitchell A., and Raghuram Rajan. 2002. "The Information Revolution and Small Business Lending: Does Distance Still Matter?" *Journal of Finance* (forthcoming).

Rossi, Clifford V. 1998. "Mortgage Banking Cost Structure: Resolving an Enigma." *Journal of Economics and Business* 50: 219–234.

Strahan, Philip E., and James P. Weston. 1998. "Small Business Lending and the Changing Structure of the Banking Industry." *Journal of Banking and Finance* 22 (August): 821–845.

Sullivan, Richard J. 2000. "How Has the Adoption of Internet Banking Affected Performance and Risk at Banks? A Look at Internet Banking in the Tenth Federal Reserve District." Federal Reserve Bank of Kansas City, *Financial Industry Perspectives*, December: 1–16.

Whalen, Gary. 2001. "The Impact of the Growth of Large, Multistate Banking Organizations on Community Bank Profitability." Washington, D.C.: Office of the Comptroller of the Currency, manuscript.

Chapter 10

The Future of Relationship Lending

Allen N. Berger and Gregory F. Udell

INTRODUCTION

The financial services industry is undergoing a dramatic transformation driven primarily by two factors—industry consolidation and technological change. Consolidation, both domestic and cross-border, is producing an industry with larger banks, more organizationally complex banks, and banks that are managed from an increasing geographic and cultural distance from their customer base. Similarly, technology is transforming the delivery of key banking products from human delivery platforms to electronic platforms. Not surprisingly, these changes have raised concern that some bank customers may suffer from this industry transformation. Included among these customers are informationally opaque small businesses that may depend on the strength of their banking relationships for their external credit.

The policy concern here is that industry consolidation and technological change might impair the ability of the banking industry to provide relationship lending services to informationally opaque small business borrowers. As discussed below, relationship lending to such firms often depends on the accumulation over time of soft, qualitative data about the firm and its owner, such as information about character, reliability, and local community standing. Consolidation may create banking organizations that are less able to deal with such information, and technological change may favor lending technologies that are based on hard, quantitative data—such as financial ratios, accounts receivable valuations, and credit scores—over relationship lending.

Consolidation of the banking industry tends to increase bank size, raise the local market shares of large banks, and increase the penetration of foreign-owned banks. Assuming that consolidation continues, each of these consequences may affect the future of relationship lending. As will be discussed, the theory suggests that these increases in bank size, changes in market size structure, and globalization of the industry could encourage some banks to reduce or eliminate their relationship lending because of organizational diseconomies and agency problems in the provision of relationship lending services and other difficulties. The empirical evidence is not as clear, and some suggestions for additional research are given in this chapter.

Technological change may also represent a threat to relationship lending in the future because advances in information processing, telecommunications, and financial technologies improve the processing, transmission, and analysis of the hard, quantitative information used in other transactions-based lending technologies much more than they help in dealing with the soft, qualitative information that is key to relationship lending. To some degree, the substitution of improved technologies for relationship lending may benefit small business loan customers as some of the cost savings and/or improvements in the information used by the banks may be passed onto the borrowers. However, the more serious threat to relationship lending from technological change is that some banks may discontinue relationship lending as it may become more profitable to focus on the set of lending technologies that use only hard information.

How serious are these threats to relationship lending? Are there countervailing forces that will negate or minimize the impact of consolidation and technological innovation on small business relationship lending? Which borrowers, if any, will be most affected? We address these questions in this chapter in an analysis of the factors that will likely affect the future of relationship lending.

Before we can discuss the impact of these factors on relationship lending, however, we need to understand the alternatives to relationship lending. Much of the academic literature has failed to make a clear distinction between *small business lending* and *relationship lending*. An exception to this perspective is a recent paper that noted that relationship lending is only one of at least four different lending technologies through which banks provide credit to small businesses, including financial statement lending, asset-based lending, and small business credit scoring (Berger and Udell, 2002). Financial statement lending emphasizes financial statement ratios in loan underwriting. Asset-based lending focuses primarily on the collateral value of accounts receivable, inventory, and fixed assets. Small business credit scoring employs statistical techniques to data gathered primarily from consumer and commercial credit bureaus. These alternative lending technologies focus on hard, quantitative information and are transactions-based (i.e., each loan stands on its own as a separate transaction), whereas relationship lending focuses on soft, qualitative, proprietary information gathered through continuous contact over time. In this chapter, we provide a more detailed analysis of each of these technologies in order to draw a clear distinction between them and the relationship lending technology. This enumeration and clarification of the lending technologies is vital to our analysis of the future of relationship lending. To the extent that banking industry consolidation and technological innovation encourages a shift out of relationship lending, it must simultaneously encourage a shift *into* one or more of these transactions-based lending technologies.

Our analysis of these competing technologies will provide an essential backdrop to our investigation of how the transformation of the banking industry will affect relationship lending and how to interpret the extant literature in that area. We begin that investigation with an analysis of the impact of bank size and bank mergers and acquisitions (M&As) on relationship lending. We consider the empirical literature that has noted the association between bank size and lending propensity that suggests that larger banks may be less inclined to make small business loans than small banks. However, we will consider more recent work which suggests that "market size structure" may be more important than bank size. That is, the quantity of relationship lending may depend more on the relative market shares of large and small banks in the local market than on the size of the lending institution. We also consider the impact of globalization on relationship lending and survey the limited literature in this area. Here we specifically address the question of whether the propensity of foreign-owned banks for relationship lending is different from that of domestically owned banks.

Our final analysis focuses on the impact of technological change. A key point of our analysis is that technological advances in information processing, telecommunications, and financial technologies improve other lending technologies more than they improve relationship lending, which may cause banks to substitute out of or discontinue relationship lending.

In the next section, we show a statistical breakdown of small business finance in order to identify the institutional sources of relationship lending and other technologies. In the following section, we describe our taxonomy of lending technologies—financial statement lending, asset-based lending, small business credit scoring, and relationship lending. Next, we analyze the two important factors that may affect the future of relationship lending—the consolidation of the banking industry and technological change. The final section presents our conclusions.[1]

THE SOURCES OF SMALL BUSINESS FINANCE

To set the stage for this analysis of the future of relationship lending, we briefly examine the sources of small business finance. This will help clarify the institutional framework surrounding the delivery of relationship lending and alternative lending technologies. Table 10.1 shows the key sources of small business finance. The data in this table are drawn primarily from the Federal Reserve's National Survey of Small Business Finance and are weighted to represent all nonfarm, nonfinancial, and non-real estate U.S. small businesses as a whole. Given the informational opacity of most small businesses, it is not surprising that Table 10.1 shows that a substantial portion of small business financing is generated internally from the firm's owners. Nevertheless, the amount

Table 10.1
A Statistical Breakdown of Small Business Finance

Sources	**Percent**
Equity:	
Principal owner	31.33
Other equity (mostly principal owner)	18.30
Debt:	
Commercial banks	18.75
Commercial finance companies	4.91
Trade credit	15.78
All other debt sources (including owners)	10.93
Total	100.00

Source: Berger and Udell (1998). The data are drawn primarily from the Federal Reserve's 1993 National Survey of Small Business Finance and are weighted to represent all nonfarm, nonfinancial, non–real estate U.S. small businesses as a whole, using the Small Business Administration classification of firms with fewer than 500 full-time equivalent employees.

of external debt financing is still quite significant. Financial institutions, specifically banks and commercial finance companies, provide almost 25 percent of total small business financing, with commercial banks providing the bulk of it (18.75%). When viewed as a fraction of total *external* funding, the role of financial intermediaries appears even more significant. Commercial banks and commercial finance companies provide about half of the external financing obtained by small businesses. Thus, by these measures, small business is quite dependent on financial intermediaries to fund their operations.

Table 10.1 is also useful in clarifying who provides relationship lending. Commercial finance companies substantially confine themselves to asset-based lending. Many commercial banks also have asset-based loan departments, particularly mid-size and large banks. Relationship lending, on the other hand, is mostly confined to commercial banks that use their ability to provide other banking products to generate relationship information about their borrowers. Small business credit scoring, the newest of the lending technologies, is also substantially confined to the commercial banking industry—mostly the largest banking organizations. Banks of all sizes provide financial statement lending.

Now that we have seen who provides these different lending technologies, we take a closer look at each one.

A TAXONOMY OF LENDING TECHNOLOGIES

Each of the four small business lending technologies discussed here—financial statement lending, asset-based lending, small business credit scoring, and relationship lending—tends to be targeted to an identifiable subset of small businesses. Nevertheless, as we will explore in a later section, the boundaries between these target firms may be significantly affected by changes in the banking industry driven by consolidation and technological innovation.

The first three lending technologies—financial statement lending, asset-based lending, and small business credit scoring—can be viewed as "transactions-based" technologies. They are transactions-based in the sense that each loan made under these lending technologies stands on its own. This is feasible because the underwriting of loans under each of these is based on hard, quantifiable data that substantially provides the measure of creditworthiness at any specific point in time. In contrast, relationship lending is based on soft, qualitative information that is gathered over time by the lending institution.

Financial Statement Lending

Financial statement lending is the most traditional and possibly the most intuitive of the four lending technologies. Under financial statement lending, bankers focus on standard financial statement analysis. That is, they utilize financial ratios to analyze historical financial statements, to analyze projected financial statements, and to analyze pro forma financial statements that estimate the impact of proposed actions, such as mergers and acquisitions.

Financial statement lenders use four broad categories of financial ratios—liquidity ratios, leverage and solvency ratios, activity ratios, and profitability ratios. Each of these categories measures some dimension of firm efficiency or risk. The financial statement lender (1) examines changes in each of these ratios over time and over different scenarios for each borrower; and (2) compares each borrower's ratios to ratios for industry peer groups either from the bank's own database or from other sources such as the Robert Morris Statement Studies data base.

Liquidity ratios, such as the current and quick ratios, are used as measures of a firm's ability to discharge its short-term obligations. Financial statement lenders look at these ratios to assess the likelihood that the normal conversion of short-term assets into cash will be sufficient to meet payment obligations on short term bank debt (typically drawn under a line of credit) and payment obligations to other short-term creditors, particularly trade creditors. Financial statement lenders are specifically looking for a substantial cushion in the form of an excess of short-term assets over short-term liabilities. In examining a firm's *leverage ratio* (e.g., its debt/worth ratio), financial statement lenders assess the insolvency risk imposed by the firm's capital structure. Financial statement lenders avoid lending to highly levered firms because the associated agency costs are too high. *Activity ratios* are used to assess the efficiency with which a firm manages its assets. Financial statement lenders are looking, for example, to see whether ratios such as asset turnover (i.e., sales/assets) are in line with industry standards. Some activity ratios, such as accounts payable turnover, can signal financial stress. Financial statement lenders shy away from companies that are paying their trade creditors slowly relative to industry standards (e.g., over 45 days). Finally, financial statement lenders examine *profitability ratios* to assess their prospective borrower's cash flow. Financial statement lenders tend to shy away from unprofitable firms with little or no cash flow.

Financial statement lenders use financial statement analysis to identify low-risk borrowers. Borrowers whose financial ratios are poor relative to industry standards are not likely to receive financial statement-based credit. Borrowers with short track records, poor financial statements, or financial statements that reflect substantial amounts of intangible assets are also less likely to get financial statement-based loans. In short, financial statement lending is reserved for small businesses that are relatively transparent informationally, have solid track records, and are relatively low risk. This, in turn, implies that moral hazard and adverse selection problems can be addressed through standard contracting features such as covenants and maturity. Collateral may be incorporated into the loan contracts used by financial statement lenders, but it is only viewed as a secondary source of repayment.

Asset-Based Lending

Some trace the history of asset-based lending as far back as the Roman Empire. It is generally agreed, however, that the earliest form of asset-based finance, factoring, had become relative commonplace by the fifteenth century.[2] Factoring is widely used today in other countries and is still used in the United States to finance some very small companies and companies in certain industries such as the textile industry. Although factoring is the economic equivalent of lending, it is technically not a loan. A factor *purchases* a client's accounts receivable and in most cases assumes both collection responsibility and credit risk (i.e., "nonrecourse factoring").

The core product of the asset-based finance industry today in the United States, however, is not factoring but asset-based receivable and inventory lending. This technology was developed at the turn of the twentieth century and has evolved from a specialty financial product offered exclusively by commercial finance companies to an industry with $300 billion of asset-based receivables and inventory loans on the balance sheets of both commercial banks and commercial finance companies (see Sherman, 1999). This compares with $90 billion of factored receivables. Not all of these assets represent loans to (or in the case of factoring, receivables from) small businesses. Nevertheless, the historically core customer base of the asset-based finance industry has been small and mid-sized companies. In addition to accounts receivable and inventory lending and factoring, equipment financing and non-auto floor plan financing are generally considered part of the asset-based lending technology.

Because asset-based lending is generally not widely understood outside of the lending industry, it may be useful to provide some detail on this technology in order to clearly distinguish it from the other lending technologies. At first blush, asset-based lending would seem to be nothing more than secured financing. Although it is true that all asset-based lending is *always* done on a secured basis, collateral is *not* the distinguishing feature of asset-based lending. The vast majority, over 90 percent, of *all* small business loans in the United States from banks and finance companies are extended on a secured basis (Berger and Udell, 1998, Table 2).[3] That is, collateral can be used in conjunction with any of the other lending technologies (i.e., financial statement lending, credit scoring, or relationship lending). What distinguishes asset-based lending from the other lending technologies is that under asset-based lending loan underwriting standards, loan monitoring and the terms of credit are all *primarily* based on collateral valuation. Thus, for example, in the parlance of commercial banking, collateral would be viewed as a "*secondary* source of repayment" in a financial statement loan. However, in an asset-based loan, collateral is viewed as the "*primary* source of repayment."

To appreciate this distinction, consider the contrast in how a line of credit is evaluated by a financial statement lender versus an asset-based lender. A financial statement lender would make its credit decision based on the four categories of ratios enumerated earlier. If the borrower's liquidity, activity, leverage, and profitability ratios compared favorably with industry peers and the trends were positive, the loan facility would likely be approved.

An asset-based lender would instead begin by focusing on the collateral. As a starting point, an asset-based lender would calculate the accounts receivable turnover ratio to get an initial assessment of the strength of its primary collateral, the accounts receivable. The next step would involve a much more penetrating analysis of the collateral. A field audit would be conducted in which asset-based audit specialists would visit the potential borrower's place of business and accumulate specific information about the accounts receivable to determine both receivable "eligibility" and an "advance rate." Eligible receivables represent the dollar amount of receivables that the asset-based lender is highly confident can be collected. Specifically, eligible receivables exclude all categories of receivables whose ultimate collection may be problematic. The audit is conducted in great part to identify these ineligible receivables. Categories of ineligible receivables include but are not limited to:

- Sales returns
- Receivables over 90 days (i.e., past due)
- Discounts
- Contra accounts (receivables from customers who are also suppliers)
- Cross agings (receivables from customers with excessive slowness)
- Excessive industry concentration
- Employee sales
- Service charges

- Bill and hold (goods ordered and produced but not shipped)
- Government receivables
- Foreign receivables
- Affiliate receivables
- Specific debtor limits

Although the asset-based lender will take all of the receivables as collateral, its loan availability will be based only on eligible receivables. A further adjustment is made by setting an advance rate less than 100 percent. Suppose, for example, that the asset-based based lender calculates total receivables at $1,250,000 and ineligible receivables at $250,000. If it imposes an 85 percent advance rate, then the maximum loan it will extend is $850,000 (= 0.85 × [$1,250,000 − $1,000,000]). This $850,000 represents the "borrowing base" for the borrower firm at a specific point in time. The advance margin (i.e., 100% minus the advance rate) is set to cover legal fees and collections costs to liquidate the receivables if necessary and to cover any dilution of the receivable base that cannot be estimated directly through the ineligibility calculation.

Another distinction between asset-based lending and the other lending technologies that employ collateral is the dynamic control over the borrowing base and the loan balance. Both are adjusted on a daily basis. The borrower submits three reports daily (often electronically): an accounts receivable assignment schedule, an accounts receivable collection schedule, and a borrowing base certificate. These reports respectively list specific new invoices, collection of outstanding invoices, and an end-of-day loan availability calculation. Further control is exercised through a cash collateral account. The borrower's customers are instructed to mail invoice remittances to a post office box over which the asset-based lender (and not the borrower) has access and legal dominion. (Normally, the borrower's customers are unaware that the post office box is "owned" by the asset-based lender.) Invoice remittances are then immediately applied to reduce the loan balance. Thus, the loan balance goes down when the collateral goes down (i.e., when the receivables are collected). New advances can be made with the generation of new invoices that are shown on the daily accounts receivable assignment schedule (followed by hard photocopies). In addition, the asset-based lender continues to conduct spot field audits using its own audit staff, usually four times per year, and regularly conducts receivables verification.[4]

The asset-based lending technology enables asset-based lenders to finance a much riskier class of borrowers than the other lending technologies (see Carey, Post, and Sharpe, 1998). In fact, companies with high leverage and negative profitability are the target customer audience for the commercial finance companies and asset-based loan departments. Many asset-based lenders specifically pursue DIP (debtor-in-possession) and pre-DIP financing as a marketing strategy. Thus, in general, a company that fails on all of the ratio measures used by a financial statement lender might be an ideal candidate for an asset-based lender if the company has tangible assets to secure its debt. It has been argued that the asset-based lending technology is ideally suited to solve an important aspect of the moral hazard problem in lending. In particular, asset-based lending can detect firm insolvency much more quickly than the other lending technologies (Swary and Udell, 1988). Thus, it can force timely liquidation before the incentive to risk-shift becomes acute.[5]

Small Business Credit Scoring

Under small business credit scoring, consumer data on the owner of the firm is drawn from the consumer credit bureaus and combined with data on the firm from financial statements and/or commercial credit bureaus. These data are processed in a model to give a credit score, or summary statistic, about the borrower's expected future loan performance. Unlike financial statement lending and asset-based lending, under small business credit scoring, both the owner and the firm are viewed as sources of repayment for the loan and as inseparable from a credit perspective.

Credit scoring and similar quantitative techniques (which we will collectively refer to here as "credit scoring") have been deployed by bankers to evaluate credit risk for over three decades. The most common of these techniques are statistical models that are used to quantify default probability or default risk classification such as linear probability models, logit models, and linear discriminant analysis.[6] Credit scoring was widely adopted in consumer lending in the 1970s. Its adaptation to commercial credit can also be traced back over three decades. The Altman Z-score model, probably the best known, was first published in 1968 (Altman, 1968). The Altman model is a discriminant function that had five financial ratios as right-hand-side variables. Data used to calibrate the model came from publicly traded companies. This made it well-suited for credit decisions associated with large corporate borrowers.[7] It may have made its adaptability to small and mid-sized commercial lending problematic, however. Consistent with this, survey data indicate that discriminant analysis and other statistical techniques were not widely used even as a monitoring device by commercial bankers in the 1980s (Udell, 1987).[8]

The adaptation of credit scoring to small business lending is a relatively recent phenomenon. By 1995, only one large bank, Wells Fargo, had been able to generate a sufficiently large loan database to develop a reliable proprietary model (Acs, 1999). Since then, however, outside vendors have developed and sold small business credit scoring models to commercial banks. A recent study found that, by 1998, over 60 percent of the largest banking organizations in the United States had adopted credit scoring for small business loans (Frame, Srinivasan, and Woosley, 2001). Interestingly, only 42 percent of those adopting credit scoring used it to make automatic approval/rejection decisions, and only 12 percent of banks used their own proprietary models. Smaller banks in particular appear not to have sufficient loan volume to develop their own proprietary models (Acs, 1999). It also appears that small banks have not as widely adopted small business credit scoring.

The adoption of credit scoring in small business lending appears to be focused on credits under $250,000—sometimes referred to as the microbusiness lending segment of the market. The largest provider of external models, Fair, Isaac, and Company, bases its models on credits up to $250,000, and the survey of the large U.S. banking organizations just mentioned found that 100 percent of those that had adopted the technology applied it to credits under $100,000, 74.2 percent applied it to credits between $100,000 and $250,000, and only 21 percent applied credit scoring to loans between $250,000 and $1 million (Frame, Srinivasan, and Woosley 2001, Table 1). Although the credit scoring models used in microbusiness lending appear to be more complex than those used in consumer lending, they still place considerable weight on factors associated with the financial history of the owner (Feldman, 1997). The personal information used in small business credit scoring models may include the owner's monthly income, outstanding debt, financial assets, employment tenure, home ownership, and previous loan defaults or delinquencies (Mester, 1997). This is consistent with the view that for small businesses, the creditworthiness of the owner is closely intertwined with the creditworthiness of the business (Ang, 1992; Mester, 1997).

Relationship Lending

Relationship lending is not a transactions-based technology and stands in stark contrast to the other three lending technologies. For a transactions-based credit, the credit decision and lending terms are based primarily on hard, quantitative information that is gathered around the time that the credit is originated. Each transaction stands on its own, and any proprietary information gathered from past contact between the lender and the borrower is substantially irrelevant. Another lender with no previous contact with the firm could grant the credit on similar terms with no significant informational disadvantage. In contrast, for a relationship credit, the credit decision and lending terms are based in significant part on soft, qualitative information that is gathered through continuous contact over time with the firm, its owner, and other members of the local community. Each credit granted or renewed does not stand on its own but is based on proprietary information gathered from past contact on a variety of dimensions. Another lender with no previous relationship with the firm would be at a significant informational disadvantage.

Under relationship lending, the lender gathers proprietary information about the firm and its owner acquired through a variety of contacts over time. In part, this information is obtained through the provision of loans (e.g., Berger and Udell, 1995; Petersen and Rajan, 1994) and deposits and other financial products (e.g., Cole 1998; Degryse and van Cayseele, 2000; Mester, Nakamura, and Renault, 1998; Nakamura, 1993). Additional information is generated through interaction with other members of the local community, including the borrower's suppliers and customers, who may give specific information about the firm and its owner or general information about the business environment in which they operate. This information also includes performance on verbal promises and commitments made by the owner that are not easily quantified or documented. These verbal promises and commitments may relate to strategies and actions of the firm or the owner. In short, relationship lending is based substantially on soft, qualitative information acquired over multidimensional dealings with the firm, its owner, and other local community members over time, and this information is not shared (and could not easily be shared) with other potential lenders.

The empirical literature suggests that the strength of the bank–borrower relationship may be reflected in a number of different measures. These alternative measures include (1) the existence of a banking relationship (e.g., Cole, 1998); (2) the temporal length of the relationship (e.g., Angelini, Di Salvo, and Ferri, 1998; Berger and Udell, 1995; Ongena and Smith, 2001; Petersen and Rajan, 1994, 1995; Scott and Dunkelberg, 1999); (3) the breadth of a relationship (e.g., Cole, 1998; Degryse and van Cayseele, 2000; Scott and Dunkelberg, 1999); (4) the degree of mutual trust between the bank and the firm (e.g., Harhoff and Körting, 1998); (5) the number of different account managers (e.g., Scott and Dunkelberg, 1999); (6) the presence of a hausbank or main bank (e.g., Elsas and Krahnen, 1998); and (7) borrowing from a single bank (e.g., Berger, Klapper, and Udell, 2001; Ferri and Messori, 2000; Harhoff and Körting, 1998; Machauer and Weber, 2000; Ongena and Smith, 2000).

Empirical evidence also suggests that banking relationships affect the pricing and availability of credit and that small businesses benefit from these relationships. Stronger relationships—with strength measured in the six different ways just enumerated—have been empirically associated with (1) lower loan interest rates (e.g., Berger and Udell 1995; Degryse and van Cayseele, 2000; Harhoff and Körting, 1998; Scott and Dunkelberg, 1999); (2) reduced collateral requirements (e.g., Berger and Udell, 1995; Harhoff and Körting, 1998; Scott and Dunkelberg, 1999); (3) less dependence on trade debt (e.g., Petersen and Rajan, 1994, 1995); (4) greater protection against the interest rate cycle (e.g., Berlin and Mester, 1998; Ferri and Messori, 2000); and (5) increased credit availability (Cole, 1998; Elsas and Krahnen, 1998; Machauer and Weber, 2000; Scott and Dunkelberg, 1999).[9]

There are two important gaps in our understanding of the relationship lending technology. First, empirical work on relationship lending has often been hindered by the inability of researchers to distinguish among different lending technologies in analyzing the benefits of relationship lending. In general, we expect that this inability would bias researchers against finding an association between the strength of the bank–borrower relationship and the availability and terms of credit, for relationship strength is essentially irrelevant for the transactions-based small business loans. This may help explain why some studies have not found a link between relationship strength and credit terms (e.g., Angelini, Di Salvo, and Ferri, 1998; Blackwell and Winters, 1997; Petersen and Rajan, 1994).The second gap concerns the extent to which the bank–borrower relationship resides with the loan officer versus the extent to which it resides with the banking organization, which cannot easily be measured. The loan officer may be the more important repository of the type of proprietary information that is associated with relationship lending because this information is difficult to transmit even within a banking organization (Berger and Udell, 2002). To the extent that this holds true, there are several implications. First, we expect that banks that specialize in relationship lending would delegate significant lending authority to their loan officers.[10] Second, this greater authority may create agency problems within the organization, with implications discussed later for the type of banking organization that might be best suited to make relationship loans. Third, if the loan officer is the repository of the soft relationship information, this may imply a portability for the bank–borrower relationship. A loan officer may be able to move from one bank to another and take their relationship borrowers with them, with some implications for the effects of banking industry consolidation as discussed later in this chapter.

One final note on relationship lending concerns the likely target customer. Relationship lending would seem to be best-suited for small businesses that (1) are quite informationally opaque and lack the strong financial ratios needed for financial statement lending; (2) need credit beyond the $250,000 microbusiness loan market served by small business credit scoring; and (3) lack sufficient tangible assets to justify an asset-based loan.

FACTORS THAT MAY AFFECT THE FUTURE OF RELATIONSHIP LENDING

Two main factors may have important effects on the future of relationship lending—the consolidation of the banking industry and technological progress. As will be discussed, the extent to which these factors threaten relationship lending is not yet clear.

The Consolidation of the Banking Industry

We consider the effects on relationship lending of three major consequences of the consolidation of the banking industry: increases in bank size, changes in market size structure, and globalization of the banking industry. Assuming that consolidation continues, each of these consequences may affect the future of relationship lending.

Increases in Bank Size

Mergers and acquisitions (M&As) in the banking industry have greatly reduced the number of banking institutions in the United States and elsewhere and increased their average size. The average size of U.S. banks more than tripled from $174 million to $584 million, and the median size more than doubled, from $34 million to $69 million over 1984–1998. A number of reasons have been given for this consolidation activity, including technological progress, improvements in financial condition, excess capacity or financial distress in the industry or market, international consolidation of markets, and deregulation of geographical or product restrictions (see Berger, Demsetz, and Strahan, 1999, for a review).

The increase in bank size of the M&A participants may lead them to reduce their relationship lending to informationally opaque small businesses. Several theoretical arguments have been put forward as to why large banks may be disadvantaged in offering relationship lending technology. First, as already discussed, relationship lending is a very different technology from the transactions-based lending technologies. Under relationship lending, banks accumulate information over time through continuous contact with the firm, its owner, its suppliers, its customers, and other members of its local community on a variety of dimensions, whereas under transactions-based lending, due diligence and contract terms are based on information that is collected primarily at the time of origination. Large banks are hypothesized to have difficulty using both relationship lending and transactions-based lending technologies in the same organization because of Williamson-type organizational diseconomies (Williamson, 1967, 1988). In addition, these diseconomies may be exacerbated because the customer bases for the two types of products are often quite different—informationally opaque small businesses for most relationship loans and large corporate customers for most transactions-based lending services. Large banks may also be disadvantaged because relationship lending often requires soft data, such as information about the character, reliability, and local community standing of the firm's owner. Such data may be difficult to quantify, verify, and transmit through the communication channels of large organizations (Stein, 2002). These difficulties may be aggravated for large banks because these banks are on average headquartered at longer distances from potential small business borrowers, which may create higher costs of generating borrower-specific information. It has been posited that relationship lending diminishes with "informational distance" because of these costs, which is likely to be associated with physical distance (Hauswald and Marquez, 2002). Finally, the accumulation over time of soft information by the loan officer may create agency problems within the organization, for the loan officer may make less effort or use the information for purposes other than maximizing banking organization value. It has been argued that small banking organizations with few managerial layers may be best at resolving these agency problems (Berger and Udell, 2002).

Some empirical research is consistent with the predictions of this theory. A number of studies have found that large banks allocate much lower proportions of their assets to small business loans than do small banks, where small business loans are usually measured as credits under $1 million (e.g., Berger, Kashyap, and Scalise, 1995; Peek and Rosengren, 1996; Strahan and Weston, 1996). A typical finding is that large banks with over $10 billion in assets allocate about 2 percent of assets on average to small business loans defined in this way, whereas small banks with less than $100 million in assets invest about 9 percent of their assets in these loans.

A number of studies have also examined the effects of bank M&As on small business lending (e.g., Avery and Samolyk, 2000; Berger, Saunders, Scalise, and Udell, 1998; Bonaccorsi di Patti and Gobbi, 2000; Keeton, 1996; Peek and Rosengren, 1998; Strahan and Weston, 1998). M&As involve dynamic effects, such as changes in bank focus or disruptions caused by the consolidation process, as well as changes in bank size. These studies usually found that M&As involving large banking organizations reduced the participating banks' ratios of small business loans to assets substantially.

The research reviewed thus far might suggest that the increase in average bank size from consolidation of the banking industry—assuming this consolidation continues—would have a substantial negative effect on the future of relationship lending. However, even if large, consolidated banks reduce their relationship lending substantially, the *total* supply of relationship credit to informationally opaque small businesses may not decline substantially. This is because there may be "external effects" or general equilibrium effects in which other banks react to any reduced supply of credit by the consolidating institutions by increasing their own supplies. That is, although some large banks may drop relationship loans after M&As, other banks or nonbank lenders may pick up some of these loans if they are positive net present value investments. Several recent studies found external effects of bank M&As in terms of increased lending to small businesses by other incumbent banks in the same local markets that offset at least part of the negative quantity effects of M&A participants (e.g., Avery and Samolyk, 2000; Berger, Goldberg, and White, 2001; Berger, Saunders, Scalise, and Udell, 1998). There may also be external effects in the form of increases in de novo entry—new banks that form in markets where M&As occur—although the evidence on this issue is mixed (Berger, Bonime, Goldberg, and White, 2000; Seelig and Critchfield, 1999). Part of these external effects may be relationship loans granted by loan officers that have moved from consolidated banks to other incumbent local banks or started de novo banks and retained some of their relationship customers. As noted earlier, this can occur to the extent that the relationship is portable in the sense that it resides with the loan officer and not the bank.

We also caution that the implications of this research hinge on the assumption that the observed associations between bank size and M&As on the one hand and small business lending on the other hand primarily reflect the effects of bank size and M&As on relationship lending, as opposed to other transactions-based lending technologies. Some additional research does support this assumption by giving evidence consistent with the proposition that large banks tend to have proportionately fewer relationship loans among the small business loans they do make. Relative to small banks, large banks were found to lend more often to larger, older, more financially secure businesses—firms that are most likely to receive transactions loans (Haynes, Ou, and Berney, 1999). It was also found that large banks tend to base their small business loan approval decisions more on financial ratios, whereas the existence of a prior relationship with the borrowing firm mattered more to decisions by small banks (Cole, Goldberg, and White, 1999). Large banks were also found to tend to make small business loans at greater distances using less personal methods of contact than small banks (Berger, Miller, Petersen, Rajan, and Stein, 2001). This finding is consistent with larger banks more often using transactions-based methods, which do not require as much geographic proximity and personal contact as relationship lending. In addition, large banks were found to lend more often to small firms that borrow from multiple banks (Berger, Klapper, and Udell, 2001). These loans are more likely to be transactions-based loans than relationship loans, for relationship lending generally requires exclusive lending arrangements to optimize the use of soft relationship information that cannot be shared among lenders.

Changes in Market Size Structure

Mergers and acquisitions in the banking industry also change the size structure of local markets. Banking market size structure refers to the distribution of market shares of different size classes of banks in a local market. Most M&As in the United States and most international M&As are of the market-extension type—joining banks with little or no local market overlap prior to the union. Such M&As do not significantly change local market concentration, but they do shift the ownership of the local banking resources into the hands of larger banking organizations. This could affect the treatment of relationship lending customers if banks behave differently in markets dominated by large banks than in markets dominated by small banks. Market size structure could matter more than the size of the lending bank itself if, for example, large banks behave more like small banks in markets with dominant market shares for small banks and/or small banks behave more like large banks in markets with dominant shares for large banks. Most studies of the effects of bank size have not controlled for the size structure of the market. This raises the possibility that some of the effects of bank market structure may have inadvertently been attributed to bank size, given that bank size and the market shares of large banks are highly correlated.

Some recent empirical evidence suggests that market size structure may matter as much or more than bank size in terms of the treatment of small business borrowers. One study found that all else being equal, the likelihood that a small business has a line of credit from a bank of a given size is roughly proportional to the local market presence of banks of that size, although there were exceptions for very small loans (credits under $100,000) and very small banks (assets under $100 million). Large banks tend to make relatively few of the very small loans, and very small banks tend to make relatively few of the larger loans (Berger, Rosen, and Udell, 2001). Similarly, another study found that the probability of a small business having a line of credit and its dependence on trade credit were not related to the presence of small banks in the market (Jayaratne and Wolken, 1999). These findings that take into account market size structure are not consistent with the prior literature that indicated that large banks generally had difficulty issuing credits of up to $1 million to small businesses.

These different results may be due to using a different methodology that takes into account market size structure and examines the issue from the perspective of the small business in its local market, rather than from the perspective of the bank. In addition, the revised methodology and new results call into question the traditional methodology for analyzing the effects of bank size that relied on the ratio of small business credits under $1 million to total assets as an indicator of the propensity to make small business loans. The traditional approach effectively takes banks' assets to be fixed and does not allow for the possibility that large banks expand their assets to take advantage of their greater opportunities to make large business loans. Large banks may make small business loans in proportion (or more than in proportion) to their local market presence, but simply have lower ratios of small business loans to total assets because these banks expand their assets to make more large business loans. That is, large banks may have low small business loans to assets ratios because the denominator of the ratio is expanded, rather than because the numerator is contracted. The traditional approach that operates from the bank's perspective also does not take into account the distribution of potential small business loan customers in the markets in which the bank is present. Some large banks may have low small business loans ratios because there are proportionately fewer positive-net-present-value small business loan opportunities in the markets in which they compete. Finally, the new results suggest that if the small business loans to assets ratio is used, consideration should be given to using cutoffs other than credits below $1 million and including market size structure as well as bank size.

Some recent evidence also suggests that market size structure may affect small business loan pricing. The results indicate that market size structure has important effects on prices—perhaps even more important than those of bank size—even after controlling for conventional market concentration and other market and firm characteristics. Banks apparently compete more aggressively and charge lower loan prices in markets dominated by large banks (Berger, Rosen, and Udell, 2001).

The new evidence on the effects of market size structure shows that the increases in the local market shares of large banks from consolidation of the banking industry—assuming consolidation continues—would have relatively little effect on relationship lending, except perhaps on lending to the very smallest customers. However, strong caveats are in order. The implications depend in part on whether these new results are replicated by future studies. The implications also depend on the assumption that the small business loan results primarily reflect relationship lending versus other transactions-based lending.

Again, there may be external effects or general equilibrium effects in which other incumbent banks or new banks take up some of the reduction created by consolidation.

Globalization

In the United States and in most regions of the world, the vast majority of M&As have involved domestic institutions within each nation, and the total banking market shares held by foreign-owned banks generally do not exceed 10 percent (Berger, Demsetz, and Strahan, 1999; Levine, 1996). However, in some parts of Latin America and elsewhere, there has been a tremendous increase in international consolidation. For example, in Argentina, the share of total assets held by foreign-owned banks increased from 14 percent to 53 percent between 1991 and 1998 (Raffin, 1999).

The foreign-owned banks that are created by globalization may have difficulty extending relationship loans to informationally opaque small businesses in part because these banks are often large and nearly always are headquartered a considerable distance from local small businesses. They may therefore suffer size- and distance-related disadvantages in delivering relationship lending similar to those of large domestically owned banks. In addition, a foreign-owned bank may be headquartered in a radically different market environment, with a different language, culture, supervisory/regulatory structure, and so forth. These market differences may make it costly to gather, process, and transmit locally based soft relationship information, thereby compounding the problems associated with size and distance.

A limited amount of recent empirical research is consistent with the notion that foreign ownership may create difficulties. One study found that foreign-owned banks were less likely to lend to informationally opaque small businesses (Berger, Klapper, and Udell, 2001). Other studies examined the efficiency of foreign-owned banks relative to domestically owned banks. Foreign-owned banks have usually been found to be relatively inefficient (see Berger, DeYoung, Genay, and Udell, 2000 for a review). This inefficiency may in part either reflect or cause the difficulties of foreign-owned banks in making relationship loans.

Any future increases in globalization may be associated with declines in relationship lending by the consolidating institutions. However, the caveats again apply. The implications depend in part on whether the limited results in this literature are replicated by future studies, on the assumption that the results primarily reflect the effects of globalization on relationship lending, and on whether or not there are strong external effects from incumbent domestically owned banks or newly formed banks.

Technological Change

As noted earlier, a second main factor that may affect the future of relationship lending is technological change. In recent years, technological change has transformed much of the banking industry. Improvements in information processing have allowed institutions to process, store, and recover information more quickly and reliably. Improvements in telecommunications, such as the Internet, have allowed banks to transmit and receive data much more quickly and easily. Finally, improvements in financial technologies have made it much easier for banks to use sophisticated models to assess risks and have provided new financial instruments and markets to help banks unbundle, repackage, and hedge these risks.

These advances in information processing, telecommunications, and financial technologies improve the processing, transmission, and analysis of the hard, quantitative information used in the three transactions-based lending technologies much more than they help in dealing with the soft, qualitative information that is key to relationship lending. To illustrate, for financial statement lending, (1) information processing technology advances have reduced the cost of analyzing financial information; (2) telecommunications technology advances have reduced the cost of transmitting financial information within the bank via intranet connections and in requesting and receiving data from the loan customer and third-party credit information producers (e.g., Dun and Bradstreet in the United States and public credit registries in other nations) via the Internet; and (3) financial technology advances have reduced the costs of managing and pricing the risks of financial statement loans, and in unbundling and packaging some of these risks for sale to other financial institutions.

Similarly, for asset-based lending, advances in information processing, telecommunications, and financial technologies have significantly reduced the cost and increased the speed of monitoring accounts receivable and inventory, transmitting this information, and analyzing and making decisions based on this information. For example, the accounts receivable assignment schedule, the accounts receivable collection schedule, and the borrowing base certificate can all be transmitted electronically. This can be augmented on a daily basis with an updated receivable aging sent via the Internet. This enables the asset-based lender to continuously adjust credit availability (i.e., the borrowing base) and to calculate nearly instantaneous changes in receivable turnover. Finally, for small business credit scoring, information processing, telecommunications, and financial technology improvements have also facilitated the analysis and transmission of consumer and business data in credit scoring models. In the future, innovations in financial technologies may permit the securitization of credit-scored small business loans, similar to the securitization of consumer credit card loans.

For relationship lending, however, it seems unlikely that similar improvements can be made in processing, transmitting, and analyzing soft, qualitative information. For example, information about the character and reliability of the firm's owner is known primarily to the loan officer and cannot be easily transmitted either within the bank or to external parties via electronic means.

The improvements in the transactions-based lending technologies may threaten relationship lending in two ways. First, there may be a substitution effect into these other technologies from relationship lending at the margin. That is, some loan applicants for which the bank is near the margin between using relationship lending and one of these other technologies may be switched into another technology. Although this may decrease the quantity of relationship lending, it may not necessarily cause a substantial change in credit availability or terms of credit, and the firms that are switched may be better off on average. That is, some firms that are switched may suffer a decline in credit availability or terms, but it is possible that even more of these firms may enjoy improved availability or terms. Presumably, the technological advances reduce costs, improve the accuracy of credit assessments, and the like, and some of the benefits from these advances may be passed onto the borrowers.

Some recent empirical evidence supports this argument. Studies of the adoption of small business credit scoring technology by large U.S. banks found that these banks increased their small business lending after adoption relative to otherwise similar institutions that did not adopt this technology (Berger, Frame, and Miller, 2001; Frame, Srinivasan, and Woosley 2001). This result suggests that on net, the switch by the bank of some loan applications from relationship lending and other lending technologies to small business credit scoring either reduced costs or improved credit assessment accuracy sufficiently that more credit was granted on average.

The second, and more serious, way in which technological improvements to the transactions-based lending technologies may threaten relationship lending is the possibility that these improvements may cause some banks to discontinue the relationship lending technology. Banks that grow large may choose to discontinue relationship lending because of Williamson-type organizational diseconomies associated with using both relationship lending and transactions-based lending technologies in the same organization. Such diseconomies may be exacerbated by improvements to the transactions-based technologies that allow the banks to make better use of hard information, but do not offer much improvement in terms of using the type of soft information employed in relationship lending. Put another way, improvements in information processing, telecommunications, and financial technologies may make it more profitable to focus on a set of lending technologies that uses only hard information and to drop the lending technology that focuses on soft information.

The extent to which technological change that favors transactions-based lending methods threatens the future of relationship lending is very difficult to determine. There is very little in the way of prior measurement of this effect. It is difficult to measure relationship lending separately from the other lending methods. In addition, the total impact of technological change also depends on external effects, or the extent to which other banks may expand their relationship lending when some banks discontinue this lending technology.

CONCLUSIONS

In this chapter, we identify two potential threats to relationship lending—banking industry consolidation and technological change, either or both of which could result in some banks significantly reducing or eliminating the use of the relationship lending technology. The increases in bank size, higher local market shares for large banks, and increased penetration of foreign-owned banks associated with consolidation may create financial institutions that are disadvantaged in gathering and using the soft, qualitative data about small businesses and their owners that are needed for relationship lending. Technological advances in information processing, telecommunications, and financial technologies may improve the processing, transmission, and analysis of the hard, quantitative information used in transactions-based lending technologies and cause banks to substitute away from or discontinue relationship lending, which is not helped as much by technological change.

Unfortunately, the available empirical research does not give a clear indication of the magnitude of either of these threats. Although there has been a tremendous amount of empirical research on the effects of banking industry consolidation on small business lending, this research is not conclusive regarding the effects of consolidation on relationship lending. Among the problems associated with this research is its use of a small business loans to assets ratio that may be misleading because the numerator may not represent relationship lending, and the denominator may not remain fixed after consolidation. In addition, little of the extant research has taken into account the effects of changes in market size structure (i.e., increases in the market shares of large banks) or globalization (i.e., increased foreign-owned bank presence). In addition, even if consolidation continues and the banks participating in merger and acquisition (M&A) behavior do significantly cut back or discontinue relationship lending, it is quite difficult to gauge the size of any external effects or general equilibrium effects in which other incumbent banks in the market or de novo entrants may react to a reduced supply of relationship credit by the consolidating institutions by increasing their own supplies. To address the issue of the effects of consolidation on the future of relationship lending, more research is needed that examines the issue from the perspective of the small business in its local market rather than from the perspective of the bank and its small business loans to assets ratio, incorporates market size structure and foreign bank ownership, and incorporates the external or general equilibrium effects of consolidation.

The empirical research problems on the effects of technological change are much more difficult. To date, some limited research suggests that the adoption of small business credit scoring technology may result in a net expansion of credit to small businesses, but there are few other measurable effects of technological change on small business lending in general or on relationship lending specifically. It is generally difficult to (1) empirically differentiate the observed small business lending among the different types of lending technologies, (2) observe the technological advances or investments in new technologies, and (3) determine how these advances or investments affect the three transactions-based lending technologies—financial statement lending, asset-based lending, and small business credit scoring—versus their effects on relationship lending. It would seem that a necessary condition for future research would be data that differentiates small business loans among the four lending technologies and data on bank investment in information processing, telecommunications, and financial technology. Any conclusions about the effects of technological change on relationship lending should incorporate the possibility of external effects in which other incumbent or newly formed banks take up the slack if some banks adopting new technologies discontinue use of the relationship lending technology.

Thus, the future of relationship lending is uncertain, but continued and improved research on the effects of banking industry consolidation and technological change may help bring it into better focus.

NOTES

1. The views expressed in this chapter do not necessarily reflect those of the Federal Reserve Board or its staff. It is based on a paper delivered at the Future of Banking panel at the Financial Management Association Meetings, October 18, 2001.

2. See Lazere (1968) and Rutenberg (1994) for a history of asset-based lending and an overview of the industry.

3. The use of collateral in commercial lending appears to have risen steadily over the past three decades. One study found that the fraction of bank commercial loans that were secured rose from 49 percent in 1977 to 55 percent in 1983 to 68 percent in 1987 (Berger and Udell, 1990).

4. For a more extensive description of the mechanics of asset-based lending, see Clarke (1996).

5. Empirical evidence, however, based on normal measures of informational opacity, fail to show a distinction between asset-based borrowers and non-asset-based borrowers (see Carey, Post, and Sharpe, 1998).

6. For a more detailed discussion of credit scoring models and other newer quantitative techniques that can be used for credit risk measurement and pricing, see Saunders (2000).

7. See Altman (1985) for a detailed discussion of the use of discriminant analysis in commercial lending.

8. A survey of 106 Midwestern banks in 1986 indicated that only 11.3 percent of all banks surveyed and only 3.2 percent of small banks surveyed used any form multivariate statistical analysis as part of their commercial loan review process (Udell, 1987).

9. These findings are consistent with the theoretical models offered by Boot and Thakor (1994) and Petersen and Rajan (1995), but inconsistent with those offered by Greenbaum, Kanatas, and Venezia (1989), and Sharpe (1990).

A downside to relationship lending is that it may create a hold-up problem by giving the lender monopoly power (see Rajan, 1992). For a more detailed discussion of the theoretical issues associated with relationship lending, see Boot (2000).

10. Empirical evidence linking relationship lending with delegation of loan authority is problematic because of the limitations of existing data. One study, however, is suggestive of such a link (Udell, 1989). This study noted that delegation of loan authority likely creates a significant agency problem between the loan officer and the bank. Consistent with this observation, the study found empirical evidence that bank expenditure

on monitoring loan officers was positively related to measures of delegation of loan authority.

REFERENCES

Acs, Z. A. 1999. The development and expansion of secondary markets for small business loans. In J. L. Blanton, A. Williams, and S.L.W. Rhine, eds., *Business Access to Capital and Credit.* A Federal Reserve System Research Conference, 625–643.

Altman, E. I. 1968. Financial ratios, discriminant analysis and the prediction of corporate bankruptcy. *Journal of Finance* 23(4): 589–609.

Altman, E. I. 1985. Managing the commercial lending process. In R. C. Aspinwall and R. A. Eisenbeis, eds., *Handbook for Banking Strategy.* New York: John Wiley and Sons.

Ang, J. S. 1992. On the theory of finance for privately held firms. *Journal of Small Business Finance* 1: 185–203.

Angelini, P., Salvo, R. D., and Ferri, G. 1998. Availability and cost for small businesses: Customer relationships and credit cooperatives. *Journal of Banking and Finance* 22: 929–954.

Avery, R. B., and Samolyk, K. A. 2000. Bank consolidation and the provision of banking services: The case of small commercial loans. Washington, D.C.: Federal Deposit Insurance Corporation Working Paper.

Berger, A. N., Bonime, S. D., Goldberg, L. G., and White, L. J. 2000. The dynamics of market entry: The effects of mergers and acquisitions on entry in the banking industry. Washington, D.C.: Federal Reserve Board Working Paper.

Berger, A. N., Demsetz, R. S., and Strahan, P. E. 1999. The consolidation of the financial services industry: Causes, consequences, and implications for the future. *Journal of Banking and Finance* 23: 135–194.

Berger, A. N., DeYoung, R., Genay, H., and Udell, G. F. 2000. Globalization of financial institutions: Evidence from cross-border banking performance. *Brookings-Wharton Papers on Financial Services* 3, 23–158.

Berger, A. N., Frame, W. S., and Miller, N. H. 2001. Credit scoring and the price and availability of small business credit. Washington, D.C.: Federal Reserve Board Working Paper.

Berger, A. N., Goldberg, L. G., and White, L. J. 2001. The effects of dynamic changes in bank competition on the supply of small business credit. *European Finance Review* 5(1): 113–139.

Berger, A. N., Kashyap, A. K., and Scalise, J. M. 1995. The transformation of the U.S. banking industry: What a long, strange trip it's been. *Brookings Papers on Economic Activity* 2, 55–218.

Berger, A. N., Klapper, L. F., and Udell, G. F. 2001. The ability of banks to lend to informationally opaque small businesses. *Journal of Banking and Finance* 25: 2127–2167.

Berger, A. N., Miller, N. H., Petersen, M. A., Rajan, R. G., and Stein, J. C. 2001. Does function follow organizational form? Evidence from the lending practices of large and small banks. Washington, D.C.: Federal Reserve Board Working Paper.

Berger, A. N., Rosen, R. J., and Udell, G. F. 2001. The effect of banking market size structure on bank competition: The case of small business lending. Washington, D.C.: Federal Reserve Board Working Paper.

Berger, A. N., Saunders, A., Scalise, J. M., and Udell, G. F. 1998. The effects of bank mergers and acquisitions on small business lending. *Journal of Financial Economics* 50(2): 187–229.

Berger, A. N., and Udell, G. F. 1990. Collateral, loan quality, and bank risk. *Journal of Monetary Economics* 25: 21–42.

Berger, A. N., and Udell, G. F. 1995. Relationship lending and lines of credit in small firm finance. *Journal of Business* 68: 351–382.

Berger, A. N., and Udell, G. F. 1998. The economics of small business finance: The roles of private equity and debt markets in the financial growth cycle. *Journal of Banking and Finance* 22: 613–673.

Berger, A. N., and Udell, G. F. 2002. Small business credit availability and relationship lending: The importance of bank organizational structure. *Economic Journal*, forthcoming.

Berlin, M., and Mester, L. J. 1998. On the profitability and cost of relationship lending. *Journal of Banking and Finance* 22: 873–897.

Berlin, M., and Mester, L. J. 1999. Deposits and relationship lending. *Review of Financial Studies* 12: 597–607.

Blackwell, D., and Winters, D. B. 1997. Banking relationships and the effect of monitoring on loan pricing. *Journal of Financial Research* 20: 275–289.

Bonaccorsi di Patti, E., and Gobbi, G. 2000. The effects of bank consolidation on small business lending: Evidence from market and firm data. Bank of Italy Working Paper.

Boot, A.W.A. 2000. Relationship banking: What do we know? *Journal of Financial Intermediation* 9: 7–25.

Boot, A.W.A., and Thakor, A. V. 1994. Moral hazard and secured lending in an infinitely repeated credit market game. *International Economic Review* 35: 899–920.

Carey, M., Post, M., and Sharpe, S. A. 1998. Does corporate lending by banks and finance companies differ? Evidence on specialization in private debt contracting. *The Journal of Finance* 53: 845–878.

Clarke, P. S. 1996. *Asset-Based Lending*. Homewood, Ill.: Irwin.

Cole, R. A. 1998. The importance of relationships to the availability of credit. *Journal of Banking and Finance* 22: 959–977.

Cole, R. A., Goldberg, L. G., and White, L. J. 1999. Cookie-cutter versus character: The micro structure of small business lending by large and small banks. In J. L. Blanton, A. Williams, and S.L.W. Rhine, eds., *Business Access to Capital and Credit*. A Federal Reserve System Research Conference, 362–389.

Degryse, H., and van Cayseele, P. 2000. Relationship lending within a bank-based system: Evidence from European small business data. *Journal of Financial Intermediation* 9: 90–109.

DeYoung, R., and Nolle, D. E., 1996. Foreign-owned banks in the U.S.: Earning market share or buying it? *Journal of Money, Credit, and Banking* 28(4): 622–636.

Elsas, R., and J. P. Krahnen. 1998. Is relationship lending special? Evidence from credit-file data in Germany. *Journal of Banking and Finance* 22: 1283–1316.

Feldman, R. 1997. Banks and a big change in technology called credit scoring. Federal Reserve Bank of Minneapolis, *The Region*, September: 19–25.

Ferri, G., and Messori, M. 2000. Bank-firm relationships and allocative efficiency in northeastern and central Italy and in the South. *Journal of Banking and Finance* 24: 1067–1095.

Frame, W. S., Srinivasan, A., and Woosley, L. 2001. The effect of credit scoring on small business lending. *Journal of Money, Credit, and Banking* 33(3): 813–825.

Greenbaum, S. I., Kanatas, G., and Venezia, I. 1989. Equilibrium loan pricing under the bank-client relationship. *Journal of Banking and Finance* 13: 221–235.

Harhoff, D., and Körting, T. 1998. Lending relationships in Germany: Empirical results from survey data. *Journal of Banking and Finance* 22: 1317–1354.

Hauswald, R., and Marquez, R. 2002. Competition and strategic information acquisition in credit markets. Working paper, University of Maryland.

Haynes, G. W., Ou, C., and Berney, R. 1999. Small business borrowing from large and small banks. In J. L. Blanton, A. Williams, and S.L.W. Rhine, eds., *Business Access to Capital and Credit*. Federal Reserve System Research Conference.

Jayaratne, J., and Wolken, J. D. 1999. How important are small banks to small business lending? New evidence from a survey to small businesses. *Journal of Banking and Finance* 23: 427–458.

Keeton, W. R. 1996. Do bank mergers reduce lending to businesses and farmers? New evidence from tenth district states. Federal Reserve Bank of Kansas City, *Economic Review* 81(3): 63–75.

Lazere, M. R. 1968. *Commercial Financing*. New York: National Commercial Finance Conference.

Levine, R. 1996. Foreign banks, financial development, and economic growth. In Claude E. Barfield, ed., *International Financial Markets: Harmonization versus Competition*. Washington, D.C.: AEI Press.

Machauer, A., and Weber, M. 2000. Number of bank relationships: An indicator of competition, borrower quality, or just size? University of Mannheim Working Paper.

Mester, L. J. 1997. What's the point of credit scoring? Federal Reserve Bank of Philadelphia, *Business Review*, September/October: 3–16.

Mester, L. J., Nakamura, L. I., and Renault, M. 1998. Checking accounts and bank monitoring. Federal Reserve Bank of Philadelphia Working Paper.

Nakamura, L. I. 1993. Commercial bank information: Implications for the structure of banking. In M. Klausner and L. J. White, eds., *Structural Change in Banking*. Homewood, Ill.: Irwin, 131–160.

Ongena, S., and Smith, D. C. 2000. What determines the number of bank relationships? *Journal of Financial Intermediation* 9: 26–56.

Ongena, S., and Smith, D. C. 2001. Empirical evidence on the duration of banking relationships. *Journal of Financial Economics* 61: 449–475.

Peek, J., and Rosengren, E. S. 1996. Small business credit availability: How important is size of lender? In Anthony Saunders and Ingo Walter, eds., *Financial System Design: The Case for Universal Banking*. Burr Ridge, Ill.: Irwin Publishing, 628–655.

Peek, J., and Rosengren, E. S. 1998. Bank consolidation and small business lending: It's not just bank size that matters. *Journal of Banking and Finance* 22: 799–819.

Petersen, M. A., and Rajan, R. G. 1994. The benefits of firm-creditor relationships: Evidence from small business data. *Journal of Finance* 49: 3–37.

Petersen, M. A., and Rajan, R. G. 1995. The effect of credit market competition on lending relationships. *Quarterly Journal of Economics* 110: 407–443.

Raffin, M. 1999. A note on the profitability of the foreign-owned banks in Argentina. *Banco Central de la Republica Argentina*. Technical Note No. 6.

Rajan, R. G. 1992. Insiders and outsiders: The choice between informed and arm's-length debt. *Journal of Finance* 47: 1367–1399.

Rutenberg, S. 1994. *The History of Asset-Based Lending*. Commercial Finance Association.

Saunders, A. 2000. *Financial Institutions Management*. Boston: Irwin McGraw-Hill.

Scott, J. A., and Dunkelberg, W. C. 1999. Bank consolidation and small business lending: A small firm perspective. In J. L. Blanton, A. Williams, and S.L.W. Rhine, eds., *Business Access to Capital and Credit*. A Federal Reserve System Research Conference, 328–361.

Seelig, S. A., and Critchfield, T. 1999. Determinants of de novo entry in banking. Federal Deposit Insurance Corporation Working Paper 99–1.

Sharpe, S. A. 1990. Asymmetric information, bank lending, and implicit contracts: A stylized model of customer relationships, *Journal of Finance* 45: 1069–1087.

Sherman, M. D. 1999. *Commercial Finance Association Marketing Survey for 1999*. Commercial Finance Association.

Stein, J. C. 2002. Information production and capital allocation: decentralized vs. hierarchical firms. *Journal of Finance*, forthcoming.

Strahan, P. E., and Weston J. P. 1996. Small business lending and bank consolidation: is there cause for concern? Federal Reserve Bank of New York, *Current Issues in Economics and Finance* 2: 1–6.

Strahan, P. E., and Weston J. P. 1998. Small business lending and the changing structure of the banking industry. *Journal of Banking and Finance* 22: 821–845.

Swary, I., and Udell, G. F. 1988. Information production and the secured line of credit. New York University Working Paper.

Udell, G. F. 1987. Designing the optimal loan review policy: An analysis of loan review in Midwestern banks. Herbert V. Prochnow Education Foundation—Prochnow Reports.

Udell, G. F. 1989. Loan quality, commercial loan review and loan officer contracting. *Journal of Banking and Finance* 13: 367–382.

Williamson, O. 1967. *The economics of defense contracting: Incentives and performance in issues in defense economics*. R. McKean, ed. New York: Columbia University Press.

Williamson, O. 1988. Corporate finance and corporate governance. *Journal of Finance* 43: 567–591.

Chapter 11

Lessons from a Bank Profitability Study for the Future of Banking

Horst Gischer and D. Johannes Jüttner

INTRODUCTION

The issue of the level of competition in banking markets has been the focus of attention for some time now at the theoretical level, and a plethora of empirical investigations have been carried out on the topic. Despite these research efforts, no unanimity exists with respect to a satisfactory model of banking competition, the available empirical results are often ambiguous, and the applied research methods differ significantly.

Researchers encounter numerous difficulties in their endeavor to model and measure competition among banks. First, banking markets may be delineated on a geographical basis, viewed from a retail or wholesale perspective, assessed within national boundaries, or placed in the international context. In addition, banking and securities markets and activities have become increasingly blurred. The spread of e-banking adds a further competitive dimension. Second, the output of banks is multiproduct in nature, while most empirical studies regard bank output as homogeneous. Third, the literature has failed to convincingly integrate market structure with competitive behavior. Thus, structure-conduct-performance (SCP) and Rosse-Panzar type investigations exist side by side. Fourth, finding an appropriate proxy variable for market power in econometric investigations has turned out to be an elusive task. The widely used three- or five-bank concentration ratios provide conflicting signals about their impact on competition in studies that control for efficiency. Fifth, the impact of risk on measures of profitability has frequently been ignored, or inappropriate proxies have been used. Sixth, the increasing globalization of banking poses new challenges, not only to active participants in the banking business but also to academic research. It appears that the literature is only slowly coming to grips with the ramifications of global competition in banking.

This chapter attempts to advance our understanding of issues concerned with the last three points. First, in order to assess competitive conditions in banking, we employ the Lerner monopoly index as a proxy for market power and measure its impact on bank profitability and interest rate margins. Our empirical estimates appear to support the notion of market power impacting positively on banks' profitability and margins. Second, our international database allows us to test hypotheses about competition on a global basis. We surmise that fee-income generating business is subject to more intense competition, especially on an international basis than interest income activities of banks. If this is so, we would expect a negative relationship from regressing bank profitability and margins on the fee-to-interest-income ratio. As it turns out, the empirical estimates confirm this conjecture. However, other factors may contribute to this relationship. If fee-based activities are more cash flow certain, the attendant lower risk may decrease required returns. Moreover, a lower required rate of return may also be due to diversification benefits that banks reap from branching out into earning fee income. Third, with regard to risk we suggest a measure that is more in tune with the concept used in the Basel value-at-risk (VaR)-approaches than the contributions in the literature. The volatility of gross bank-income appears to capture the uncertainties of banking; it exerts a consistently positive influence on bank profitability and margins.

In this chapter we review the literature on the topic of competition, market structure and various measures of profitability and interest rate margins. We also highlight the importance of using consistent databases to measure the international dimension of competition. Other sections formulate and analyze estimation equations; discuss the variables used and the role they play in the testing of the hypotheses; discuss the estimation results; and present the conclusion, suggestions for further research, and implications for the future of banking. The empirical estimates employ OECD Banking Profitability statistics on an aggregative cross-country basis.

REVIEW OF THE LITERATURE

Competition typically exerts its influence on banks on input and output prices (interest rates), on their cost structure, product mix, technological progress, and profit margins. Bank profitability ratios and interest rate margins are most frequently used as the summary measures on which competition and other factors exert their influence.

Risk in Bank Profitability and Interest Margin Studies

Since our own and most other studies are based on accounting measures of assets and income/expenditures, the dependent variables, namely, profitability and interest rate margins, are not risk adjusted. Since finance theory postulates a positive relationship between return and risk, we have to include a risk proxy among the independent variables.

Risk impacts on bank profitability and interest margins in two ways. First, bank managers and shareholders may exhibit different degrees of *risk aversion* across the various kinds of banks (large and small, universal and specialized, domestic and international, etc.). Most studies ignore this component of risk, thus implicitly assuming uniformity of risk aversion among banks or hypothesizing risk neutrality. Where risk aversion is mentioned (e.g., Saunders and Schumacher, 2000), the risk uniformity assumption is explicitly made, presumably because of the difficulties in finding an empirical proxy for bankers' risk aversion.

Second, the banking business involves various kinds of risk such as credit risk, market risk, and operational risk. Finance theory predicts a positive relationship between risk and return. Only a few banking studies include among the determinants of bank profitability or interest rate margins risk factors, and Saunders and Schumacher (2000) is one recent interest rate margin study that considers risk. They attempt to break down the risk of a bank into credit risk and intermediation risk. The capital to assets ratio reflects, on the one hand, regulatory costs that banks try to shift onto customers, and on the other it purports to measure credit risk. However, because the Basel capital requirement is based on risk-adjusted assets, while the authors use raw asset data, the resulting positive relationship between this ratio and the interest margin lends itself to ambiguous interpretation. Take, for example, two banks with the same capital to assets ratio. On the basis of risk-adjusted assets, the bank with the riskier assets would have a much higher capital/risk-adjusted assets ratio than the bank with the lower ratio and thus require a larger margin. To boot, the capital base supports a much broader range of banking business than just interest earnings activities. For example, trading in securities and derivatives requires capital and generates mainly fees but little or no interest income. As banks have tended to replace interest income by fee revenue, the positive link between the interest margin and a rising capital ratio could be spurious.

In a similar vein, Molyneux and Lloyd-Williams (1994) include the ratios of capital to assets and loans to deposits as risk variables in their SCP-estimation equation. As one would have expected, the risk variables are either not consistently significant or show the wrong sign. Take, for example, the capital/assets ratio. According to the authors, its influence on profitability is expected to be negative, but the estimated coefficients turn out consistently positive and statistically significant. This nonsensical outcome is hardly surprising since the capital account does not allow us to slot banks into risk groups. This is so because banks deemed to carry risk-assets on their balance sheets are required by the Basel Capital Accord 1988 to hold capital commensurate with the risk grade. Thus, while capital in the ratio is risk-adjusted, assets are not. As a consequence, banks with riskier assets will tend to have higher capital ratios, making this ratio unsuitable as a risk gauge. However, even if the denominator of the ratio were risk adjusted, the capital-to-assets ratio would still be completely useless as a risk measure as the Basle capital requirement in fact equalizes ratios across banks. That is, banks with riskier assets still have to hold 8 percent of their risk-adjusted assets in the form of capital. However, accounting data do not record assets on their risk-adjusted basis in balance sheets.

Returning to the risk elements of Saunders and Schumacher's study, we see that they capture intermediation risk relating to interest rate margin business by including the volatilities of the borrowing and lending rates as determinants of the interest rate margin. As expected, higher volatilities cause margins to widen.[1]

Competition and Market Power

In the traditional structure-conduct-performance (SCP) literature, competition in banking markets, or its absence, is commonly measured by the market power of banks. Market power is proxied by the Herfindahl Index (HI) or various concentration ratios. The HI is obtained by summing the squares of the market share of each bank as regards total assets or deposits. The three- or five-bank concentration ratio measures the market share (in terms of assets) of the three or five largest banks in a region. The HI is generally considered a more pertinent market power measure because it captures both the number and size distribution of all firms in the market. Researchers subsequently infer from market structure the level of competition among banks in that market. The higher the HI and the x-banks concentration ratio, the lower the degree of competition and vice versa. Thus, banks in more concentrated markets are expected to earn higher profits for collusive or monopolistic reasons than under more competitive conditions. However, a concentration ratio contains information about the few included banks but completely ignores the competitive impact on the market of the remaining firms. Both measures are mute about the possibility that the degree of competition might be completely unrelated to market structure.

The SCP hypothesis has been modified to include the impact of efficiency differences on market power. The so-called efficient-structure hypothesis (ESX) contends that banks with lower cost structures (due to managerial superiority and more advanced output technologies) and more attractive products will turn higher profit. Banks can use these efficiency/output advantages to enlarge their market shares, which breed market power. According to this line of investigations, one has to control for the role of efficiency in profitability equations (see Berger, 1995).

Numerous studies base the market structure variable on deposits. This no longer adequately reflects the realities of banking. Banks raise funds through a variety of debt instruments, and their output is more appropriately indicated by the size of their balance sheet. Assets not only reflect on-balance-sheet activities, but they also include those done off-balance sheet and both are linked through the latter's impact on regulatory capital.

International Competition and Market Power

Another criticism of the market power delineation refers to the omission of overseas competition in most studies. Hardly any bank is shielded form the impact of global competition, which makes its presence felt in a number of ways. First, domestic banks may have branches or subsidiaries in foreign jurisdictions, while foreign banks may establish their presence in foreign local markets through the subsidiary/branch structure. A correct research strategy requires a check of the geographical coverage of any data used. The OECD bank data stretch over a disparate range of country-specific definitions as Table 11.1 demonstrates. However, even if subsidiaries of foreign banks and foreign subsidiaries of domestic banks are not included in a data set, the foreign banks' impact on the home turf of local banks and the domestic banks' experience from trading overseas presumably affect the business behavior of local banks. Second, banks in general, regardless of where they are located, are touched in various ways by the competition prevailing in financial and capital markets on a global basis. Banks, investment houses, and other nonbanks trade in bonds, currencies, and derivatives, they underwrite debt securities, provision credit cards, and offer a range of other financing services. Consequently, generous spreads, margins, and fees cannot be preserved behind national borders.

Despite these compelling reasons for casting the competition net wider, very few econometric studies actually try to capture the impact of foreign competition on profitability. Claessens et al. (2001) are one exception. They document the presence of foreign banks in 80 countries, assess relevant performance differences between domestic and foreign banks, and investigate the impact of foreign bank entry on profitability and interest rate margins. Their findings that foreign bank entry tends to reduce profitability and margins of incumbent domestic banks appear to support the notion of the pro-competitive impact of foreign bank entry.

Entry of foreign banks into a domestic market may be made for other reasons than exploiting the opportunities promised by a low competitive environment and inefficient cost structure. For example, tiny Luxembourg ranks second in the number of foreign banks and first by share of total banks. Tax avoidance and evasion reasons are the main motivators. These considerations would also apply to Belgium, Switzerland, and even the UK, where many large banks underwrite and trade bonds free of withholding tax.

Contestable Markets and Competition

The various market share and concentration measures in profitability studies have been criticized for being static, and concentration ratios may not be predictably related to competition. Although the reservations regarding the snapshot depiction of market structure can be tempered by including a measure of changing market structures in any SCP-estimation equation, the core problem with

Table 11.1
Geographical Coverage of OECD Bank Data

Country	1	2	3	4	5	6	7	8	9	10
Australia							X			
Austria										X
Belgium				X[a]						
Canada										X
Czech Republic									X	
Denmark								X		
Finland	X									
France						X				
Germany					X					
Greece		X								
Hungary							X			
Iceland	X									
Ireland			X							
Italy		X								
Japan		X[b]								
Korea		X								
Luxembourg										X
Mexico		X								
Netherlands				X						
New Zealand								X		
Norway								X		
Poland								X[c]		
Portugal										X
Spain								X		
Sweden									X	
Switzerland						X				
Turkey						X				
United Kingdom		X								
United States				X[d]						

1 = domestic banks only; 2 = domestic banks and their foreign branches; 3 = domestic banks and their foreign subsidiaries; 4 = domestic banks and their foreign subsidiaries and branches; 5 = domestic banks and their foreign branches, and foreign bank subsidiaries; 6 = domestic banks and their foreign branches, and foreign bank branches; 7 = domestic banks and subsidiaries of foreign banks; 8 = domestic banks and subsidiaries and branches of foreign banks; 9 = domestic banks and their foreign branches and subsidiaries and branches of foreign banks; 10 = global consolidation.

[a]for credit institutions.

[b]excludes affiliates.

[c]subsidiaries and branches of foreign banks are regarded as commercial banks.

[d]data for foreign controlled banks that are chartered under U.S. laws are included.

Source: OECD Data Bank.

this approach persists, namely, its tenuous link with the competitive behavior of institutions. A shrinking or rising number of firms may not necessarily be a reliable indicator of faltering or increasing competitive pressures, respectively. Even a single incumbent bank may behave competitively if it fears the potential entrance of rivals. At the polar end of the spectrum, a market populated by many banks may lead us to expect a highly competitive environment when in fact they either enjoy the fruits of a "quiet life" or, worse, collude.

In response to the shortcomings of the market structure approach, Bain (1956) introduced the concept of potential competition and Baumol et al. (1982) further developed this idea into the *contestability hypothesis*. This approach eschews any market power measure but instead allows the direct measurement of competitive behavior by market participants whether few or numerous. Studies in the Panzar and Rosse (1987) mold employ reduced-form revenue equations. They are developed at the firm level and based on the idea that firms operating in a competitive environment have no scope to absorb input cost increases, unlike monopolies or firms in monopolistically structured markets that can curtail revenues or profits in response to cost pressures. Accordingly, it is hypothesized that the sum of the elasticities of the factor input prices with respect to revenue would be negative for a monopoly, less than one for monopolistic competition and equal to one for firms operating in a perfectly competitive market where firms are price takers. Thus, market power is reflected by the extent to which factor price changes are absorbed through revenue adjustments. Applications of this technique to the banking industry include Nathan and Naeve (1989), Molyneux et al. (1994), and De Bandt and Davis (2000). Murat et al. (2001) employ this method to the property/casualty insurance.

ESTIMATION APPROACH

This study investigates the relationship between bank profitability and competition in banking markets on the basis of OECD data using a modified SCP approach. Due consideration is given to other important determinants of bank performance besides competition, such as the risk of banking business and banks' cost structure. We also attempt to evaluate the degree to which banks have replaced traditional interest rate margin business with fee-generating activities. As these activities have become increasingly important especially for banks in industrialized countries we attempt to measure the impact of the share of fee income on profitability. Therefore, we propose the following core estimation equation:

$$\begin{aligned}\text{profitability}_i = {} & \alpha + \beta_1(\text{market power})_i + \beta_2(\text{fee income})_i \\ & + \beta_3(\text{cost structure})_i + \beta_4(\text{risk})_i + \varepsilon\end{aligned} \tag{11.1}$$

where profitability is defined as profits before tax divided by total assets (ROABT). Alternatively, we regress the same set of independent variables on the net interest rate margin (NIM) which is calculated as the difference between interest income and interest expenses divided by total assets:

$$\text{NIM}_i = \alpha + \beta_1(\text{market power})_i + \beta_2(\text{fee income})_i + \beta_3(\text{cost structure})_i + \beta_4(\text{risk})_i + \varepsilon \qquad (11.2)$$

The independent variables are defined as follows:

Market power is represented by an adapted Lerner monopoly index (LMM)

$$\text{LMM} = \frac{P - MC}{P} \qquad (11.3)$$

where P stands for price (proxied by interest revenues divided by total assets) and MC stands for marginal costs (given by interest expenses divided by total assets).

The *fee income* variable is represented either by the quotient of fee income to gross interest income (FGII) or by the ratio of fee income to net interest income (FII). These variables proxy a mixture of changes in the product palette, technological advances of banks, and the competition they face in wholesale and global markets. The *cost structure* is described by the ratio of operating expenses to gross income (OEGI). *Risk* is measured by the volatility (standard deviation) of gross income (RISK); ε stands for the stochastic error term and i for the particular country.

On the basis of our subsequent discussion, we would expect the estimated parameters of the variables to have the following signs:

$$\beta_1 > 0,\ \beta_2 < 0,\ \beta_3 < 0,\ \beta_4 > 0, \text{ with } \varepsilon \sim N(0, \sigma^2).$$

We experiment with different functional forms, a range of additional variables, and combinations, as well as alternative proxies for variables, data availability permitting.

VARIABLE ANALYSIS AND DATA

Our empirical estimates of equations (11.1) and (11.2) are based on the OECD data set on Bank Profitability (2000) from 1993 to 1999. Data details are presented in Appendix 1.

Market Structure

The market structure in which banks operate determines their ability to influence price and output. A bank with market power may pay lower borrowing rates on its liabilities and extract higher yields from its assets than would be possible under perfect competitive conditions. We prefer the Lerner index of market power to the behavior-free concentration indices. The size of banks, whether measured in terms of deposits, relative size of their balance sheets, or income generated, might not necessarily capture appropriately the degree of competitive behavior. The Lerner index provides more pertinent information about the actual price-setting behavior of banks in relationship to their cost structures than static market power measures are able to convey. However, this summary index fails to distinguish between banks' exposure to domestic and wholesale/global competition.

As is well known, the wholesale and international activities of the larger banks in a country are most likely exposed to global competition in wholesale trading, debt, and currency markets, their funds management business, and investment banking activities. In each country, domestic banks compete with foreign subsidiaries and branches of foreign banks on their domestic turf and with foreign banks located abroad. This global competitive influence does not depend on whether domestic banks operate foreign branches or subsidiaries inasmuch as certain lines of banking business have become global. Take, for example, the case of Iceland in our sample. Icelandic banks own no foreign subsidiaries or foreign branches, and no foreign banks have subsidiaries or branches in Iceland. However, arranging an interest rate swap or trading in foreign currency would immediately expose them to global competition as these markets are highly integrated. Furthermore, foreign subsidiaries are more inclined to compete in the market for fee business than interest income activities. We therefore have to search for a complementary proxy that promises to reflect global exposure to market forces.

Fee-to-Interest-Income Ratio

Increasingly, banks have moved away from focusing on generating interest income toward the earning of fees. Several factors have been driving this process. First, deregulation of interest rates forced banks to cease cross-subsidizing certain of their activities. For example, the removal of a ceiling on deposit rates induced banks to price deposit and loan rates in line with market forces. Previously, the below-market rates on deposits allowed banks to offer lower loan rates than would have been otherwise the case and to compete for depositors and loan customers on nonprice terms. Greater freedom in the setting of interest rates resulted in the curtailment of services as well as the unbundling and separate pricing of costs. Banks also branched out into credit cards. Second, financial deregulation, advances in computer/telecommunication technologies, and the development and application of advanced financial models encouraged trading and dealing in currencies, securities, commodities, and their associated derivatives. Third, the rise of direct and indirect personal wealth spawned fee-generating funds management activities. Fourth, the rapid growth of international trade provided opportunities for the earning of fees (e.g., letter of credit). Fifth, the expanding demand for investment banking services emanating from M&As, corporate restructuring, and other financial consulting prompted many banks to move into this growth area.

The fee-to-interest-income ratio thus appears to measure the degree to which banks have adjusted to the new financial deregulated environment. The higher the ratio, the more advanced their palette of products and services. However, this modern face of banking does not necessarily promise to boost the return on assets (ROA). Fee-income generating banking business tends to be domiciled in wholesale markets and is more global in nature than interest-based activities such as retail deposit taking and loan granting. *A priori* reasoning suggests that such banks are exposed to a level of intense competition in wholesale markets and at the international level that any purely domestically based market power variable is unlikely to reflect. Furthermore, broadening the range of banking activities beyond the focus on interest-generating businesses entails diversification benefits. Diversified banks are less risky than those with a narrow range of products. The ratio of fee income to total income captures the tradeoff between return and risk. Moreover, fee-income generating activities involve less credit risk, are more cash flow certain, but have lower margins than interest income business. However, as DeYoung (1994) pointed out, on a risk-adjusted basis, profits may be enhanced.

In our estimation equation, we interpret the fee/income ratio as a gauge for technological advance and product-mix change in banking, as a measure of banks' exposure to international competition, and as an expansion of low-risk activities. We expect the fee/interest-income ratio to exert a negative impact on bank profitability in our test equation. This is so because one dollar of assets deployed in fee-business generates less ROA than it earns in the domestic market's interest income business. This effect would be particularly pronounced during a period when banks shift their activities from interest-income to fee-income activities. Although our approach does not allow us to clearly separate out domestic from international market power, it is conducive to capturing aspects of global competition. Omitting this structural supply-side variable would attribute its impact on profitability to market power. Note: Concentration ratios, market shares, or the Lerner index fail to capture the domestic banks' exposure to this broader level of competition.

Cost Structure

Efficiency in delivering banking services constitutes an important determinant of the profitability of banks. Although operating expenses form the logical numerator of cost structure ratio, we experiment with several variables as the denominator, namely, liabilities, assets, and total income. A lowering of the cost structure ratio logically increases profitability. As we are using country data, a relatively high value of this variable would cost-inefficiency, perhaps related to overbanking.

Table 11.2
Descriptive Statistics of Data Set (number of observations: 147)

	Mean	Median	Std.Dev.	Maximum	Minimum
ROABT	0.87	0.78	0.92	4.80	-2.76
FII	0.57	0.54	0.49	4.52	-0.50
FGII	0.17	0.16	0.14	1.22	-0.10
NIM	2.74	2.23	2.15	12.83	0.57
OEGI	63.99	63.93	14.51	199.64	37.93
LMM	0.32	0.32	0.12	0.61	0.08
RISK	0.56	0.51	0.36	1.33	0.07

Risk

Economic agents, including financial institutions, are commonly risk averse. However, our accounting-based measures of profitability are not adjusted for risk. We would therefore expect the ROA or NIM to be positively related to risk. Riskier banks have to compensate their stockholders with the promise of higher rates of return. The major risks of banks include market, credit, and operational risks. An ideal measure of risk would utilize value-at-risk (VaR) data for countries' banking systems. Alas, data of this nature are not available. To start with, so far only VaR measures pertaining to market risk are computed, but not published, by internationally active banks; credit risk indicators are missing.[2]

ESTIMATION RESULTS

Our estimations are based on annual panel data for the years 1993 to 1999. Since the European banking industry changed with the opening of a common banking market within the European Community in 1992, we abstained from using data for the period before 1992. Due to data unavailability, our sample includes 21 countries of the 29 countries listed in Table 11.1. Appendix 2 contains the sample countries and the descriptive statistics for each country. The corresponding information of the country averages of the variables is given in Table 11.2. In Appendix 3 we present a correlation matrix of the variables.

The first series of estimations was carried out with ROABT as the dependent variable and FGII and FII as alternative measures of fee income, respectively (Table 11.3) as well as OEGI and RISK as independent variables. Both models were tested with and without an additional dummy variable to control for time effects. Furthermore, we applied both one-stage Generalized Least Squares (GLS) procedures and two-stage Weighted Least Squares (WLS) estimations.

Table 11.3
Common Intercept Estimations for ROABT and NIM

	ROABT GLS estimates		**ROABT WLS estimates**		**NIM GLS estimates**		**NIM WLS estimates**	
C	2.10 (6.88***)	2.35 (7.30***)	2.07 (7.06***)	2.32 (7.48***)	2.77 (4.10***)	3.86 (5.74***)	2.93 (4.31***)	3.89 (5.74***)
LMM	1.42 (2.82***)	1.28 (2.56**)	1.37 (2.72**)	1.19 (2.46**)	2.46 (2.20**)	0.79 (0.76)	2.72 (2.53**)	1.18 (1.16)
FGII	0.08 (0.31)		0.13 (0.33)		-2.86 (-3.32***)		-3.20 (-3.71***)	
FII		-0.21 (-1.77*)		-0.20 (-1.71*)		-1.42 (-5.81***)		-1.36 (-5.74***)
OEGI	-0.04 (-8.97***)	-0.04 (-9.28***)	-0.03 (-9.16***)	-0.04 (-9.65***)	-0.04 (-4.39***)	-0.04 (-5.04***)	-0.04 (-4.33***)	-0.04 (-4.92***)
RISK	0.96 (6.03***)	0.93 (5.93***)	0.92 (5.98***)	0.92 (6.00***)	3.74 (10.66***)	3.67 (11.18***)	3.69 (10.79***)	3.57 (11.29***)
adj. R^2	0.46	0.47	0.46	0.48	0.51	0.57	0.55	0.60
DW	1.93	1.80	1.91	1.79	2.10	1.92	2.04	1.91
F	31.77***	33.22***	32.53***	34.92***	38.91***	49.97***	46.27***	55.34***

t-values are reported in parentheses.
***, **, * denote significance on a 1 percent, 5 percent, or 10 percent level, respectively.

Both techniques are especially suitable for data sets where serial correlation and/or heteroscedasticity might be present (Pindyck and Rubinfeld 1991, 129 ff.).

Our findings for both ROA measures lend credence to our approach. All coefficients show the expected signs, and most are significant at the commonly accepted levels. Both market power and risk impact positively on profitability. As expected, the cost structure variable influences bank profitability negatively and in a statistically significant way. Both fee to income ratios are weakly significant in only two of the four regressions. The time dummy variable is insignificant; the adjusted R^2 falls in the upper range of values reported in similar studies. Furthermore, the results are virtually unaffected as far as the method of estimation is concerned. All of the values of the coefficients lie in a similar range regardless of whether GLS or WLS is applied. Furthermore, the highly significant F-values suggest an appropriate specification of the overall model. In conjunction with the value of the DW-statistic there is no apparent evidence for structural changes.

The estimation outcome improves appreciably when NIM is chosen as the dependent variable (Table 11.3). The overall best result is achieved in the WLS model when FGII is taken as a measure of the fee-to-gross-income ratio; all coefficients are significant at the 1 percent level. Once again the time dummy variable is insignificant; therefore, we omit it in further estimations. Since we are using panel data, our models might lead to inadmissible conclusions unless we test for separate intercepts for each year included in our data pool (fixed effects estimation). The modified results are displayed in Table 11.4.

Obviously, the fixed effects method does not change our main results, although the coefficients of the intercepts CY_j, $j = 1993, \ldots, 1999$, vary. Since they are relatively close together on average, we can reject the presence of structural breaks between the years. With NIM as dependent variable and using WLS, the findings suggest a positive impact of market power and of risk on profitability and the expected inverse relationship between fee income and cost structure, respectively, and profitability.

We also estimated equations (11.1) and (11.2) using a broader measure of the Lerner index where we use gross income to total assets for P and total expenses to total assets for MC. This broader definition attempts to measure the market power of banks regarding their entire on- and off-balance-sheet business activities. However, the estimation results with this broader variable of market power are poor in comparison with the narrower definition. This negative outcome lends support to our view that total bank incomes and costs, which presumably also relate to their global operations, are exposed to international competition, eroding any price-setting ability of banks.

CONCLUSIONS AND IMPLICATIONS FOR THE FUTURE OF BANKING

The major parts of our estimation results provide strong support for our hypotheses. All our models are highly significant, with overall adjusted coefficients

Table 11.4
Fixed Effects Estimations

	ROABT GLS estimates		ROABT WLS estimates		NIM GLS estimates		NIM WLS estimates	
LMM	1.52 (2.94***)	1.39 (2.70***)	1.43 (2.86***)	1.30 (2.63***)	2.35 (2.05**)	0.75 (0.70)	2.60 (2.35**)	1.12 (1.08)
FGII	0.06 (0.16)		0.11 (0.29)		-2.70 (-3.04***)		-2.99 (-3.37***)	
FII		-0.22 (-1.83*)		-0.21 (-1.81*)		-1.40 (-5.57***)		-1.34 (-5.48***)
OEGI	-0.04 (-8.88***)	-0.04 (-9.22***)	-0.03 (-9.08***)	-0.04 (-9.62***)	-0.04 (-4.30***)	-0.04 (-4.97***)	-0.04 (-4.24***)	-0.04 (-4.84***)
RISK	0.95 (5.91***)	0.93 (5.81***)	0.91 (5.85***)	0.91 (5.85***)	3.75 (10.55***)	3.67 (11.07***)	3.61 (10.67***)	3.57 (11.16***)
CY1999	2.01	2.29	1.98	2.27	2.42	3.55	2.62	3.59
CY1998	2.24	2.52	2.21	2.49	2.88	4.01	3.09	4.08
CY1997	2.13	2.40	2.10	2.37	2.61	3.72	2.80	3.78
CY1996	2.17	2.47	2.14	2.44	2.81	4.01	3.02	4.05
CY1995	2.19	2.43	2.16	2.40	2.76	3.79	2.95	3.85
CY1994	2.03	2.27	2.01	2.25	2.94	4.02	3.12	4.07
CY1993	2.06	2.30	2.04	2.28	3.09	4.145	3.27	4.19
adj. R^2	0.44	0.46	0.45	0.47	0.50	0.56	0.54	0.59
DW	1.96	1.83	1.94	1.82	2.14	1.96	2.09	1.95
F	41.87***	44.00***	43.05***	46.70***	51.52***	66.02***	60.02***	72.66***

t-values are reported in parentheses.
***, **, * denote significance on a 1 percent, 5 percent, or 10 percent level, respectively.
CY = fixed effects constant coefficients.

of determination in the range of 0.5, and there is no evidence of mispecification or structural changes. We find strong support for the expected impacts of risk and cost structure on the return on assets after tax as well as on the net interest margin, regardless of the model specification or the applied estimation techniques. Although the relationship between costs and profits is not really surprising, the insight that a risk variable measured by the volatility of gross income affects profitability is both novel and instructive. It might be a promising task to include this kind of risk measure in already existing models of the SCP-type.

Although the coefficient of the market power proxy LMM is not significant in every single estimation, our findings nevertheless provide broad support for the positive influence of competitive conditions in the banking industry on profitability and interest rate margins. On average, a 1 percent increase in the Lerner index leads to a more than 3 percent increase of the interest rate margin and an approximately 1 percent increase in the return on assets, respectively. Since there is no indication of structural changes in the data during the period under review, we cannot be confident that increasing competition on a global basis might alter the results in the future.

Interpreting the fee-to-interest-income ratio as a measure of competition in the wholesale markets, we also find strong evidence for its expected inverse impact on the interest rate margin, whereas the expected influence on profitability is not uniformly supported by our estimates. On average, every percentage increase in FII decreases the net interest margin by approximately 1.25 percent. To strengthen our arguments of diversification and reduced risk exposure by banks shifting activities from interest income to fee income business, additional research will be needed to see whether our risk measure, the volatility of gross income, continues to exert its moderating influence on bank profitability.

From our econometric test results and the literature dealing with international competition, we distill the following tentative predictions for the future of banking. Those predictions pertain to the collective trends, which are discernible for the range of countries included in this study. First, the pronounced negative impact of the fee-to-interest income ratio on the interest rate margins of banks entails the separate costing of bank services previously compensated for in relatively wide interest rate margins. This trend appears to continue. Second, we linked the expanding fee-income business and the shrinking interest rate margins to increased competition. The fact that the Lerner monopoly index is only weakly significant has led some analysts to support our view. However, in order to disentangle the domestic from those of international competitive forces, we introduced in a followup paper (Gischer and Jüttner, 2001) a scaled variable (foreign assets plus foreign liabilities) measuring the financial openness of a country to global competition in financial markets. The inclusion of the new proxy for global competition in our profitability equations wipes out any statistical significance that the domestic monopoly index previously attained. To the extent that the level of competition in global financial markets among banks and nonbank financial institutions in trading of securities, currencies, and derivatives increases, the rate of return before tax (ROABT) and interest rate margins (NIM) are bound to shrink in the future. Foreign bank entry, and not only exposure to global financial markets, adds to the competitive pressure on incumbent banks (Claessens et al., 2001). The question of separating domestic from global competition clearly requires further research.

Third, obviously cost reductions cushion the negative impact of more intense competition on bank profitability and interest rate margins. Bank mergers, especially in overbanked countries such as Germany, will continue to result in branch closures and associated labor shedding. Moreover, migration of services to the Internet can be expected to feature prominently in the future. Consumer acceptance of e-banking, however, depends on whether their security concerns can be convincingly alleyed, as well as on the availability of reasonably priced Internet access services.

Fourth, since capital ratios are now used as prudential banking policy instruments, they have lost their value as risk indicators. Capital ratios now already cover unexpected market, credit, and operational risks for those banks that comply with the New Basel Capital Adequacy Requirement. Future bank profitability studies have to search for alternative risk proxies. Fifth, our study remains mute about whether the competitive process involving global financial markets and foreign bank entry is self-sustaining, or whether it will result in a weeding out of marginal banks/investment houses and the development of financial conglomerates with global market power.

Appendix 1
Symbols and Variables (Item numbers corresponding to OECD data tables)

ROABT: return on assets before tax = profit before tax in percent of balance sheet total [item 48]

NIM: net interest rate margin = net interest income in percent of balance sheet total [item 42]

LMM: market structure proxy (Lerner monopoly index) = (interest income in percent of balance sheet total minus interest expenses in percent of balance sheet total) divided by interest income in percent of balance sheet total [(item 40 − item 41)/item 40]

FII: fee to interest income ratio = noninterest income divided by net interest income [item 4/item 3]

FGII: fee to gross interest income ratio = noninterest income divided by interest income [item 4/item 1]

OEGI: operating expenses to gross income ratio = operating expenses in percent of gross income [item 55]

RISK: standard deviation of gross income in percent of balance sheet total = $\sigma_{[\text{item } 44]}$ (1988–1997)

Appendix 2
Descriptive Statistics of Country-Specific Data (all items in percent)

	ROABT			NIM			FII			FGII			OEGI			LMM		
	min	max	mean	min	max	mean	min	max	mean	min	max	mean	min	max	mean	min	max	mean
BELGIUM	0.33	0.45	0.39	1.07	1.35	1.19	0.40	1.00	0.58	0.05	0.14	0.08	63.50	71.72	66.69	0.13	0.15	0.14
CANADA	0.68	1.20	1.02	2.07	2.80	2.40	0.50	0.99	0.68	0.18	0.35	0.25	63.74	67.86	64.92	0.31	0.42	0.36
DENMARK	0.00	1.41	0.88	1.86	3.94	2.86	-0.14	0.61	0.39	-0.07	0.24	0.16	51.09	72.51	59.36	0.37	0.59	0.44
FRANCE	0.02	0.47	0.22	0.74	1.33	1.02	0.60	1.43	0.98	0.11	0.20	0.15	64.75	71.28	67.95	0.13	0.61	0.28
GERMANY	0.38	0.71	0.54	1.48	2.18	1.85	0.24	0.55	0.33	0.08	0.16	0.10	57.60	67.75	62.90	0.28	0.32	0.30
ICELAND	0.10	1.33	0.81	3.30	5.00	4.18	0.43	0.70	0.55	0.19	0.28	0.24	63.19	72.59	68.18	0.35	0.53	0.45
ITALY	0.28	1.02	0.60	2.23	2.99	2.59	0.25	0.60	0.40	0.09	0.30	0.16	60.36	69.07	65.06	0.32	0.50	0.37
JAPAN	-0.76	0.28	-0.12	1.25	1.45	1.35	-0.19	0.14	0.00	-0.10	0.08	0.00	62.34	91.79	74.13	0.29	0.57	0.41
KOREA	-2.76	1.03	-0.18	1.86	2.34	2.13	-0.50	1.34	0.54	-0.10	0.38	0.16	51.64	199.64	82.35	0.19	0.31	0.26
LUXEMBOURG	0.51	0.58	0.54	0.57	0.77	0.67	0.49	1.23	0.76	0.05	0.10	0.07	37.97	46.54	43.60	0.08	0.11	0.09
MEXICO	-0.62	2.28	0.59	3.28	6.37	4.88	0.28	0.80	0.47	0.05	0.13	0.10	53.37	75.90	63.71	0.14	0.32	0.22
NETHERLANDS	0.61	0.78	0.72	1.70	1.89	1.80	0.40	0.74	0.58	0.11	0.19	0.15	66.56	70.78	67.98	0.24	0.28	0.27
NZ	1.23	1.51	1.37	2.20	2.85	2.59	0.57	0.64	0.59	0.16	0.23	0.19	55.71	71.48	65.55	0.25	0.36	0.31
NORWAY	0.90	1.36	1.16	2.32	3.73	2.84	0.23	0.39	0.34	0.11	0.17	0.14	50.41	69.49	64.42	0.34	0.46	0.41
PORTUGAL	0.40	0.86	0.71	2.00	3.19	2.33	0.28	4.52	0.98	0.08	1.22	0.28	55.42	64.94	60.22	0.27	0.37	0.30
SPAIN	0.36	0.96	0.81	2.23	3.29	2.69	0.27	0.47	0.38	0.10	0.23	0.14	59.65	63.23	61.42	0.31	0.49	0.37
SWEDEN	0.33	1.33	0.94	1.33	2.96	2.18	0.54	1.27	0.87	0.17	0.35	0.27	64.28	106.51	78.08	0.28	0.41	0.33
SWITZERLAND	0.11	0.90	0.55	1.08	1.86	1.33	0.95	1.66	1.37	0.30	0.57	0.42	48.64	66.14	56.79	0.28	0.34	0.31
TURKEY	1.13	4.80	3.81	8.96	12.83	10.95	-0.29	0.19	-0.06	-0.10	0.04	-0.02	37.93	56.26	47.17	0.22	0.41	0.31
UK	0.76	1.35	1.14	2.05	2.45	2.22	0.63	0.80	0.70	0.22	0.29	0.26	53.99	64.09	60.68	0.34	0.39	0.37
USA	1.56	1.92	1.71	3.39	3.73	3.54	0.47	0.69	0.56	0.25	0.35	0.29	60.57	64.91	62.73	0.49	0.55	0.51

Appendix 3
Correlation Matrix of the Variables

	ROABT	FII	FGII	NIM	OEGI	LMM	RISK
ROABT	1.0000	-0.1057	0.0137	0.7299	-0.5263	0.2102	0.3837
FII	-0.1057	1.0000	0.8816	-0.3656	-0.1375	-0.1987	-0.1149
FGII	0.0137	0.8816	1.0000	-0.2548	-0.0671	0.1805	0.0199
NIM	0.7299	-0.3656	-0.2548	1.0000	-0.2035	0.1991	0.6509
OEGI	-0.5263	-0.1375	-0.0671	-0.2035	1.0000	0.0652	0.0400
LMM	0.2102	-0.1987	0.1805	0.1991	0.0652	1.0000	0.1789
RISK	0.3837	-0.1149	0.0199	0.6509	0.0400	0.1789	1.0000

NOTES

Research for this chapter was carried out while Horst Gischer was a Visiting Professor at Macquarie University. Financial support by the Volkswagen Research Foundation (VolkswagenStiftung) is gratefully acknowledged. James Woolford provided excellent research assistance.

1. However, the relationship between risk and profitability of banks is more complex than textbook finance suggests. When certain banks face insolvency, their managers and shareholders may be tempted to abandon the carefully chosen tradeoff between return and risk and seek excessive risk as a survival method. If the gamble pays off, the bank may work its way out of near bankruptcy and continue operating. If not, or if it does not take the gamble, the institution is doomed. Due to the limited company form, the size of the damage bill that is left in the wake of a disastrous outcome is of no financial consequence for the gamblers. Likewise, deposit insurance or expected bailout actions by national or supranational authorities may corrupt a whole banking system by providing banks with an incentive to gamble.

2. The Basel Capital Accord requires banks to uniformly hold capital against risk-adjusted assets.

REFERENCES

Bain, J. S. 1956. *Barriers to New Competition.* Cambridge, Mass.: Harvard University Press.

Baumol, W. J., Panzar, J. C., and Willig, R. D. 1982. *Contestable Markets and the Theory of Industry Structure.* New York: Harcourt Brace Jovanovich.

Berger, A. N. 1995. "The Profit-Structure Relationship in Banking—Tests of Market-Power and Efficiency-Structure." *Journal of Money, Credit, and Banking* 27: 404–431.

Claessens, S., Demirgüc-Kunt, A., and Huizinga, H. 2001. "How Does Foreign Entry Affect Domestic Banking Markets?" *Journal of Banking and Finance* 25: 891–911.

De Bandt, O., and Davis, E. 2000. "Competition, Contestability, and Market Structure in European Banking Sectors on the Eve of EMU." *Journal of Banking and Finance* 24: 1045–1066.

DeYoung, R. 1994. *Fee-Based Services and Cost Efficiency in Commercial Banks, Bank*

Structure and Competition. Chicago: Federal Reserve Bank of Chicago, pp. 501–519.

Gischer, H., and Jüttner, D. J. 2001. "Global Competition, Fee Income, and Interest Rate Margins of Banks." Mimeo, Macquarie University.

Lloyd-Williams, M. D., and Molyneux, P. 1994. "Market Structure and Performance in Spanish Banking." *Journal of Banking and Finance* 18: 433–443.

Molyneux, P., Lloyd-Williams, M. D., and Thornton, J. 1994. "Competitive Conditions in European Banking." *Journal of Banking and Finance* 18: 445–459.

Murat, G., Tonkin, R., and Jüttner, D. J. 2001. "Competition in the General Insurance Industry." Mimeo, Macquarie University.

Nathan, A., and Naeve, E. H. 1989. "Competition and Contestability in Canada's Financial System: Empirical Results." *Canadian Journal of Economics* 22: 576–595.

OECD. 1999. *Bank Profitability, Financial Statements of Banks*. 1999 Edition. Paris: OECD.

OECD. 2000. *Bank Profitability, Methodological Country Notes, Finance and Investment*. Paris: OECD.

Panzar, J. C., and Rosse, J. N. 1987. "Testing for 'Monopoly' Equilibrium." *Journal of Industrial Economics* 35: 443–456.

Pindyck, R. S., and Rubinfeld, D. L. 1991. *Econometric Models and Economic Forecasts*, 3rd ed. New York: McGraw-Hill.

Saunders, A., and Schumacher, L. 2000. "The Determinants of Bank Interest Rate Margins: An International Study." *Journal of International Money and Finance* 19: 813–832.

Chapter 12

Strategic Alliances: An Alternative to Mergers

Benton E. Gup and Louis Marino

INTRODUCTION

In the past, it was generally thought that firms could grow on their own, or they could grow through mergers and acquisitions. Now a third choice is available to them—strategic alliances. Strategic alliances were virtually unknown in the early 1980s.[1] Since then, however, there has been a virtual explosion of strategic alliances by firms of all sizes in almost every industry, including air transportation, financial services, media/entertainment, and pharmaceuticals. The growth in alliances has been attributed to a number of factors, including technology, globalization, and the increasing complexity and diversity in markets. Perhaps more important is that strategic alliances are being used instead of mergers to accelerate corporate growth. In 2000, there were more than 10,000 alliances, almost double the number four years earlier.[2] During 1990–1999, there were 3,005 joint ventures and strategic alliances involving the financial sector.[3] Most of them were in North America (1,640), followed by Europe (823) and the Pacific Rim (542). The UK accounted for 401 alliances in Europe. Almost half of these strategic alliances occurred in 1998 and 1999.

As the competitive landscape of the new economy evolves, traditional boundaries between industries are beginning to blur and new capabilities are required to succeed in the converging markets. To meet these challenges, alliances are being viewed by many organizations as essential to their firms' very survival. According to David Ernst, a consulting partner at McKinsey & Co., "For most companies, the basis of competition has shifted to groups of companies competing against groups of companies" (Sparks, 1999). In the current environment, it is becoming increasingly uncommon for larger firms to have a multitude of cooperative agreements. Oracle, for example, has more than 15,000 alliances, while Visa and MasterCard each have arrangements with more than 21,000 financial institutions around the world ("Trust Us," 2000).[4] Alliances partners are not limited to vertical partners in a firm's value chain. For example, some firms have alliances with competitors. For example, 15 international airlines that are direct competitors in some cases have formed the Star Alliance to provide better services for their customers and to enhance their revenues.[5]

The growing popularity of alliances is directly proportionate to the perceived benefits of these agreements. However, firms entering into these agreements must also be prepared for challenges they might encounter. Parkhe (1993) found that alliances are subject to instability and poor performance, and may be dissolved. Dyer, Kale, and Singh (2001) estimate that nearly half of all alliances fail. But the termination of alliances should not be *prima facie* evidence of failure because one of the advantages of alliances is flexibility, and the ability to dissolve them can confer substantial benefits to both partners.[6] To promote the success of alliances, Dyer and Singh (1998) argue that alliance partners' interests should be aligned in terms of their investments, knowledge, and capabilities.

In considering the role that alliances will play in the future of financial institutions, this chapter examines the nature of strategic alliances, the potential benefits and challenges of these agreements, and the current state of alliance usage in financial institutions.

STRATEGIC ALLIANCES DEFINED

The term *strategic alliance* has been used to describe cooperative agreements ranging from repeated arms-length transactions to equity arrangements just short of mergers. It follows that there are various definitions of alliances. Mockler (1999) states that strategic alliances are arrangements in which two or more entities unite and form important associations in order to further their common interests. Gilroy (1993) defines an alliance as a formal and mutually agreed upon commercial collaboration between companies. Gulati (1998) defines strategic alliances as voluntary arrangements between firms involving exchange, sharing, or co-development of products, technologies, or services. Alliances can take the form of equity positions or contractual arrangements including but not limited to collaborative agreements, licensing agreements, joint ventures, consortiums, partnerships, and other forms of collaboration.[7]

Harbison and Pekar (1998) developed a matrix that described different types of alliances based on the length of the commitment and the degree of ownership. In the case of short-term transactional alliances of five years or less involving distribution agreements, R&D programs, and so on, firms may share information, resources, and some funding. In longer-term alliances, the degree of funding and ownership increases. In permanent alliances, the funding ranges from cross-equity, such as the Japanese keiretsu, to wholly owned subsidiaries.

REASONS FOR ALLIANCES

Three theoretical approaches have been applied in the strategic management literature to help explain the motivations to enter into strategic alliances: real options theory, resource dependence theory, and transaction cost economics.

Real Options

Strategic alliances can be thought of in terms of real options granted to the parties in the alliance (Chi, 2000). Copeland and Antikarov (2001) define a real option as the right, but not the obligation, to take an action (e.g, deferring, expanding, contracting, or abandoning) at a predetermined cost during the life of the option. In the context of alliances, each of the parties can make choices and adapt to changes as the relationships progress over time. For example, they may decide to invest more funds, to wait, or to withdraw from the relationship.

Resource Dependence Theory (RDT)

Resource Dependence Theory (RDT) offers another view on the formation of alliances. It rests on the fundamental premise that organizations seek to maintain flows of critical resources (e.g., capital and raw materials) originating from the external environment by effectively managing dependencies and power differentials between firms (Astley & Fombrun, 1983; Finkelstein, 1997; Pfeffer & Salancik, 1978). Strategic alliances are one tool that can be used in managing these resource flows and in reducing uncertainties related to external environment. From this perspective alliances serve as linkages between the firm and outside entities that allow the organization to "access resources, stabilize outcomes and avert environmental control" (Pfeffer and Salancik, 1978, 144).

Transaction Cost Economics (TCE)

Transaction Cost Economics (TCE) focuses on the acquisition of assets. This approach is commonly attributed to Williamson (1975, 1985), and it is similar to resource dependence theory. TCE, however, centers on examining economic problems where unrecoverable investments are made in highly specialized assets that cannot be deployed to alternate uses (i.e., asset specificity). This unit of analysis in TCE is the transaction, and the primary question addressed is whether a given transaction should be conducted in the external market through an arms-length transaction, internalized within the organization's boundaries, or governed by a hybrid organization structure somewhere between the market and the internal hierarchy. The decision rests on the level of asset specificity and the costs related to the transaction. These transaction costs include both *ex ante* costs such as identifying partners and writing contracts and *ex post* costs such as monitoring partners' behaviors to detect opportunism (i.e., self-interest seeking with guile) and to enforce the contract, if necessary. Proponents of TCE argue that as asset specificity and transaction costs increase, transactions require governance structures that afford the firm more control (e.g., joint ventures or equity agreements versus market transactions); and at the highest levels, the transactions should be internalized within the boundaries of the firm.

Other Advantages of Alliances

Other advantages of alliances are listed below (Culpan, 1993; Harbison and Pekar, 1998; Mockler, 1999; Sparks, 1999; Willman, December 6, 2000):

- Access to new markets, materials, and technologies
- Acquisition of needed proprietary resources (outsourcing)
- Alternative to mergers
- Economies of scale and scope
- Focus on "core competencies" and outsource other aspects of the business
- Market access
- Minimized costs of research and development
- Minimized transaction and production costs due to economies of scale
- Organizational learning of new processes, skills, or competencies
- Risk sharing
- Trial marriage before merging

Firms in the same industry use alliances or acquisitions to accomplish similar goals. By way of illustration, consider the strategies that two UK banks—Barclays and Lloyds TSB Group[8]—used to sell life insurance and savings products through their distribution networks. Barclays formed a strategic alliance with Legal & General Life Insurance Company, while Lloyds TSB bought Scottish Widows Life Insurance Company. In this case, Barclays has more strategic options open to it than Lloyds TSB. A study by Anderson Consulting found that bank and insurance mergers are more successful than those in other industries (Mackintosh, 2000). The study did not address strategic alliances. Only time will tell which model worked best for these firms.

SELECTED FINANCIAL SERVICES INDUSTRY ALLIANCES

The following reveals how some alliances are being used by banks and businesses around the globe and in selected countries. This is not intended to be a complete listing of alliances involving financial services. It is only for purposes of illustration to show their widespread uses.

Global

Identrus™ LLC provides an example of a global alliance for banks and businesses in more than 133 countries.[9] Indentrus is the world's leading provider of identity trust in business-to-business Internet commerce. It facilitates electronic signatures; validates identities of buyers, sellers, and third parties; provides various payments options, and so on. More than 30 domestic and foreign financial institutions have Identrus Certificate Authority to use their services. These include ABN Amro, Abbey National PLC, Bank of America, Deutsche Bank, HypoVereinsbank, Wells Fargo & Co., and other financial institutions. Identrus is also allied with Sun Microsystems and iPlanet E-Commerce Solutions, a Sun Netscape alliance that provides technical services.

Seven of the leading financial institutions in the world formed a multidealer foreign exchange service called FXall.com to provide foreign exchange services ("Banks Form Exchange Site," 2000; Condon, 2000). The institutions include Bank of America, Credit Suisse First Boston, Goldman Sachs, HSBC, J. P. Morgan, Morgan Stanley Dean Witter, and UBS Warburg ("Banks Form Exchange Site," 2000; Condon, 2000). Some of these same institutions have formed another alliance, Market Axess, which offers institutional clients a place to obtain new issues, trading, and global credit products.[10] These trading partners include ABN Amro, Bear Stearns, Credit Suisse, First Boston, Deutsche Bank, J. P. Morgan, Chase & Co., Lehman Brothers, and UBS Warburg.

Another group of 50 other banks, including Chase Manhattan, Citibank, and Deutsche Bank, formed an alliance called Atriax to deal in foreign exchange (Marlin, 2001). The size of the market is estimated to be $1.5 trillion daily, making it the largest financial market in the world.

German insurer Allianz Holding formed a joint venture with Singapore's United Overseas Bank to explore asset management opportunities in China ("Asia/Pacific," 2000).

Deutsche Bank (Germany) formed alliances with Yahoo!, Nokia, SAP, AOL, Lycos, and others as part of their Global E strategy to deliver their bank's products and services worldwide (Deutsche Bank, 2000).

Merrill Lynch & Co. and HSBC, the UK banking group, launched an online bank in Canada to deal with high net worth individuals (Willman, 2000).

IBM and telephone service provider Alltell, of Little Rock, Arkansas, formed an alliance to provide online banking systems to financial service firms in Europe (Luening, 2001). The joint venture, to be called Alltel Corebanking Solutions, will be based in London. Alltell will provide the core banking systems that will run on IBM equipment.

United States

Bank of America, Chase Manhattan Bank, and IBM have established a unit called Viewpointe Archive Services to facilitate the exchange of check images among banks. It provides the foundation for consumers to retrieve digitzed check images from the web ("Banks, IBM Team Up," 2000).

Citibank had acquired AT&T Universal Card Services from AT&T, and both firms signed a 10-year agreement to co-brand and jointly market their products.

Citigroup signed an alliance with Microsoft to allow MSN users to use the Internet to make money transfers (Beckett, 2001). It also made agreements with AOL to provide money transfer services.

AmSouth Bank's subsidiary AmSouth Investment Services has alliances with various mutual funds (Fidelity, Kemper, Putnam, etc.) and with insurance companies to provide annuity products to investors.

American Express and Charles Schwab Corporation have an alliance. American Express offers Schwab's network of mutual funds to its customers, increasing its offerings from 500 to 2,900 funds (Sparks, 1999). Schwab has also entered into an alliance with AOL to increase its distribution in domestic and international markets (Cameron, 2000).

Fidelity Investments is one of the largest mangers of mutual funds. However, Fidelity has hired Deutsche Bank Asset Management to manage its $32 billion Fidelity index funds (O'Brian, 2001). Use of subadvisers, such as Deutsche Bank Asset Management, gives investors access to a wider variety of funds than they would otherwise have.

In another alliance, Fidelity Investments and General Motors are going to offer in-car trading of securities through the latest version of GM's OnStar communications system (White and Tomsho, 2001). The voice-activated system will allow drivers to trade securities. The OnStar service costs $199 to $299, depending on the level of service. The cost for using the wireless internet will be between $0.18 and $0.35 per minute.

Merrill Lynch & Co. has lots of partners to provide a wide variety of services.[11] In the technology area there are AT&T, Cisco, IBM, Microsoft, and others. Data providers include Standard & Poor's, Dow Jones, Intuit, and others. Service providers include Works.com, Financial Engines, and D.E. Shaw Financial Technology.

This listing is not complete, but it illustrates the widespread use of alliances.

European Union

Banco Santander Central Hispano (BSCH), Spain's largest bank, has cross-holdings with the Royal Bank of Scotland in the UK, Societe Generale in France, Commerzebank in Germany (Willman, August 2000). BSCH's holdings in Societe Generale helped that bank fend off an unwanted bid from Banque National de Paris, and its holdings in Royal Bank facilitated that bank's bid for National Westminster Bank.

BSCH has formed an alliance with AOL, and Banco Bilbao, Vizcaya Argentaria (BBVA), Spain's second largest bank, formed with Terra Networks to give them access to the Internet (Cameron, 2000). BBVA also has formed an alliance with Telefónica—a giant telecommunications company—so that they can combine their customers. BBVA provides financial content, and Telefónica provides the communications portal.

Germany's Commerzbank AG, U.S. Nationwide Mutual Insurance Co., and UK's Prudential PLC and Switzerland's Zurich Financial Services formed an online mutual fund supermarket joint venture ("EU Approves Online Joint Venture," 2000).

Japan

In Japan, three major insurance companies (Nippon Life Insurance Co., Mitsui Marine and Fire Insurance Co., and Sumitomo Marine and Fire Insurance Co.) formed an alliance to market each other's products under their own brand names. In addition, three other insurers (Tokio Marine and Fire Insurance Co., Nichido Fire and Marine Insurance Co., and Asahi Mutual Life Insurance Co.) formed an alliance to integrate operations ("Report: Japan Insurers," 2000). Finally, Dai-Ichi Mutual Life Insurance and Yasuda Fire & Marine Insurance Co. Ltd. took equity positions to form an alliance to take advantage of each other's distribution channels ("Japanese Insurers to Tie," 2000).

Sony, NTT DoCoMo, Sakura Bank, the Bank of Tokyo-Mitsubishi, Toyota Motor, Denso, and KDDI have joined a joint venture to provide prepaid electronic money services that focus on small settlements ("Sony, Group Launch Money-Services Pact," 2000).

United Kingdom

Barclays, the UK bank, and Legal & General (L&G), the UK's third largest life insurance company, formed an alliance to sell L&G branded life and pension products through Barclay's distribution network (Croft, January 16, 2001). In essence, Barclays is getting the advantages of having life insurance products without the cost of buying and operating a life insurance firm. Part of those benefits are reduced costs because they are reducing their labor force and dealing in well-known, brand-name products to enhance their revenues.

In a separate deal, L&G signed an agreement with Alliance & Leicester, the former UK building society with 309 branches, to distribute long-term savings and investment products (Croft, February 22, 2001).

Egg, the UK internet bank, announced in early 2001 that it was looking for partnerships in Europe to expand its market. In particular, it was interested in telecom companies or Internet portals that would give access to Egg products and services (Croft, February 19, 2001). Launched in October 1998, Egg was created by Prudential, the UK-based financial services company.[12]

Zurcih Financial Services, a Swiss insurer, formed an alliance with Bank of Scotland to allow both firms to cross-sell mortgages, loans, credit cards, and bank accounts to Zurich's 4.5 million customers in the UK.[13]

PERFORMANCE MEASURES

Keys to Success

Measures

Prior to examining the keys to successful alliances, it is first necessary to define success. Measuring alliance success is a daunting challenge. For example, a 1999 Anderson consulting study found that only 51 percent of companies that use alliances had developed formal measures of success for these agreements, and of these only 20 percent felt that the metrics employed were appropriate (Dyer, Kale, and Singh, 2001).

Longevity of alliances is the most simplistic measurement of performance that has been employed. This measure is based on the assumption that if an alliance is terminated, it must not have been successful. The shortcomings of this measure should be obvious. There are times when alliances are terminated because they have been successful and have met partner expectations (e.g., new market entry or new product development).

Financial performance is another measure of the success of alliances (e.g., joint venture performance). Measuring the success of strategic alliances purely in terms of financial performance for many types of agreements is not only problematic for many types of agreements but it is also shortsighted. Although there are a limited number of agreements, such as new market entry which can have a clear effect on firm performance, there are many alliances for which financial measures of performance are inadequate. This should be evident based on a review of the motivations to enter alliances previously discussed. It would be difficult, if not impossible, to quantify the value of organizational learning in either the short or long term.

Framing performance in terms of the extent that the agreement has lived up to predetermined *partner expectations* is a measure of alliance performance that has gained acceptance. Although expectations may evolve over the course of agreement, employing this approach affords a more flexible and comprehensive measure of alliance performance. This measure has been further enhanced by the use of weighted measures that allow firms to prioritize preferred outcomes and then compare performance based on these outcomes. However, to gain the potential benefits afforded by alliances, it is necessary to proactively manage these agreements.

Organizations

Participating in an alliance requires new ways of thinking about organizations. A study by Weber and Barrett (1999) revealed that successful alliances between pharmaceutical firms required clearly defined roles, common interests, and hands-on experience. The alliances that didn't work had conflicting aims, mistrust, and arrogance. These same factors may also apply in financial services.

Another difference between conventional organizations and alliances is that people have to manage "laterally" rather than a typical "hierarchical" structure of organization ("Trust Us," 2000). In addition, all of the parties must agree on well-defined goals and on how to measure the results. All of these factors take time, and they are best done gradually. Equally important, companies with more experience in alliances tend to have returns that are two to five times greater than companies doing them for the first or second time (Jaruzelsk, Volkholz, and Horkan, 1999). One reason companies with multiple experiences with alliances may have greater success is that there is a steep learning curve. Part of that learning curve is that the parties must learn to operate in a different environment and recognize in turn that for the flexibility they receive in terms of access to additional options, the interdependence that is created between the partners can result in decreased independence for the firm and the potential loss of some control over what their alliances do.

Perhaps the steep learning curve can be reduced by examining the growth of Internet companies. Rosabeth Moss Kanter's (2001) book about firms evolving in the Internet age provides some important insights about alliances. She states that established companies must undergo deep internal changes from the old ideas about how businesses are run. Consistent with this perspective, Spekman, Isabella, and MacAvoy (2000) identify five alliance competencies firms must develop if they are to be successful:

1. Alliance management know-how.
2. The development and maintenance of supportive processes and structures that facilitate knowledge transfer and learning.
3. An alliance management mindset that promotes a reputation as a good partner and engenders trust from potential partners.
4. Sufficient alliance-relevant skills and managerial talent to support the partnership.
5. Institutional mechanisms that facilitate the recognition and dissemination of alliance-related skills throughout the organization.

In addition, Kanter (2001) identified eight qualities that characterize successful partnerships:

1. The best company should be chosen as partner.
2. The top tier of partners are the most important and need to be treated as such.
3. Successful partners invest in each other.
4. Partners may compete, but need each other's services in the long term.
5. Performance measures and information must be shared.
6. There must be joint marketing and operational integration.
7. Contractual relationships must be carefully observed.
8. Partners must act to benefit each other rather than just benefiting themselves.

Potential Problems for Banks

The Office of the Comptroller of the Currency issued an OCC Bulletin (2001–2012) to discuss the risks associated with bank-provided account aggregation services. Account aggregation is a service that gathers customer information from various web sites and presents that information in a consolidated form to the customer. The information can vary from publicly available information to nonpublic information that is available to banks and brokers. Banks typically outsource the aggregation service, thereby forming an alliance. And the aggregator, in turn, may outsource some of its activities, such as bill payment, software that analyzes customer files and suggests financial products and advice, and others. The OCC points out that aggregation carries with it certain risks. For example, the aggregator may not be financially sound or able to provide reliable service. There are security risks associated with financial transactions and with gathering data from web sites. And there are compliance risks—complying with various laws and regulations. Such laws and regulations cover electronic funds transfer (Federal Reserve Regulation E), privacy under the Gramm-Leach-Bliley Act of 1999, and asset management under the Bank Secrecy Act. Thus, while a strategic alliance between banks and aggregators may simplify some aspects of providing a wider range of financial products to customers, it also opens the door for litigation and additional risks that banks must take into account.

Unwinding Alliances

While some new alliances are forming, others are coming to an end. As noted previously, alliances can be thought of in terms of real options, and one of those options is quitting. Therefore, the termination of an alliance is not necessarily a failure. Alliances can be ended for reasons ranging from failure to live up to partner expectations to the successful attainment of partner goals (e.g., new product development) to a shift in circumstances such that the alliance is no longer necessary. Germany's Dresdner Bank and France's Banque National de Paris (BNP) formed a partnership in 1993 to do commercial lending in Bulgaria, Croatia, the Czech Republic, Hungary, Poland, and Russia (Willman, September 24, 2000). However, BNP was acquired by Paribas, and it expanded its investment banking operation. Dresdner also expanded its investment banking operation, and it intends to reduce its retail operations and close some branches. Thus, Dresdner and BNP Paribas are now competitors in investment banking and are placing less emphasis on commercial lending. The original alliance is no longer needed.

WHAT THE FUTURE HOLDS

Clearly, alliance usage is increasing in virtually every industry, and the banking industry, is no exception. Equally important, alliance usage is growing in almost every stage of the banking industry's value chain. As this phenomenon continues to escalate, three trends will be especially significant:

1. *Formalization of the Alliance Function.* The proliferation of alliances has made it increasingly common for individual firms to have multiple alliances, while it has simultaneously made it unlikely for any individual agreement to provide a firm with a sustainable competitive advantage. Many firms are likely to experience less than satisfactory performance from their cooperative agreements as the number of agreements in which they participate grows. To combat this situation, an increasing number of firms will adopt the best practice of those firms that are reaping the greatest benefits from their strategic alliances by forming a dedicated strategic alliance function with a vice president or director of strategic alliances that commands an independent staff and the resources necessary to build alliance-related competencies (Dyer, Kale, and Singh, 2001).

2. *Proliferation in Alliance Types.* Strategic alliances are a means by which firms can effectively respond to opportunities and challenges in the external environment. Thus, as the banking industry evolves, so too will alliances in which banks engage both in terms of content and in the form of alliances employed. Three types of agreements that are likely to become more common include:

a. Alliances that facilitate the integration of technology service providers such as those formed by Microsoft and Merrill Lynch, Microsoft and Citigroup, Citigroup and AOL.

b. Alliances that facilitate cross-border activities. Alliances such as Citibank's agreement with the Japanese postal system that gives the bank access to an otherwise inaccessible consumer market will become more common as technology advances and globalization demands continue. Not only will banks increasingly engage in foreign commerce, but they will also find themselves cooperating with new types of partners.

c. Interimistic Alliances, alliances that are short term and formed to address a specific, transient, but important challenge or opportunity (Spekman, Isabelle, and MacAvoy, 2000). These alliances may be formed to allow firms to repel a competitive threat such as a new market entrant, to influence regulatory changes, or to capture an opportunity such as acquiring a specific type of knowledge or developing a specific new product or service. For example, in the Fall of 2000 Bank of America and SAP teamed up to develop and test methods for using Extensible Markup Language (XML) to allow Bank of America customers who are also SAP clients to access their statements online (Middlemiss, 2000). This alliance covers only this transaction, and both partners are free to explore similar opportunities with other firms. This type of alliance will grow increasingly common as firms develop alliance management competencies and leverage the flexibility inherent in interimistic alliances.

3. *Strategic Alliance Portfolio Management.* One of the primary duties of the dedicated strategic alliance function will be to manage the entirety of the organization's cooperative agreements as a coherent portfolio. This will become

especially challenging as alliance types proliferate. In managing these portfolios, managers need to focus not only on the number of agreements and the portfolio's extensiveness, but also on the portfolio's flexibility and its complexity. The flexibility of the portfolio can be especially important in maintaining the organization's agility and managing interdependencies among firms. For example, when faced with technological or political uncertainty, a firm may prefer to craft flexible alliances so that the terms of the agreement can be altered or terminate the alliance should the need arise. The complexity of the portfolio, or the diversity in the array of agreements the firm has, is also important, for the firm must balance the need for a broad enough range of agreements to meet the demands of the environment against the resources required to manage and integrate this variety. Management of portfolio complexity management will become especially important to firms in the banking industry as integration of technology service providers such as Microsoft and Merrill, Microsoft and Citigroup, Citigroup and AOL becomes a key to success in the banking industry and as cross-border activities grow.

CONCLUSION

Strategic alliances have become an accepted part of the business models of many financial institutions. Use of strategic alliances will continue to accelerate as organizations realize their benefits. Financial institutions that benefit the most from alliances will be those that manage them as a portfolio rather than dealing with them in a piecemeal fashion. In building strategic alliance portfolios, firms must ensure that they allocate sufficient resources to the endeavor and consider establishing a separate alliance function in the organization. Furthermore, they must add new alliance partners when opportunities arise, and prune those that are no longer necessary and those that are underperforming. By adopting this proactive posture, firms will develop a competitive advantage based on a portfolio of strategic alliances that ensure critical flows of resources while providing the flexibility to meet emerging treats and opportunities.

NOTES

1. See Harbison and Pekar (1998).
2. Data are from Schifrin (2001), p. 26. Forbes's *Best of the Web* (May 21, 2001) was a special issue about strategic alliances.
3. *Consolidation in the Financial Sector* (2001), Table A.18, p. 403.
4. For details on Visa and Mastercard, see www.visa.com and www.mastercard.com.
5. The airlines include: Air Canada, Air New Zealand, All Nippon Airways, Ansett Australia, Australian Airlines, British Midland, Lauda Air, Lufthansa, Mexicana Airlines, SAS, Singapore Airlines, Thai, Tyrolean Airways, United, and Varig. United and Lufthansa are the players in this alliance. Other airline alliances include Oneworld (Ameri-

can, British airways, others), Sky Team (Delta, Air France), and Wings (KLM, Northwest).

6. The term *strategic flexibility* has been used in this connection. See Sanchez (1997).

7. Mockler (1999) states that a firm granting a license for using technology in exchange for a royalty is *not* a strategic alliance except where there is continuing contribution and control among two or more independent firms.

8. In 1995, Lloyds Bank merged with Trustee Savings Bank Association and formed Lloyds TSB Group, Plc. (www.lloydsdstsb.com).

9. See "Identrus Member Financial Institutions," September 11, 2000; "Global Financial Institutions," December 2000; and www.identrus.com for further information.

10. See www.marketaxess.com for further details.

11. Spriro (1999).

12. For more information, see www.egg.com.

13. Croft, March 16, 2001.

REFERENCES

"Asia/Pacific." *Wall Street Journal*, September 8, 2000, A15.

Astley, W. G., and Fombrun, C. J. "Collective Strategy: Social Ecology of Organizational Environments." *Academy of Management Review* 8 (1983): 576–587.

"Banks Form Exchange Site." CNNfn, cnnfn.com, June 6, 2000 (visited 6/7/00).

"Banks, IBM Team Up." CNNfn, cnnfn.com, November 1, 2000 (visited 11/1/00).

Beckett, Paul. "Citigroup, Microsoft Sign Pact Allowing MSN Users to Make Web Money Transfers." *Wall Street Journal*, May 1, 2001, B6.

"Best of the Web—B2B, Banking." *Forbes*, May 21, 2001, p. 72.

Cameron, Doug. "Charles Schwab and AOL in Online Alliance." FT.Com, *Financial Times*, October 31, 2000 (visited 10/31/00).

Chi, Tailan. "Option to Acquire or Divest a Joint Venture." *Strategic Management Journal* 21 (2000): 665–687.

Condon, Tom. "Dueling Forex Titans." *U.S. Banker*, December 2000, 55–60.

Consolidation in the Financial Sector. Group of Ten, Basel, Switzerland, Bank for International Settlement, 2001.

Copeland, Tom, and Antikarov, Vladimir. *Real Options: A Practitiioner's Guide*. New York: Texere, LLC, 2001.

Croft, Jane. "Bankassurance Deals Boosted." FT.com, *Financial Times*, February 22, 2001 (visited 2/22/01).

Croft, Jane. "Barclays and L&G in Alliance." FT.com, *Financial Times*, January 16, 2001 (visited 1/16/01).

Croft, Jane. "Egg Looking to Grow Through European Partnerships." FT.com, *Financial Times*, February 19, 2001 (visited 2/19/01).

Croft, Jane. "Zurich in BoS Joint Venture." FT.com, *Financial Times*, March 16, 2001 (visited 3/16/01).

Culpan, Refik, ed. *Multinational Strategic Alliances*. New York: International Business Press, 1993.

Deutsche Bank IR Release. Analysts Meeting, February 21, 2000. www.public-deutsche-bank.de (visited 12/18/00).

Dyer, J. H., Kale, P., and Singh, H. "How to Make Strategic Alliances Work." *MIT Sloan Management Review* 4, No. 42 (2001): 37–43.

Dyer, J. H., and Singh, H. "The Relational View: Cooperative Strategy and Sources of Interorganizational Competitive Advantage." *Academy of Management Review* 23, No. 4 (1998): 660–679.

"EU Approves Online Joint Venture to Create Mutual-Fund 'Supermarket.' " WSJ.com, September 5, 2000 (visited 9/5/00).

Finkelstein, S. "Interindustry Merger Patterns and Resource Dependence: A Replication and Extension of Pfeffer." *Strategic Management Journal* 18 (1997): 787–810.

Gilroy, Bernard Michael. *Networking in Multinational Enterprises*. Columbia: University of South Carolina Press, 1993.

"Global Financial Institutions Keep Promise, Deliver Internet Trust to Corporate Banking Customers." Press Release, December 11, 2000, www.identrus.com (visited 1/9/01).

Gulati, Ranjay. "Alliances and Networks." *Strategic Management Journal* 19 (1998): 293–317.

Harbison, John R., and Pekar, Peter, Jr. *Smart Alliances*. San Francisco: Jossey-Bass Publishers, 1998.

"Identrus Member Financial Institutions Develop Internet Payment Initiation Services." Press Release, September 11, 2000, www.identrus.com (visited 1/9/01).

"Japanese Insurers to Tie." CNNfn, cnnfn.com, August 28, 2000 (visited 8/28/00).

Jaruzelsk, Barry, Volkholz, Klaus, and Horkan, Gerald. "The High-Tech Challenge: Sustaining Rapid & Profitable Growth." Booz-Allen & Hamilton, 1999.

Kanter, Rosabeth Moss. *Evolve! Succeeding in the Digital Culture of Tomorrow*. Cambridge, Mass.: Harvard Business School Press, 2001.

Luening, Erich. "IBM Forms Venture for Online Investing." CNET New.com, March 13, 2001, http://news.cnet.com/news (visited 3/13/2001).

Mackintosh, James. "Banks and Insurers Combine Best." FT.com, *Financial Times*, August 6, 2000 (visited 8/7/00).

Marlin, Steven. "50 Leading Banks Kick Off Online FX Venture." *Bank Systems and Technology*, Issue 3801, January 1, 2001, www.banktech.com (visited 1/11/01).

Middlemiss, J. "Bank of America and SAP to Test XML Document Transmission." *Bank Systems & Technology*, Issue 3711, 2000, 32.

Mockler, Robert J. *Multinational Strategic Alliances*. Chichester, U.K.: John Wiley & Sons, 1999.

O'Brian, Bridget. "Some Fund Managers Hand Reins to 'Subadvisers.' " *Wall Street Journal*, August 31, 2001, C1, C17.

"OCC Bulletin, OCC 2001–12." Office of the Comptroller of the Currency, February 28, 2001.

Parkhe, A. "Partner Nationality and the Structure-Performance Relationship in Strategic Alliances." *Organizational Services* 4, No. 2 (1993): 301–324.

Pfeffer, J., and Salancik G. R., *The External Control of Organizations*. New York: Harper & Row, 1978.

"Report: Japan Insurers Plan Alliance." *The Washington Post Online*, October 22, 2000 (visited 10/23/00).

"Sanchez, Ron. "Preparing for an Uncertain Future." *International Studies of Management & Organization* 27, No. 2 (Summer 1997): 71–94.

Schifrin, Matthew. "Partner or Perish." *Forbes Best of the Web*, May 21, 2001, 26–28.

"Sony, Group Launch Money-Services Pact." *Wall Street Journal*, December 26, 2000, A7.

Sparks, Debra. "Partners." *Business Week*, October 25, 1999, 105–112.

Spekman, R. E., Isabella, L.A., and MacAvoy, T. C. *Alliance Competence, Maximizing the Value of Partnerships*. New York: John Wiley and Sons, 2000.

Spriro, Leah Nathans. "Merrill's E-Battle." *Business Week*, November 15, 1999, 256–266.

"Trust Us." *Economist*, August 26, 2000, 54.

Weber, Joseph, and Barrett, Amy. "Volatile Combos," *Business Week*, October 25, 1999, 122.

White, Gregory L., and Tomsho, Robert. "Fidelity, GM to Offer In-Car Trading Via OnStar." *Wall Street Journal*, February 14, 2001, A6.

Williamson, O. E. *The Economic Institutions of Capitalism: Firms, Markets, Relational Contracting*. New York: Free Press, 1985.

Williamson, Oliver E. *Markets and Hierarchies: Analysis and Antitrust Implications*. New York: Free Press, 1975.

Willman, John. "Dresdner and BNP End Pact." FT.com, *Financial Times*, September 24, 2000 (visited 9/25/00).

Willman, John. "Freeze or Jump? That Is the Question," Financial Times Survey: Banking in Europe/Mergers. FT.com, *Financial Times*, August 2000 (visited 9/5/00).

Willman, John. "HSBC and Merrilol's Online Bank Is Launched." FT.com, *Financial Times*, December 6, 2000 (visited 2/26/01).

Yoshino, Michael Y., and Rangan, U. Srinivasa. *Strategic Alliances*. Boston: Harvard Business School Press, 1995.

Chapter 13

The Future of Banking at Synovus Financial Corporation

Richard Anthony

The competitive environment for financial services has never been more intense than it is today. Nonbank competitors such as brokerage firms, insurance companies, mutual funds, and credit card issuers have gained control of a significant portion of individually owned financial assets in the United States at the expense of the banking industry. Not only is banking's share of total financial assets declining, but the industry's share of deposits has shrunk as well. A brief look at the history of banking over the last several decades gives a clear explanation for the current environment.

Prior to 1980, certain banking revenues were protected by federal mandate. The government controlled interest rate ceilings on numerous types of deposit accounts, and many states limited interest rates on loans to individuals. The resulting "net interest margin," the difference between interest charged and interest paid, was largely influenced by law.

The Depository Institutions Deregulation and Monetary Control Act of 1980 ended the "cozy regulatory cocoon" banks had once enjoyed. The competition that resulted from deregulation exposed various problems plaguing the country's banks such as inefficiency, overcapacity, eroding revenues, and loss of market share.

In the 1980s, the U.S. market was saturated with banks that now had lost some regulatory protection. Consolidation within the banking industry accelerated, and acquirers sought to improve performance by reducing jobs and other types of noninterest expenses. At times such consolidators were viewed as having a "slash and burn" mentality. Financial performance at these institutions was indeed enhanced in the short term, but morale in the employee ranks suffered, resulting in diminished customer relationships and weaker revenues over the long term.

As the consolidation movement continued, banking increasingly became viewed as a commodity business. Many experts believed that economy of scale was the answer in that survivors would have to compete on a low-cost basis. Such a view led many competitors to believe that aggressive cost control and scale had to become their differentiator in the marketplace in order to achieve financial goals.

Since that time, the industry has become more polarized. Today, we see money center banks, such as Citibank and Bank of America, on one end of the spectrum, while community banks are on the other. In the middle are a few regional and super-regional institutions including the new Wachovia, SunTrust, and Wells Fargo. These large institutions today represent a significantly greater concentration of banking assets than was the case 20 years ago. In such an environment, developing personal relationships with customers can be a challenge for larger providers who are more concerned with scale and efficiency than distributed authority to the field.

Synovus Financial Corporation fits into a separate category which has few peers. This form of organization is best described as a mid-sized regional network of decentralized community banks. Synovus's 38 affiliate banks across Georgia, South Carolina, Florida, and Alabama are each separately chartered and branded, retaining local boards of directors, local management, and local decision making. Strong customer relationships, an emphasis on personalized service, and active community involvement lead to high levels of trust from customers. Synovus provides its affiliate banks with an array of sophisticated financial products and services that community banks sometimes find uneconomical to offer. Products like debit and credit cards, wealth management services, mortgage banking, corporate cash management, international banking, leasing, and investment banking are good examples. In addition, larger lending capabilities are available to a Synovus affiliate in serving substantial customers.

This heavy emphasis on decentralization places a Synovus bank in the unique position of being able to mold its personality and create strategies to match the needs and opportunities within its own community. "One size fits all" is not in the Synovus vocabulary! For instance, Synovus affiliates serving smaller, more rural communities typically have a style and approach that differs from tactics used in urban, metropolitan markets. Synovus has banks in these types of markets as well as others with even different characteristics. Market share of Synovus affiliate banks also ranges from low to high, resulting again in varying tactical approaches to the marketplace.

Synovus has a strong foundation of historically providing exceptional, personal service to its customers in all markets, although style can vary. In recent years, many other institutions have seemed to frequently change business models, looking for better performance through massive cost-cutting and completely new and different delivery systems. Over the years, Synovus has held true to its primary objective of offering high levels of service and developing customer relationships through stability, consistency, and an emphasis on people. Synovus bank customers should feel that their bankers are not frequently transferred from city to city, resulting in a feeling of stability within the bank. These customers have experienced limited change and little disruption, other than having greater access to a wider range of more sophisticated products in recent years.

Although Synovus has had success and enjoyed superior financial performance, competitive pressures are now mounting. The status quo will not suffice. Continuous improvement is necessary if the company is to excel in the future. The Synovus response to today's environment will be a heightened emphasis on sales and expanding customer relationships in its affiliate banks.

Synovus banking operations have recently developed and implemented a new Sales Management System that is intended to reinvigorate the banking franchise. The desire is to create a true sales culture on top of an existing strong customer service foundation. Sales per se have not historically been touted by the company as an attribute that contributes most to its success. This program was crafted by the top eight banking executives without the use of outside providers or consultants. This internal approach created a high sense of ownership and buy-in within this management team. In unfolding the Sales Management System to team members in the 38 banks, each bank's CEO is striving to create a much higher level of individual accountability for sales production than previously existed. Team members at all levels are encouraged to preserve the sense of teamwork that has historically existed, but individual performance expectations are much clearer than in the past. These expectations would include goals in the following areas: customer profiles, outside calls, referrals to specialty product areas, and traditional product sales. A new sales tracking system has been created to measure individual performance against these goals.

The Sales Management System has a number of elements but one important fundamental priority. Every salesperson is expected to sell products based on customer needs. Product pushing just for the sake of creating revenues is not tolerated if the customer's best interests are violated. This needs-based approach encourages front-line team members to understand and evaluate customer needs, filling any gaps with Synovus financial services. Such an approach will be made easier in the future as profiling capabilities are enhanced.

Needs-based selling is supported by Synovus's strong culture of valuing the worth of every individual. This value helps team members feel more positively about their work life and the opportunity they have to make other people successful, whether they be fellow team members or customers. In this spirit, when communicating to team members the banking leadership always tries to stress the importance of making our customers successful rather than the importance of generating revenues for the company. The approach will allow each affiliate bank to create a vibrant sales culture on top of a meaningful service foundation. Synovus Management sees the winners in the financial services industry over the next 20 years as those banks that are distinguished in delivering both superior service and effective sales. Sales and service are not mutually exclusive. The best sales organizations in the world have the strongest customer service. Service and sales should complement each other rather than creating the perception of conflict in the minds of team members on the front line.

A major component of the Synovus Sales Management System is the leadership element. The COACH model is designed for use by bank sales leaders, such as branch managers, senior lenders, and CEOs. Units within both business banking and consumer banking participate. COACH is based on the following points:

- Communicate effectively: hold weekly sales planning meetings, set goals for customer contacts, set personal goals for product and service sales.
- Observe: watch how team members interact with customers and meet their goals. Find opportunities for improvement, support, praise, and advice.
- Assess results: hold followup meetings to discuss results, successes, failures, problems, and challenges. Synovus is developing a software platform to track sales and referrals, allowing each subsidiary to compare results with individual goals. Extensive reporting will follow, including comparisons across the entire banking operations.
- Coach: one-on-one discussion and evaluation sessions with an emphasis on personal growth and development.
- Hold scheduled sales and development meetings: continue the cycle. As the sales team develops, schedule training that identifies strengths and improves weaknesses. Discipline is necessary to adhere to the regular schedule over a long period of time.

The system enables and encourages rigorous business planning at the bank level based on market research and customer segmentation. Market segmentation calls for defining each individual market's geographic area, while customer segmentation compares each bank's client base to customer segments for the market. As a result, each bank can evaluate whether it is maximizing the potential of each profitable customer segment. Tactical adjustments can be made where segments are underserved by the bank.

Through this process, Synovus Product Development and bank management identify the ideal combination of services to meet each segment's needs. Sales efforts on the front line strive to match products to the prospect's needs, depending on the segment in which the individual "resides." For instance, Synovus affiliates have an opportunity to meet the investment needs of the Upper Affluent segment as well as the transaction needs of the Mass Market segment, and the cash management needs of the Large Corporate segment as well as the lending needs of the Small Business segment.

At the heart of Synovus's segmentation strategy lies a plan to integrate wealth management into traditional banking. Within the affluent consumer segments great potential exists to offer investment management services to individuals who bank with affiliates or own businesses with commercial lending relationships with Synovus banks. Synovus sales leaders will stress the opportunity and need for relationship managers to migrate these customers into brokerage, trust, and insurance services.

Another aspect of the planning process is that each Synovus bank continuously reevaluates its own facilities and infrastructure as a part of this annual business planning process. Looking at the physical condition, layout and location of branches, effectiveness of customer service areas, growth and performance of offices, and level of staffing and talent within each branch helps each Synovus bank better determine potential to perform as a sales organization.

Incentive compensation is also being revised and is key to the Synovus sales formula. Salaries without an incentive component are not effective in an attempt to establish individual accountability for production. Prior to development of the Sales Management System, many affiliates did not offer production bonuses to its relationship managers. At this time, in the interest of local autonomy, templates for incentive compensation are strongly suggested to affiliate banks, but final details and elements are not mandated from the corporate level. Synovus also focuses heavily on nonfinancial rewards and recognition both corporately and at the individual bank level.

Finally, Synovus has created an overarching set of quantitative objectives by which our entire banking operation can measure progress and success under the new program. Goals have been established for three consolidated measures. The company's current aggregate penetration rate of services per household has been examined, and a goal has been set to increase this measure from a current level of approximately two services per household to four over the next four years. Synovus's customer acquisition rate has historically been good, but even this measure can be strengthened going forward. Customer count currently grows at about 1.5 percent each month. The rate of lost customers must be managed toward lower levels. Synovus would like to see a net gain of 6 percent in customers each year in the future, this figure representing the difference between annual growth and attrition. Each bank can have different goals, but the entire banking operation will manage toward these consolidated objectives.

Synovus's vision is to be the finest financial services company in the world. For Synovus, this vision can be attained only if each of its 38 banks fully embraces and successfully implements this new Sales Management System. The financial services industry today is too competitive for any company not to place sales at the top of its strategic agenda. After almost a full year of implementation work, Synovus's banking operations have significantly strengthened its capabilities in every aspect of the sales process. Much work remains to achieve its vision, but Synovus's bank management believes that sales effectiveness can become its banks' significant differentiator in the competitive days ahead.

Chapter 14

The Future of Swiss Banking

Teodoro D. Cocca and Peter Csoport

INTRODUCTION

The formally conservative and easily predictable banking sector is in the midst of a radical change. What was unthinkable five years ago has to a large extent already occurred. Both external observers and the sector itself agree that this phase of change is far from completed. This contribution discusses this change from the point of view of the Swiss banks and the Swiss financial center. In a first step, the structure and development of the Swiss banking sector will be described. The forces of change in banking will then be shown and placed within a framework. Using various provocative hypotheses, the future development of Swiss banks will then be discussed. The emphasis of this chapter is on private banking, for this represents the most influential factor in forming the image of Swiss banks, both internationally and nationally.

STRUCTURE AND DEVELOPMENT OF THE SWISS BANKING SECTOR

Characteristics of the Swiss Banking Industry

Swiss banks look back on a very long tradition. The oldest, the private banks, were founded 200 to 250 years ago as individual enterprises, collectives, or limited partnerships. Over time, they have served as loan creditors and financial administrators to monarchies, empires, and governments in Europe and other continents. Today, the clientele of Swiss banks are domestic and international private persons, companies, institutional clients, and corporate enterprises. Because of its federalist structure, Switzerland has a decentralized banking system with a large number of independent institutions. Characteristic of the Swiss banking industry are its major national economic importance, its density, the dominant universal banking system, its strong international involvement, and its heterogeneity.

Development of the Banking Sector

At the beginning of the 1990s, the structure of Swiss banking changed dramatically as a result of acquisitions, mergers, and liquidations. Between 1990 and 1999, the number of employees decreased by 9.6 percent. The number of institutions declined by 40.5 percent and the number of branch offices decreased by 32.2 percent. However, within the same time span, the total of the banks' personnel costs increased. This was due to higher average wages and bonuses. Despite this process of concentration in the banking market, the sector maintained its important position with the Swiss national economy. Currently, the banks' share in total added value in Switzerland is approximately 11 percent and thus around twice that of Germany, France, or the United States. In 1998, labor productivity gross value added per employee for banks was 240,000 CHF. The only sector that came close to this figure was the chemicals industry with 228,000 CHF per person. The exceptional performance of the banks is due to the high labor productivity. In 1998, the net added value of banks was achieved with only 3.8 percent of all Swiss employees.

Declining Bank Density

The traditionally high density of banks in Switzerland has shown a tendency toward decline since 1990 (see Table 14.1). The following comparisons show this clearly: at the end of 2000, Swiss banks numbered 375 (1990: 625). In the same year, these had 2,903 branch offices in total (1990: 4,387) and of these, 2,801 (1990: 4,297) had their domicile in Switzerland. Placing the number of national branch offices in relation to the population, this means that in the year 2000 there was one branch per 2,570 residents (1990: 1,625). Despite this development, compared internationally, Switzerland still has a higher than average number of banks and, moreover, one of the most dense networks of branch offices.

Universal Banking System

A special feature of the Swiss banking sector is the universal banking system. It is characterized by the fact that every bank is allowed to, though not obliged to, carry out all banking transactions. Universal banks are also permitted to offer nonbanking services (and are therefore not subject to the supervision of the Federal Banking Commission), such as insurance services (bancassurance). Thus, almost all institutions of major national importance that are active on the

Table 14.1
Number of Banks and Branch Offices, 1990–2000

Year	1990	1991	1992	1993	1994	1995	1996	1997	1998	1999	2000
Number of banks	625	592	569	529	494	413	403	394	376	372	375
Number of branch offices	4,387	4,357	4,262	4,117	3,922	3,771	3,645	3,439	3,199	2,973	2,903
domestic	4,297	4,264	4,169	4,027	3,821	3,666	3,543	3,335	3,101	2,873	2,801
abroad	90	93	93	90	101	105	102	104	98	100	102
Residents per (domestic) branch office	1,625	1,637	1,674	1,734	1,827	1,904	1,970	2,093	2,251	2,430	2,570
Population in 2000 (in 1,000)											7,204

Source: Swiss National Bank (2001, 20).

Swiss market (big banks, cantonal, regional, Raiffeisen [loan associations], and commercial banks) are universal banks. This does not prevent them from concentrating on particular lines of business (e.g., mortgages, commerce, money management, foreign trade) or market areas. Generally speaking, it is the investment banks and private banks, as well as the foreign banks, that do not operate as universal banks.

International Positioning

Initial conclusions on international integration can be drawn from the proportion of foreign assets and liabilities. For almost every group of banks, foreign assets outweigh foreign liabilities. Accordingly, Swiss banks invest more money overseas than they receive from overseas clients. This is a remarkable fact that is often overlooked. The exceptions are the cantonal, regional, and Raiffeisen banks—which are forced to partly refinance their national activities with foreign investment—as well as the branch offices of foreign banks. The external importance of the Swiss banking sector is clearly expressed in the current account balance. The banks' exports are registered in the balance sheet for service transactions (almost half the balance is the result of overseas bank commissions) and the balance sheet for earned and capital income. The most important sources of this surplus in the banking sector are closely connected to brokerage fees and fiduciary commissions for asset management, as well as earnings from issue activities. The latter are based on the higher than average placement power of the banks due to asset management.

Tables 14.2 and 14.3 show the potential of the two Swiss big banks in international comparison. It is remarkable that a small country such as Switzerland has not one but two banks that are considered among the largest in the world.

The extensive spread of stock investment in Switzerland is also striking. This is empirically substantiated by an international comparison. Of those countries considered, Switzerland has the highest number of direct equity owners, following Australia and Sweden (see Figure 14.1).[1]

Value Creation in the Banking Sector

Swiss banks have not been sufficiently successful in increasing company value in the long term. McKinsey analyzed the value increase in the Swiss banking sector for the period 1985–1994. Taking all banking groups into consideration, a diminution in value—depending on the beta figures applied—of between 11.9 and 15.5 billion CHF was ascertained. This is the equivalent of a value depreciation of 1.2 to 1.6 billion CHF per year. To simply cover the equity risk costs, banks' profits would have needed to be 25 to 30 percent higher to prevent a value diminution (Brunner 1996, 81–96; Vettiger, 1996, 99). As shown in Figure 14.2, a comparison for the period January 1, 1990 to October 25, 2001, marked by massive restructuring in the banking sector, results in an

Table 14.2
Largest Banks According to Total Assets

Rank	Name	Country	Total Assets[1]
1	Mizuho Financial Group	Japan	1,259
2	Citigroup	United States	902
3	Deutsche Bank	Germany	875
4	J.P. Morgan	United States	715
5	Bank of Tokyo-Mitsubishi	Japan	676
6	HSBC	Great Britain	674
7	Hypo Vereinsbank	Germany	667
8	UBS	Switzerland	665
9	BNP Paribas	France	646
10	Bank of America	United States	642
11	Credit Suisse Group	Switzerland	603
12	Sumitono Bank	Japan	541

[1]Total assets in billions of U.S. dollars for fiscal year 2000.

Table 14.3
Largest Banks According to Market Capitalization

Rank	Name	Stock Exchange	Market Capitalization[1]
1	HSBC	London	110
2	Bank of America	New York	96
3	J.P. Morgan	New York	89
4	Wells Fargo	New York	79
5	UBS	Virt-x	64
6	Lloyds TSB	London	56
7	Royal Bank of Scotland	London	54
8	Barclays	London	52
9	Credit Suisse Group	Virt-x	49
10	Mitsubishi Tokyo Fin. Group	Tokyo	48
11	Sumitomo Mitsui	Tokyo	46
12	Deutsche Bank	Frankfurt	45

[1]Market capitalization in billions of U.S. dollars as of June 30, 2001.

Figure 14.1
International Comparison of Direct Equity Investors

Country	Percent of direct equity investors
Australia	41
Sweden	35
Switzerland	32
New Zealand	31
U.K.	30
U.S.	26
Canada	26
Denmark	22
Norway	21
Germany	10
Austria	6

0 10 20 30 40 50

Percent of direct equity investors

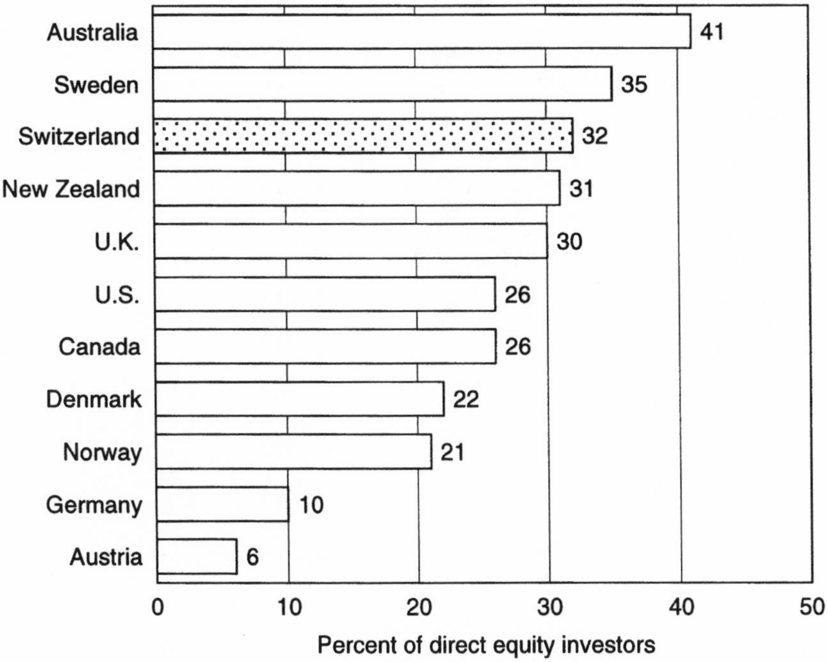

Source: Cocca and Volkart (2000, 12). Reprinted with permission.

average yearly appreciation in prices of 12 percent for the Swiss Market Index.[2] The two big banks produce yearly earnings of merely 8.56 percent (UBS) and 8.32 percent (Credit Suisse Group). As the equity costs for big banks amount to at least 8 percent per year long-term, the generation of value is insignificant.

A comparison of the Swiss banks with the North American banking sector shows that the U.S. banks realized an average yearly earnings for the period January 1, 1990 to October 25, 2001 of 14.9 percent (Swiss banks 8.9%) and therefore achieved a better generation of value (see Figure 14.3).

Heterogeneous Banking Scene

The banks in Switzerland form an unequal group: only one in four banks has total assets of more than one billion CHF; 95 percent of total assets falls to these approximately 100 banks. The distribution of off-balance-sheet operations is even more one-sided. The Swiss National Bank categorizes the banks according to a system of statistics into big banks (UBS, Credit Suisse Group), cantonal banks, regional banks, Raiffeisen banks, other banks (commercial, investment, small loan, and foreign-dominated banks) and private banks.

Figure 14.2
Comparison of Stock Prices (UBS, CS Group, SMI)

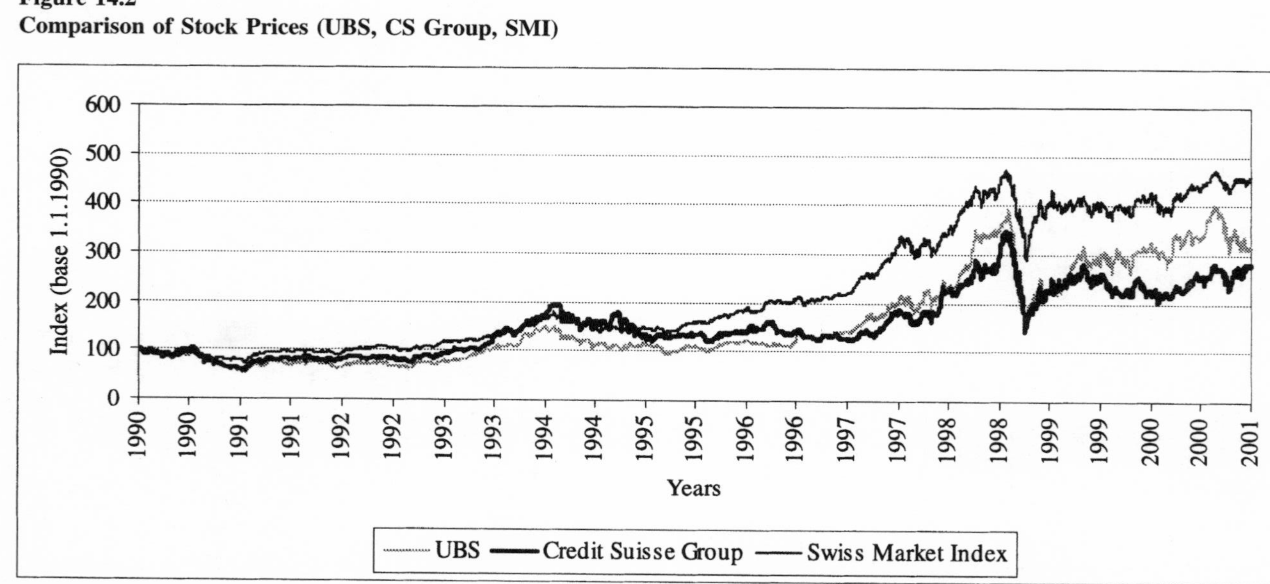

Source: Authors/Datastream.

Figure 14.3
Comparison of Indices (Swiss banks versus U.S. banks)

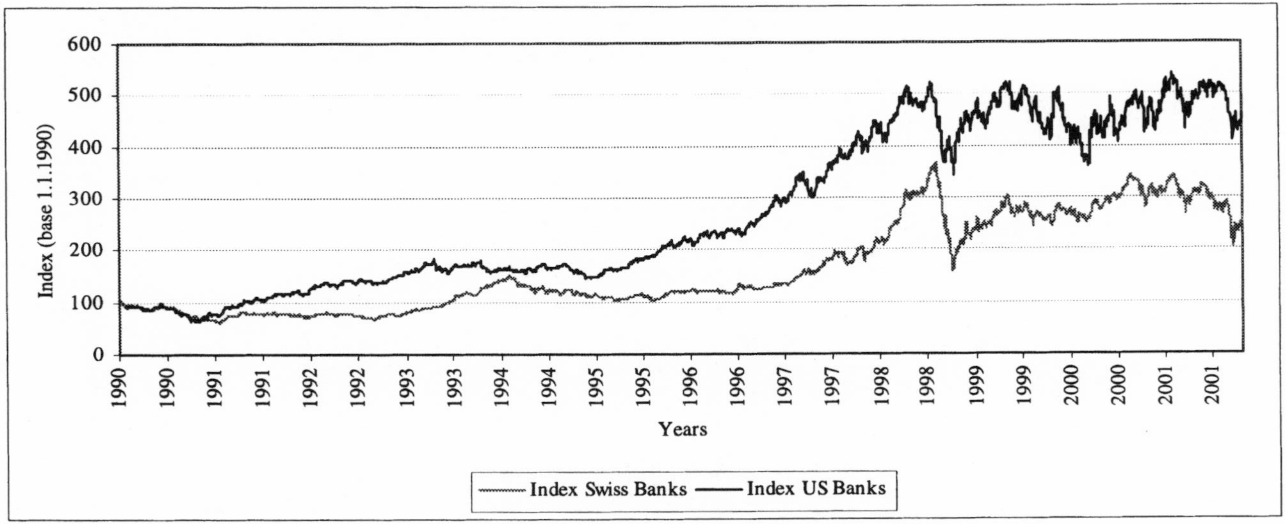

Source: Authors/Datastream.

Measured according to total assets, the big banks dominate more than two-thirds of the total banking market in Switzerland and, taken together with the cantonal banks, cover over 80 percent of the market. However, measured according to the off-balance-sheet operations "fiduciary transactions," it is no longer the big banks who head the list but the foreign-dominated banks (included in the category "other banks" above) (see Table 14.4).

Mergers and Acquisitions

The following discussion of mergers and acquisitions considers those events surrounding the big banks which are relevant from an international perspective. The merger between the UBS and the Swiss Bank Corporation, which was announced in December 1997, represents a milestone in the history of Swiss banking. The new UBS moved up to third place in the list of financial corporations active worldwide with a market capitalization of 94 billion CHF, putting a temporary end to a jostling for position between domestic big banks. Asset management played the key part in this: in 1997 the group managed 1300 billion CHF, more than any other institute in the world. The UBS became active again in July 2000 when it acquired the U.S. investment house PaineWebber. At that point, PaineWebber was the fourth-largest brokerage in the United States. The company had more than 20,000 employees, 7,600 of who were financial advisors, and managed U.S. $452 billion in customer deposits. This acquisition allowed the UBS to tap the lucrative private and investment banking area on the U.S. market and to strengthen its investment bank subsidiary, UBS Warburg.

The Credit Suisse Group realized its expansion strategy with the acquisition of Winterthur Insurances in August 1998. The emphasis of this takeover was on the creation of a comprehensive financial services package (bancassurance) for private and company customers within a single group worldwide. Just a few weeks after the major UBS takeover on the U.S. market, the Credit Suisse Group acquired the American investment bank Donaldson Lufkin & Jenrette (DLJ) in August 2000. The aim of this acquisition was to considerably strengthen the position of the CS Group investment bank subsidiary, Credit Suisse First Boston (CSFB), as a global investment bank.

FRAMEWORK

The worldwide banking and financial sector is currently in a phase of change and upheaval, the end of which is not yet foreseeable. As can be seen in Figure 14.4, we consider six causal trends that affect the elements of banking.

Next, the most important trends from the point of view of the Swiss banks (in particular the big banks) will be examined.[3] The analysis of the effects of these trends on the changeable elements of the banking world (market structure, products and processes, and investor behavior) allow various hypotheses to be formulated. The latter form the basis of the discussion on the future development of Swiss banks.

Technology

The banking and financial sector is primarily an information processing branch of the economy. The developments in information and telecommunications technology and its swift dissemination in business and society are the most important forces of change for banks long term. The financial sector is, for example, subject to more fundamental change than the manufacturing industry. The added value of the banks, and thus the economic justification of their existence, is based on a guaranteeing of various transformation and transaction functions within the scope of financial intermediation. Developments in information technology have caused time and distance to collapse. These developments are the most important parameters for the production and distribution of financial products. This technological development has caused the banking sector to become a highly investment-intensive sector of the economy within the last quarter of a century. Specialization, critical mass, as well as a large number of scale, network, and platform effects play a decisive role.

The consequences of technological change can be seen in three areas in particular:

1. *Production*. The way in which financial services are produced is changing radically (processes, structures). The traditional value chain has been broken and assembled differently. The depth of product range in the banking sector is being radically reduced. The new motto is "market replaces hierarchy."
2. *Products*. Information technology allows the construction of new financial products by reorganizing the transformational elements. These new products often meet customers' needs better than traditional products, which allowed (former) suppliers to realize high yields with low capital commitment.
3. *Marketing, customer bonding*. The electronic distribution channels compete with traditional channels in various ways: the necessity for spatial proximity is overcome, services are available immediately and around the clock, interfaces are standardized, the distribution costs are significantly reduced, various "technical intermediaries" appear between the bank and its customer.

All three developments not only change the competitive situation between existing competitors but also allow a multitude of various new suppliers to enter the traditional sphere of banking.

There are various reasons that this does not develop more swiftly:

- Such fundamental innovation processes naturally necessitate a certain amount of time to assert themselves. The innovation cycles have, however, become dramatically tighter when compared to earlier technological innovations (e.g., the telephone).

Table 14.4
Key Figures for the Swiss Banking Sector (2000)

Group	Institute	Branch Offices	Total Assets		Employees	
	(Number)	(Number)	Mio. CHF	Employees in %	Number	Employees in %
All banks	375	2,903	2,124,880	100.0	124,998	100.0
Cantonal banks	24	748	303,385	14.3	19,190	15.4
Big banks[1]	3	630	1,340,310	63.1	59,114	47.3
Regional banks and savings banks	103	390	75,808	3.6	5,451	4.4
Raiffeisen banks[2]	1	537	77,142	3.6	4,999	4.0
Other banks	204	544	290,968	13.7	30,912	24.7
Subsidiaries of foreign banks	23	27	18,843	0.9	1,243	1.0
Private banks	17	27	18,424	0.9	4,089	3.2

Group	Foreign Assets		Foreign Liabilities		Fiduciary Transactions		
	Mio. CHF	in % of Assets	Mio. CHF	in % of Liabilities	Mio. CHF	in % of Total Assets	Market Share in %
All banks	1,196,189	56.2	1,111,380	52.2	411,641	19.3	100.0
Cantonal banks	18,843	6.2	24,981	8.2	8,975	3.0	2.2
Big banks	983,062	73.3	916,591	68.4	74,656	5.6	18.1
Regional banks and savings banks	604	0.8	1,378	1.8	486	0.6	0.1
Raiffeisen banks	2,381	3.1	3,260	4.2	260	0.3	0.1
Other banks	172,436	59.2	147,374	50.6	274,001	94.1	66.6
Subsidiaries of foreign banks	10,735	57.0	12,398	65.8	9,056	48.0	2.2
Private banks	8,128	44.1	5,399	29.3	44,207	239.9	10.7

1 Formally speaking there are three big banks, commercially speaking there are two (Credit Suisse First Boston (CSFB) and Credit Suisse are considered individually in bank statistics as they are legally independent).

2 One organization with 582 associated institutes as of end of 1999.

Source: Swiss National Bank (2001).

Figure 14.4
Forces of Change

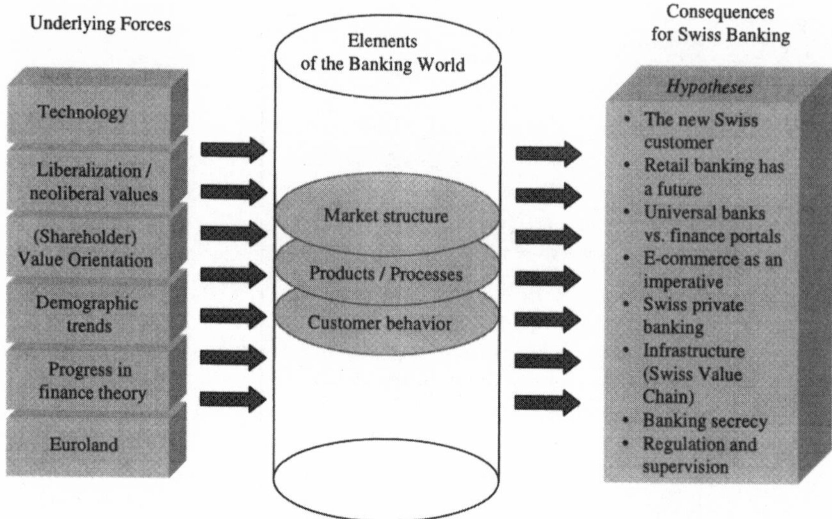

- The industry is protected from new competitors by supervision and regulation, which results in a significant delay in the adoption processes. This cannot, however, prevent these processes long term.
- The customers, particularly private persons, are conservative in their financial behavior, and many changes may well only be accepted and adopted by the next generation of clients.

Value Orientation in the Banking Sector

In Switzerland, too, various factors have led to the fact that the creation of corporate value (shareholder value) has been propelled into the center of entrepreneurial behavior. This trend has not left the banking sector untouched. Today, banks in particular are forced to meet owners' demands for preservation of capital and appreciation in value.

In contrast to the Anglo-Saxon countries, where the primacy of corporate value has been securely anchored since Modigliani and Miller's fundamental contributions, the shareholder value approach became important in Continental Europe only at the beginning of the 1990s. This rudimentary change was accompanied by polemical discussion. The following factors have strengthened the trend toward value-oriented corporate management:

- The tendency toward globalization has also forced Continental European corporations into meeting the requirements of Anglo-Saxon investors.

- The increase in institutional asset management, which is a result of the demographic structure of Switzerland, has led to a strengthened position of institutional investors and, as a result, to increased performance pressure for corporations.
- One can also observe a general emancipation of private investors, who increasingly invest their money according to performance and risk factors.

In addition to the above-mentioned fundamentally value-oriented factors, a number of points indicate a specific value-orientation of the banking sector:

- Banking services are always transformational. Therefore, risk and the fixed time structure of a bank's balance sheet play central roles. Modern financial market theory approaches are in a position to quantify the value of a bank's compensation for carrying these risks.
- Due to their business activities banks have specialized knowledge at their disposal in the area of appraisal and, in particular, in the area of risk management. Compared to other sectors, the adoption of modern concepts of value-oriented corporate management is easier in this area.
- The application of modern financial market theory for banks is relatively straightforward—in comparison to an industrial concern—as the bulk of the balance sheet is made up of financial assets and liabilities.

Sociodemographic Developments in Switzerland

Since many banks function entirely according to close customer proximity, client analysis is given high priority. This section presents the most important sociodemographic changes relevant to the Swiss financial center:

- Ageing of the population and decreasing security networks. As with other highly developed countries in Europe and America, one can also observe a demographic ageing in Switzerland due on the one hand to increased life expectancy and on the other to a decline in the birthrate. This development is intensified by a migration movement. The result is that a continually declining number of employees are set against a growing number of people in education and in retirement.[4] As this development challenges the financing of state retirement schemes, the necessity for individual retirement financing is increasing.
- More singles, single parents, and couples with double incomes and no kids yet ("dinkies"). Insecurity due to state retirement schemes increases as the traditional family with its security function is less and less represented. Falling marriage rates are set against drastically increasing divorce rates. Not only singles and single parents (mainly women), but also those couples living together have other financial needs compared to the traditional family.
- High education levels. Generally speaking, one can say that the level of education in Switzerland has increased. In 1998, the portion of 25- to 34-year-olds who had only completed the obligatory school years was a mere 13 percent; the equivalent level of education in 55 to 65 year-olds was 29 percent. These observations are also valid for

those with higher education and professional training where the numbers steadily decline for all age groups. Whereas the share is 25 percent in the age category 25–34, the portion of 55- to 65-year-olds is 18 percent. Significant gender differences in education levels can be observed. While 12 percent of men have a university degree, only 6 percent of women have the same level of education. The development in high-school diploma rates suggests that this will change (Bundesamt für Statistik, 2000, 391).

- Income increase. The nominal gross national income as a macroeconomic income aggregator more than doubled between 1980 and 1996. This corresponds to an actual increase of more than 20 percent during this time period. However, private household salaries increased in total by 80.5 percent, or 10.2 percent p.a. Although income development in Switzerland has seen constant growth since World War II, salaries have actually stagnated since 1992. For the segmentation of bank clientele, the development of the average salary is less relevant, although its change influences the division of total income in transaction and speculation components. Of relevance is the distribution of income.
- Increasing polarization. Although the Swiss population has generally become more affluent, the distribution of assets is becoming visibly more polarized. Whereas the well-educated are receiving increasingly higher premiums for their work, those workers with poor education are progressively being forced into unemployment or badly paid part-time work.
- Ever-increasing leisure activities and opportunities, changing values, new forms of work (home-office) and working-hour models are having considerable effects on the factors of time, availability, and use of financial services. These must be faster, more flexible, and more available, better-oriented according to primary client consumption, or rather, investment, needs and the customers' values (leisure and consumption behavior). Leisure time is increasing in value and becoming more and more important. Apart from the desire to conduct banking transactions swiftly and at any time of the day or night, it is becoming clear that some customers (in contrast to day traders) do not want to spend their valuable time with continual monitoring of their asset situation. On the other hand, a trend has recently become established: Consumption in itself has a satisfying effect on the customer. Thus, a consumer group can be defined who enjoys conducting their stock transactions personally. New mediums such as the Internet underline this combination of investment and entertainment ("investainment").

Euroland

With the introduction of the Euro, a large and solvent European financial market is born. The volume of bond issues, stocks and bank assets of the 11 participants of the monetary union had already reached U.S. $21 billion in 1995, roughly the same value as in the United States. The market capitalization of a European Union-wide stock market constitutes 31 percent of the U.S. market and is therefore larger than the Japanese or British market. However, the structure of assets is varied: in the EU almost 60 percent are bank assets, whereas it is only 20 percent in the United States. In the European Union the process of disintermediation will be accelerated accordingly. It will be impossible for Switzerland to avoid this trend of "away from the balance sheet towards the market."

There are two possible scenarios for Switzerland and the Swiss franc:

1. The Swiss franc remains an alternative to the Euro and offers security in insecure times. An over-valuation of the franc would, however, have consequences for the export and domestic economy. The banks would "profit" from such a development but perhaps at the cost of the quality of their credit portfolio.
2. The Swiss franc follows the Euro, it develops into a parallel currency of the Euro, it loses a large part of its special status. The differences in the financial markets should decrease, in particular with respect to interest rates. For the Swiss real economy this would be on balance a favorable development. This would increase the Swiss economy's demand for all types of Euro banking services, also domestically. The special role of the Swiss financial center would decline in importance, unless it could maintain its leading position in the area of infrastructure (SIC, the stock exchange, SIS, etc.) for Euro-denominated contracts.

The banking sector will be most affected by the newly emerging currency. The banks need, on the one hand, to guarantee Euro compatibility in all areas of business and, on the other, to develop new business potential. The transition to a single currency implies adjustment of payment transfers, account management, securities, exchange commerce, money market and foreign exchange trading, derivatives, and asset management.

For Swiss banks, investment operations (both institutional and private) will gain in importance. As a result of the establishment of the European Union and the introduction of a single currency, an integrated financial market will emerge, which will significantly increase price transparency in the European economy. Financial investments within the EU will no longer carry a currency exchange risk for EU-based investors. Thus, an increase in transparency in the comparison of alternative asset investments in general and of various companies in particular will be the result. Competition in the various business areas will mount. The margins in standardized asset management will decline due to increasing price transparency, high capital mobility of institutional investors, and technical progress.

HYPOTHESIS

The New Swiss Customer

Central to the market performance of a financial institute is the customer and his or her needs. The approach developed here assumes that the sociodemographic developments will cause a change in bank-relevant client requirements. If the financial services supplier is not in a position to satisfy the changing needs of customers, he will be in danger of losing his position in the market. The following analysis concentrates on the investment process from the client's viewpoint and covers the private customer business area (retail and private banking) of a Swiss big bank.

Importance of Client Analysis

Developments that cause the foundations of an industry to be changed completely are called "killer applications" (Downes and Mui, 1999). They are defined as a new product or service that fundamentally changes the norms of an industry. A classic example is the personal computer. Killer applications have begun to penetrate all markets and industries. Internet banking shows huge potential for becoming a killer application in the financial services area. This does not mean to imply that development in technology is necessarily also a killer application. Rather, one should distinguish between "sustaining" and "disruptive" technologies (Christensen, 1999, 108). Developments in the area of "sustaining technologies," are concerned with the improvement of the performance of established products and are seldom accompanied by pioneering changes to the industries. The "disruptive technologies," on the other hand, bring enormous consequences in their wake. They redefine the situation for all market participants, and they become a dominant customer need at an unforeseeable point in time in the future.

The following phenomenon should also be observed in this connection (Christensen, 1999). Well-run corporations, whose company management keeps close watch over the requirements of their customers, invest in the further development of current products under consideration of all basic economic laws and can still lose their market leadership position when such killer applications appear. Many of the generally well-accepted management principles have only situative validity and are no guarantee for the long-term success of a company. Classical approaches are not in a position to recognize the indications of disruptive killer applications and are therefore taken by surprise by the changed customer requirements. Thus, the role of management is to become familiar with these developments, to recognize the implications for specific management activities, and to put these into practice. It is necessary to do two things simultaneously. On the one hand, one should avoid neglecting the needs of those traditional groups of customers who have existed up until that point. At the same time, the focus of attention must also be on the requirements of groups of customers who will be dominant in the future in order to fulfill these needs at the correct point in time. (Then when these client groups are dominant, the killer application must become a necessary feature of the bank's services.)

Features of the New Client

The client is the focus of attention. His or her basic financial needs will be the same in the future as in the past. The private customer needs four types of financial services: (1) financial investments, (2) financing, (3) payment transfers, and (4) risk coverage. Does this mean that everything will remain the same with the customers in the future? The answer is a threefold no.

- First no: The retail client is not a purely rational monetary being. Increasingly, he or she is on the lookout for fun and entertainment in money matters: F & F, "fun and finance," could be the new slogan, particularly in the investment business. Yahoo! promotes its services with "make money and have fun." Others talk of "generation me"—those who work hard, earn extremely well, and want to have a lot of fun at the same time. Financial requirements seem increasingly connected to lifestyle needs. Of course, the traditional private customer is also not a purely monetary human being. He or she often values time as much as money. Time is not considered here as the speed of a transaction but as a dimension of attention that is given in the form of contact time with the bank's most precious resource: qualified personnel.
- Second no: The retail customer is equipped with new technology. Already over half the population in Switzerland has access to the Internet, and in three years this figure will increase to more than 60 percent. Today's retail client possesses a debit and more often than not a credit card. In three years' time, these cards will be armed with new functions based on chips and will also have a digital signature.
- Third no: The retail client is better informed. He or she knows the financial products and services on offer, has easy access to financial information, and compares prices and offers. The loyal savings customer has developed into a critical investor. The client is less loyal than in the past and has various bank connections at the same time. Of course, there will also be old customers in the future, and increasingly so. Even these, however, will come closer and closer to the profile described. The age of the Internet has arrived for all retail clients.

Consequences for Swiss Banks

Clients are more prepared to use nonbank or independent advisor information services if the quality and price are right. Banks currently enjoy the trust of investors, but this can change in future generations. The generation that is growing up with trademarks such as Microsoft, Amazon, or E-Trade will use the financial services of these companies. A recent example is Sony's advance into private and retail banking. In particular, those companies that have a large customer base (AOL), and that dominate a distribution channel (Nokia, Psion) and/or have special marketing capabilities, will be the ones that increasingly compete with the banks. Within banks a new development in customer segmentation is beginning to emerge. It is no longer the extent of the assets, but the service in demand (customers who require advice or administration and individual customers) that is of importance. The market is increasingly developing according to the wishes and needs of the customers. Since the customers have better know-how and real alternatives, they are in a much stronger position than ever before.

The bank's role as a supplier of information is therefore changing. It is no longer simply the financial institute that is used as a source for well-founded financial information. In addition, as a result of this development, the subject of money and investment will lose its mystique as elite merchandise and become consumer goods. Improved access to information and the investor's increased ability to process information will lead the investor to make independent decisions. The customer will also more consciously compare services and prices and will therefore change banks more frequently, or rather will have more than one banking connection (reduction in bank loyalty). Dissimilar treatment of small and large investors will increasingly be looked upon with distrust. The small investor also wishes to have high-quality services at a fair price. The fact that future investors will have already learned how to deal with modern technology in their first years of school will ensure the unproblematic use of the personal computer and the Internet.

Changes in age structure will have an effect on both the qualitative and quantitative composition of the private customer segment and the structure of requirements of the financial services in demand. Senior citizens will represent a dominant demographic force in the future. An "implosion of the world population" is currently being discussed (Wallace, 1999). Apart from advisory services and products modeled according to the phases in clients' lives, the demand for individual solutions will also increase. The baby-boomer generation (those born between 1946 and 1964) is coming closer to retirement age, a time when accumulation of assets is at its peak. This group will become the dominant group of investors. Differences in behavior from that of earlier generations can be observed according to the example of Internet banking. Those in the mid-thirties execute the greatest number of banking transactions on the Internet. This generation will invest a large portion of their assets through institutional investors or through direct investment on the stock exchange. In Switzerland, it is the baby-boomers who hold a higher than average amount of stocks (32% versus the total average: of 29%) (Cocca and Volkart, 2000, 11). The volume of business will increase with the next generation. Generations X (those born between 1965 and 1981) and Y (those born after 1982) have technological know-how, are more skeptical of state retirement schemes, will trade much more often than their parents, and will invest their money on the stock exchange much earlier.

Disposable income in Switzerland has developed rather stably. In contrast, monetary assets have greatly increased due to the bull market at the end of the 1990s. Despite the corrections in 2000–2001, the demand for financial services will grow owing to the awaited transfer of assets to the so-called inheritance generation. In addition, one can assume that the beneficiaries, in contrast to their predecessors, will have different advisory needs as well as different investment behavior (a tendency toward risk since the assets are not a result of their own labor). With increasing assets to invest, private customers' involvement in and demand for financial services will grow. The client wants comprehensive and individual advice according to his or her phase of life.

As can be observed in Figure 14.5, the number of investments carried out by the investor personally will increase.

Figure 14.5
Development of Active Investors in Switzerland

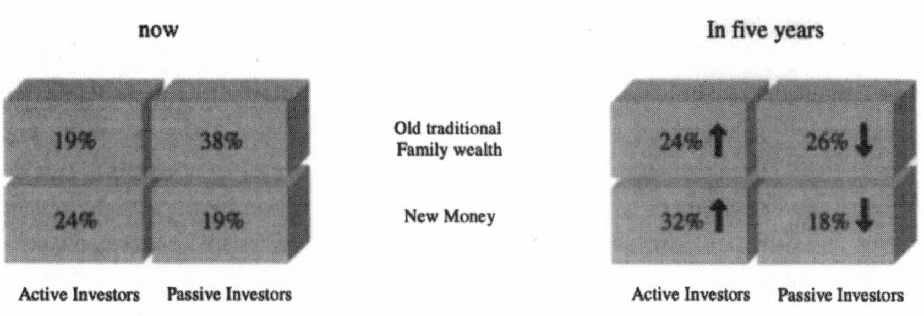

Source: PriceWaterhouseCoopers (1999, 28). Reprinted with permission.

These developments have had the following consequences for retail banking. First, due to the longer time required for education, income for young people and adults will decrease and be more dependent on their parents' asset and income situation. As a result of the increase in the number of women who, now better educated, have more demanding and more lucrative jobs, a new customer segment will emerge for banks. Delays in marriage and first pregnancies are consequences of this development, as are demands for new products emanating from the changed image of women. Finally, customers, particularly those with a business education, will demand better advice as they are in a position to themselves assess the product risks and judge competitive products. The banks will be forced to invest more resources in training their personnel.

The changes illustrated exert a wide-ranging influence on the behavior of future customers. A common denominator will be a call for a modular spectrum of products with integrated insurance benefits and a desire for more flexibility. However, differences will remain in the choice of distribution channel. The traditional customer will continue to use the channel of habit—particularly the cost-intensive bank window—and value personal contact with bank representatives. The innovative new bank client, on the other hand, will increasingly use new distribution channels such as the Internet and call centers. Although this technology reduces costs, the danger of decreasing customer loyalty and product interchangeability should not be underestimated.

The most important point to realize is that demand often grows more slowly than technological opportunities. The result is an initial uncertainty of the market participants. The future demographic core customer group will, however, reduce this difference in time. "Disruptive technologies" and Internet banking will therefore be the market requirements of the future, even if the majority of today's most important clients do not yet consider them a basic requirement. This is a distinctive feature of "disruptive" killer applications: they are always appreciated first by the customers who are least profitable for the company.

Retail Banking Has a Future

The following hypothesis is dedicated to the future of Swiss retail banks, the retail customer, and their relationship. We understand retail banking here as banking business with private customers whose asset portfolios go up to a certain limit (250,000 CHF for example). In many countries, retail banks typically cultivate business with small and medium-sized business customers. This aspect is not analyzed here.

The New World of Retail Banking

Although the four fundamental financial requirements of customers will remain the same, almost everything will change for banks in the future. Today's retail banking suffers from excess capacity in personnel, production, and distribution systems, locations, and perhaps capital as well. In the coming years, this excess capacity will need to be reduced further. The construction and development of the information and business systems of retail banks will become increasingly expensive and, in contrast, the variable costs of additional business volume will greatly decrease. Thus, on the one hand, the best retail banks will have the opportunity to increase retail banking profitability due to high volumes, as the current high variable personnel costs will sink dramatically. On the other hand, technological development requires a complete restructuring of the value chain on the production side, especially with the universal banks. Most banks must reduce their vertical range of products, increasingly acquire services from outside specialists, and concentrate on a number of core competences (close to the client). The speed of restructuring is crucial for the success or survival of retail banks. Banking regulations and supervision periodically protect retail banks from new competitors; however, this will not be a lasting function. Finally, in the coming years, one can expect that large European retail banks will emerge, helped along by the European Monetary Union. Despite Switzerland's autonomous currency area, the Swiss banking market will not likely avoid this development.

The Client Relationship

Crucial to the future of retail banking is its ability to satisfy the customer's future requirements at a profit. Central to this ability is a solid relationship with the customer. Banks have developed new concepts in this area, such as bancassurance and one-stop shopping. A well thought-through customer segmentation by the bank is the foundation of such concepts. But if the customer is always right, and if the Internet serves to strengthen his or her position in this case, then the efficacy of this approach seems doubtful. It will not be important how the bank divides its customers into segments, but how the retail customers divide up their suppliers and how they choose their financial services suppliers.

Domination of the electronic interfaces to the customer is a question of survival for every retail bank. The role of personal contact with the retail client in the future is widely recognized. The type of contact will be similar to that of an appointment at the doctor's or with a lawyer, rather than the current cost-intensive *ad hoc* usage. Through the electronic distribution channel, retail banks are increasingly faced with new competitors from other industries, which are also attempting to meet the new requirements. Examples of these are Internet and telecommunication network operators, manufacturers of operating systems, browsers, and software applications, Internet portal operators, as well as retail trade companies with large customer bases. There is a risk that retail banks will effectively lose the direct contact to the client and will be relegated to the rank of suppliers to other companies who have conquered customer interfaces. In this connection, a question arises as to what role the banks want to play for their customer in the future. Two well-established models are the product specialist "online broker" and the "finance portal." The business model "pure online retail bank" has been assessed as having little chance in the near future. The prerequisites to become such a finance portal are not only extreme professionalism, but also a strong trademark and a flexible architecture. In the online business scene of tomorrow, banks will also be media corporations: a corporation that relieves its clients of various aspects of information management, reduces and structures the information overflow, and is available to customers around the clock. "The client advisor as navigator in this world" could be the motto.

Finance Portals—The New Competitors of the Traditional Universal Bank

The universal bank with its comprehensive range of products has successfully asserted itself in Continental Europe and in Switzerland in particular. In the age of e-commerce, however, few banks have successfully positioned themselves as specialists in providing only one part of the entire value chain. Is the Swiss universal bank model no longer viable due to theoretical considerations in a time of Internet–based financial services? A transaction cost theory analysis between the universal bank and the virtual finance portal will serve to answer this question.

Information technology is leading to a disaggregation of the value chain in the financial services sector (Janssen, 1999). Digitalization has made it possible to break down the value chain into its individual parts and to reassemble it according to customer needs. In this case, a customer can use a finance portal that will allow him or her to purchase each part in the chain from the best supplier (see Figure 14.6). Thus, the composition of the chain is flexible so that each part (financial service) is interchangeable. Until now, a customer had to choose between various suppliers or service providers (P1, P2, P3, P4, P5) who offered a bundle of products. This product bundle was made up of a fixed combination of financial services (S1, S2, S3, S4, S5). Universal banks are such service providers. In this way, the customer could not choose individual services

Figure 14.6
New Composition of the Value Chain through a Finance Portal

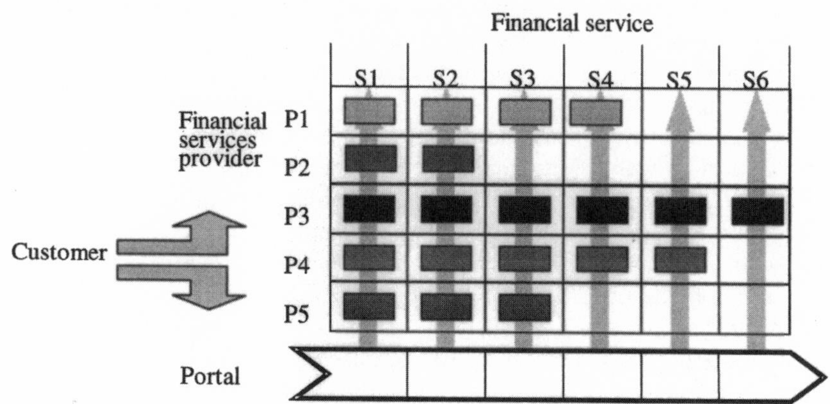

Source: Based on Janssen (1999).

as was possible through a finance portal. Rather, the decision was for the service provider (universal bank) with the relevant offer.

Transaction Cost Analysis

On principle, transaction costs arise from exchange processes.[5] How high they are affects the type of organization and the realization of economic processes. Transaction costs result from both the execution of a market transaction (e.g., the use of a finance portal) and the internal coordination within a corporation (e.g., a universal bank).[6] The structure of an economy is dictated by the relationship between the relative transaction costs of providing a service on the market compared with the production of the same service by a company.[7] The form of coordination that reduces transaction costs will prevail. Transaction costs can be divided into the following categories: initiation costs, negotiation and decision costs, processing costs, and monitoring and implementation costs:[8]

- *Initiation Costs*. Search and information costs arise from communication between possible exchange and trading partners as well as in the form of costs for the collection of information on prices, quality, and specific characteristics of financial products. If a product is purchased through a universal bank, the customer profits from a range of goods offered by a single source (one-stop shopping/one face to the customer). The risk of an overlap in the benefits of two products that a customer purchases at the same time is less likely. The reputation of a universal bank, or rather a satisfactory previous business relationship, reduces the monitoring costs in the case of future purchases from the same bank. The alignment of the client advisor according to customer requirements can reduce the search costs. On the other hand, the finance portal allows the customer an extensive and comprehensive overview of the whole market at any time. This increases transparency and reduces search costs significantly.[9] In addition, it is possible to put appropriate tools at the client's disposal, which allow him or her a (simplified) comparison and assessment of the products on offer. However, with complex and new types of products, or with specific customer requirements, the information supply through the portal may be inadequate.

- *Negotiation and Decision Costs.* Drawing up written contracts incurs costs, as does their negotiation and the processing of available information. There are also opportunity costs for the customer. These costs are the result of a difference between the best possible offer and the best one found in the limited time available. The negotiation process with the universal bank can be advantageous because only two parties are involved and these are known to one another. With the use of a finance portal, the actual provider of the product and the product quality are often unknown to the customer, or only become apparent at a later date. Possible individual customer questions, which must be answered to allow a purchase decision to be made, only reach the product's supplier with difficulty. This is because it is in the portal's interest to keep the identities of buyers and sellers unknown. Business with a universal bank allows questions to be informally answered by taking up contact with a client advisor. Purchase through a finance portal gives the customer the opportunity to choose the best possible product (best choice) according to his or her needs due to exclusive access to the whole market. A significant disadvantage of the universal banking solution, therefore, lies in the risk that the customer takes that his or her decision is not for the best possible product offered on the entire market (second-best solution). This risk (opportunity costs) increases accordingly as the number of possible suppliers grows. A recent study concluded that every American household could save U.S. $900, if the best possible financial product were chosen (Singer, Stephenson, and Waitman, 2000, 29). It is necessary to remember that the customer's decision-making process is seriously complicated, if not made impossible, by too much information. If the portal is equipped with an effective search function, this problem becomes less significant. The complete closure of contract is not yet possible when a number of products are purchased (e.g., opening of an account or valid closure of an insurance policy). This stems from the fact that a comprehensive (international) legal regulation does not yet exist and that security doubts from a technological point of view are an issue. The costs involved in taking up a partnership with an additional supplier can count as "investment costs" and limit the choice.
- *Processing costs.* Fulfillment of the contractual obligations, or rather control of the transaction process, also incurs customer costs. At most, two parties participate in processing the transaction through a universal bank and there is, therefore, a tendency toward lower processing costs. Often, completion of contract and processing occur simultaneously. With the portal solution, one can assume that the portal only takes over the search and comparison functions and that the customer possibly begins a business relationship with a number of parties of different origin. Higher processing costs are the consequence. As additional interfaces are created as a result of this multipartner relationship, the possibility that mistakes occur in processing increases. Generally, the advantage of the portal solution is extremely dependent on the existence of common standards with suppliers.
- *Monitoring and Implementation Costs.* The customer must monitor deadlines and the quality and amount of the product and services acquired. Should the supplier not fulfill the contract according to the specifications, then the customer incurs additional costs

trying to realize the contractual content. With the universal bank solution, there is only one partner to monitor whose legal domicile is clearly stated. If irregularities occur, then it is only necessary to take action against this party, which is reflected by lower implementation costs. Should processing take place through a portal, then it is necessary to consider that regulation is not watertight. One such aspect is the regulation of digital signatures. If a number of parties have a share in value creation and could also be domiciled in different countries, it is often not completely clear who is to be sued for defects. This further complicates the assertion of legal rights.

The comprehensive evaluation of transaction-specific advantages and disadvantages shows that in the initiation, negotiation, and decision phases the finance portal is at an advantage. Transactions through the universal bank in the processing, monitoring, and implementation phases have proven to be more advantageous. The following basic conclusions can be drawn:

- The transaction-specific advantages of the portal are predominant in standardized products and those that are easy to explain. The customer is well-informed in advance of the functions and characteristics of the products.
- The higher the variability and specification of a product, and the more difficult the update of its characteristics, the more problematic its processing through the portal.
- If a product is in low demand, then the distribution via portal is less advantageous.
- The higher the customer's affinity to modern technology, the more likely it is that he or she will use the portal.
- The higher the customer-specific time costs for the assembly of a product through a portal, the more likely it is that the offer of a universal bank is purchased.
- The larger the customer's know-how of financial transactions, the stronger the likelihood that he or she uses a portal.

Convergence Theory

Evaluation of the transaction cost analysis shows that, in principle, neither of the two business models is superior to the other when taken to the extreme. From this point of view, both the finance portal and the universal bank can continue to exist parallel to one another. Competitive pressure suggests a convergence of the two types of offers. The finance portal, which in effect allows the pick of the best products, prefers specialized, efficient product suppliers. In order not to suffer cost disadvantages, the universal bank will have to reduce its range of products. In addition, it will have to concentrate on those areas of business where it can generate a competitive advantage. The increasingly focused universal bank will have to hive off production functions (outsourcing), cooperate, and network within the value chain. This is particularly important where there are no core business areas, or rather where fewer product features are compensated by the market. To counter the disadvantage of a tight (focused) product range compared with that of the finance portal, the universal bank is forced to offer products from outside contractors. Its Internet presence will therefore increasingly adapt to that of the finance portal.

These shortcomings of the finance portal, as well as the impossibility of comprehensively servicing the market in practice, allows one to expect that competitive pressure will force the supplier who was initially conceived as a "general-purpose portal" to adjust their strategy. Also in this case, a focusing on specific products, or rather customer requirements, is taking place (vertical portals). In addition, a number of portals will attempt to increase their product range by, for example, cooperating more closely with individual banks, or even by taking on the status of a bank themselves. Thus, finance portals will try to overcome the problem that their service range currently only covers the information or initiation phases. By expanding their product range, transactions without intermediaries are much easier to realize. Convergence is therefore justified on both sides: finance portals have a tendency toward an increasing product range as well as a specialization in a specific product offer; universal banks tend to aim toward a reduction in product range and to increasingly include products from outside contractors in their sales mix. How close the two intermediary forms come to one another remains to be seen.

Market Trends

One of the main trends in the area of e-finance is the current development from portals to aggregators, and this in a much wider sense than has existed on the market until now. For example, the customer can observe the aggregated bank balances of a number of accounts with various financial institutes via a web site and have direct control over them via the Internet. In this way, the private investor should be in a position to optimize the management of his or her assets and liabilities. This service should represent a real need when set against a backdrop of declining customer loyalty and the associated high average number of bank connections. In Europe, the Credit Suisse Group's Insurance Lab, an interactive database for insurance products, is among the pioneers in this area. It is possible to access information on insurance products from Swiss Life Direct, CS Life, Winterthur Life, Allianz, Basler Versicherung, Helvetia Patria, National and Zurich Financial Services. Zurich Financial Services, the Rentenanstalt, and Bank Vontobel all intend to introduce similar products to the Swiss market. Whereas the Credit Suisse Group's Fundlab was a first step toward offering third-party products (over 830 funds from 32 different suppliers), new products are currently coming on the market. In September 2000, the Deutsche Bank launched Moneyshelf.com, a finance portal that allows private investors to monitor their entire financial situation. Access to the bank accounts with various institutions is just as possible as the comparison of the investment funds offered by numerous suppliers.

Egg, the second-largest British Internet bank, allows customers the choice of 220 funds from 17 different suppliers. Not a single product is from Egg itself. Cooperation between banks and portals represents promising alliances. The aggregation of banking data for numerous suppliers is not only an additional customer service in the form of "convenience." It also allows the development of completely new tools that are currently only available to major customers (risk management, asset allocation, and portfolio management tools). These allow consideration of the investor's entire asset situation. Was the possibility of carrying out transactions over the Internet (stock market orders, payment transfers) only the beginning of the Internet revolution? This is most certainly the case. For banks, however, aggregation and consolidation of customer data over finance portals will be of more importance. This fact gives us an idea of how the future virtual finance world could look: the customer constructs his or her own (virtual) universal bank!

E-commerce as an Imperative for the Banks

What is the importance of e-commerce for the banks? If one consults the signals from the stock exchange as the largest, most liquid "opinion market," the picture is clear (see Figure 14.7). E-commerce is of major importance to the banking world. The E-Finance Index[10] has reached a yield of 69 percent since January 1, 1998. For the same period, the total for all Internet suppliers has developed less favorably with −16 percent and −7 percent for the banking sector in general.

Network of Networks

Information and communication technology offer a wide variety of instruments that support the transaction phases of goods and services in e-commerce. Thanks to the Internet, great progress has already been made in the information phase. Product transparency has, at negligible cost, improved immensely. Many product and service markets are already very close to the conditions needed for a perfect market. The weakest point so far is the negotiation and decision phase on the commodity markets. As a comparison, banking instruments exist for every electronic trading phase, although only for bilateral use between bank and customer. Initial contracting, or the formal side of customer acquisition (opening an account), is the aspect that is the least, or not at all, supported phase. The spread of the digital signature and the accompanying registration and certification could also open up e-commerce in this important transaction phase. Today, e-commerce transactions are generally divided into two main categories:

- B2B: Business to Business
- B2C: Business to Consumer

This classification is incomplete. Theoretically, it is also necessary to include the groups C2C and C2B for the commodities markets. However, these are of little importance today. Of importance is the extension of the classification for

Figure 14.7
The "Opinion" of the Stock Market

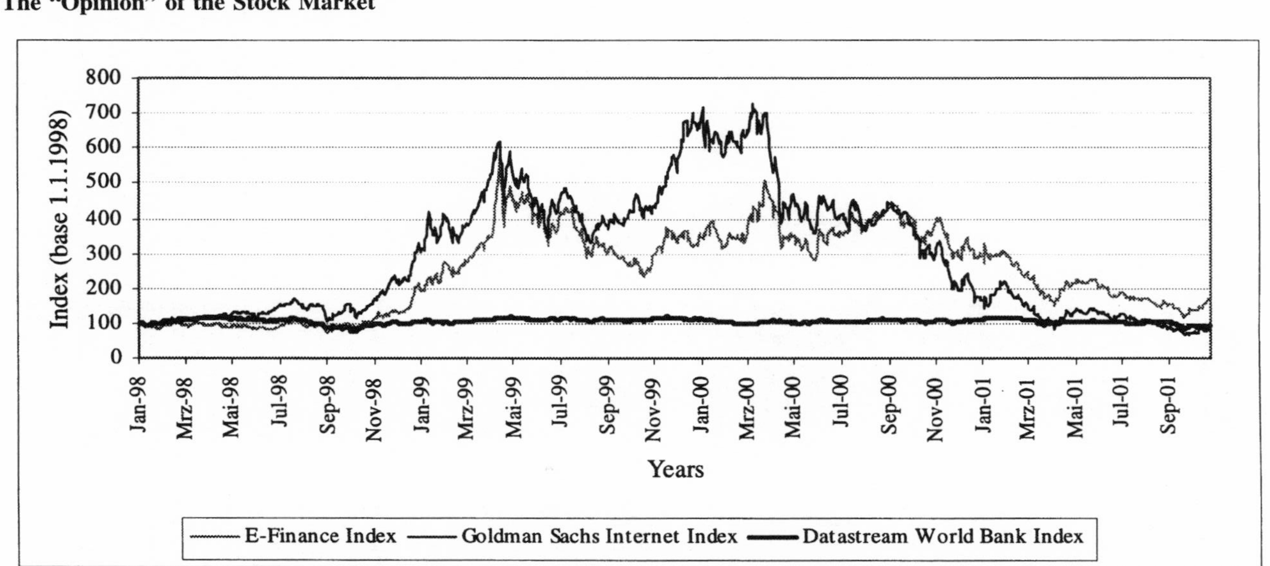

Source: Datastream.

Figure 14.8
The Six E-commerce Banking Spheres

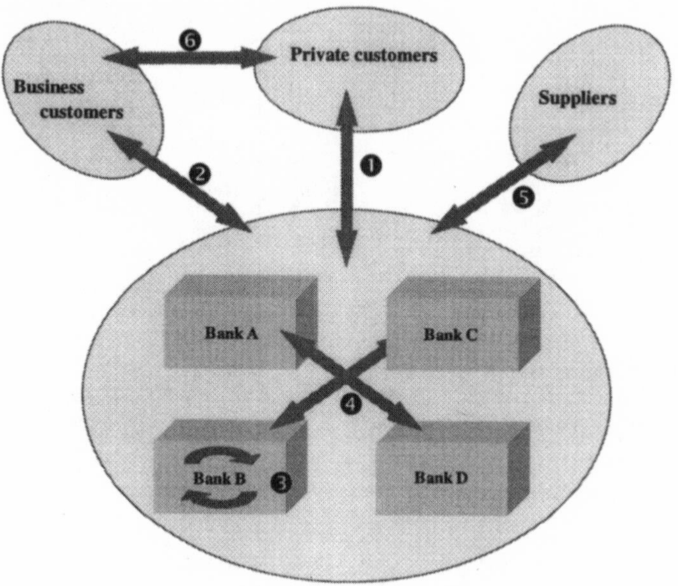

the financial market. In the area of banking e-commerce, it is necessary to include the classification of transaction with banks (distinguished by the Greek β). This results in the following additional types of transactions:

- β2C: Bank to Consumer (private customers)
- β2B: Bank to Business (business customers)
- β2β: Bank to Bank (business between banks)
- β'2β': Secondary internal banks or "street-side" transactions that are necessary to process primary banking transactions

When considering the subject of banking e-commerce, one first thinks of Internet banking, the electronic relationships and transactions between private customers and the bank (Figure 14.8: Relationship 1: β2C). Customer relations is justifiably at the center of attention; however, the limitation to only this aspect impairs the overview and with it the recognition of all the opportunities and risks. The picture does not show the whole subject, and it neglects other important aspects as well as the connection between the various aspects.

There are five other e-commerce banking spheres in addition to Relationship 1, the relationship to private customers, which was just considered (β2C); Relationship 2, to business customers (β2B), makes other demands than private customers. Relationship 3, within a bank or a banking group, is increasingly

Figure 14.9
Value Chain in Asset Management

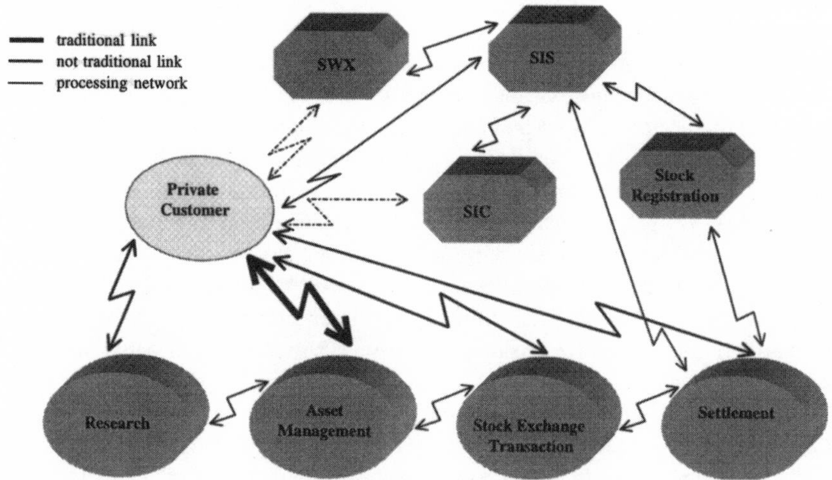

regarded as a market relationship, particularly with major corporations. Relationship 4 is primary or secondary business with other banks (β2β) and relationship 5 is to the bank's suppliers. Relationship 6 is the potential business area between the bank's customers and their customers. This is traditionally an area in which the banks did not participate. A series of banking transactions are not primary transactions for the bank's customers, who simply need them to process their own primary transactions. A classic example of this is payment transfers, but a car loan also belongs to this category. E-commerce opens up new opportunities for the banks for those transactions that are considered secondary from the customer's point of view. Current examples are electronic billing (bill presentment and payment) or the procurement of digital signature access and the maintenance of the corresponding registration. All six business spheres are important to consider when evaluating the possibilities, risks, and opportunities of e-commerce banking.

Change in the Asset Management Value Chain

The relationship to customers is quite rightly at the center of attention for Swiss banking e-commerce. Traditionally, banks have direct contact to their clients, be it through branch offices, over the telephone, or by post. After-sales service includes important regulatory duties and responsibilities, customer identification, and the guarantee of other necessary diligence. In Switzerland, the product range was and remains high in the banking sector where, traditionally, the bank covers the entire value chain itself. Figure 14.9 illustrates this aspect with the area of asset management.

Up until now, private asset management has been vertically integrated. The bank looks after its customer, providing research, asset management, and investment advice, stock transactions, and processing. It may even develop and produce new products, such as investment funds and structured products. Banks have exclusive access to customers. In the networked world of e-commerce, each link in the value chain becomes an independent business area in which not only the integrated bank but also specialists are present. In this world, banks increasingly specialize in certain functions, preferably in customer relationship management; reduce their product range; and procure services from other suppliers. Examples are research, stock transactions, or processing through a transaction bank or global custodian. This reduction of product range can be considered analogous to outsourcing in the auto or electronics industries. However, in the networked world of e-commerce, each of these suppliers can offer its services to the customer electronically and can attempt to establish a direct business relationship to the customer, be it with better prices or better services, or even by avoiding conflicts of interest. This has not yet occurred to a great extent in private banking for a number of reasons. The value chain in institutional asset management began to break up some time ago. Today, the separation of transaction processing, or "technical asset management" from "financial asset management," is common. The fact that disintermediation in the value chain is not yet more significant is due, in part, to a number of these service suppliers being in possession of the banks, and the latter refusing them direct access to their customers. In principle, the opportunities mentioned of reducing the product range and of competing for customers exist at all stages of the value chain.

Internet Banking in Switzerland

Switzerland already has a number of finance portals that offer a wide range of services. Various suppliers, such as Borsalino, Consors, E-Sider, Finanzinfo, or Swissquote, offer, among other things, current account, deposit, and stock information, as well as payment transfers and stock transactions. The big banks offer a wide product selection with Youtrade (Credit Suisse) and UBS Tradepac. The cantonal banks have jointly produced Internet solutions to save setup costs through synergies. This is also the case with the regional banks which have outsourced their information services to the cooperative RBA-Service AG, which loads and maintains their Internet sites. At the beginning of 2001, the Raiffeisen banks cooperated to develop a central Internet solution that allows each bank an individual presence on the net.

Swiss E-commerce Is Better

Banking in the age of information technology is subject partly to past success factors and partly to completely new ones. The competitive advantages of Swiss banks with regard to an international alignment of Internet banking can be identified as follows:

- A major condition for success in e-commerce is the customer's confidence in the bank or the bank's reputation. In addition, the customer of the future will not simply conduct

Table 14.5
Assets under Management in Switzerland, 1998–2000

Assets under Management:		Domestic	Foreign	Total
Billion CHF	1998	1,400	1,600	3,000
	1999	1,591	1,847	3,500
	2000	1,661	2,056	3,716

Source: Swiss National Bank (2000, 49).

his or her banking transactions with the cheapest supplier. Analyses of Internet purchasing behavior show that even with unproblematic and standardized products, such as books or music CDs, customers often do not buy from the cheapest supplier but from the one they know and trust (Bailey, 1998). Time and spatial separation between customer and supplier seem to increase the need for trust when compared to the more traditional ways to purchase items (Smith, 1999, 12). The trust factor could lead to the largest and best-known banks having the best chances of success in e-commerce. Trademarks receive more importance in the new world, although well-known brands do not necessarily have to have their roots in banking. A good rating will also be of importance for e-commerce banks, which goes beyond evaluating debt instrument creditworthiness. Similarly, the quality of the financial center and the banking supervision, to which e-commerce banks are answerable, will be an important element of trust, as will be the technical security of the information technology solution and the protection of the client's privacy. All these aspects are traditional strengths of Swiss banks and could be put on the quality label of "Swiss banking".

- As Switzerland has four national languages, the web presence is already in French and German. A "smooth" market penetration of its neighboring countries is therefore easier to achieve.
- The Internet offerings of the two big banks already count among the best solutions worldwide. They can therefore profit as first movers owing to their experience and are in an excellent position to conquer a large share of the internet market.
- The financial strength of the Swiss banks allow, first, the financing of numerous own projects and, second, the takeover of successful e-finance suppliers, should these pose a serious threat to their business prospects.
- The technologically well-advanced financial infrastructure of Switzerland simplifies the implementation of Internet technology advantages for a wide area of the entire value chain (Swiss value chain).

Swiss Private Banking

Asset management for private and institutional investors is currently experiencing a golden age (see Table 14.5). Private banking has never had so many assets at its disposal. In 2000, the market was estimated at around U.S. $25 trillion worldwide—2.5 times what it was 10 years ago.

The Swiss financial center plays a leadership role in this market and thus doubtlessly contributes to the worldwide degree of familiarity of domestic institutions. The Swiss share of international cross-border wealth management[11] is estimated at between 25 and 30 percent. Private banking is a lucrative business. Along with the high profit margins, a revenue dynamic allows yields to grow "automatically" through increasing depository value. As only limited capital is necessary, the profitability of this business is extremely attractive. The revenue per employee is around 600,000 CHF. The Swiss banks' ROE (after tax) in asset management is between 19 and 34 percent, while for other areas of business profits are between −8 and 6 percent.

There are a number of indications that the traditionally wealthy bank client is changing. It could well be that elegant meeting rooms with expensive paintings will soon be a thing of the past, but opinions in Switzerland are very different. One thing is certain, however: change will also be continual in private banking. The increasing number of competitors points to tough competition. Simply gathering money is no longer enough. In the past, private investors were easily divided into "onshore" and "offshore" clients. However, for many years now, new customer segments with differentiated requirements have been developing (companies that have become rich through an initial public offering or takeover; executives who have accumulated huge assets with options; trading-oriented customers who make their own investment decisions).

Successful Private Banking Strategies

The new challenges demand clear strategies. Three elements are of prevailing importance:

- It is necessary for many institutes to focus their market positioning. The maxim is no longer to offer everything to every customer segment. Now it is to serve those segments whose requirements can be met by a specific private bank who, thanks to its special abilities, has a unique product. A clear distinction from suppliers in the top retail segment makes sense. Image and branding considerations play a part here, as does the insight that most private banking institutions do not have a cost structure that allows them to profitably serve these segments.
- The architecture must be more flexible. It is still the case that many private banks only sell their own products and services and abstain from selling products from other suppliers. The value of a private bank that conducts its business with customers' interests in mind must result from giving their clients an overview of the products on a market that is almost impossible to keep track of. In addition, evaluation of products and their risk-adapted performance and construction of a customer-specific overall solution is necessary.
- Intangible capital (employees, networks, and trademarks) are more difficult to develop. Private banking remains, for the time being, fixed on personnel. Employee continuity and quality have a decisive influence on success. Innovative career models and compensatory plans need to be offered in order to recruit and keep top personnel. Networks will significantly increase in importance, set against a background of a tendency toward

"unbundling." As a network provider, private banks coordinate various product and service suppliers (e.g., news, research, and reporting instruments). The network should be in a position to offer the customer the best possible overall solution and the participating partners the opportunity for increased value. With growing competition, a stronger focus on specific customer segments, and increased cooperation, a strong trademark with a clear message is indispensable. Until now, Swiss suppliers in private banking have leaned heavily on the reputation of "Swiss private banking." However, this term could become too general to develop as intangible capital in the future. In addition, private banks will have to develop their own trademarks which clearly communicate their position on the market. Apart from the element of personality in the customer–bank relationship, which is influenced by particular employees, an institutional personality should be developed in order to win the customer's favor.

Size Matters in Private Banking—But in What Way?

It seems to be a given that large institutes have scale and scope effects that allow them to work more efficiently than smaller ones. That this is not the case for commercial banks is confirmed by numerous empirical analyses. Highly diversified large institutes have high coordination and administration costs that reduce or completely cancel the advantage of size. Swiss private banking was able to avoid the worldwide mergers in the banking sector that were so prevalent over the past years. Technological development has affected this business sector much less than it has others. Table 14.6 shows how Swiss private banks' company size has had a significant effect on profitability and success.

One can see that banks in the 250–500 employees category on average work most profitably and economically. The second-best group are banks with over 500 employees, and banks with under 50 employees fare the worst. These figures are not simply the result of varying performance but also reflect different business models. Big banks offer comprehensive services and produce all the elements of the value chain themselves. Smaller banks concentrate more on close customer investment advice and asset management. The potential for value creation is high in the immediate vicinity of the client. As this distance increases, so the profit margins decrease. The value chain becomes more industrial and is increasingly subject to scale effects. The figures seem to indicate that the market offers space long term for large as well as for small competitors. The large are based on close client contact, whereas the small are based on differentiation through efficiency advantages.

How Much Internet Can Private Banking Cope With?

The Internet has unsettled the traditional strengths of private banking—the informational lead over the customer. Today's investors have a great variety of information at their disposal, and all of it is free of charge. Part of the bank's value creation is therefore obsolete or of diminishing importance. Online brokers put pressure on established institutes on the transaction side. This point of view faces a more traditional one, however: the majority of private banking custom-

Table 14.6
Key Figures According to Company Size, FY 1998

	< 50 Employees (N = 8)	50–100 Employees (N = 8)	100–250 Employees (N = 5)	250–500 Employees (N = 5)	> 500 Employees (N = 5)
Revenue/employee[1]	453	542	515	621	637
Costs/employee[1]	238	268	269	263	308
Gross profits/employee[1]	215	274	246	357	329
Net profits/employee[1]	98	147	174	294	230
Managed assets/employee[2]	52	40	42	50	53
Equity/employee[1]	1,120	993	945	1,125	1,178
Revenue/managed assets[3]	1.02	1.37	1.28	1.27	1.31
Costs/revenue[3]	52	51	54	44	49
ROE (gross profits)[3]	23	28	28	47	29
ROE (net profits)[3]	10	15	18	39	21

[1]in 1,000 CHF.
[2]in million CHF.
[3]in percent.

Source: Geiger (2000).

ers—with varying intensity—still want to have personal contact with the private bank.

Empirical data for the Swiss market show that private bank customers use the Internet mostly to collect information. Transactions via the Internet are carried out particularly by investors with higher than average incomes and assets: the traditional private banking clientele. Today, these investors use the web offers of suppliers outside private banking because the latter are only slowly introducing Internet solutions to the market.

Incompatibility between the Internet and personal advice is not necessarily given. On the contrary, the Internet will increase the quality of personal customer contact in as much as online advice will be integrated by the client advisor into the offline advice using intelligent tools. Since the customer has the same information and tools at his or her disposal as the advisor, passing on information will no longer be the priority of both parties. The aim will be to get the best possible results with the information available. The client gains access to all the products on the market. Internet tools and the advisor assist the customer in finding the right product. Tomorrow's customer who is looking for advice is well-informed and more demanding with respect to performance but also advice, both in content and time. Clients want to deal with the bank via the Internet and call centers and to execute transactions themselves. Whether the customer advisor is central to this or one of many equal channels depends on the institution's chosen strategy.

If one understands private banking as the area of business in which the customer is offered the very best (such as, for example, the luxury category in the car industry), then it is clear that the Internet belongs to this—and with the best of what is on offer. Private banking can cope with the Internet as much as their best customer—and that is a lot.

"Swiss Value Chain" of Securities Settlement

The architecture of the Swiss financial sector is characterized by three associations: the Swiss Exchange (SWX), the national central securities depositary SegaInterSettle (SIS), and the payment system Swiss Interbank Clearing (SIC). Those transactions executed through the trading platforms Virt-x or SWX are transferred directly to SIS as locked-in-trades, without the business partners having to issue a separate processing order. The payment system SIC is linked to SECOM (Sega Communication System) via a delivery-versus-payment connection. Each transaction is processed in real time continuously and singly according to the principle of delivery-versus-payment. The model is based on an automated connection between the securities transfer system and the payment system. These ensure that the delivery follows only if payment is also carried out. This integrative automation of securities trading and processing is unrivaled worldwide and is therefore described as the Swiss value chain. The credit risk is eliminated during settlement not only with respect to the parties but also to the system providers. The connection between the associations allows a comprehensive "straight through processing" (STP) and results in a higher settlement quality with an extremely low error rate. The London Clearing House (LCH), as the central counterparty for settlement, now guarantees the settlement of Virt-x transactions. Planned is a best possible netting.

The consolidation of the clearing and settlement infrastructure and the connected reduction of interfaces and standards will result in increasing productivity in a heterogeneous European financial center architecture. On the one hand, the issue is a massive reduction of the complexity; on the other, capacities are provided for an increasing volume of trade which will be managed at substantially lower costs and risks.

The question of the final form of the future infrastructure for the clearing and settlement of securities in Europe cannot yet be answered. It is clear that a new infrastructure model will be essentially different from those solutions that exist today. Despite all the advantages that consolidated infrastructures bring, there will also be weighty disadvantages. Enormous project costs and risks, monopolistic behavior, and a reduction in choices for market participants should not be overlooked. It would seem that a network of numerous clearing points and central counter parties for various European market segments is more likely midterm than the realization of a single central solution. With the Swiss value chain, the Swiss banks are in a promising position to be involved in the design of a future trading and settlement infrastructure. The Swiss model represents a solid base for an efficient cross-border solution; such a solution is the aim of the pan-European stock exchange Virt-x.

Banking Secrecy

The individual's privacy is legally protected in Switzerland. Thus, it is the bank's duty to exercise complete discretion in every aspect concerning their clients. Banking secrecy was embodied in the law on banks and savings banks in 1934. This law states that whosoever acts as agent, employee, representative, liquidator, or commissioning agent for a bank, as an observer for the Federal Banking Commission, as agent, or as employee of a recognized auditor is not allowed to disclose any information entrusted by a client to him or her in this capacity. Banking secrecy, however, should not offer criminals protection. Banks issue information particularly to domestic and foreign penal authorities on the basis of proceedings bound by law. Numerous measures have already been taken to impede criminal usage of Swiss banking secrecy:

- Professional financial intermediaries are under obligation to know their customers ("know your customer principle"). The aim is to identify contractual partners and determine the person with economic authorization. This should allow ostensible partners to be identified. Deficient identification is a criminal offense.
- Since 1990, a person who acts in a way that obstructs investigations into the origin, tracing, or confiscation of assets which he or she knows or assumes to result from a crime (money laundering) is subject to punishment.
- Should a financial institute perceive assets to result from a crime, it is bound by duty to inform the penal authorities without coming into conflict with the banking secrecy act or other rights of its customer.
- Persons who participate in a criminal organization and keep its structure and composition of personnel a secret and aims to commit a crime or to enrich themselves by criminal means are subject to criminal prosecution.
- The corruption laws were rearranged and tightened in 1999. Bribes to foreign officials are now liable to prosecution.
- Despite what numerous crime novels tell the reader, there are no anonymous bank accounts in Switzerland. Moreover, it is required that the customer of a numbered account be identified and known to the bank.

Banking secrecy does not, therefore, offer protection to the person who deposits money in a Swiss bank obtained from a criminal act punishable by Swiss law.

Tax Evasion

In a discussion on Swiss banking secrecy, it is necessary to differentiate between criminal activities and tax evasion. Tax collection in Switzerland is based on personal declaration. Based on this special tax relationship between citizen and state, the (mild) form of tax evasion is not a criminal offense. Punishment follows in the form of administrative fines and a withholding tax of 35 percent on capital revenues as a pledge. On the other hand, tax fraud is a criminal offense (tax fraud in connection with further criminal offenses such as falsification of documents, for example). Tax discipline in Switzerland is high. It shows that the administrative measures are sufficient and that this practice is relevant to the country's circumstances. Compared internationally, Switzerland has by far one of the smallest shadow economies, although direct fiscal drain on private income is higher than average in the OECD.

The principle of equal treatment of nationals and foreigners, and therefore of domestic and foreign investors, is uncontested in Switzerland. The EU accepts those measures in trade with third-party states that aim toward "equality." The automatic notification procedure desired by the EU and the structure of the connected supervisory instruments contradict the Swiss liberal governing principles, and would therefore erode privacy.

Successful with and without Banking Secrecy

Government administration and the Swiss economy still vouch for banking secrecy. The Swiss Federal Constitution and referendum rights stand as a guarantee for the continued existence of banking secrecy. In recent public opinion polls, 77 percent were in favor of continued banking secrecy, and 72 percent of the population even wanted to support it against the will of the EU. Independent of this finding, Swiss banks must be in a position to do business even without banking secrecy. Despite this, or because of it, Switzerland must and can protect people's privacy with banking secrecy in the future. There is no contradiction in these demands and in how they can be achieved.

The EU, the OECD, and others have made Switzerland's banking secrecy a target of attack. The official reasons are given as the fight against tax evasion and "unfair tax competition." These attacks on banking secrecy also a reflect envy of the Swiss banks' leadership position in the lucrative private customer business, but this is not expressed. The EU states have also promised their citizens the free movement of capital along with the other three freedoms. It remains unstated that the states can keep their citizens and their assets only if the demands and services of the state are attractive. This principle is valid with or without Swiss banking secrecy. As important as a favorable environment for the success of private banking is, the banks cannot make their future strategy for success dependent on the institution of banking secrecy. Swiss banks must conduct their business so that they can be successful without this for the following reasons.

A European opinion poll carried out by PriceWaterhouseCoopers in 1999 confirms the fundamental structural change of the private banking clientele. The emphasis has moved from old wealth to new, from the passive to the active investor. Service quality and investment performance are the preferences, with confidentiality and banking secrecy losing their importance. The young generation of investors knows that black money is less valuable than taxed money and is unsuitable for many purposes. This generation recognizes that, in addition to the financial risks of tax evasion, reputation is also at stake. The wealthy are also in a position to reduce the tax burden legally in numerous ways. One can assume that under the pressure of the electorate and the market, the EU countries will reduce their inflated state shares and excessive income taxes, making tax evasion even less attractive. Thus, onshore private banking will became more important than offshore activities, with the expansion opportunities in servicing private domestic clients. Swiss banks want to be successful through competitive services and not through gaps in taxation laws. For years, the diligence agreement has prohibited active support of capital flight and tax evasion. From a political point of view, banking secrecy will become a less attractive target of attack when it becomes plausible that the dominant position of Switzerland and its banks in private banking is not dependent on it.

Banking secrecy is, however, an important local factor of Switzerland's banking sector. Also important are political stability, general conditions, and professional competence, infrastructure, and the moral integrity of Swiss banks. It is the best customers who demand this integrity, for at the end of the day it is also their own.

Regulation and Supervision

A number of features of the "new banking world" are apparent. These question the fundamental assumptions of the conventional supervision environment.

How Much Regulation Is Too Much?

From the point of view of supervisory bodies, the emphasis is on the protection needs of investors and the entire system. For suppliers, however, the development of innovative business models is central. Restrictive admission handling meets the needs in the areas of investor and system protection. This goal faces two possibly important disadvantages:

- The supervisory law can also function as a substantial entrance barrier for new suppliers. The requirements are set so high that new suppliers are not in a position to cover the cost of meeting them.
- Protection of a system that is too restrictive encourages the status quo and impedes innovation. This results in the protection of established suppliers from new challengers.
- The administrative burdens of supervision can be so extensive that smaller banks can no longer carry the costs. The result is that a tough regulation treats big banks preferentially.

Relaxation of the regulation is preferable from the point of view of the services supplier. However, this solution is not necessarily the best one with respect to the development of financial services on the Internet. Thus, it has been observed that the opportunity of using less strict regulatory regimes is not realized by Internet services suppliers, although, from a technical point of view, it would be unproblematic. The reasons for this can be found in the specific features of the Internet and financial services. Users of financial services over the Internet are faced with the difficulty of having to do business with a partner who, first, has no physical presence and, second, often operates out of a foreign country. These aspects increase the customer's insecurity with respect to the fulfillment of contractual conditions. Another aspect of insecurity is that suppliers of new business models are often market newcomers whose reputation cannot yet vouch for the seriousness of the offer. The market participant's trust in new Internet services is of utmost importance. For market newcomers it is a vicious circle. On the one hand, their reputation is not good enough to convincingly offer services, and, on the other, they do not yet have a range of services that allows them to build up their reputation. If suppliers can show that their services are subject to official supervision, then their reputation improves and they escape the above dilemma. Legal regulation in general and supervision by the relevant bodies in particular can therefore not be considered as impeding innovation a priori.

One of the most significant approaches in supervisory law is the principle of competitive neutrality: official intervention should not have a market-distorting effect.[12] A supervisory system that supports innovation must follow the principle that the costs of regulation do not "strangle" market newcomers. If this is not considered, then the regulatory requirements act as market entrance barriers and result in (unwanted) distortion of competition. In addition, unequal (also distortive) treatment of financial services suppliers should be avoided, and innovation should be given room to flourish. It is necessary to find rules that can be adapted to the phases of development of new marketplaces and allow the legislator the possibility of differential regulation. The question that can be posed is whether similar activities that have the same risks and general conditions can consciously receive different treatment. Differentiation of qualitative (number of suppliers affected) and quantitative criteria (risk for the investor) should help answer this question.

Regulating the Aggregators and Portals

Changes in the banks' production, distribution, and organization functions have wide-ranging consequences that are difficult to put in concrete terms from a supervisory viewpoint. The removal of the vertically and horizontally integrated financial supplier due to a new business model complicates the task of regulatory bodies.

The portals (aggregators) that aggregate financial services in order to cover specific customer needs could soon be subject to the critical eye of regulatory bodies. Provided that, for example, a clear division between the portal's service and a broker is given, then there is no supervisory control problem. However, as soon as a portal functions as an aggregator for various accounts and stores customer account numbers and passwords, then control through a supervisory body should be considered. Thus, the American bank regulatory body, Comptroller of the Currency, and the Basel Committee on Banking Supervision have already posed the question as to whether these aggregators should not also be put under supervision. The aggregator can be either a bank or a nonbank. For example, the customer gives the aggregator his or her bank account numbers and passwords. By way of a process that is called "screen scraping," data are collected and filtered from the web site of a third party (often without their knowledge) and passed on. Aggregation and "screen scraping" are currently offered in the United States in particular. Within a few years, such methods will probably be part of standard service in Europe. Apart from the strategic aspects that result from this technical possibility, security, legal, and reputation questions will become an issue for the financial institutions affected. Even if banks have no control over who carries out "screen scraping" of their web sites, they can be made responsible for the misuse of information.

Switzerland's banking secrecy in particular can be a hurdle to such aggregate solutions from unsupervised suppliers. If a bank loses customer interface to an aggregator, then the question of "know your customer" regulation is challenged. Who is responsible for a client's identification if the bank is degraded to the position of product supplier? In this constellation, only the aggregator would be in such a position. Should only a small number of aggregators who control customer interface manage to become established on the market, then the protection of the system is also subject to discussion. If an aggregator that controls the interface between the product suppliers and millions of customers were to break down for technical reasons, then the whole system could be in danger. The more well advanced the integration of individual services through an aggregator, the more likely it is that the supplier must be subjected to supervision. However, according to current legislation, it would only be possible for a supervised financial intermediary to be in a position to offer a fully integrated solution. Following from this point of view, banks would be in a very favorable position to realize this function. The supervision of an aggregator would be justified by the need to protect the customer from the misuse of his or her banking data. Because investments are not executed directly with the aggregator, protection of creditors is not an issue. However, supervision can be justified for protection of the system.

Media portals are classic examples of nonbanks that attempt to control the information phase of the customer and then transfer that information to the relevant supplier of transaction services. The procurement of informational content and connection via links is not a relevant case for legal supervision and would be spared from regulation. This, however, would be the case, only as long as the information services are clearly separated from the transaction services. If portals control customer interfaces and the client no longer recognizes from which supplier (bank) a product has been purchased, then the supervisory body could be tempted to set the media portals the task of informational duty according to the Swiss Stock Exchange Act, for example. The media portals could then come under pressure if, for example, during a comparison of outside supplier products, obvious conflicts of interest were to emerge and the legislator believed that it was necessary to protect the investor according to consumer protection.

SUMMARY AND CONCLUSIONS

The Swiss financial and banking center, like other financial centers, will continue to develop under the sign of e-commerce and will have to meet new challenges. It is difficult to predict which old and new suppliers of financial services will emerge from this transformation process as winners. Another prediction seems easier: the customer will be the biggest winner. Adam Smith's "invisible hand" will make sure of this in the electronic market. The Swiss financial center is often accused of leaning too heavily on banking secrecy and of neglecting technological and strategical change that would be needed to meet the new customer needs. According to our assessment, Switzerland has an excellent infrastructure, advantageous general conditions, and therefore a good position as a worldwide competitor. The "Swiss banking" trademark is probably strong enough to keep its position in international private banking for the next five years. What is more crucial is whether the Swiss banks can also continue to extend their comparative strengths: their trademark is not so much private banking, but management of the private client relationship.

ACKNOWLEDGMENTS

The authors are grateful to Prof. Dr. Hans Geiger and Prof. Dr. Rudolf Volkart, Professors in Finance and Banking at the University of Zurich for their many constructive comments.

NOTES

1. The following differentiation is used to calculate the percentage of equity ownership in Switzerland. Investors who invest directly in equities are defined as those respondents who say they own equities directly, own equities through employee stock ownership plans (ESOPs), or both. The percentage of investors investing indirectly in equities also includes the number of investors in pure equity funds.

2. It comprises the highly liquid shares of up to 30 of the most important large-cap Swiss companies, which represent approximately 80 percent of the total market capitalization.

3. The aspects of liberalization and progress in finance theory are not discussed here in detail. In the opinion of the authors, these elements have a general effect on all banks and do not represent a speciality of Swiss banking. However, both elements influence the later discussion of the other points.

4. Currently, the relation of over-65-year-olds no longer in employment to those employed (20- to 65-year-olds) is 25 percent. This ratio could realistically increase to 45 percent by 2050 (see http://www.statistik.admin.ch).

5. Williamson (1985, 1) states that a transaction occurs "when a good or service is transferred across a technologically separable interface. One stage of activity terminates and another begins."

6. This is also the reason there cannot only be one "big firm" (Coase, 1937, 394).

7. Williamson (1985) or Richardson (1972) do not limit themselves to this two-dimensional viewing but point towards intermediate forms of coordination through co-operation between companies (contracts, franchising, cooperatives).

8. See Richter and Furubotn (1996, 51). A somewhat different categorization can be found in Freixas and Rochet (1997, 18); Carlton and Perloff (1994, 5); Scholtens (1993, 122); and Fuchs (1994, 43).

9. The time necessary to search for a certificate of deposit can be reduced by telephone (60%) and again by the Internet (90%) (see Butler et al., 1997).

10. Calculated by the authors, this market-weighted index (in U.S. dollars) consists of the titles Swissquote (Switzerland), Consors (Germany), Direkt Anlage Bank (Germany), Comdirect (Germany), Charles Schwab (USA), Intuit (USA), E*Trade (USA), Ameritrade (USA), and JB Oxford (USA).

11. Under cross-border wealth management, asset management on behalf of customers with a foreign domicile is understood.

12. Competitive neutrality: basically, the state should treat all companies equally (competitive neutrality). This equal treatment is interpreted as proportional equality. This means that (1) the legislator and authorities must employ the principle of differentiation. Specifically, regulation and supervision must consider the range of products and volume of business of each services supplier. (2) Regulation and supervision should be in line with the functional approach. Accordingly, comparable activities that are in a competitive relationship on product markets and show the same risks should be regulated similarly—is provided that two different regulatory approaches are not consciously allowed to give the customer freedom of choice (Expertengruppe Finanzmarktaufsicht, 2000, 36).

REFERENCES

Bailey, J. P. 1998. "Intermediation and Electronic Markets: Aggregation and Pricing in Internet Commerce." Doctoral Thesis, Technology, Management and Policy, Massachusetts Institute of Technology.

Brunner, C. 1996. "Value Based Management—Zentrale Herausforderung der Bankführung." In H. Geiger, C. Hirszowicz, R. Volkart, and P. F. Weibel (eds.), *Schweizerisches Bankwesen im Umbruch.* Bern/Stuttgart/Vienna: Verlag Paul Haupt, pp. 81–96.

Brynjolfsson, E., and Smith, M. D. 1999. "Frictionless Commerce?" Research Paper, Sloan School of Management, MIT, Cambridge.

Brynjolfsson, E., and Smith, M. D. 2000. "Frictionless Commerce? A Comparison of Internet and Conventional Retailers." *Management Science* 46, No. 4 (April): 563–585.

Bundesamt für Statistik. 1999. *Statistisches Jahrbuch 2000.* Zurich: NZZ Verlag.

Butler, P. et al. 1997. "A Revolution in Interaction." *The McKinsey Quarterly*, No. 4: 4–23.

Carlton, D. W., and Perloff, J. M. 1994. *Modern Industrial Organization*. New York: HarperCollins.

Christensen, C. M. 1999. *The Innovator's Dilemma*. Boston: Harvard Business Review Press.

Coase, R. H. 1937. "The Nature of the Firm." *Economica* 4 (November): 386–405.

Cocca, T. D., and Volkart, R. 2000. *Equity Ownership in Switzerland 2000*. Zurich: Swiss Banking Institute, Versus.

Downes, L., and Mui, C. 1999. *Unleashing the Killer App*. Boston: Harvard Business Review Press.

Expertengruppe Finanzmarktaufsicht. 2000. *Finanzmarktregulierung und-aufsicht in der Schweiz*. Bern.

Freixas, X., and Rochet, J.-C. 1997. *Microeconomics of Banking*. Cambridge/London: MIT Press.

Fuchs, W. 1994. "Die Transaktionskosten-Theorie." Doctoral Dissertation, University of Trier.

Geiger, H. 2000. "Welche Grösse braucht eine profitable Bank?" *Neue Zürcher Zeitung*, May 16, p. B11.

Geiger, H. 2001. "Schweiz: Erfolg ohne Bankkundengeheimnis?" *Finanz und Wirtschaft*, April 28.

Janssen, M. 1999. "How to Optimize Costs Management in Private Banking Through Focused IT Investments." Conference Presentation, Private Banking, Le Défi de la Technologie, Geneva.

PriceWaterhouseCoopers. 1999. *European Private Banking Survey*. London.

Richardson, G. B. 1972. "The Organization of Industry." *Economic Journal* 82: 883–896.

Richter, R., and Furubotn, E. G. 1996. *Neue Institutionenökonomie*. Tubing: Mohr Siebeck.

Schmid, B. F., and Lindemann, M. A. 1998. "Elements of a Reference Model for Electronic Markets." 31st Annual Hawaii International Conference on Systems Science (HICCS '98).

Scholtens, L.J.R. 1993. "On the Foundation of Financial Intermediation." *Kredit und Kapital*, No. 1: 112–141.

Schumann, J. 1987. "Die Unternehmung als ökonomische Institution." *Volkswirtschaftslehre*, No. 4: 212–218.

Singer, M., Stephenson, J., and Waitman, R. M. 2000. "Click and Save." *The McKinsey Quarterly*, No. 3: 28–33.

Smith, M. D., Bailey, J., and Brynjolfsson, E. 1999. "Understanding Digital Markets: Review and Assessment." Working Paper, MIT Sloan School, Boston.

SNB. 2001. *Die Banken in der Schweiz*. Zurich.

Stäger, C. 1999. *Multi Channel Management—Mehrdimensionale Optimierung der Kundenbeziehung zur nachhaltigen Steigerung der Profitabilität im Retail Banking*. Bern/Stuttgart/Vienna: Verlag Paul Haupt.

Vettiger, T. 1996. *Wertorientiertes Bankcontrolling: Das Controlling im Dienste einer wertorientierten Bankführung*. Bern/Stuttgart/Vienna: Verlag Paul Haupt.

Wallace, P. 1999. *Agequake: Riding the Demographic Rollercoaster Shaking Business, Finance, and Our World*. London: Nicholas Brealey.

Williamson, O. E. 1985. *The Economic Institutions of Capitalism*. New York: Free Press.

Chapter 15

Microcredit for the Poorest Countries

Kiyoshi Abe

INTRODUCTION

The world consists of developing as well as developed countries. The income gap between them is getting wider and wider. With the majority of the world's population living in developing countries, it is unreasonable to ignore the developing countries in discussing future banking in the world. Are any finances particularly suitable to the poorest people on the planet? What types of banks are appropriate to developing countries? How different are these banks from conventional banks of advanced countries? This chapter attempts to answer these questions.

RICH VERSUS POOR COUNTRIES IN FINANCIAL INTERMEDIATION

All economies in the world rely on financial intermediary functions to transfer resources from savers to investors. In developed market economies, this function is performed by commercial banks and capital markets. Millions of poor households in developing countries want similar financial services, and they want them for the same reasons as everyone else. In many developing countries, however, capital markets are still at a rudimentary stage, and commercial banks are reluctant to lend to the poor. Commercial banks typically do not serve poor households because of the high cost of small transactions, the lack of traditional collateral, geographic isolation, or simple social prejudice. And even those institutions that provide financial services to the poor are limited in scale. Commercial lenders in rural areas prefer to deal mainly with large-scale farmers. Complicated loan procedures combined with a lack of accounting experience limit the access of poor people to formal sources of credit.

CONVENTIONAL VERSUS NONCONVENTIONAL LENDING

In most developing countries, traditional financial sectors ignore the informal sector, and they repress the sustainability of member-based financial institutions at the community level. It has become clear that traditional World Bank and International Monetary Fund (IMF) macro-investment strategies, based on the Washington Consensus theory of economic liberalization, have failed to improve the livelihoods of the poorest communities in developing countries. This market liberalization theory obstructs community-level investment opportunities, failing to develop appropriate rural financial institutions for the poor in backward countries. It represents the classic top-down approach to development in which local communities and even governments have little or no say in the process. These policies have benefited the urban sector and those people in the top 10 percent of the income distribution in developing countries. This top 10 percent includes bankers, consultants, government bureaucrats, and owners of large businesses, but not the poor.

The absence of commercial banks for poor people has led to nonconventional lending schemes. The recent prominence given to microcredit owes much to the success of a relatively few microcredit programs. The most prominent of the successes now reaches over 2 million people, with cumulative lending of about $2.1 billion. Similar successful examples are known in Latin America and Africa. These schemes are characterized by relatively small loans, with a rather short repayment period. Women are a major beneficiary of their activities, and the funds go primarily to agriculture, distribution, trading, small craft, and processing industries. The impact of microcredit lending varies widely between rural areas and urban areas.

Participatory Structure and Limits

In many developing countries, overall interest rates are relatively high. Rates charged by microlending schemes are quite high when the risk premium is added. Many of these micro-institutions claim a high rate of repayment. This is attributable to the informal participatory structures, which create an atmosphere in which debtors respect their obligations. Everyone is involved as peer. The administrative structure is generally light, and the entire process is participatory in nature. Although this phenomenon is certainly true of better-run institutions, it is not possible to verify whether this is a universal feature.

Some studies show that there are limits to the use of microcredit as an instrument for eradicating poverty. They include difficulties in identifying the poor and targeting credit to reach the poorest of the poor. In addition, many people, especially the poorest of the poor, are usually uneducated and are not in a position to undertake an economic activity because they lack business skills, experience, and even the motivation for business.

DEFINITION AND ORIGIN OF MICROCREDIT

Much of the current interest in microcredit stems from the Microcredit Summit held on February 2–4, 1997, in Washington, D.C. The summit adopted the following definition of microcredit: Microcredit is a program designed to extend small loans to very poor people for self-employment projects that generate income, allowing them to care for themselves and their families. Some of the defining criteria common to all countries include: (1) size (loans are micro, or very small in size), (2) target users (microenterpreneurs and low-income households utilization), (3) the use of funds (income generation and enterprise development, but also for community use (such as for health/education), and (4) terms and conditions (most terms and conditions for microcredit loans are flexible and easy to understand, and suited to the local conditions of the community).

Microcredit is thus the extension of small loans to entrepreneurs who are too poor to qualify for conventional bank loans. It has proven an effective and popular measure in the ongoing struggle against poverty, enabling those without access to traditional lending institutions to borrow at bank rates and to start small business. Microcredit has been used as an "inducer" in many community development activities, as an entry point in a community organizing program, or as an ingredient in a larger education/training exercise.

Origin of Microcredit: Grameen Bank

In the early 1970s, after earning a Ph.D. in economics at Vanderbilt University, Dr. Muhammad Yunus returned to Bangladesh to settle into a life as a professor. But a famine in 1974 ravaged the country, leading Dr. Yunus to alter his thinking and his life profoundly. What good were complex theories when people were dying of starvation on the sidewalks and porches across from his lecture hall? Nothing in the economic theories he taught reflected the life around him.

Armed with a lofty dream to end the suffering around him, Dr. Yunus started an experimental microcredit enterprise in 1977. It began with a simple loan. After witnessing the cycle of poverty that kept many poor women enslaved to high-interest loan sharks in Bangladesh, Dr. Yunus lent a total of $27 to 42 women so that they could purchase bamboo to make and sell stools. In a short time, the women were able to repay the loans while continuing to support themselves and their families. With that initial eye-opening success, the seeds of the Grameen (named for the Bengali word for "rural") Bank, and the concept of microcredit, were planted. By 1983, the Grameen Bank was officially formed.

The idea behind the Grameen Bank is ingeniously simple: extend credit to poor people, and they will help themselves. This concept strikes at the root of poverty by specifically targeting the poorest of the poor, providing small loans (usually less than $300) to those unable to obtain credit from traditional banks. At Grameen, loans are administered to groups of five people, with only two receiving their money up front. As soon as these two make a few regular payments, loans are gradually extended to the rest of the group. In this way, the program builds a sense of community as well as individual self-reliance. Peer pressure works well. Most of the Grameen Bank's loans are to women, and since its inception, there has been an astonishing loan repayment rate of over 98 percent. The Grameen Bank is now a $2.5 billion banking enterprise in Bangladesh.

Noteworthy is the spread of microcredit to other countries including some advanced countries. The microcredit model has diffused to over 50 countries worldwide, from the United States to Papua New Guinea, from Norway to Nepal. It has now become the world's hot idea for reducing poverty. Ever optimistic, Yunus travels the globe spreading the belief that poverty can be eliminated. His efforts prove that hope is a global currency.

It is difficult to argue with Dr. Yunus's achievements in building the world's best-known microcredit institution called Grameen Bank. The well-known ability of the Grameen Bank to fight poverty in one of the world's poorest countries has done more than anything else to legitimize the field of micro-finance, which now is part of a well-coordinated worldwide movement trying to reach 100 million of the world's poorest families by 2005.

Part of the success may be the bank's relentless innovation and flexibility in organizing itself to work in the challenging setting of rural Bangladesh. Another part may be the bank's co-op structure, in which borrowers are called "members" and make up the key block of its shareholders. Yet another part may be the desire to be only minimally profitable and to return as much of its earnings as possible to those very people. Whatever the reason for success, the Grameen process as a whole works well. Peer pressure and equal participation unquestionably lead to success.

A Grameen Bank starts off with a nonprofit orientation and a desire to fill an important niche in the local development picture, but intends to convert to a for-profit status within a few years. The best established of of Grameen Banks, Grameen Uddog ("Rural Initiative"), finances local women's purchases of yarns and dyes to weave on traditional handlooms and then links them with Bangladesh's thriving textile export business. The production capacity is currently a million yards per month, with more than 15 million yards of the fabric exported to date. Lately, Dr. Yunus has used Grameen Bank as a springboard into other innovative business ventures intended to create new opportunities for poverty reduction.

Here is a summary of the bank called Grameen, according to the International Finance Corporation of the World Bank:

Name of the Bank: Grameen Bank

Managing Director: Muhammad Yunus, Bangladesh

Size of Bank: Approximately $100 million in equity; $275 million outstanding loan portfolio; has lent more than $2 billion to 2.3 million low-income borrowers in rural Bangladesh, 94 percent of them women

Start of Commercial Operations: 1983

Loan Size: Average is local currency equivalent of $160, it but can range from $1 or less to $300 or more

Ownership: Grameen borrowers 93 percent, government 7 percent

Use of Loans: To finance purchase of ducks, cows, geese, basket-weaving material, and other inputs for self-employment projects of borrowers who otherwise would have little economic opportunity; also some housing loans

Business Strategy: Lends without collateral to small groups of peers, not individuals, via a system based on "mutual trust, accountability, participation, and creativity"

How It Works: If any member of the group defaults, all are cut off from new lending until the outstanding debt is repaid

Repayment Rate: 98 percent

Number of Villages Served: 37,000

Number of Employees: 12,000

Portion of Borrowers Who Have Escaped Poverty: 33.3 percent (World Bank/Grameen estimate)

EMPOWERING THE POOR THROUGH MICROCREDIT IN BANGLADESH

The provision of small loans for income-generating self-employment activities can make all the difference for poor families. The World Bank is supporting Bangladesh's microcredit movement, the Poverty Alleviation Microcredit Project. The International Development Association (IDA) within the World Bank plays a key role in supporting the poverty-reduction mission. The IDA's assistance focuses on the poorest countries, to which it provides interest-free loans and other services. The organization depends on contributions from its wealthier member countries for most of its financial resources.

The IDA's interest-free credit is to be repaid by the Government of Bangladesh in 40 years with a 10-year grace period. The government, in turn, gives this money to the Palli Karma Sahayak Foundation (PKSF) at 1 percent interest to be repaid in 20 years. The money flows as follows:

IDA(WB) → Government of Bangladesh → PKSF → 170 Microcredit NGOs

The PKSF is an innovative quasigovernment poverty foundation that lends to promising small and medium nongovernmental organizations (NGOs) to expand their microcredit programs. The government helps the PKSF and the microcredit NGOs who borrow from it to become financially viable through training, research, and dissemination of best practices on increasing cost effectiveness. The project has helped more than 170 NGOs extend microcredit to an estimated 1.4 million poor borrowers, most of whom are women. "Microfinance has tremendous potential as an instrument for poverty reduction," says Shahid Khandlers, Senior Economist at the World Bank Poverty Reduction and Economic Management Network. "The project supports the Bank's twin objectives of poverty alleviation and broad-based economic growth."[1]

PROSHIKA, for Education and Training for Human Development

PROSHIKA is an acronym for three Bangla words that stand for training, education, and action. It is an NGO offering educational and training programs for human development. It has been more than two decades since PROSHIKA, now one of the largest NGOs in Bangladesh, took its first step. The PROSHIKA development process started in a few villages of Dhaka and Comilla districts in 1975, and the organization formally emerged in October 1976.

Rural areas are beyond the reach of formal financial institutions, but the hunger for microcredit is tremendous. Severely short of capital, the rural poor have proven that they can change their destiny if cash flows into their hands. "Demand is expanding so fast that we initially could not provide all our group members with credit," says Dr. Qazi Faruque Ahmed, president of PROSHIKA.[2]

Aminul Islam, director of the Bangladesh Rural Advancement Committee (BRAC), echoes this sentiment. "The demand for funds is increasing fast. Once a woman finds that credit can change her lifestyle, she dreams of going higher and higher, and the demand also grows. We found that grant money couldn't keep up with the large demand. So we opted to take funds from PKSF." Now that PKSF is providing a new source of funding, NGOs are able to meet the demand for microcredit. Meanwhile, more and more members of NGO groups are taking out new loans everyday.

Case History: Ranzida Khatun's Story

One NGO, the Association for Social Advancement (ASA), specializes in credit programs in Bangladesh. The organization is committed to empowering landless and disadvantaged poor villagers. It disburses credit through small groups, which serve to promote solidarity and awareness-building. ASA has developed a credit service to women's groups that is highly standardized and very economical. The repayment rate is almost 100 percent and covers not only all field expenses but overhead expenses as well. The organization runs nearly 800 branches in Bangladesh. With almost half of their loans resulting in default, Bangladesh's commercial banks have much to learn from Ranzida Khatun.

Ranzida Khatun, a small peanut trader, is a member of Keya Bhumihin Women's Group in the village of Kuliarchar, Bangladeshi, and has taken out four loans from ASA. Not once has she defaulted. "The first time I borrowed only Tk 2,000 to see if I can really make use of it. Since it was successful, I found the courage to borrow another Tk 3,000, then Tk 4,000, and finally Tk 5,000 eight months ago," says Ranzida. "I have already paid 32 installments on my last loan and have 13 more installments to go." The NGOs that have been giving loans to these women are also regularly repaying their lender. "We place top priority on paying back loans to PKSF," says Shafiqual Haque Choudhury, managing director of ASA. "Our loan recovery rate is 99.82 percent." Explaining the secret to their success, Choudhury says, "We are able to maintain such a high rate of loan recovery by providing training to borrowers before giving them loans. Projects are also vigorously scrutinized by our staff before giving loans and these are constantly monitored," he added.[3]

Bangladesh Rural Advance Commission

Bangladesh Rural Advance Commission (BRAC) is an NGO with programs in microcredit, primary health care, and nonformal primary education for the landless rural poor. It is currently engaged in relief operations for flood victims and the landless rural poor. BRAC was established as a relief and rehabilitation organization in 1972 after the Bangladesh Liberation War spearheaded by Fazle Hasan Abed. Over the years, BRAC has gradually evolved into a large, multifaceted development organization with the twin objectives of alleviating poverty and empowering the poor. It targets people living below the poverty line (mostly landless). BRAC focuses mainly on women and has developed its own strategy to take resources and services to the grassroots level.

Case History: Jamila Begum and Her Small Hotel

"Monohori Hotel," reads a freshly written sign on the top of the tin shed beside the dusty road. From inside wafts the mouth-watering smell of fish curry. Between the narrow gap of the two rows of stretched tables and benches, Jamila Begum moves along deftly with a bowl of rice in one hand and curry in the other. Customers, mostly cattle traders who came to sell their animals in the market a few hundred yards away, eat heartily. "The hotel is my brain child," Jamila says while serving her customers. "First, I borrowed Tk 1,000 from BRAC and started a poultry farm. But when I found out that those hotels near the market were booming, I thought, well, if they can sell food to the cattle traders, why can't I? I am a good cook, and I can offer them better food at cheaper prices. So I took out another Tk 6,000 loan from BRAC and along with the profits from the poultry invested in this hotel." "Before starting the hotel, I used to work as a maid in other people's houses," recalls Jamila. "I had to work from dawn to late night almost for a pittance. We used to live in temporary housing made of straw. Those terrible days are now behind me. Now, I have replaced my old house with a tin shed, and my two children are attending primary school."[4]

GRAMEEN BANK AND ITS REPLICATIONS IN THE WORLD

There are two different kinds of banks: conventional commercial banks based on distrust and unconventional microcredits based on trust. Grameen Bank (GB) has reversed conventional banking practice by removing the need for collateral and creating a banking system based on mutual trust, accountability, participation, and creativity. GB provides credit to the poorest of the poor in rural Bangladesh, without any collateral. At GB, credit is a cost-effective weapon to fight poverty, and it serves as a catalyst in the overall development of socioeconomic conditions of the poor who have been kept outside the banking orbit on the ground that they are poor and hence not bankable. Professor Muhammad Yunus reasoned that if financial resources can be made available to the poor on terms and conditions that are appropriate and reasonable, "these millions of small people with their millions of small pursuits can add up to create the biggest development wonder." His reasoning proved to be right.

Currently, GB is the largest rural finance institution in Bangladesh. It has more than 2.3 million borrowers, 94 percent of whom are women. With 1,128 branches, GB provides services in 38,951 villages, covering more than half of the total villages in Bangladesh. The repayment of its loans, which average US$160, is over 95 percent. Grameen Bank's positive impact on its poor and formerly poor borrowers has been documented in many independent studies carried out by external agencies, including the World Bank, the International Food Research Policy Institute (IFPRI), and the Bangladesh Institute of Development Studies (BIDS).

Grameen Bank has inspired people and institutions throughout the world with its success in alleviating poverty. More than 4,000 people from some 100 countries have gone through Grameen's training/exposure programs over the last 10 years. Some of those visitors have returned to their countries and replicated the Grameen Bank financial system to help the people in their own country to overcome poverty. A total of 223 Grameen replication programs in 58 countries were established during the 1990s, reaching several hundred thousand poor borrowers with credit around the world.

Grameen Banks in the United States and the United Kingdom

The success of the Grameen Bank in Bangladesh has been much heralded, and with Hilary Clinton's visit to the Grameen Bank in April 1995, U.S. policymakers began to consider the applicability of this experiment to the low income, inner-city neighborhoods of the United States. At its advent, the Grameen Bank developed strong enforcement structures through group lending and borrowing which ensured a high rate of repayment. Recently, the Bank has made use of the latest advances in information technology, permitting better contact with borrowers and more accurate monitoring of repayment. The development of information communication technology appropriate for streamlining micro-finance and making it more attractive to high street banks makes this an opportune time to consider developing micro-finance with the low-income communities in the United Kingdom and elsewhere. Grass-roots micro-finance initiatives already developed within the United Kingdom include Full Circle in Norwich and the Rebuilding Society Network in Birmingham. Thus, the merits of micro-finance are not limited to the developing countries; it is now universally recognized.

MICROCREDIT SUMMIT AND COMPARATIVE DATA

The Microcredit Summit Campaign was established in 1997 in response to the desperate need of hundreds of millions of women in developing countries. The Campaign seeks to reach 100 million of the world's poorest families, especially the women of those families, with credit for self-employment and other financial and business services by 2005. During 1997–1999, a total of 1,065 microcredit institutions reached 13.8 million poorest clients, 10.3 million or 75 percent of whom were women. At the time of the 1997 Microcredit Summit, it was estimated that 8 million poorest clients were being reached. The survey for the year 2000 indicates an increase of more than 6 million poorest clients being reached over a two-year period (January 1, 1998, to December 31, 1999), an increase of 82 percent. Of the 512 programs reporting data covering January 1, 1999 to December 31, 1999, the growth in the number of poorest women being reached over the preceding year was 1.4 million, an increase of 16 percent. Although this progress is impressive, the Campaign still has a long way to go to fulfill its mission over the next six years.

Four Core Themes: Setting the Direction

At the launch of the Microcredit Summit, many in the field of micro-finance argued for a focus on building financially self-sufficient institutions at the expense of reaching the poorest families. However, members of the Microcredit Summit Campaign are demonstrating that there does not have to be a tradeoff. Combining institutional financial self-sufficiency with reaching the poorest is attainable.

The Microcredit Summit Campaign has four core themes:

1. *Reaching the Poorest*. The Summit recognizes that the field of micro-finance includes institutions that provide financial services to constituencies usually overlooked by the traditional banking sector. However, the Summit specifically focuses on reaching the poorest families, defined in the Summit's *Declaration and Plan of Action* as families in developing countries among the bottom 50 percent of those living below their nation's poverty line. Another way of looking at this target is to see the 1.2 billion people living in absolute poverty as comprising some 240 million families. These 240 million families

comprise the group from which most of the Microcredit Summit's target of 100 million poorest will come. Within industrialized countries the Summit focuses on all of those living below their nation's poverty line.

2. *Reaching and Empowering Women.* Experience shows that women are a good credit risk and that woman-run businesses tend to benefit family members more directly than those run by men. At the same time, earning an income gives women a higher status in their homes, communities, and nations.

3. *Building Financially Self-Sufficient Institutions.* The *Declaration and Plan of Action* emphasizes the importance of programs in developing countries reaching financial self-sufficiency. Experience has shown that microcredit programs in developing countries can improve their efficiency and structure, as well as their interest rates and fees, to eventually cover their operating and financial costs. Day-long courses offered by the Campaign at global and regional meetings held from 1999 through 2001 trained practitioners in this area. Although the economic context in industrialized countries is radically different, the Summit encourages programs in industrialized countries to explore ways of becoming self-sufficient, so that their operating costs will be covered through direct revenue from program services.

4. *Ensuring a Positive, Measurable Impact on the Lives of Clients and Their Families.* Although financial measures such as program repayment rates indicate the strength of a microcredit institution, the Microcredit Summit is committed to programs that have a positive, measurable impact on the lives of the very poor. Two impact assessment studies conducted by the nongovernmental microcredit organization Freedom from Hunger showed that current clients of its affiliate institutions in Honduras and Mali experienced positive program impact at the individual, household, and community levels. The studies demonstrated that when compared to nonclients, current clients were more likely to have larger enterprises; to experience an increase in personal income and household food consumption; to have personal savings; and to feel a greater sense of empowerment and higher self-esteem.

Micro Summit Campaign Programs report having reached 82 percent more poorest clients (over 6 million more poorest families) during the two-year period from January 1, 1998 to December 31, 1999. The numbers increased from 7.6 million at the end of 1997 to 13.8 million at the end of 1999. The 512 programs are reporting a 16-percent increase in the number of poorest *women* reached in the past year (January 1, 1999 to December 31, 1999), an increase of 1.4 million poorest women.

A total of 1,065 established microcredit practitioners responded to the survey. These programs report reaching 23,555,689 active clients. According to the information these programs provided, they are currently serving 13,779,872 of the *poorest* families, 75 percent of whom are women (see Table 15.1).

Table 15.2 shows that of the world's 1999 microcredit clients, 79 percent are in Asia, followed by Africa with 16 percent and Latin America and Caribbean with 5 percent (see Figure 15.1). The concentration in Asia is not surprising in

Table 15.1
World Summary of Microcredit Clients

Year	Total Number of Clients Reported	Number of "Poorest" Clients Reported	Number of "Poorest" Clients Who Are Women
12/31/98 1,065 institutions	20,938,899	12,221,918	8,839,706
12/31/99 1,065 institutions	23,555,689	13,779,872	10,273,900

Source: Microcredit Summit Campaign.

view of their birthplace. Their first success in Bangladesh is being spread around to its neighbors in Asia. Interestingly, their spread is not limited to the developing countries. Poor people live in developed countries as well and can benefit by microcredits, which are now borderless.

Table 15.3 shows that Bangladesh is most active in microcredit, with more than five million clients, followed by Thailand. The ratio of women to the total number of poorest clients in Bangladesh was 90 percent in 1998 and 91 percent in 1999. The ratio in Thailand was smaller—58 percent in 1998 and 60 percent in 1999. Bangladeshi women appear to be more active in small business than Thai women. In 1999 this ratio was 33 percent in Nepal, 65 percent in India, and 90 percent in Cambodia. Women in Cambodia are apparently as active in micro-finance and small business as are Bangladeshi women. Grameen Bank's replication programs now operate in 19 countries in Asia; in India alone there are over 20 Grameen Banks.

In Africa (see Table 15.4), Ethiopia remains the leader, although the total number of poorest clients in Ethiopia in 1999 was only 7 percent that of Bangladesh.

The ratio of women to the total number of poorest clients in Ethiopia was 43 percent in 1999, far below that in Bangladesh. The ratio in Nigeria was similar. (Data on other countries are taken directly from the Microcredit Summit Campaign web site.)

CENTRAL BANKERS AND MICROCREDIT

The Asia and Pacific Region Microcredit Summit Meeting of Councils was held on February 1–5, 2001, in New Delhi, India, and attended by many central bankers from Asian countries. Dipendra Purush Dhakal, governor of the Central Bank of Nepal, reports that micro-finance institutions now play an active role

Table 15.2
Microcredit Clients in the World by Region

Region	Number of Programs Reporting	Number of Clients Reported, 1998	Number of Clients Reported, 1999	Number of Poorest Clients Reported, 1998	Number of Poorest Clients Reported, 1999	Number of Women Poorest Clients Reported, 1998	Number of Women Poorest Clients Reported, 1999
Africa	455	2,974,318	3,833,565	2,149,517	2,617,861	1,142,614	1,526,267
Asia	352	16,798,605	18,427,125	9,513,544	10,498,656	7,350,121	8,316,313
Latin America and Caribbean	152	989,800	1,109,708	452,436	531,228	290,364	355,253
Middle East	16	44,225	46,925	28,071	28,807	15,501	15,680
Developing World Totals	975	20,806,948	23,417,323	12,143,568	13,676,552	8,798,600	10,213,513
North America	48	40,439	46,925	28,071	28,807	15,501	15,680
Europe and NIS	42	40,439	43,750	16,566	18,519	11,144	13,022
Industrialized World Totals	90	131,951	138,366	78,350	103,320	41,106	60,387
Global World Totals	1,065	20,938,899	23,555,689	12,221,918	13,779,872	8,839,706	10,273,900

Source: Microcredit Summit Campaign.

Figure 15.1
Microcredit Clients by Region, 1999

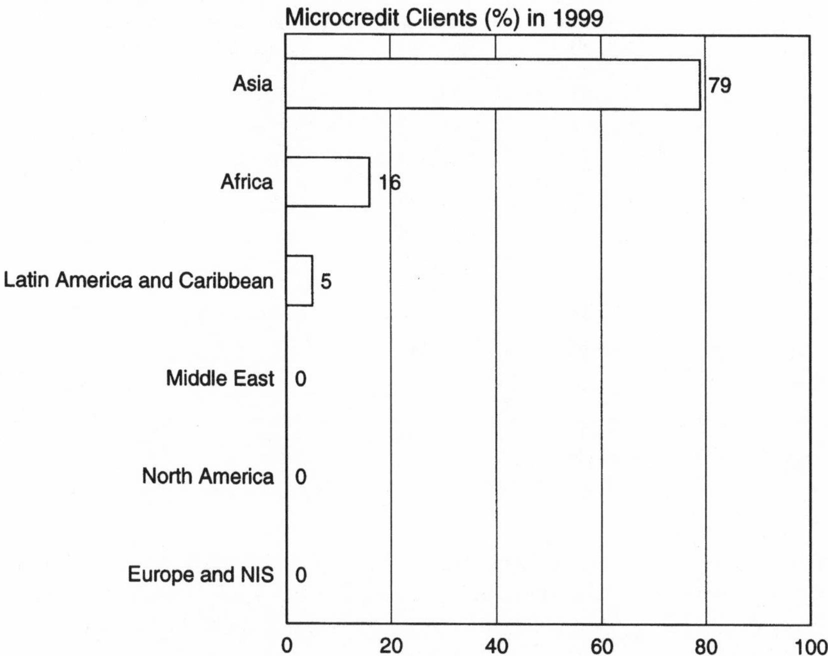

Table 15.3
Major Microcredit Clients in Asia by Country

ASIA Country	Total Number of Poorest Clients as of 12/31/98	Total Number of Poorest Clients as of 12/31/99	Total Number of Poorest Women as of 12/31/98	Total Number of Poorest Women as of 12/31/98
Bangladesh	5,165,069	5,801,699	4,645,862	5,261,566
Thailand	1,502,644	1,528,245	871,534	916,947
Nepal	176,742	186,576	54,275	61,613
India	151,288	168,211	86,114	109,524
Cambodia	69,724	71,646	64,125	64,200

Source: Microcredit Summit Campaign.

Table 15.4
Major Microcredit Clients in Africa by Country

AFRICA Country	Total Number of Poorest Clients as of 12/31/98	Total Number of Poorest Clients as of 12/31/99	Total Number of Poorest Women as of 12/31/98	Total Number of Poorest Women as of 12/31/98
Ethiopia	272,123	385,373	113,038	164,895
Nigeria	299,052	262,999	115,816	110,123
Malawi	272,123	120,703	49,196	55,541
Mali	67,871	82,898	67,871	82,898
Burkina Faso	30,806	35,000	29,266	31,500
Morocco	16,055	30,000	16,055	30,000
Benin	7,205	9,444	4,683	6,327
Kenya	5,686	9,060	5,686	9,060
Congo	1,568	1,778	1,490	1,689

Source: Microcredit Summit Campaign.

in poverty eradication. The Central Bank of Nepal, in support of this goal, is assisting relevant programs in hopes of expanding the micro-finance institutions in Nepal. According to Dhakal, the role of the Central Bank is related not only to credit, but also to social intermediation.

Dr. Ishrat Husain, governor of the State Bank of Pakistan, states that Pakistan wants to promote micro-finance institutions as a partnership between the public sector, the private sector, the communities, and NGOs. Interest rates and service charges will be at a level determined by the market, not subsidized; these institutions will not be under government supervision and regulation.

Other central bankers in Asia express similar opinions, demonstrating that in poor Asian countries, central bankers believe microcredit institutions are important in poverty reduction. The Central Bank of Pakistan supports this goal and stresses the partnership role of micro-finance institutions.

FUTURE OF MICRO-FINANCE

The Microcredit Summit Campaign, headquartered in Washington, D.C., seeks to ensure that 100 million of the world's poorest families, especially the women of those families, will receive credit for self-employment and other financial and business services by the year 2005. A crucial part of any future effort will be to strengthen the administrative structures of the existing microcredit institutions. Economies of scale are important in microlending, as are dynamic leadership and management staff. The provision of information on available services to the poor is critical, but has not yet been achieved even in some advanced developing countries. Information on services for the poor is seldom readily available.

The long-term financial sustainability of microcredit operations merits particular attention. In the absence of long-term sustainability, microcredit operations become a welfare or charity operation. Although welfare sometimes has its place in development, it should not characterize microcredit institutions. Microcredit institutions are not charitable organizations.

There is now considerable consensus that lending to the poor can succeed provided it is accompanied by other services, especially training, information, and access to land. An OECD study, for example, emphasizes that credit needs to be supplemented with access to land and appropriate technology. But such activities require strong support from the public sector. In some of the lowest income countries, lack of access to land is the most critical single cause of rural poverty in those countries. The success of microcredit will depend on the availability of accompanying services from the public sector. Governments and central banks will need to be involved to some extent.

Future historians will hopefully look back at the last decades of the twentieth century and the early decades of the twenty-first as an important transformational period for humankind during which the microcredits shattered a myth regarding alleviating poverty: Notably, the myth that women are not bankable. Bagladeshi women have turned out to be productive members of society, as has been found to be the case in many other countries in Asia and Africa in particular. The incredible success of microcredit programs in Bangladesh and other countries will continue to give hope and encourage networking of mutual help.

Microcredit is about trading, selling, processing, and getting some return on an investment in days or weeks. The microcredit summit's target group is not farmers but small entrepreneurs. The next microcredit summit is to be held in New Delhi, in 2005. At the Asia Pacific Region Meeting of the Microcredit Summit Meeting of Councils, in New Delhi, on February 1–5, 2001, Dr. Yunus highlighted some of Grameen's successes in utilizing technology to benefit the poor, including Grameen Phone and Grameen Shakti (Energy). Information technology will continue to be used in the future for the benefit of the poorest.

NOTES

For more information about the Microcredit Summit Campaign, please contact Nathanael Goldberg, Microcredit Summit, 440 First Street NW, Suite 460, Washington, DC 20001. Phone: (202) 637–9600, Fax: (202) 637–3566. E-mail: info@microcredit summit.org, Web: www.microcreditsummit.org.

1. World Bank news release No. 99/2063/SAS, Dhaka, Bangladesh, January 14, 1999.

2. *Fighting Poverty through Microcredit* (Dhaka, Bangladesh: World Bank, June 10, 2000).

3. The World Bank Group, *Empowering the Poor Through Microcredit: The Bangladesh Poverty Alleviation Project*, 2000. http://wbln1018.worldbank.org/SAR/sa.nsf/All/450FC8A2FAD5479885256865007197CF?OpenDocument.

4. Ibid.

REFERENCES

Adams, Lise, Anna Awimbo, Nathanael Goldberg, and Cristina Sanchez. "Empowering Women with Microcredit." *2000 Microcredit Summit Campaign Report.*

Ahmed, Salehuddin. "Creating Autonomous National and Sub-regional Microcredit Funds." *Microcredit Summit Campaign Publications and Resources*, January 2001.

Asia and Pacific Region Microcredit Summit Meeting of Councils, February 1–5, 2001, New Delhi, India.

Client Perspectives: The Sustainable CEO. "Different Kind of Banker, Different Kinds of Bank." Impact Summer 1998, International Finance Corporation, World Bank, Washington, D.C.

Dunford, Christopher. "Sustainable Integration of Microfinance with Education, in Health, Family Planning, and HIV/AIDS Prevention for the Poorest Entrepreneurs." Freedom from Hunger Discussion Paper, commissioned by the Microcredit Summit Campaign, August 2001.

Hatch, John. "Microcredit: Where We've Come, Where We're Going." RESULTS, Microcredit Summit, 1999.

Kamal, Mustafa. "Impact Evaluation Mechanism of the Association for Social Advancement (ASA) in Bangladesh." *Microcredit Summit Campaign Publications and Resources*, January 2001.

"Thaneakea Phum Village Banking." Catholic Relief Services, Cambodia, n.d.

Chapter 16

The Future of European Stock Exchanges

Jean-Pierre Paelinck

Europe is on the verge of an equity revolution, that will force market participants to forge international strategic alliances. Stock exchanges are and will remain the symbol of capitalism, providing the meeting place of strengths and weaknesses of the market economy. The stock exchange system also offers safety and confidence to investors and issuers.

It is not easy to guarantee a level playing field in a multicultural European society characterized by a number of institutions with different features evolving in a world of increased competition.

Although European stock exchanges use sophisticated electronic trading systems, they still need to work hard if they want to prevent alternative securities trading systems from taking over part of their business. Stock exchanges realize that if they do not put more emphasis on efficiency, electronic communications networks (ECN) might come to dominate.

This chapter presents a preview of the future landscape of the securities world in Europe. There is some danger that alliances would reduce choices for investors and contain some possibilities of anticompetition, but experience has shown that concentration leads to increased competition between stronger and more powerful entities to the benefit of investors.

MAJOR PLAYERS: OVERVIEW OF CURRENT DEVELOPMENTS

Stock Exchanges: From Regulated to Organized Markets

For a long time European stock exchanges failed to define a strategy adapted to the global world. New types of stock exchange managers emerged with new ideas or with other economic and political interests to serve, apart from their own ambitions.

The aim for Europe is to have orderly and efficient trading facilities, with decent infrastructures. Organized markets are trading systems with transactions concluded in accordance with formal rules, procedures, and regulations, whereby prices are determined and transactions take place on a regular basis, with systems matching multiple orders.

Regulated markets (stock exchanges) are part of the organized markets system. Regulated markets focus on fair and orderly trading rules for market participants and efficient price formation and transparency; they protect investors against counterparty defaults and play an essential role in admission to listing and licensing of intermediaries. Stock exchanges get more commercialized. This makes it less appropriate to allow them to continue to exercise regulatory powers.

Stock exchanges, also called regulated markets in the European context, have been around for many years. For most of the time they were essentially in the hands of brokers and dealers, professionals who were recently removed on the basis of the principle that corporatism is detrimental to free trade and competition.

The Internet has modified the competitive environment in which the exchanges of the future will have to work.

Stock exchanges move toward the money-making model to satisfy their own shareholders. According to the chairman of Euronext (Paris-Brussels-Amsterdam, and, eventually Portugal), money of stock exchanges (in the case of Euronext) comes essentially from:

Commissions on transactions[1]	25%
Clearing and settlement charges[2]	30%
Turnover in derivatives	12%
Admissions of securities to the exchange	7%
Sale of technology	13%

The bank ABN AMRO calculated that 75 percent of the costs of Euronext were fixed, and not sensitive to the volume of business. Euronext is the result of the cooperation between three well-established exchanges that realistically decided to cooperate. It is much easier to swallow smaller exchanges (Warsaw, for instance) than to cooperate with other giants who might like to replace the chiefs in place. The danger for Euronext's smallest exchange (Brussels) is that it tends to evaporate between the two powerful partners who for each service offer an alternative that can replace what Brussels did, when it was still independent.

The London Stock Exchange puts emphasis on performance and on remaining independent from rival exchanges. It had to undergo the proposals expressed by the chief executive of the German Exchange and had to fight the advances of the Swedish technology firm OM Gruppen. The OM Gruppen own 60 percent of JIWAY, an alternative securities trading system, which is intended to serve the interests of individual investors but so far has had an insufficient volume of transactions.[3]

London has by far the most visible international presence as a financial center. The community of British bankers with their international expertise are the basis of excellence in investment banking services worldwide. Yet the London Stock Exchange has experienced an incredibly long list of mistakes at the managerial level for which few Board members accepted the blame. It is only by a miracle and given the strength of the City of London, as the unchallenged financial capital of Europe, that this institution could survive the Taurus and other strange episodes of unrealistic appointments and sackings. The London Stock Exchange earns 44 percent of its income from distribution of information.[4]

The German exchange is feared by a number of European exchanges because of its affluent cash, which could allow the Germans to invade other financial places. The German exchange particularly intimidates some profitable smaller exchanges and a number of emerging markets, which do not want Germans to decide how to improve their market.

In 2000, the International Securities Markets Association (ISMA) launched COREDEAL, a pan-European electronic trading system for international securities. COREDEAL is an investment exchange run by the United Kingdom's Financial Services Authority (FSA) and is a regulated market under the European Union Investment Services Directive (ISD).[5]

Clearing and Settlement

The present patchwork of depositories and clearing and settlement systems should evolve toward a more consolidated and integrated system. The existing international systems, highly specialized in fixed income financial instruments, moved into the equity business and are fighting a crucial battle for supremacy of their service.

The present fragmented system will sooner or later be replaced by a more integrated system. Clearing and settlement will play an essential role in determining the future of stock exchanges in Europe.

Alternative Trading Systems

Exchanges tend to see alternative trading systems (ATS) as squatters within their walls. Securities trading firms matching multiple client orders on proprietary electronic trading systems offer alternative services to the execution on the exchange. They belong to the infrastructure of organized markets and are in competition with the traditional securities exchanges. There should be no discriminatory treatment for either kind of organized market.

For the Committee of European Securities Regulators (CESR), previously called Forum of European Securities Commissions (FESCO), an ATS is a non-exchange entity operating a trading system which results in contracts that cannot be unilaterally revoked. (CESR actually refers to "irrevocable" contracts). Some exchanges feel endangered by the potential and existing competition of ATS and suggest a number of tactical moves such as prohibiting shares already listed on a regulated (stock exchange) market to be traded on an ATS. Bourses online such as Instinet, Island, Bloomberg Tradebook, Redibook, and Archipelago enter the securities markets of the world. They are not exchanges but offer trading facilities worldwide. Night and day Electronic Communication Networks function nonstop. This is one of their major advantages. They distribute information to the benefit of their members (brokers and traders), who pay a subscription fee for this service.

Stock exchanges reacted to ATS by extending trading hours and by distributing information to their correspondents and to the public.

Alternative trading systems are serious rivals of exchanges but do not have the prestige of the well-established bourses with regulatory and official prerogatives. Financial managers like to refer to official institutions and must justify their investment decisions on the basis of reliable information (from sources known to be reliable) and with transactions protected by trustworthy clearing and settlement systems as well as by well-supervised trading systems. This works in favor of the traditional exchanges.

Eventually, the public might fail to distinguish between electronic securities trading systems and stock exchanges, but it should still be informed about differences, if any, regarding supervision, arbitrage, and guarantees (investor compensation funds).

Some would like to see both exchanges and other trading systems monitored and controlled in the same way in a spirit of transparency and creation of a level playing field.

To be successful and profitable, ATS need to reach a sufficient level of liquidity. The official regulated market (stock exchange) Tradepoint (now Virt-x, which is a combination of Tradepoint and the Swiss exchanges) experienced major difficulties in reaching a sufficient volume of business, notwithstanding the very high quality of its team. Instinet (Reuters), Virt-x, and OM (the major shareholder of NOREX) all fight for sufficient liquidity and profits. From June 2000 to June 2001, Jiway lost 40 percent of its business.[6] Jiway is fully owned by OM. There seems to be substantial interference between the software seller (OM) and the exchanges (Stockholm and Jiway) they control.

Alternative trading systems operate in the EU under the supervision of their national authorities. Since they operate internationally, it is difficult to control them effectively. We expect them to be treated eventually the way exchanges are presently supervised. Their strength lies in their innovative techniques and skills, in their capacity to adapt to new needs, in the rapidity of reaction as compared to classical systems. To neutralize the ATS market or to avoid confusion and fragmentation of markets, it was proposed that trading on ATS be prohibited in financial instruments once admitted on a so-called regulated market, as described in the Investment Services Directive. This was considered to be a concentration regulation "through the back door."

Sometimes the level playing field as viewed by the European Commission under the strong influence of stock exchanges appears to mean a level playing field whereby alternative trading systems would only be left with the choice between becoming a stock exchange and dying under suffocating reporting costs, obligations, and bureaucratic burdens.

The real answer to the existing and future problems is to be found in realistic transparency, with efficient and inexpensive reporting techniques by which organized markets, both regulated and alternative, can function to the benefit of all concerned. This assumes that all systems should cover their share of the administrative and functional burdens, such as costs related to the licensing of intermediaries and of admission to listing, investor compensation schemes, and arbitrage provisions.

The main problem associated with Electronic Communication Networks is their difficulties in attracting a sufficient number of investors and issuers. They manage to attract intermediaries by way of higher commissions, while investors still enjoy the advantage of lower transaction costs.

ATS and traditional stock exchanges have caused some dispersal of liquidity. Not all of them are expected to survive.

A level playing field that organized markets require for all participants follows the market rules, conduct of business rules, laws, and regulations to the benefit of the integrity of markets and efficiency. CESR did an excellent job in writing a set of standards for conduct of business rules and was careful to make investor protection a basic element of its work. Overregulation had to be avoided, but the interests of shareholders needed safeguarding, effective monitoring, and realistic reporting. Concentration rules whereby all transactions are to be executed on the "regulated market" are overprotective and are no longer applicable to the real world. Reporting by ATS to their main rival (the regulated market) seems to be more an attempt to eliminate the potential competition than to serve the integrity of the market.

Investment firms might well be required to participate in investor compensation funds and be able to give supervisors efficient audit trails to combat malpractice and fraud.

The New Markets

The new economy has had a strong but limited impact on the European stock markets. Easdaq (now NASDAQ Europe) did the right thing in trying to set up a pan-European market for high-tech growth companies. They had contacted the stock exchanges (essentially Paris) to work together with the view of helping Europe realize the first high-tech, high-risk trading system. The stock exchanges preferred to create such a market on their own. Europe in fact did not need two new market systems (NASDAQ Europe and Nouveau Marché). The tech bubble was responsible for the consequent mistrust of tech shares throughout Europe. For quite a time the new markets did well. Young, brilliant, but inexperienced executives supported the market by inducing investors to buy the so-called Technology-Media-Telecoms (TMT) shares. The owners of growth companies saw in the new markets a way out, allowing them to get rid of their overvalued shares. A conflict of interest (between organizers of the new markets and the investors) was inevitable. Investors were warned about the risks in the prospectuses, though warnings are sometimes ignored as is the case even for cigarettes where health warnings don't seem to work.

Corporate governance is proclaimed everywhere, but use of shareholders' money is frequently not in line with the shareholders' interests.

The Long-Awaited Revolution of Shareholders

Until recently, there was not much of a securities culture in the European Union, apart from the United Kingdom (where more than a quarter of the population owns shares). Privatization, stock options, and fiscal incentives helped to increase the number of shareholders throughout Europe, but much remains to be done.

Until very recently, CESR had to speak on behalf of shareholders since investors were barely organized. Shareholders were not always treated with much esteem, however. They came after a long list of more privileged partners in the securities game: boards, managers, staff, brokers, banks, and so on.

The collapse of the stock markets in 2000–2001 led to reduced capital spending due to eroded personal wealth. As everyone knows, there is no such thing as a market without investors. Confidence in the securities business was strongly affected by the collapse of a number of European mushroom companies.[7]

Euroshareholders, the European federation of associations (representing 18 European countries), defends the interests of shareholders, especially minority shareholders. This association is increasingly involved in the defense of shareholders' interests, including matters such as takeover bids, corporate governance, and mutual funds. Companies now have to care about shareholder value if they want to avoid major criticism from these associations.

Much emphasis needs to be placed on reliability and availability of information, especially in the case of allotments and information on the occasion of initial public offerings (IPOs).

Online Traders

Internet-based stock brokering has internationalized trading. Internet widened the horizon of European investors, a phenomenon that introduced more competition between exchanges and alternative trading systems.

In France, Dubus S.A. of Lille and the Real Bank, in Belgium, are currently offering worldwide trading facilities at a fraction of the costs charged by traditional intermediaries. This does not prevent them from providing advice and studies on which fund managers or traders can base their investment decisions. These two examples are mentioned here because they were pioneers in this field. Internet brokerage helped to diversify investments internationally over the various industrial sectors. Internet gives information on benchmarks, index performance data, charges, allocation models, and performances of portfolios.

Issuers in Search of Liquidity

Large corporations require stock exchanges of high standards and substantial fund-raising capacities. Some leading issuers have threatened to abandon their stock exchange if they do not acquire fund-raising capacity. Stock exchanges had to make deals and to forge alliances to increase liquidity to meet the requirements of issuers, and fund managers. For some issuers, the stock exchange represents an exit formula for their own shareholdings. Even if major shareholders pledge not to sell their shares in the company they control, experience in Europe shows that these promises are not always kept and that such obligations are very difficult to monitor.

There have also been a number of successful operations whereby a bank was able to improve the financial structure of its clients, enabling the same bank to continue to service them with loans and credits in accordance with the rebalanced balance sheet, to the benefit of all concerned.

Banks and stock exchanges can help good projects to succeed, but this requires a lot of homework in the field of assessment of the value of the shares to be offered to the public.

The Future of Investment Funds and Companies

The problem with investment funds and companies is related to the difficulty in assessing their performance, in choosing benchmarks, in giving sufficient information on scientific investment policy, and in getting a realistic and transparent explanation of prices and costs.

In and out trading benefits the brokerage company (not the investors) that usually happens to be directly or indirectly part of a financial group. The performance of investment funds is often disappointing. The fund industry is still doing well for a number of reasons:

- trust in the success of the fund in the longer run
- passivity
- not realizing how much gets lost in charges and management fees
- preference of risk spreading over high returns
- fiscal incentives

Pension Schemes

We foresee an increase in privately funded pensions and retirement schemes. The "pay as you go" system means that the present workers will pay for the pensions of the colleagues who have stopped working. It means that the pensioners' savings for their pensions have been used for other purposes and that their contributions are gone, forever! This is what is called "deficit spending."

In the United Kingdom, the prevailing idea is the introduction of the stakeholder pension, a halfway house between a full private pension and a company scheme. Following the uncertainties of the securities market that have been experienced, there is also a move going from defined benefits (usually a percentage of the average salary of the last five years) to a defined contribution system (whereby the financial institution does not run into difficulty in the event of a depreciation of its portfolio). The risk is shifted from the financial institution or governmental organization to the weaker party—in this case the employees.

Pension funds are expected to play an essential role as major players in the securities markets.

ONGOING AND EXPECTED DEVELOPMENTS

Mergers and Acquisitions of Stock Exchanges

Agreements, alliances, and mergers between stock exchanges are widespread in Europe. A number of memoranda of understanding were the prelude to the present consolidation process. This led to an increase of linkages of various types but made it difficult to respect all engagements and promises.

Rivalry between top managers and chairmen matters a lot in mergers and acquisitions. Behind official proclamations of corporate governance, personal ambitions can hardly be hidden. Leaders who have managed to replace the securities professionals are in most cases able but very ambitious managers. In the old days stock exchanges were chaired by unpaid brokers who performed their services for prestige and goodwill.

Mergers and acquisitions in the stock exchange world have shown how difficult it is to assess and understand value of shares. Each time a new stock exchange is added to a group, the readjustments are difficult to calculate and to realize.

The drama starts when there is an agreement for merger between large exchanges. Despite corporate governance rhetoric, only one leader can be the top man.

Derivatives

The European derivatives markets are more in the province of institutional investors than of individual investors. Interestingly, some countries (the Netherlands and the United Kingdom, for instance) have more derivatives cultures than others (e.g., Belgium). In the Netherlands one of the reasons derivatives were so successful can be found in the personality of the founder and promoter of the European Options Exchange. On the other hand, the lack of success in Belgium was partly due to the fact that the overwhelming success of the Dutch derivatives market induced Belgians to trade in Amsterdam.

The Blurring of Geographic and Professional Borders

During years of positive developments, little criticism was heard about globalization. Globalization spread wealth and put in place new supply chains within multinational groups choosing cheaper and more effective industrial localizations for their production.[8] But being united does not mean that failure is not possible. In an interconnected world, stock exchanges know that a small spark in one market can ignite their market. During affluent times, globalization allows economies to gain from other countries' favorable developments. In times of recession, interconnections facilitate the transfer of unemployment and market downturn.

Securities markets are global in the sense that wholesale markets are interconnected to retail markets; this is true throughout the world. Smaller markets graduate around larger ones, and the securities of new and smaller companies can grow to the level of blue chips at major stock exchanges.

THE CRUCIAL CHOICE REGARDING EXCHANGES IN THE FUTURE

There is not much of a consensus about how exchanges will evolve in the next decade. A number of smaller exchanges have to look at their future position in present fast-moving circumstances. A first reaction often consists in merging whatever seems to be directly related to the securities business locally. After such a move, the consolidated entity should feel stronger in merger and acquisition talks.

A second idea is to find an agreement with a partner exchange abroad. A nationalistic attitude leads to protective measures to keep the symbol of financial strength in the hands of national entities. For instance, the famous Wimbledon effect consists of organizing the business in Great Britain, regardless of the nationality of players. Foreign tennis players often win in Wimbledon, but Wimbledon is still a British world sport event. On the basis of this realistic approach, the British were able to become and to remain the main financial center of Europe.

The Lamfalussy Report

Professor Alexander Lamfalussy is a Hungarian-born Belgian who enjoys general esteem in finance and industry. He put in place what is now the European Central Bank. A capable and intelligent person, he is also modest and friendly. All these qualities helped him to get his report as chairman of the Committee of Wise Men accepted by market organizers and participants. Some of his proposals had already been dealt with in European directives. His report will speed up long-awaited reform of securities markets in Europe.

In short, the Lamfalussy report proposes that in the future regulated markets in the EU have only one supervisory authority per country. (Presently there are several.) Uncoordinated national approaches could give rise to regulatory inconsistencies and could be harmful to the integration of the European capital market. The Lamfalussy report recommended measures to be taken such as to avoid conflicts of interest within commercial operators of securities trading who play an institutional role as well as a commercial one. It also tried to find a solution for the international control, which is presently, still based on a home/host country control mechanism by putting in place a real coordination of supervisory authorities, not to mention at this early stage a kind of European Securities and Exchange system.

The Investment Services Directive in the Process of Redevelopment

The European legal framework is no longer adapted to the capital market on the continent. The Investment Services Directive (ISD), in the course of being updated, should be adapted to securities markets (exchanges and trading systems) as they will be in approximately 10 years. This reflects a need for durability. The ISD revision will introduce the single passport for investment firms and increase harmonized high levels of investor protection.

The ISD was adapted to the traditional stock exchanges and contributed significantly to the opening of exchanges to the entire EU market. This was not easy, with some countries requiring a bank as intermediary and others prohibiting a bank from performing that function. A lot of vested interests were concerned. The first ISD internationalized the market and introduced more potential competition.

The more the ISD came under scrutiny, the more the document became unworkable following a number of technological developments. The new ISD proposal has become too complex following intensive lobbying of interested parties and wants to serve too many purposes, taking into account too many vested interests and political interference.

A number of other directives (money laundering, listing particulars directive, insider trading, investors compensation funds, Undertakings of Collective Investments in Transferable Securities, takeover bids) govern the European capital market. There should also be room for a directive on asset management in view of the extremely important role asset management plays, especially in the institutional context.

PREVIEW OF THE EUROPEAN INVESTORS AND THE ISSUERS-DRIVEN SECURITIES MARKET

A New Relationship Between Organized Systems and Investors

Conflicts of interest between shareholders of the profit-minded stock exchange and users of the trading facilities are expected. When exchanges proudly announce exceptionally high profits, the market should understand where the money comes from. In a way, stock exchanges have moved from organizations, which served essentially the interests of brokers and other intermediaries, to companies which serve essentially the interests of new owners and management.

A serious threat to European stock exchanges has come from their dual "institutional-commercial" status by which they no longer enjoy privileged treatment toward electronic securities trading systems that focus on efficiency and business, while stock exchangers want to continue to play some prestigious regulatory role.

Investors are interested in the most efficient trading facility. There is a serious difference between listing (where there is a contract between the issuer and the exchange which receives a fee for the listing service) and an admission to trading (exchanges and securities trading systems organizing trading for which there is demand in the market). The investors want to be able to choose the place where they will trade.

It is time for the European stock exchanges to show a willingness to plan a system by which liquidity gets increased, clearing and settlement are made more efficient, and investors are better informed and protected against malpractice and the greed of other interested parties.

Stock exchanges have to regain influence, and securities trading systems have to realize that the market has become more demanding. European shareholders are ready to monitor business at the company and stock exchange levels.

Industrial Sector-Based Investment Policy

Many investors will invest according to an asset allocation model (over industrial sectors, currencies, bonds and shares, real estate, countries etc.). The London Stock Exchange, which lists stocks by industrial sector, not by country, will become the approach of the main European stock exchanges of the future. An alphabetical list (such as that of EURONEXT) does not promote consideration of the European market by industrial sector. Worse, a division between so-called growth stocks and value stocks can be terribly misleading and does not help to spread risks wisely.

Investors require timely and reliable information. They need market research information coming from good sources. The manager of an institutional investor must be able to justify his investment decisions. Equity analysts need to be independent and to be seen in that way. Very few investment advisers are paid only by their clients.

E-markets and International Supervision of Financial Transactions

E-markets are closely linked to the emergence of highly sophisticated and efficient electronic securities trading systems that might threaten the classical exchanges. The Electronic Communications Network is a securities market where securities get traded.

Access to the Internet cannot be easily controlled, and Internet access providers cannot easily be sued. Skilled users tend to circumvent laws and regulations, including investors' protection rules. Internet might become a patchwork of overlapping regulations,[9] with "local laws that respect local sensibilities, supplemented by higher level rules governing cross-border transactions and international standards."

Central and Eastern European Perspectives

Eastern European stock exchanges got worthwhile assistance from their colleagues in the West. Software packages were adapted to Central and Eastern European circumstances, and a number of executives were trained by discussing matters with their Western counterparts. The European Commission programs (PHARE, TACIS), the British "Know-how" fund, and the German Fördergesellschaft have done excellent work, assisted by the very high standards of the pioneers of the Central and Eastern European emerging capital markets. The Eastern markets often show the way to cooperation and efficiency when it comes to trading in low volumes with restricted financial means.

The eastern part of the European securities business has received international recognition but most still cope with insufficient liquidity, as well as financial reporting that is not sufficiently transparent. The core asset of these exchanges is the quality of their management and staff and their ability to attract national and international funds. The combination of lower than expected revenues and higher than expected returns was the major problem in the first period of development of these emerging markets. Some were able to adapt their ambitions and investments to their means, whereas others ended up in the hands of authorities or partners with an appetite for acquisitions. Central and Eastern European exchanges are expected to form alliances of their own with some international input from more advanced regions in terms of money and marketing.

The International Watchdog and Fraud

Intermediaries have to provide the best execution to the benefit of their customers. This is not the same as ensuring the best price only. The Lamfalussy report falls short of recommending a centralized supervisory system in Europe. In fact, in the international securities business, it has become increasingly difficult to follow up on transactions. Prospectuses can be professionally so misleading and distorted that even auditors of the highest standards contradict each other at press conferences.

The best way to maintain the integrity of the market still requires that the acceptance of the players be highly selective. Admission to listing is one of the most essential and powerful tasks of an exchange or, in some countries, of the supervisory authority. To have black sheep on a list is detrimental to the credibility of an exchange, notwithstanding the position of a number of people who believe investors should find out themselves ("caveat emptor") whether they should or should not buy a given stock. The other task of paramount importance is the admission of intermediaries after careful examination of their skills and honesty. Both tasks are the cornerstones of the integrity of the market.

Money laundering and thefts are major problems in the capital market sphere. In most cases, the authorities in Europe lack the central point of action to investigate and to enforce the law. Moreover, even if the expertise is available, the authorities lack the means and the time to trace stolen or illegal funds and securities. In a matter of minutes, securities and funds can move from one place to another, from one institution to another, from one market to another, from one owner to another. This is so true that even extremely capable financial detectives, usually working for international lawyers at the request of major banks or financial corporations need months and years—at a high cost and as much as 50 percent of the value of the stolen securities—to retrace and block the funds. The cooperation between financial detectives, stock exchanges, and authorities is not made easy by the (exaggerated) protection of privacy laws

There is definitely a need for more continuity and for more effectiveness in supervision and control of markets. Measures must be taken rapidly since crooks don't wait for authorities in search of their criminal funds. This was confirmed when the United States requested that the funds of terrorists be frozen and some small European countries answered that such a move had to be taken at European level (while funds and securities can be transferred to exotic destinations in a matter of minutes!).

Reporting

The days of propagandistic annual reports seem to be over. Users want reliable and understandable information. Shareholders will increasingly require honest assessments of risks and opportunities. They will not easily forget the deceptive company news of some high-tech, low-transparency ventures with political ingredients designed to support authorities in search of success stories to gain votes during elections. Companies in their wisdom don't wish to be overvalued. They do not want to disappoint their investors at a later stage since they understand how difficult it is to regain confidence.

Profit warnings and honest information help the market to stay close to reality, but their impact is difficult to foresee. Unfortunately, investors tend to overreact, even to objective and scientific company news.

Taxation

Why do European governments insist on harmonization of taxation, when it is difficult to imagine that such an intention would not kill existing flourishing financial centers in Europe? Does the business community really wish to eradicate business in Luxembourg, Jersey, Dublin, or the Isle of Man? Do governments really believe funds now in those locations would fly back to their vaults? Would better budgetary behavior not be more effective?

Excessive taxation reduces the attractiveness of financial marketplaces and favors investments in offshore centers. It is a common practice to put funds in offshore trusts in order to reduce tax and inheritance liabilities. Many offshore banks are offshore in name only and are actually controlled and run by third parties in traditional financial centers. Distance banking is facilitating certain operations.

Taxation considerations have led investors to place their portfolios out of reach of their fiscal authorities or to diversify their securities geographically in the major banks of EU and non-EU countries. Investors are afraid of a number of offshore banks and investment firms that are related to banks situated in their own tax environment (where they don't trust the taxman and the way their country's finances are handled). They also fear the risks involved with insufficiently supervised exotic financial offshore centers.

The time has come to distinguish between serious and well-run centers from poorly operated centers. Luxembourg, for instance, has good governmental handling of finance and can afford to have a friendly and realistic attitude toward savings. The country is in good budgetary hands. It does not invest in sumptuous proliferation of the number of ministries as some of their neighbors did and has accumulated expertise in bonds, investment funds, and international portfolio management. Luxembourg attracts monies from neighboring countries which have mainly themselves to blame because of unpredictable taxation, budgetary deficits, politically motivated extravagant governmental, and subgovernmental regional spending. Capital flight is certainly detrimental to some and beneficial to others, but can we really blame portfolios, which fled countries with overspending tendencies and extravagant taxation policies?

Everybody can be better off with a more successful European capital market.

The Future of Small Exchanges and Trading Facilities

Small can be beautiful, but in this case the range of services on offer has to be restricted and specialization needs to be adapted to the needs of listed companies and interested investors. In this context, the excellent example of the Luxembourg stock exchange should be mentioned. Luxembourg has developed an extraordinary expertise to the benefit of investors and issuers.

For exchanges with a vision, with strategies adapted to size and means, there is a future. It is difficult not to think of Luxembourg, Zurich, and Dublin in this respect. These three are financial centers of the highest order, where expertise and international networks function to the benefit of a number of important financial players. Each of these centers has its own merits. Luxembourg has traditionally had a pragmatic and realistic approach to financial business by all local political parties. Luxembourg's main luck has been the shortsightedness of neighboring governments, which introduced unreasonable taxes to finance their unreasonable and unnecessary administrative costs and other extravagant expenses.

The second asset is Luxembourg's ability to quickly implement reforms and legislation while their neighbors seem incapable of introducing new systems quickly enough as they need to satisfy too many political appointees and administrations in search of power and justification of existence. The third asset is a multinational population of experts and banks.

Notwithstanding their strengths, the Luxembourg institutions fear for their future, given the rivalry and jealousy of a number of EU and OECD countries that dream of recovering what once immigrated to Luxembourg. Fortunately for Luxembourg, the EU's fiscal directives still require a unanimous vote, but there are threats of blackmailing, such as the intention to withdraw institutions (European Investment Bank, Court of Justice, Court of Auditors, etc.) from Luxembourg. In response, Luxembourg could accept fiscal harmonization, provided all taxes would be the same (value-added taxes, inheritance dues, income taxes, taxes on fuel and gasoline, etc). It is well known that other countries have developed budget deficits while Luxembourg has followed an orthodox budgetary policy. In addition, Luxembourg (nor for that matter the other EU countries) does not want to see its funds migrating to the Cayman Islands and other exotic paradises outside Europe.

Gibraltar does not consider itself to be an offshore center. It is part of the EU and follows EU rules.

Tax competition can also be healthy.

There is no harmonization of fiscal rules in the European Union, neither is there such a thing in the United States.

It may well be that smaller exchanges in Europe will survive and may even have to play a crucial role in admitting to their listing locally well-known companies, leaving the blue chips to the world markets. Smaller exchanges may have to cooperate technically and to participate in alliances. Sometimes it pays to develop your own software and to remain in a situation whereby you decide for yourself what is good for you. This was the course of action successfully followed by a number of Central European exchanges.

Impact of the Euro on European Stock Exchanges

The European authorities believe that the credibility of the Euro depends on how strong institutions such as stock exchanges seem to stick to their commitments to support the new currency. Stock exchanges have to be recognized for their excellent acceptance of the Euro and the integration of the European market. We do not think the European organized capital markets of the Euro-zone should be replaced by one central system: rather, they should remain adapted to the colorful cultural and economic variety of circumstances of language and uses, get modernized continuously—as this certainly is currently the case—but remain close to issuers and determined to protect investors, whatever their origin. When all this is achieved, it still will not be good enough. Such a system has to be reported, advertised, and sold to the world of investors interested in Euro-zone investment opportunities.

THE FUTURE LANDSCAPE OF THE SECURITIES MARKETS IN EUROPE

Stock exchanges will continue to play a vital role in the economy by facilitating the very essential process of fund raising by listed companies, to the benefit of banks, shareholders, issuers, intermediaries, and other stakeholders.

Modern exchanges and trading systems in Europe want to gain international recognition, get into the global securities business, improve liquidity, increase efficiency, concentrate and rationalize whenever feasible. Stock exchanges should try to continue to play their institutional and regulatory role even in the present and future commercial circumstances. From all these objectives, the institutional goals seem to be more difficult to maintain in the context of the internationalization of the supervisory function.

Many exchanges in Europe have to take into account the opinions not only of the usual market participants but also their own owners/shareholders. These sometimes consist of a not so harmonized group of people and institutions, ranging from software producers to intermediaries, politicians—brokers, issuers, and fund managers. To decide on a vision in such circumstances is not the easiest of tasks. Even if a number of recently appointed exchange managers are not so familiar with the business they run, they often have excellent managerial capacities and outside political support to impose common views. To avoid conflicts of interest remains a daily task.

The financial place of the future must and will inform the market correctly and comprehensively or will be replaced by other systems. Organized markets of the future will be the markets that will be able to ensure that operators have the necessary skills and means to support efficient transparency and price formation, market integrity, and investor protection (e.g., investor compensation funds). It should not matter if these organized markets are ATS or classical stock exchanges as long as business is done on a level playing field and with a focus on investor protection and issuers' interests.

The main question asked in Brussels on the occasion of an ISD hearing by the German delegate (of the Deutsche Boerse A.G.) in September 2001 was whether securities exchanges could trade in securities they would not have on their own list (listed elsewhere). The answer of the European Commission was that this was indeed feasible. Competition between stock exchanges and other trading institutions will definitely increase. The European capital market has to be seen by all trading providers as a complex and hybrid market in the process of integration, offering excellent opportunities to spread risks and to have investment policies based on industrial sectors and on geographic allocation of investments in a global perspective.

Schematically, we foresee the following will happen to the major players.

Organized Markets

1. Innovation
   - Emergence of new innovative trading systems and an increased use of innovative alternative trading systems.
2. Mergers, partnerships, and alliances
   - Between ATS and stock exchanges, Europe-Asia-the United States.
   - The more exchanges become commercial, the more one can expect mergers and acquisitions that characterize commercial business.
3. Information
   - More notification, more distribution of information, more reporting services to enhance transparency and profitability of commercial trading systems and exchanges.
4. International competition
   - Coexistence of classical institutional securities exchanges (even of mixed economy "public/private") with commercial exchanges and trading systems.
   - Increased worldwide competition between all kinds of organized markets.
5. Clearing and settlement
   - Clearing houses to merge and consolidate operations to save costs and increase efficiency/order routing systems to be fully controlled and improved.
   - Costs of clearing to be substantially reduced (presently much higher than in the United States).
   - Combinations and mergers at the international level of clearing and settlement systems.
6. Efficiency
   - Need for further improvements on efficiency in linking companies with savings.

Issuers

1. Liquidity
   - More emphasis on liquidity requirements/ability to raise funds in good conditions (at a low cost).

- Wish to see markets less fragmented and welcome consolidation movements between organized trading systems.

2. Investors' relations
   - Emphasis on investors' relations in the context of the global market.
3. Efficiency
   - Emphasis on performance, modern technology, well-functioning clearing and settlement, rapid and reliable information, and efficiency in transactions.
4. Reporting
   - To adapt to International Accounting Standards (IAS).
   - Need for increased transparency.

Intermediaries

1. Online
   - More online brokerage but with financial advice and services adapted to customers/e-commerce.
2. Over the counter
   - More off-exchange business between banks and other intermediaries.
3. Portfolio
   - More portfolio management entrusted to specialized institutions (under stricter supervision).
4. Conduct of business rules
   - More harmonized (and better enforced and monitored) conduct of business rules.
5. Organized markets
   - New and more realistic relationship between intermediaries and organized markets based on needs and requests of intermediaries and end-users (issuers and investors).

Investors

1. Investment policy
   - More funds invested in bonds and related business but with diversification on the basis of risk and currencies.
   - More sophisticated investment policies and less confidence in nonindependent advisors.
   - More and better diversified portfolios with more emphasis on real estate and connected investments.
   - Fewer investments in shares of companies without sufficient care of investors.
2. Corporate governance
   - Imposing corporate governance.
   - Monitoring management and boards.
3. Shareholder activism
   - Active participation to general assemblies of shareholders via shareholders associations.

- Organized and intervening in EU matters via Euroshareholders.
- Cooperation with financial analysts.
- Imposing efficiency and requiring the best execution of orders.
- Choosing themselves as the intermediary and the financial place to trade.

4. Information
   - End of distinction between institutional and individual investors when defining the needs for understandable, reliable, and timely information on listed companies.

International Supervision

1. Self-regulation and cooperation with supervisory authorities
   - There has always been a struggle between self-regulators and supervisors. We foresee increased cooperation between all those who really want to maintain and to improve the integrity of markets.
   - Organized markets and supervisors will unite and respect each other's domain in favor of efficiency and realistic audit trail possibilities, with the cooperation of financial detectives and courts (the latter missing time and means to trace criminals and dirty funds). The supervision will become increasingly difficult in view of the many institutions, intermediaries, exotic financial places, and the cleverness of legal and other financial advisors.
   - More cooperation between securities markets supervisors/work on antiterrorism as encouraged by the European Commission.[10]
   - New types of supervisors with international business experience.
   - More "keep it simple" legislation with less politically motivated bureaucratic rules.
   - End of the home/host country control theory and introduction of high-tech international supervisory techniques and bodies.
   - Friendlier attitude toward new initiatives in the trading business, provided they serve the interests of market participants and the economy.
   - Further harmonization of laws and regulations throughout Europe (EU + other European countries) while accepting diversity in cultures.
   - Avoiding bureaucratic measures that would drive the Eurobond market out of Europe.[11]
2. Dirty money
   - Finally, a distinction will be made between dirty (criminal origin of money, drugs, arms deals, pirates, hijackers, terrorists) and black (tax evasion) money.
   - Fiscal paradises will continue to exist as long as there are fiscal hells.
   - More but better-defined and chosen disclosure requirements will be imposed on more institutions and intermediaries to the exclusion of unnecessary data, which nobody really cares for, in order to reduce costs and bureaucracy.
3. Enlargement
   - To ensure that EU enlargement takes place successfully.

In the global world, European stock exchanges are afraid that if they followed excessively bureaucratic EU directives business might leave the European region for other locations where trading could be more efficient and cheaper. For that reason, European organized markets and their practitioners are warning the European Commission that too many (and sometimes unnecessary) reporting requirements could be detrimental to the economy of the European financial sector. In this perspective, the war waged by exchanges (still called regulated markets) against other organized markets (ATS) in Europe, by way of bureaucratic imposition of costly and cumbersome reporting obligations, doesn't make a lot of sense. Back-door concentration obligations won't work in a world context.

The answer to international competition lies in the field of efficiency and the professionalism of practitioners who can enhance the way trading is done. The European post-Lamfalussy stock exchanges and trading systems are currently highly efficient.

Europe still lacks a securities culture. Only in the United Kingdom do investors show interest in the government's budget and in company profit warnings, whereas in the United States there seems to be a certain degree of overreaction to this kind of information.

In some major exchanges, intrigues led to a substantial loss of expertise. A number of centers of finance and industry are working together to achieve more efficiency to the benefit of the market.

The future European directives will need to foresee sufficient adaptability to market circumstances by way of the so-called comitology technique, which entrusts to *ad hoc* technical committees the care of adapting provisions to the reality of business. On the other hand, durability is also required by the securities industry, which no longer accepts overloading by too complicated and too frequently modified European regulations.

The process of consolidation of stock exchanges and trading systems will most probably continue. Exchanges and other trading systems will have to coexist. We may also expect a period of emergence of new innovative efficient techniques. The systems able to deliver liquidity and efficiency will lead the European market globally. We expect further international cooperation between exchanges, trading systems, supervisors, issuers, investors, and intermediaries to the benefit of the integrity of markets, especially in the context of the fight against terrorism and dirty money.

It is expected that a number of organized markets and alliances of exchanges/trading systems will be competitive and strong enough to have a long-term, independent future in Europe and in the broader world context.[12]

NOTES

1. *De Financieel Economische Tijd*, August 31, 2001, p. 7.
2. *De Financieel Economische Tijd*, September 13, 2001, p. 5, of *Aandelen Tijd*.
3. Between July 6, 2001 (when Euronext was launched) and September 13, 2001, OM lost 33 percent of its market capitalization, according to *Aandelen Tijd*, September 13, 2001, p. 5.

4. *Aandelen Tijd*, September 13, 2001, p. 5

5. John Langton, "Do Exchanges Meet the Needs of the Markets They Serve?," speech delivered on the occasion of the fifth European Investment Services Association (EURISA) in Ljubljana on October 13, 2001.

6. *Aandelen Tijd*, September 13, 2001, p. 5.

7. Example: Lernaut & Hauspie, Leper (Belgium). This company managed to deceive investors with inaccurate information. It received subsidies from regional politicians who got strongly involved in the publicity the company enjoyed.

8. *Time*, September 3, 2001, p. 47.

9. *The Economist*, August 11–17, 2001, p. 10.

10. Crispin Waymouth, Securities and Organized markets unit of the European Commission, speech delivered in Ljubljana on the occasion of the EURISA meeting on October 13, 2001.

11. John Langton, October 13, 2001.

Index

About the Contributors

KIYOSHI ABE is a Professor of International Economics at Chiba University, Japan. His research interest is international economics. Abe has taught at Sophia University International Division, Tokyo and Takushoku University, Tokyo, and he has been a research fellow at the Kiel Institute of World Economics in Germany. He is the author of two books dealing with economic development, and he serves on the board of directors of the Japan Society of International Economics.

RICHARD ANTHONY is the Vice Chairman of the Board of Synovus Financial Corporation, a $15 billion financial services company. He was the Chair of First Commercial Bank of Birmingham, Alabama, when it was acquired by Synovus. He is responsible for the management of all of its affiliated banks and its full-service mortgage company. He has a B.S. from the University of Alabama and an M.B.A. from the University of Virginia.

ALLEN N. BERGER is Senior Economist at the Board of Governors of the Federal Reserve System and a Senior Fellow at the Wharton Financial Institutions Center. He is editor of the *Journal of Productivity Analysis* and associate editor of the *Journal of Banking and Finance* and the *Journal of Financial Services Research.* He has published more than 80 articles in leading economics and finance journals.

TOM C. H. CHAN is a Research Assistant at the Melbourne Business School, Melbourne, Australia. He is employed by Accenture as an analyst in their Strategy and Business Architecture consulting service.

MARIA GLORIA COBAS is a Senior Financial Economist at the Office of the Comptroller of the Currency, where she writes policy analysis and prepares testimony on a variety of subjects including financial modernization, the Community Reinvestment Act, and fair lending.

TEODORO D. COCCA is a Senior Research Assistant at the Swiss Banking Institute (Zurich, Switzerland) and lecturer at the University of Zurich. He formerly worked for Citibank Switzerland in investment and private banking. He has published articles dealing with electronic markets and shareholder behavior.

PETER CSOPORT is a Senior Research Assistant at the Swiss Banking Institute (Zurich, Switzerland) and lecturer at the University of Zurich. He has served as a consultant at SegaInterSettle concerning the Swiss Clearing and Settlement architecture and is a member of the Swiss Repo Advisory Board of the Swiss Exchange/Eurex.

ROBERT DEYOUNG is a Senior Economist and economic advisor to the Federal Reserve Bank of Chicago. Prior to joining the Federal Reserve he was a financial economist with the Office of the Comptroller of the Currency. He lectures on finance and economics at the Kellstadt Graduate School of Business at DePaul University. DeYoung's widely published research focuses on the changing structure of financial markets and the performance of firms in those markets.

HORST GISCHER is Professor of Economics at the University of Magdeburg, Germany, where his research interests deal with monetary theory, capital markets, and political economy.

BENTON E. GUP holds the Robert Hunt Cochrane–Alabama Bankers Association Chair of Banking at the University of Alabama. He also held banking chairs at the University of Tulsa and the University of Virginia. Dr. Gup is the author of 21 books and more than 90 articles about banking and financial topics. He has served as a consultant to government and industry. In addition, he teaches a course at the University of Melbourne, Australia.

IAN R. HARPER holds the position of Professorial Fellow in the Melbourne Business School at the University of Melbourne, Australia. He is the Principal of a consulting firm, Harper Associates Australia, a Senior Consultant with Charles River Associates, and a consultant with KPMG and the Commonwealth Bank of Australia. He served on the Wallis Inquiry and is one of Australia's best known academic economists.

SUSAN HINE is an Assistant Professor in the Department of Agricultural and Resource Economics at Colorado State University. Previously she operated a western wear/feed store in Colorado and a horse sale consignment company, and was vice president of financial services at a large Colorado Bank. Her current research focuses on cooperatives and other agribusiness structures, both from a marketing and a financial perspective.

WILLIAM C. HUNTER is Senior Vice President and Director of Research at the Federal Reserve Bank of Chicago and an associate economist on the Federal Open Market Committee. Previously he was vice president at the Federal Reserve Bank of Atlanta and served on the faculties of the University of Georgia, Emory University, Chicago State University, and Northwestern University. He is co-editor of *Research in Banking and Finance*, serves on several editorial boards, and is the editor of five books.

D. JOHANNES JÜTTNER is a Professor of International Finance at Macquarie University, Sydney, Australia. He is the author of 12 books and more than 90 articles in academic and professional publications. He has held visiting professorships in the United States and Europe and has acted as a consultant to the OECD/Paris, the German Council of Economic Experts, the Australian Financial System Inquiry, and private sector firms. He also served as a guest scholar at the German Bundesbank in Frankfurt.

LOUIS MARINO, Assistant Professor of Strategic Management at the University of Alabama, received his Ph.D. from Indiana University. Professor Marino's research interests include strategic alliances, the development of strategic alliance portfolio theory, and international alliances usage and their performance in small to medium-sized organizations. His articles have been published in *The Academy of Management Journal* and the *Journal of International Business.*

LARRY R. MOTE is a Senior Financial Economist at the Office of the Comptroller of the Currency. Mote also teaches financial economics to bank examiners. Previously he was economic advisor and Vice President in the Research Department of the Federal Reserve Bank of Chicago. He also served as a visiting scholar at the University of Oregon and at the Congressional Budget Office.

JEAN-PIERRE PAELINCK has a doctorate in economics from the University of Ghent and lectures at the Hautes Etudes Commerciales de Liège (European economics). He is Secretary General of Euroshareholders (a federation of shareholders associations) and managing director of S.A. Europrivec (financial consultancy to emerging markets).

RONNIE J. PHILLIPS is Chair and Professor of Economics at Colorado State University. He has been a Visiting Scholar at the FDIC, the Comptroller of the Currency, and at the Jerome Levy Economics Institute of Bard College. He is a past president of the Association for Evolutionary Economics (AFEE). His publications on financial system issues have appeared in books, academic journals, newspapers, magazines, and public policy briefs.

STEVEN A. SEELIG is a Financial Sector Advisor at the International Monetary Fund. Previously he was Deputy Director of Research and Statistics at the Federal Deposit Insurance Corporation (FDIC), as well as editor of *The Banking Review*. He also served as Director of the Division of Liquidation and was the Chief Financial Officer for the FDIC. He has taught at George Washington University and Fordham University.

BERNARD SHULL is a Professor Emeritus at Hunter College of the City University of New York and a Special Consultant to National Economic Research Associates, Inc. He specializes in banking, financial institutions, competition, and regulation, and has published widely in scholarly journals. He is the author of numerous books and monographs. Prior to his current affiliation he held various positions in the Board of Governors of the Federal Reserve System, the Federal Reserve Bank of Philadelphia, and the Office of the Comptroller of the Currency

GREGORY F. UDELL is the Bank One Chair of Banking and Finance at the Kelley School of Business at Indiana University. He was formerly a Professor of Finance and Director of the William R. Berkley Center for Entrepreneurial Studies at the Stern School of Business at New York University. He is the co-author of *Principles of Money, Banking and Financial Markets* (10th ed.) and an associate editor of *Journal of Money and Credit*, Banking, *Journal of Financial Services Research*, *Small Business Economics*, and *Business Horizons*. He also has an extensive list of publications.

JAMES A. WILCOX is the Kruttschnitt Professor of Financial Institutions at the Haas School of Business at the University of California, Berkeley. He served as Chief Economist at the Office of the Comptroller of the Currency, Senior Economist on the President's Council of Economic Advisers, and Economist at the Board of Governors of the Federal Reserve System. He has published extensively in leading journals. He received his Ph.D. from Northwestern University.

ARTHUR E. WILMARTH, JR. is a Professor of Law at George Washington University. Before joining GW's law faculty he was a partner in a major Washington, D.C., law firm. He has written numerous articles on banking law and regulation and is co-author of a book on corporate law. Wilmarth has been an advocate before the U.S. Supreme Court and other federal courts and he has testified before Congress on banking issues.